BROME, Vincent

The Other Pepys

B
PEP
BRO

The Other Pepys

Also by Vincent Brome

Biography
H.G.Wells
The Way Back: Albert-Marie
    Guérisse
Freud and His Early Circle
Ernest Jones – Freud's Alter Ego
Frank Harris
Aneurin Bevan
Jung – Man and Myth
J.B.Priestley
Confessions of a Writer

History
The International Brigades

Essays
We Have Come a Long Way
The Problem of Progress

Novels
The Last Surrender
Sometimes at Night
Acquaintance With Grief
The Revolution
The Surgeon
The World of Luke Simpson
The Embassy
The Brain Operators
The Happy Hostage
The Day of the Fifth Moon
London Consequences

THE OTHER
PEPYS
VINCENT BROME

Weidenfeld & Nicolson
London

First published in 1992 by
George Weidenfeld & Nicolson Ltd (the Orion Publishing Group)
2–5 Upper St Martin's Lane
London WC2H 9EA

ISBN 0 297 81270 X

Typeset in Great Britain by BP Integraphics Ltd, Bath, Avon
Printed and bound by The Bath Press Ltd, Bath, Avon

British Library Cataloguing in Publication Data is available

Contents

Contents

Illustrations

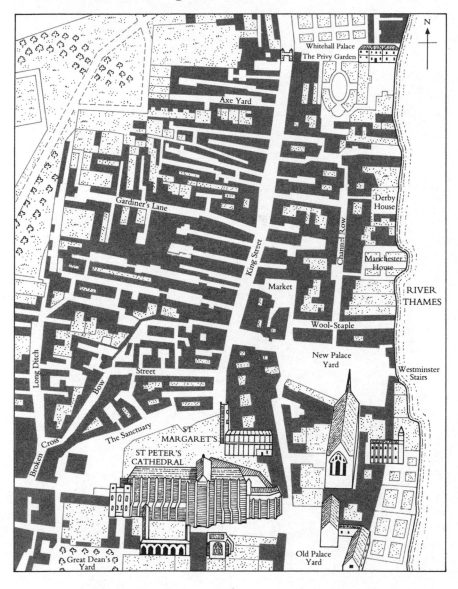

To Jackie Edelman who made it possible

Preface

Anyone entering the labyrinth of Pepysian studies must acknowledge among scores of sources the pioneering work of H.B. Wheatley, J.R. Tanner and R.C. Latham. They opened up a wealth of documentation which illuminates Pepys's family life and social background.

Sir Arthur Bryant's three-volume work towers over the biographical landscape and is another indispensable source. Richard Ollard's biography, published in 1974, threw fresh light on that landscape. Scholars whose work is indispensable to any understanding of Pepys include J.R. Tanner (*Private Correspondence and Miscellaneous Papers of Samuel Pepys, Further Correspondence of Samuel Pepys* and *Mr Pepys*); H.B. Wheatley (the first complete edition of the Diary and *Pepysiana*); R.G. Howarth (*Letters* and *Second Diary*); Walter H. Whitear (*More Pepysiana*); H.T. Heath (*The Letters of Samuel Pepys and his Family Circle*); Edwin Chappell (*The Shorthand Letters of Samuel Pepys*); The Rev. John Smith (*The Life, Journals and Correspondence of Samuel Pepys*). American scholarship contributed, among others, two volumes by Professor Rudolph Kirk and his wife – *Mr Pepys and Mr Evelyn*, and *Mr Pepys Upon the State of Christ's Hospital*. When Richard Ollard's biography was first published in 1974 the definitive edition of the Diary prepared by Robert Latham and William Matthews still needed two volumes for its completion. Since then they have become available and the ten volumes represent a monument of rigorous scholarship which are the basis for any study of the first eleven years of Pepys's life.

There remains considerable unpublished material among the Rawlinson mss in the Bodleian, Oxford; the Pepysian mss in the Pepys Library, Magdalene College, Cambridge; the mss in the British Museum and Public Record Office; letter books and other documents held by the Maritime Museum, Greenwich.

I am indebted to Robert Latham and Mrs Mary Coleman for access to Magdalene's incomparable collection. The librarians at the Bodleian were equally accommodating. The Maritime Museum at Greenwich opened its records, including those of the Navy Records Society. The British Library supplied a steady flow of material over three years and tolerated my presence for many more. Senate House Library also made available certain works. Innumerable other sources are identified either in the bibliography or the notes.

Although Bryant printed for the first time some of the *lingua franca* from the Diary which concealed Pepys's sexual life, he did not translate it, and I am indebted to John Greecon who disentangled many complexities. The result is printed here for the first time. I am indebted to Sarah Stockwell for her work in the Bodleian archive and John Hansman, who solved a number of problems in the Pepys Library at Cambridge. Grace Dempsey overcame some complex translation problems. Justin Champion read and corrected a number of historical passages. Natalina Bertoli's editorial work was indispensable. Excerpts from the Diary are reprinted by permission of The Peters, Fraser and Dunlop Group, and quotations from the Rawlinson manuscripts reproduced by permission of the Bodleian Library. For the rest, this biography sets out to give a reassessment of Pepys's life and work which does not burke the darker issues.

Prologue

Examine in depth the complexities of a person as rich as Samuel
Pepys and contradictions multiply. Consider a portrait so black that
the average reader would fail to recognise the warm, Dickensian
confessor of the Diary who evoked a response in millions of readers.
He is a squat, bewigged person, very aware of the grand coach from
which he steps, displaying a new silken jacket.[1] He is dining with
Lord Sandwich and comes to the occasion with some embarrassment
since he has written His Lordship a letter questioning his moral behaviour with a certain lady of easy virtue, while still involved himself
with many of the ladies of the town.[2] He has spent the day as a
distinguished bureaucrat in the Admiralty where some regard him
as authoritarian. His wife does not accompany him because she occu-
pies an ambiguous place in his social life.

Jealously watching every step she takes, he has an affair behind
her back with the new maid, Deborah, exercising remarkable
ingenuity to cover his traces. His wife remains, as is customary, a
second-class citizen whose birthday never gets celebrated in the Diary
and he blames her for their childless marriage – although it is he
who is sterile.[3] On one classic occasion he gives his wife a black
eye and makes no bones about beating a recalcitrant servant.[4] He
is not above indulging a woman against her will,[5] and deceives his
wife about his affairs with one lie after another. His deepest commitment to repentance is followed quickly by fresh transgression. His
spirit is 'very poor and mean as to bearing with trouble';[6] in too
many situations he cannot say no;[7] he is a self-acknowledged coward;[8]
and he knows there is 'something of ill nature in him'.[9] A skilled
hypocrite, he practises double standards in many areas. Prepared to
accept presents and bribes from victuallers who supply the Navy,
he simultaneously damns their corruption. He deliberately diverts
money intended for paying seamen in the King's service to his own

privateer, the *Flying Greyhound*,[10] while he hears the lamentable moan of poor seamen 'starving in the streets'. He is preoccupied with protecting confiscated goods he acquires illicitly. In pursuit of his own ends he is not above blackguarding a colleague simply because he rivals his own chosen candidate for prestigious position.[11] He once traded a delinquent black servant for as much wine and food as possible, condemning him to a form of slavery then socially acceptable.[12] Not one but two such black servants were sent packing to the colonies on what seem the flimsiest pretexts. His friend Evelyn's inborn compassion rose above the values of the day and recoiled from such behaviour.

Preoccupied with money, Pepys gloats over the steady accumulation of his capital and keeps minute accounts, recording every detail down to the last penny. His wife complains of his meanness and in one government inquiry he deliberately records his salary as nil – a blatant lie.[13] Capable of shutting the door in the face of a servant who has stayed out late, he imposes a Puritan regime on his household and continues to play the *boulevardier* himself. He eats dinner with an ordinary naval carpenter, sends him packing on some invented mission and in the meantime seduces his wife.[14] He toadies to the King in just proportion to custom and constantly sings the praises of his sovereign even while he finds him wanting on several counts.

Writing a Diary of tremendous length, he meets people of the calibre of Boyle and Isaac Newton without recording one word of their new scientific thinking. Although he is speculative about religion, he never reflects on the nature of the Universe or the deeper places of his own mind. His honesty about his own cowardice redeems it in the eyes of his friends,[15] but he raises no objection when highwaymen go to the gallows for robbing him of a pittance,[16] and in the classic trial of the bishops for seditious libel in 1688, his evidence becomes ambiguous.[17] His shortcomings have been explained away by biographers as socially acceptable in his day, but some men – as with Evelyn – rose above such values. Even the great Diary does not escape censure from R.L.Stevenson in his magisterial *Cambridge History of Literature*. 'It is generally supposed that as a writer Pepys must rank at the bottom of the scale of merit.'[18] He is not averse to enjoying a 'good execution' and on one occasion books a special room on Tower Hill to witness the death of Sir Henry Vane.[19] He cuts short a visit to his closest friend Sir William Coventry in the Tower, because it is not circumspect to be seen too much in his company.[20] When one of his eldest nephews marries a girl Pepys thinks unsuitable, banishment is the only answer.[21] He has elevated the British Navy from its impoverished doldrums into an internationally feared force, but fundamentally he enshrines the virtues of the civil servant.

Unscrupulous selection of individual characteristics makes it possible to produce this black profile of Pepys. However, there is another side to Pepys, next to which everything is said to pale into insignificance. This is a self-made man who has broken away from his lowly roots to become a distinguished public servant. He is vivid and amusing company, a great talker, given to vice no worse than is widely fashionable, and able to write with such skill that he produces a unique multi-volume work. He has the gift of evoking – intimately – those unformulated responses to everyday experience which, mediated through his sensibility, strike a chord of recognition with the immediacy of the experience itself in millions of readers. For all his 'fumbling sexuality' he has known the nature of true love and has a 'strange slavery to beauty'.[22]

Insatiably curious, hard-working and with a practical cast of mind, he is a highly cultured man with a deep interest in the arts and music. The *Philosophical Transactions of the Royal Society* in his library reveals the source of Evelyn's scepticism: 'This molehill on which we mortals crawl and keep such a stir ... [was] created for us little vermin.'[23] His shortcomings with women, his corruption and hypocrisy are socially acceptable and widely practised in his day. They do not invalidate his great work in reconstructing the British Navy which subsequently changes the course of British history. He remains in London at high risk during the Fire and the plague, comes closer to death when he undergoes brutal surgical operations, survives the Popish Plot, incarceration in the Tower and narrowly escapes the gallows.[24] He enthrones reason as the god of wise action; he believes that the mind is the man; he has learnt toleration of others; and he remains at heart a warm, generous person, loyal to friends and relatives and so revered by highly placed company that he becomes President of the Royal Society. Above all, he has the endearing weaknesses of the common man, and a boyish delight in simple things persists at the height of his sophistication. 'But Lord, to see how much of my old folly and childishness hangs upon me still that I cannot forbear carrying my watch in my hand in the coach all this afternoon to see what o'clock it is one hundred times.'[25] There remains a candour about his weaknesses which almost converts them into virtues.

How can these two so contradictory personae be reconciled? It is the biographer's perennial problem that at precisely the point where he imagines the essence of his subject to be within his grasp, it dissolves again. Pepys is a rich example of all these complexities and distilling the essence of the man is a stimulating problem. This biography applies itself to that task and attempts a new reconciliation.

The Other Pepys

Chapter I

The small years

Step down into the early seventeenth century and enter the house in Salisbury Court, London, where Samuel Pepys was born on 23 February 1633. 'Most such . . . houses had a cellar, a shop and a kitchen on the ground floor, two or three floors above and a garret in the gable.'[1] There were two garrets in John Pepys's house where his children slept and woke at dawn to the steadily mounting roar of traffic from adjoining Fleet Street. Carts and horses rumbled down cobbled streets, with apprentices bawling their wares and drumming wheels swallowing up conversation. Wooden houses leaned across narrow streets almost within a hand-shake of one another, and shops projected across byways where carts and horses frequently confounded one another.

Almost within earshot of the house, London's 'noble river' flowed majestically through the chaos of dirty streets 'brimming with craft and commerce'; it was bisected by London Bridge, no longer quite so choked by houses that once massed along its length.[2] The gardens and palaces beside the Thames rendered long stretches of the riverside beautiful, St Paul's asserted its soaring splendour, and certain citizens were busy writing great literature. Sewerage ran freely in many streets, the death rate was high, infectious disease a continuous threat and medicine still not free from medieval superstition.

John Pepys, Samuel's father, came from a long line of Pepyses reaching back two hundred and fifty years to the Abbey of Crowland in the Fen District where they served as ordinary reeves, rent collectors and haywards.[3] Their administrative skills developed to the point where they despised manual labour and broke away from their roots. In 1569 John Pepys of Cottenham married Editha Talbot who inherited her father's possessions.[4] 'My sovereign of gold and chalis of silver and six silver spoons and a covering to a salte of silver double gilt with all my messuages lands etc. in the Fen . . . and elsewhere

3

in the Isle of Ely with my messuage at Impington which I lately bought.' Thus richly endowed, John Pepys in turn bought the Manor of Impington and left the property to his offspring. When he died he put his six-year-old son Talbot under the guardianship of his elder sons John of Cottenham, Apollo, and Thomas the Black and Thomas the Red.[6] Black then married Mary Day of Wisbech, producing three daughters and three sons. Born at Impington in 1601 the youngest son, John Pepys the father of Samuel, decided, for reasons which are not clear, to leave his beloved Fenland where for centuries the family had accommodated the mists, lazy rivers, fog and damp.[7] Perhaps the fight against the 'legion of the unknown' born of the 'hideous Fen' which haunted the imagination of many a Fen-man, and his slow rise in the social hierarchy, drove John to consider the warmth and comfort of faraway London, where it was said a man could make a new life with comparative ease. Alternatively, the large and evergrowing circle of Pepyses intensified competition and forced him to leave an area where he constantly encountered skills of his own kind.[8]

Once in London it was necessary for him to serve four years' apprenticeship as a tailor before he could establish his own business. Even then he failed to become a privileged member of the Guild of Merchant Tailors since he had not been born in London. It was no easy matter to break into a jealously guarded trade full of people with different accents and to some extent culture. Whether he had capital to spare is not known, but he risked taking a long lease on the house which abutted St Bride's to the west and Salisbury Court to the east. Eight years went by before this 'meek, mild, pious man', who was 'never quite equal to the occasion',[9] proposed to Margaret Kite, a woman of such humble stock that she had once been a washmaid. Whatever her origins she had considerable personality, and her profound piety, which matched her husband's, did not prevent her quarrelling explosively. Physically, she must have been strong because she bore him eleven children in quick succession – all unaware that the fifth child, Samuel, was to become an international figure whose fame re-echoed down the centuries to the present day.

Meanwhile, a dramatic marriage had taken place elsewhere in the family which was to have lifelong repercussions. In 1618 John Pepys's aunt, Paulina, was married to Sidney Montagu, brother of the Lord Treasurer. The Montagu family possessed lands, preferments and connections which gave them high status and wide influence, but the real benefits of such privileges were to be reserved to John's son, Samuel. Paulina's marriage sent a stir across all branches of the Pepys family. It was good news to have such a connection even at several removes.

As the years slipped away John Pepys built up his trade. In 1662 Mrs Pepys discovered – with dread foreboding – that she was pregnant again. On 23 February 1633 Samuel Pepys was born. Eight days after his birth Samuel was taken to St Bride's and baptised into the Anglican Church. Already there were two other children, Mary and John; Tom arrived in the summer of 1634 and Sarah in the following year. There is no record of John Pepys's tailoring business, but his finances must have strained to feed the children who numbered seven by 1638. Overrun with young life, the somewhat leaky house had a cellar used as a lavatory, and there was scant privacy. Such shortcomings were easily accommodated under the precepts taught by Samuel's parents. The translation of the Bible into the vernacular had worked on the unsophisticated English middle class to produce that mighty force called Puritanism which believed in an ordered, hard-working way of life dimly controlled by a divine mission. Churches proliferated everywhere and church bells were a constant background to Samuel's childhood, which combined a litany of prayers with voracious competition in business.

Not even the sacred precincts of St Paul's were free from money-changers, salesmen, sharks, courtesans and servants advertising their services. Bookshops crowded close on the churchyard and multifarious trades openly publicised their wares on sacred pillars. This was the scene which Samuel Pepys came to know as he looked out in the dawn from his garret. Below stairs, his father's workshop was busy from dawn to dusk, with the obligatory observance of Sunday in sanctimonious certitude. It was common for paternalistic employers to rule over the lives of their apprentices, who sometimes held them in respect.

John Pepys was loyal to an unrelenting creed which regarded card-playing and dancing as no less evil than entering an alehouse or dressing in order to allure. Occasional indulgence might find redemption but persistent 'coarse-living' led straight to destitution in this world and hellfire in the next. Man only raised himself above the level of the animal if he forswore such indulgences and paid strict devotion to God, even if it meant waiting in the crush of the faithful anxious to hear the fire and brimstone of a popular preacher. Every Sunday the children were crowded into the family pew at St Bride's and every weekday had the virtues of punctuality, tidiness and solvency impressed on them.

Much of the family shared John Pepys's Puritan values. Uncle

Thomas Pepys brought up his family with a severity approaching fanaticism and exercised a cunning disciplinary code. Aunt Jane, 'a poor, religious, well-meaning, good, humble soul', talked 'of nothing but God Almighty and that with so much innocence that mightily pleased me'.[10] Fishmonger William Wight, John Pepys's half-brother, Fenner the blacksmith and Kite the butcher, all reflected this hard-working decency. The relatives of Samuel's mother were equally impoverished but none the less exemplars of Puritanism.[11] Sundays became exhausting days which Samuel never forgot, when the family in high hats and sober garb gathered after the midday meal to indulge in mild gossip and mutual prayers before long and elaborate afternoon services.

There is no certain evidence, but a boy of average high spirits might easily rebel against such drab conformity, and certainly there were a growing number of distractions for him around the house in Salisbury Court. The Globe Theatre had been burnt down and rebuilt at Bankside with a tiled instead of thatched roof, and here Shakespeare's plays continued to attract large audiences. According to Bryant, the growing boy went to Bankside where he acquired a lifelong love of the theatre, but all theatres were closed in 1644 by the Puritans, which meant that by the time Samuel reached his eleventh year there were none available. That he developed very early in life a taste for the theatre remains clear. The Bear Garden offered the brutal but dramatic spectacle of dogs being tossed by bulls to their blood-spattered deaths. Cockfighting and bear-baiting produced equally sadistic pleasures for all kinds of people. On the river one could enjoy the thrill of shooting the rapids under the bridges and local constables frequently carried off malefactors to the stocks to be pelted pitilessly.

St Bartholomew's annual fair brought half of London to gape at the total violation of Puritan principles: girls in tights openly flaunting their limbs, monkeys dancing on tightropes and conjurors risking obscene performances. For a boy, simply to slip between the buckled shoes, silk stockings and satin finery of the gentry must have had its own particular excitement. There were also trips to grand houses – as when he visited Sir Robert Cooke's mansion and later wrote: 'Ever since I was a boy Arethusa's part, which I was to have acted at Sir Robert Cooke's, was very pleasant to me, but more to think what a ridiculous thing it would have been for me to have acted a beautiful woman.'[12]

Much more dramatic, there remained the chance of a hanging, standing tip-toe on a cart or wall with the victim prolonging his prayers and protestations, hoping for reprieve. Socially acceptable in Pepys's day, the drawing and quartering which followed meant that those guilty of treason were cut down from the gallows while still alive, publicly disembowelled and the writhing remnants torn into four, before being consigned to the flames.

Family deaths were another matter. Of Samuel's ten brothers and sisters only three survived beyond early childhood and we have very little evidence of their relationships. The stray references in the Diary are frequently inspired by some topographical coincidence, as when a Sunday excursion carried Pepys to the village of Kingsland near Hackney where 'I have not been many a year, since a little child I boarded there. Thence to Kingsland by my nurse's house ... where my brother Tom and I was kept when young.'[13] There are references to playing games, to shooting bows and arrows, carrying clothes for his father's customers and once – a time of great alarm – when he hurried, as a very small boy, through Horsley, intent on finding his father feared lost on a return passage from Holland. The Pepys heritage spread its tentacles widely and nearby in Salisbury Court was the house of another John Pepys, a lawyer, who rode in a beautiful coach to his country estate at Ashstead. It was a great pleasure for Samuel to be invited to what seemed a grand establishment where he gorged himself on fruit from the gardens, played blindfold games and giggled at a sermon delivered by a pompous parson.[14]

We know more about Samuel's health than his state of mind. Every summer he suffered from pricklings and itchings – probably eczema – while winter colds were supposed to 'stop his water' and wind gave him great pain. More significant perhaps, he was liable to pain in the kidneys which could express itself in distressing symptoms. 'I remember not my life without the pain of the stone in the kidneys (even to the making of bloody water upon any extraordinary motion) till I was about twenty.'[15]

When his brother John died Samuel was seven years old. He had lost his best playmate. But death became a familiar experience to a boy who quickly accustomed himself to the funeral cortege. December of the same year saw the death of thirteen-year-old Mary, a year later Barbara Williams, the family servant, died, and Sarah Pepys, aged five, followed both to the grave.

Such personal tragedies were overtaken in the wider scene where events which changed the course of British history were in the making. Across Europe a new spirit was astir of which Pepys later became very conscious. It was the spirit of the late Renaissance, still shaking itself free to consider new and exciting perspectives which were to culminate in scientific speculations only fully understood by men of the calibre of Sir Isaac Newton. It remained true that seventeenth-century religion and politics were inextricably linked. Religion permeated public duty which the state was expected to preserve and if necessary enforce. People saw historic events from a religious perspective.

In the realm of politics, the Long Parliament had met on 3 November 1640, declared extra-parliamentary taxation illegal, abolished the Star Chamber and established that Parliament could not be dissolved without its own consent. The shifting fortunes of Charles I took a turn for the worse when the pamphleteering lawyer Prynne was released from prison and rode in triumph from Westminster through a crowd of thousands crying 'Reformation!' Demonstrating against Charles, the hordes invaded Westminster Hall, insulting the Lords, sneering at the King's officers and pushing leeks into the face of Archbishop Laud. The fever of rebellion ran high, and in the spring of 1641 the Earl of Stafford's execution was watched by thousands on Tower Hill.

According to Veronica Wedgwood,[16] Stafford bore himself with great dignity and declared that he had never spoken against Parliament or professed any faith but that of the English Church.[17] It was a measure of the atmosphere of Samuel's childhood that as the executioner lifted the bleeding head from the block a tremendous cheer broke from the crowd and horsemen rode off shouting 'His head is off!' to the delight of the spectators.

In the following year, 1642, King Charles, with a company of armed men, moved into Westminster to arrest the five sitting Members, but the independent capital decided to shelter them. Thrust and counter-thrust in the battle of supremacy ensued until the royal path was barred by the twenty-five thousand pikes of London apprentices; barricades were flung across Chelsea High Street; and even Hyde Park accommodated a bristling new fort with trenches dug on Constitution Hill. The King's attempt to take control of Parliament failed. He withdrew from London and on 22 August 1642 he declared war on Parliament, raising his standard at Nottingham.

These events in Samuel's ninth year widened his perspectives. In that year Samuel escaped from London to re-join his fellow countrymen in the Fens. His great uncle, Talbot Pepys, still ruled Impington Manor in Elizabethan style. Having grandly risen to the position of Bencher of the Temple, Recorder of Cambridge and for a time Member of Parliament, he remembered those who had cared for him and befriended their grandchildren, including Samuel. There

were other influential relatives living at Priory House, Hinchingbrooke, just two hours' ride away from Impington. As we have
seen, one of Talbot's sisters had married Sir Sidney Montagu, who
bought Priory House from a world-weary Sir Oliver Cromwell. The
Montagu family was to have a deep influence on Samuel's fortunes,
but Walter Whitear argued that it was another relative, John Barton,
who placed Samuel in the Free School at Huntingdon, a provincial
grammar school which had once coped with the wilder eccentricities
of the youthful Oliver Cromwell.[18]

Samuel's sojourn in Huntingdon was shortlived, covering the year
1663–4, a year in which Captain Oliver Cromwell arrived in Huntingdon to recruit the company of 'honest, sober citizens' who became
the kernel of his Ironsides. There were divided loyalties in the Pepys
family, with John Pepys committed to the Cromwellian cause, Uncle
Robert a captain in the Parliamentary militia, and Uncle Appollo
'accustomed to honour the King's majesty'.[19] The young Edward
Montagu, like many of his generation, was eager for reform and
passionately committed to his neighbour Oliver Cromwell. Growing
up in the midst of these contradictions Pepys found himself swayed
by the arguments of his father and Edward Montagu. The school
at Huntingdon reaffirmed Samuel's education as a Roundhead.[20]

By the year 1644 Samuel was back once more in London and
entered St Paul's school, which was deeply committed to classical
learning. Five minutes' walk from Salisbury Court, St Paul's stood
amongst the bookshops crowding the precincts of the cathedral, surrounded by the traffic of the inner city. Samuel Cromleholme, the
High Master, was a distinguished scholar who had built his own
remarkable library and Pepys quickly came under his influence.
Cromleholme's philosophies were enshrined in the Latin inscriptions
on the walls of the vestibulum engraved by the school's founder,
Dean Colet. Scholars were invited to read and follow the dictums
of Livy, Virgil, Cicero, Thucydides and Aristotle. Here, in a world
of classical austerity which did not exclude the frequent use of the
cane, the young boy Pepys set out to become a Perfect Grammarian
married to Oratory and Poetry, centred on the learning of Hebrew,
Latin and Greek. He lived in two totally contradictory worlds –
one, the outside world of the streets with its traffic, hawkers, prostitutes, booksellers and money-lenders; the other a sanctuary of learning
where the highest Puritan principles were propounded with ruthless
consistency. Repeating the catechism became an inescapable ritual
and translating Cicero's *Oration against Catiline* a test of his endurance.
The redoubtable High Master Cromleholme remained a presence

throughout Pepys's life. Several references were to be made to him in the Diary from the day when 'he did drink more than he used to do',[21] despite which 'I honour the man and he doth declare abundance of learning and worth.' Later Pepys's opinion changed and Cromleholme became a ridiculous and 'conceited pedagogue'.[22]

No less influential was the Puritan antiquarian Dr Langley. His overpowering presence 'struck mighty respect and fear into scholars' which lost something of its effect as familiarity revealed a gentler person concealed within.[23] There are also references in the Diary to a number of new friends including the witty, erratic Jack Cole and honest Richard Cumberland. Cumberland was also a tailor's son destined to become a mathematician, philosopher and bishop.

There developed in St Paul's a boy with a liberal view of life who was to face the interrogation of the examiners in Hebrew, Latin and Greek before the forbidding assembly of governors of the Mercers' Company of merchant tailors. These gentlemen not only had the power to decide Samuel's fate but as Bryant commented: 'A tailor's son with the learning of the ancient republican world at his fingertips could see nothing incongruous in the spectacle of stern and inspired graziers, attorneys and cobblers 'sitting in judgement on an annointed king'.[24]

It was the King who faced the executioner's axe shortly afterwards. Samuel was to stand in Chancery Cross Street to watch the head of Charles I dripping with blood. While it was held high in exultation for all the populace to see, the snow of a bitter winter fell on the upturned faces of a thousand spectators.[25] He was now fifteen years old and, with the arrogance of youth, announced that if asked to comment on the King's death his text would be 'the memory of the wicked shall rot'.[26] Classical learning, the poetry of Milton, the politics of Cromwell and the republicanism of Sir Harry Vane – these for the time being were his gods.

Chapter 2
School days and early marriage

A young man in his mid-teens, Pepys was some 5′1″ in height with 'large enquiring eyes' and clothes which matched his sober upbringing. His early poverty and classical training had produced conflicting characteristics. The son of a Puritan tailor, his conversation was cautious, although artificial restraints on language were temperamentally alien to him. His gift for mixing with people, ready tongue and vitality, all of which sprang from someone greedy for life, remained repressed. He presented to his tutors a controlled sobriety and a disapproval of dancing, drunkenness and swearing, setting a high store on duty.

Such a person in February 1650 confronted the Master and Wardens of the Mercers' Company in their magnificent hall. He had come to petition for one of their exhibitions which could open the gates to Cambridge and a whole new way of privileged life.[1] It must have been an even more tense moment for Pepys because the execution of King Charles I had not encouraged the tailors' trade or the fortunes of tailors' sons. The merchant tailors had lost business against a background of increasing taxes, and they now petitioned the Lord Mayor to exclude the so-called 'foreign tailors' of Salisbury Court, which created great anxiety for his father John Pepys. When John Pepys tried to record his vote for the public offices of the next year, he was told that he no longer had the right to do so since he was no longer a freeman. Driven by mixed motives, in January 1650 he decided to humble himself and petition the merchant tailors to admit his son even if it meant paying a considerable sum of money.[2] Without his father's official recognition there seemed no hope of higher education for Samuel. Against all the accumulating evidence, the Mercers granted him a Robinson exhibition and Pepys was admitted as a sizar to Trinity Hall, Cambridge, on 21 June.[3] Clearly, his scholastic record must have impressed the governors, but now an element of luck supervened to transfer him to Magdalene College. Intellectual life in England was undergoing a purge and university teachers were subjected to republican tests which could invalidate appointments and lead to expulsion. Adjoining Trinity Hall was Magdalene College where a new Master, John Sadler, deeply committed to the Puritans, had been appointed. Already republican Town Clerk of London he combined many qualities, including a flair for administration which rendered him, at the age of thirty-six, sympathetic to the government. By sheer accident he was also a neighbour of John Pepys in Salisbury Court and it is likely that he knew the Pepys family. Whether he exerted any influence is not clear, but two weeks after Sadler's appointment as Master, Samuel moved from Trinity Hall to become a sizar at Magdalene, on 5 March.[4] Within a month he was also a scholar on the Spendluffe Foundation.[5]

Despite its Puritan ethos, Cambridge remained a free university and Pepys plunged into a student routine which has not greatly changed down the ages. Lectures, disputations and tutoring were everyday 'encumbrances' to be accommodated by students without too much show of boredom in case disciplinary action followed. The services in the chapel were prolonged and obligatory, but given the right degree of fervour, which in many was genuine, a student could take them in his stride.

University teaching was still founded on the scholasticism of the Middle Ages. Formal logic in rational argument expressed itself through verbal displays called disputations, where one group proved and the other disproved chosen propositions. They could take place in public or private, sometimes achieving a theatrical quality with the tutor as director. Students were expected to make a written record of entire lectures and some, including Pepys, frequently had recourse to Shelton's system of shorthand called Tachygraphy, a system later immortalised by him in his Diary.

The young Pepys, thirsting for knowledge, quick in mind and combative when challenged, flourished in seventeenth-century Cambridge.[6] Certainly, the scholastic technique could produce a tiresome preoccupation with minutiae and a plausibility in logic not far removed from sophistry. Thus John Hall in 1649: 'Where have we anything to do with Chimistry which hath snatched the keys of Nature from the other seats of philosophy ... where any manual demonstrations of Mathematical Theorems or instruments.'[7] Pepys never complains in his Diary, but he was lucky with his tutor, Samuel Morland, a man who reconciled a number of seemingly incompatible roles. Mathematician, diplomat, inventor, double agent working for

Charles II in Thurloe's secret service, and cryptographer, Morland epitomised the polymath versatility of some intellectuals of the day. He was relatively new to the donnish life when Pepys became his student, but his influence was profound.

The Vice-Chancellor of the university, Benjamin Whichcote, was, like Morland, surprisingly tolerant of dissenting views in an age when ten years of civil war had reduced academic learning to cautious conformity. Echoes of their teaching continually reappeared in Pepys's later personal and professional life. Morland had a mind open to experimental philosophy and Whichcote escaped fashionable bigotries to practise reason with a courtesy not customary in the religious arguments of the day. So much for Pepys's tutors. What of his fellow students? Several were to become famous later in life, including Bob Sawyer referred to in the Diary as 'my old chamber-fellow', who rose to the rank of Attorney General.[8] Another and closer friend, Richard Cumberland, assiduously climbed the tortuous religious ladder to reach high office as Bishop of Peterborough. It would falsify the atmosphere of Magdalene in Pepys's day to represent the students as immaculate exemplars of the Puritan spirit dedicated to rising in public life. Kit Anderson, a fellow student in medicine was later referred to in the Diary as having 'an eye for an exceeding pretty lass and right for the sport'.[9] Others exploded into bouts of drinking and indiscipline. Stars like Dryden, the poet, and Stillingfleet, the Gospel poet, failed to qualify for later mention in the Diary, but John Peachell, who liked the taverns, and John Skeffington, who was too aristocratic for common company, were both remembered nostalgically.[10] On one occasion they discussed their careers at length with Pepys and he was pleased that none had 'sped' better than himself.

Most leisure activities were innocent enough. A walk through the meadows discussing the nature of the Universe would end at Madingley, or a ferry ride across the river in overloaded boats would finish with stewed prunes from Goody Mulliner. They lived frugally in bare chambers, they worshipped God at all appropriate moments and sweated away at studies which seemed remote from life, but one pastime remained which could enliven their evenings and sometimes ruin their aspirations – drink. One evening Samuel was 'solemnly admonished with a companion for having been scandalously over-served with drink on the previous night'.[11] Bouts of heavy drinking continued to worry him in his early career, but now another and quite different leaning expressed itself for the first time – writing. He committed to paper a romance called *Love a Cheat* which clearly expressed disillusion with that experience and left its author so dissatis-

fied that he simply tore it up on 31 January 1664.[12] Bryant in his
biography indulges romantic speculation about long evenings when
'a boatful of boys might ferry across [the river] to stand for a moment
silenced as the magic of a summer's evening caught up their spirits
among the ruins of Barnwell Abbey'.[13] Given Pepys's imaginative
sensitivity it is a reasonable speculation, but it is completely undocu-
mented.

Outstanding in Pepys's memories of walking beside the river was
an altogether different event. On a hot summer's day he stopped
with his friends to drink several draughts of cold water from Aristotle's
Well and was driven to pass water. Returning to his room in Magdalene he was attacked by a savage pain which coincided with passing
blood when he made water. He recorded the event and its consequences in the Diary:

I remember not my life without the pain of the stone in the kidneys
. . . till I was about twenty years of age, when upon drinking an
extraordinary quantity of conduit water out of Aristotle's Well . . . the
weight of the said water carried, after some days' pain, the stone out
of the kidneys, more sensibly through the ureter into the bladder from
which moment I lived under a constant succession of fits of stone with
the bladder till I was about twenty-six years of age.[14]

For the rest, Pepys's days at Magdalene were characterised by the
enforcement of Puritan precepts which did not produce an unhappy
adolescence. He did not entirely escape the coarse bluntness of the
Cambridge taverns and his cousin Barnardistan of Cottenham introduced him to a Mrs Aynsworth, a barmaid, who quickly made sly
remarks to the near-blushing boy and taught him to sing a song
'Full Forty Times Over'. It was a healthy antidote to his upbringing
which had produced a prolonged inability to refer directly to sexual
matters. Lowly born, without money or privilege, he sailed relatively
unperturbed through the hazards of a period torn by war and dissen-
sion before his first skirmish with love.

There was an interval after university when he returned to his
father's home in Salisbury Court and played some role in the tailoring
business. Whether it amounted to anything more than helping to
deliver garments to customers is unclear, but according to an entry
in the Diary its recollection on one occasion embarrassed him.

Spying out of the coach Collonell Charles George Cock, formerly a
very great man and my father's customer whom I have carried clothes
to but now walks like a poor sorry sneake, and [I] light to him. This
man knew me which I would willingly have avoided so much pride

I had, he being a man of mighty heighth and authority in his time
but now signifies nothing.[15]

Snobbery came and went in Pepys's early life as it would any man
following the social mores of his day.

It would understate the case to say that Pepys was easily attracted
to women and of the three who remained in his memory only one
was to have much influence on his life. Betty Archer inspired a
brief entry in the Diary: 'Went to the opera and saw the last act
of *The Bondsman* and there find Mr and Mrs Mary Archer, sister
to the fair Betty whom I did admire at Cambridge.' The second
lady he held in great regard 'and did make an anagram or two upon
her name',[16] Elizabeth Whittle, lived in Salisbury Court close to
the Pepys family, unaware that she was to become the grandmother
of Charles James Fox.

The third woman, Mrs Hely, clearly stirred deeper feelings than
her predecessors. 'Down by Minnes Wood with great pleasure view
my old walks ... where Mrs Hely and I did use to walk and talk,
with whom I had first sentiments of love and pleasure in woman's
company ... taking her by the hand, she being a pretty woman.'

Then came the woman destined to dominate the next twenty
years of his life – Elizabeth St Michel.[17] It happened suddenly and
unexpectedly with all the force of a *coup de foudre*. Where he met
her is unknown, but he found himself swept off his feet and nothing
would satisfy him but marriage post-haste to secure her against any
rival. The precepts by which he lived emphasised financial, professional and personal prudence, but now at one stroke he broke
out of all three.

In person, Elizabeth St Michel justified his reckless behaviour,
although beauty, youth and personality carried very few other men
in the seventeenth century into anything so final as marriage. 'She
was *very* beautiful with a little round face of an almost unearthly
pallor set in curls.'[18] Otherwise she had every possible disadvantage.
She was of foreign origin (French), penniless, with no prospects,
and her family connections were worthless. A mere fifteen years
old, she knew nothing of life, although this was not seen as a disadvantage because many girls married in their early teens. He was seven
years older, and as unattractive a future husband as she was wife,
being himself penniless and without prospects. Such considerations
were of no consequence to a completely infatuated Pepys who loved
her so passionately that the thought of losing her made him feel
physically sick.

Marriage to the daughter of a French Huguenot who had
fled to England with Queen Henrietta Maria was completely out
of keeping with family tradition. They married into their own kind
and were accustomed to haggle for bigger and better dowries.
However, he must have her here and now. Her father was in no
position to object, being himself impoverished and full of impractical
notions such as the paramount importance in life of perpetual
emotion. His grand name, Alexander le Marchant, matched his lowly
position and Pepys was a not unreasonable suitor: he was at least
a solid Protestant. Elizabeth had earlier in her native country
shown signs of coming under the influence of Popery and the young
Pepys would eradicate such heresies with his learning and commitment. Questioned by her father about her beliefs later in life, she
replied, kissing his eyes as she loved to do: 'I have now joined a
man ... too wise ... to suffer my thought to bend that way any
more.'[19]

They were married finally on 10 October 1655 with Pepys providing a ring he had saved money to buy from a New Exchange gold-
smith.[20] The wedding dinner followed in a tavern and must have
been distinguished from most such occasions which were celebrations
of property and dowries. This was a love match and, probably, one
of those romantic occasions with an unforgettable combination of
passion, extreme youth and high expectations. Whether the marriage
was consummated that night remains uncertain because Elizabeth
and Pepys did not live together, according to the Diary, until 10
October 1656. This was the date Pepys recorded in his Diary as
his wedding night. Meticulous in keeping all anniversaries, Pepys
can be taken as reliable for such a crucial event. The delay is inexplicable. Ollard believed it might be due to the extreme youth of the
bride, but consummation was commonplace at even earlier ages.
Perhaps a lack of suitable accommodation played its part, because
Pepys was unable to afford more than a single room.

Seen through modern eyes the marriage should have ended in
disaster: an innocent child and painfully young man, quite ignorant
about each other, were committing themselves to a lifelong partnership without a penny to meet possible exigencies. One simple justification remains. Since the average expectation of life was forty-five,
to live every day as if it were your last became a widely accepted
dictum and at twenty-two Pepys had already lived half his expected
life.

There were other, more serious complications. Elizabeth brought
with her a number of encumbrances, some of which Pepys was never

to escape. In addition to an incompetent father-in-law who could not live up to his high-flown name, her lazy and almost delinquent brother Balthazar was to saddle them with an impossible burden. The economic stringencies of this period were revealed later in the Diary. 'Lay long abed talking with pleasure with my poor wife how she used to make coal fires and wash my foul clothes with her own hand for me, poor wretch, in our little room ... for which I ought for ever to love and admire her and do, and persuade myself she would do the same thing again if God should reduce us to it.'[21]

Evidence of Pepys's activities from 1654 when he left Cambridge until we find him living in one room with his wife in the house of his cousin Edward Montagu is scarce. As we have seen, Montagu had become his cousin through marriage in 1618. Now the connection was doubly fortunate, for Montagu offered Pepys a lowly post in the hierarchy of his servants. Pepys became his factotum or resident steward, with a watching brief over the maids and a responsibility for making payments on Montagu's behalf.[22] Pepys and his wife occupied a little turret garret overlooking the gateway at the centre of the ancient palace of Whitehall, the original residence of the Protector Cromwell's government. It was an insignificant home in a grand household.

Despite the social gap between them, 'from the outset the two men were most intimate. Pepys was in Montagu's confidence ... and endeavoured to keep his patron's affairs out of a tangle during a most troublesome time.'[23] Challenged much later in the House of Commons about his early days, Pepys elevated these activities under the title secretary and it is easy to understand the conversion. Here he was occupying the housekeeper's room in Montagu's house in menial service, when his talents and education qualified him for a much higher role. No wonder he emerges from his letters as a somewhat idle and certainly disgruntled person. Professional status in Montagu's day was greedily sought. Later in life, Pepys's Puritan upbringing drove him to work with unstinting commitment, but now frustration and a sense of displacement dissipated his energies at work. Pleasure became a prerequisite of reconciling himself to his lot.

Edward Montagu was already a member of Cromwell's Council of State, the fifteen-man executive which exercised wide powers independently of Parliament, when Pepys joined his household. A resolute, but conciliatory politician, he had become a Treasury commissioner. Pepys followed, with fascination, his skilled advocacy of government policies in the vital debates on the Navy. It was Pepys's first acquaintance with the intricacies of naval politics which were to become his metier, and he must have been disappointed to see the government defeated despite his cousin's efforts. In the event, the defeat was of little moment because Cromwell overturned that Parliament but retained Montagu's services. In 1655 Cromwell then selected him as understudy for Admiral Robert Blake, whose command of the fleet was threatened by ill health.

The year 1655 also saw Montagu created General-at-Sea. He was not a seaman but then six out of seven such powerful appointments were landlubbers, and the Navy's performance under their command unremarkable. Pepys was lucky to be born into a period when such anomalies were commonplace, with the administration continuously revising its techniques in the light of new knowledge. It was a time full of contradiction, taking poverty, violence and starvation in its stride, but riding high on a new confidence inspired by an awareness of possibilities hitherto unthinkable. Such an optimistic climate made possible the future careers of Montagu and Pepys.

Like Pepys, Montagu had married young, and unlike Pepys, against his father's wishes, but he had been wise enough to choose a wife whose family enhanced his political career. The next step in that career was reflected in Pepys's when the new General-at-Sea employed him in the equivalent of the Admiralty, first as paymaster and receipts clerk. Pepys's acute powers of observation and analysis quickly enlarged his activities and gradually he developed into a political commentator feeding Montagu with scraps of political intelligence. 'The common vogue', he wrote to Montagu, 'is the old story of the Protector's kingship.'[24] This reflected a move made early in 1657 by members of Cromwell's Council when they came forward to offer the crown to Cromwell, earning the title 'kinglings'.[25] According to three members of the Council – Montagu, Broghill and Disbrowe – this method of monarchy had worked in the past and its resurrection might solve the country's present problems. Early in the spring they drew up a document – 'Humble Petition and Advice' – discussing the monarchy, Privy Council and second Chamber. Pepys had his ear to the ground during these momentous events and sometimes detected undercurrents of which Montagu was unaware.

Meanwhile, Pepys's marriage had already gone awry. A picture emerges from the Diary of the usual anxieties and quarrels which attend any two young people attempting to discover and adjust to each other under economic duress. Elizabeth was untidy, Pepys mean, she served badly cooked meals,[26] he swamped her with his learning and he worried too much about housekeeping accounts.[27] Their quarrelling reached a climax when he referred to her abusively one day and she retaliated calling him a 'prick-louse'[28] (for he was the son of a humble tailor who earned his living with the needle). Clearly from his later record, Pepys had powerful sexual appetites and these were inhibited from the outset by Elizabeth's menstrual problems. Periods left her prostrate for several days and were complicated by mysterious 'humours and swellings' in the vagina.[29] A very young uninitiated bride found difficulty in responding to his ardour when she was suffering. 'When I came home I found my wife not very well of her old pain in the lip of her *chose* which she had when we were first married.'[30]

Their tastes in literature differed diametrically and, when he read serious books to her on Sunday evenings, her response was poor. She preferred interminable French romances and had an unfortunate habit of dragging in her latest reading among his friends, who could not stop her recounting boring narratives in detail. He set out to broaden her mind and culture to match his own but she had different ideas. None of these differences were characteristic of their normal relations. He, the besotted husband still hopelessly in love with her, and she a person fundamentally affectionate and generous, experienced periods of contentment if not happiness – until one serious break occurred whose cause remains unknown. At some point in the first two years, one or the other could no longer take living together and Elizabeth went off to join friends at Charing Cross. Pepys referred to Mrs Palmer in the Diary. When he was just married she became 'an acquaintance of my wife' who lodged with her at Charing Cross 'during our differences'.[31] Later he referred to 'some old papers of differences between me and my wife'.[32] His reputation as a roué might have grown during his first married years, but, given his total absorption in his wife and his natural jealousy, infidelity seems an unlikely explanation. A child of fifteen years who had serious menstrual troubles must have presented problems to a man equally inexperienced in love-making. Whatever the cause, he hated to be reminded of the break and it did not last long.

When Montagu as General of the Fleet went to sea in 1657, Pepys continued to keep him informed of any event which seemed politically significant. Moving at the centre of political life in Whitehall, he brushed shoulders with important people and witnessed significant events. He saw the Lord Protector set out in state to meet his Parliament, heard much talk of possible kingship, and recorded the new regulations for visitors to the palace. For all this Pepys remained a humble person whose companions were mostly carpenters, cooks, maids and coachmen. His finances remained limited; once he was forced to pawn his lute which meant a great sacrifice because music had begun to play a major role in his life. 'I played also ... and at last broke up and I to my office ... being too much taken with musique.'[33] 'Here the best company for musique I ever had in my life and I wish I could live and die in it ... I spent the night in an ecstasy almost.'[34]

There remained in his possession his father's old bass viol with which he was accustomed to accompany himself singing simple couplets like:

My mind to me a kingdom is
Such perfect joy therein I find.

Unembarrassed in public he would sit in St James's park piping his flageolet or he would take the risk of river-boat company. Singing bawdy choruses with friends in the tavern or hymns at bedtime gave him pleasure, providing the company had voices to match his requirements.

Suddenly, his life was radically altered. An event occurred which was never eradicated from his memory and left him with a new reverence for life and God. As we have seen, he 'lived under a constant succession of fits of stone with the bladder till I was about twenty-six years of age' he wrote in the Diary and when he entered his twenty-sixth year the pain became unendurable. There was nothing for it but an operation – a major operation which meant penetrating the bladder with crude unsterilised instruments, without anaesthetic, and with a success rate of less than twenty-five per cent.[35] Post-operative infection was misunderstood, surgeons did not wash their hands and bloody cloths were used indiscriminately. John Evelyn evoked the ordeal chillingly:

There was one person ... had a stone taken out of him bigger than a turky's egg: the manner thus: the sick creature was stripped to his shirt and bound arms and thighs to a high chair, two men holding his shoulders fast down: then the chirurgion with a crooked instrument prob'd til he hit on the stone, then without stirring the probe which had a small channell in it, for the edge of the lancet to run in ... he made an incision through the scrotum ... then he put his forefingers to get the stone as near the orifice of the wound as he could, then with another instrument like a crane's neck he pulled it out with incredible torture.[36]

Despite all this, lithotomy was a branch of surgery more advanced than others and at St Thomas's hospital, Hollier, a 'stone specialist', had a success rate higher than any equivalent practitioner. We have no direct record of how Pepys prepared himself for the ordeal, but his constant commemoration of the event indicates that he regarded his survival as remarkable. It is not difficult to imagine the feelings of his young bride trying to adjust to a husband who promised her emotional and economic security at a time when neither was easily replaced for a person of her background. Whether it was all too much for her or whether his cousin Jane Turner's house better suited the operation, it was at Jane's house that the grim process took place.

There is every reason to believe – as Ollard suggested – that such a crude operation would render Pepys sterile. He blamed his wife for their inability to have children, exploiting the trouble she had with her periods as a possible explanation. At the age of twenty-six, with the limitless expectations of youth and a firm belief in his own fertility, he could not imagine that he was responsible for their childlessness.

According to Sir D'Arcy Power,

the operation by injuring both his *vasa deferentia* (the tubes by which
the semen is driven into the prostate) left him sterile but not impotent,
and throughout the Diary he shows himself to have been in a state
of constant sexual excitement – desirous but incapable of satisfying his
lust with all the pretty but immodest women of his acquaintance.[37]

Power's distaste for Pepys's sexual behaviour is clear and the picture he draws of Pepys unable to ejaculate is probably misleading. The seminal fluid which carries the semen through the prostate would delude Pepys into believing that his ejaculation carried spermatazoa. Instead, seminal fluid alone would pass. Power was writing in 1930 but modern surgical knowledge tends to bear out his diagnosis of the operation if not its full consequences. It did not necessarily follow that Pepys could not satisfy his lust. It is clear from the Diary that he was anything but a frustrated man. If he had been unable to ejaculate he would have said so vehemently. Instead his ability to ejaculate and feel satisfied remained but no spermatazoa passed in the process.

Whatever the truth, the operation slowly found a perspective in a life which had placed his foot firmly on the professional ladder, brought him a beautiful wife and threatened him with premature death.

Chapter 3
The Diary begins

In 1658 Pepys was proud to migrate from his single room in Montagu's chambers to a small house in Axe Yard on the westside of King Street. It consisted of a bedroom, dining room and study, a dressing room – highly prized as a status symbol – and garret. The yard at the back of the house had possibilities of rearing pigeons and easily accommodated the piles of uncollected rubbish which multiplied so readily. Compared to the garret, it all had a certain splendour. Although the Diary records its disadvantages ruthlessly – with the Thames liable to flood the cellar, the soldiers billeted nearby given to bawdy songs, and dogs who would bark right through the night[1] – the house became a new and fascinating delight to Pepys and his wife, now returned from Mrs Palmer. They began to live more spaciously than ever before. Already Pepys had managed to save money from his £50 a year salary to be invested with his uncle, the forerunner of a saving habit which never deserted him. His ordinary black apparel accompanied by sober stockings and shoes was now replaced on special occasions by a silver lace coat, a suit with wide skirts, a fine cloak and buckled shoes. Much more important to Elizabeth was the acquisition of Jane Wayneman in August 1658 as a maid who smoothed the life of the family for the next three years. A plain, gentle girl whose sensitivities sometimes irritated Pepys – as when she refused to decapitate a turkey – she shared Elizabeth's untidiness, but fulfilled many duties. Work would sometimes begin for her at two in the morning which for some reason seemed the ideal time for washing clothes, but, according to Bryant, she might also be out late at night as a link 'boy' lighting her master through the dark streets.[2]

It was customary for servants like Jane to share the intimate details of the household. She would 'put her master to bed', sit in his bedroom combing his hair, or continue to sit sewing while he slept. She also, on occasion, instructed his boy servant Will in the art of putting his master to bed, an undertaking which we can only suppose involved some degree of undressing. Although Bryant believes Jane lit her master through the streets, this duty probably fell to the boy.

Already Pepys had developed a gift for making friends. All classes of people interested him, and his avid response to life was matched by his ability to catch its presence — hot-foot and alive — on the written page. Strolling through the crowds at Westminster Hall, picking up news or buying occasional wares, he talked to everybody and sometimes stopped to gossip for hours. There were many passing acquaintances, but when he was presented with a pretty woman his interest was immediately concentrated. Books, music, politics were important but a pretty woman — even if it meant no more than admiring her — could always arrest his attention. It was so with Betty Martin (*née* Lane) who had just married a linen draper from Westminster Hall. A cheerful, buxom young woman, she was not averse to drinking in the Trumpet tavern and given to quick responses.

Thence to Westminster and to Mrs Lane's lodging to give her joy. And there she suffered me to deal with her as I used to do: by and by her husband comes, a sorry simple fellow and his letter to her which she proudly showed me, a simple, silly nonsensical thing. A man of no discourse and I fear married her to make a prize of . . . And a sad wife I believe she will prove to him for she urged me to appoint a time as soon as he is gone out of town to give her a meeting next week.[3]

Mrs Lane was the beginning of a series of amours, sometimes casual, sometimes sustained, which were to enliven the Diary disguised in three languages and which ceaselessly disturbed Elizabeth.

The routine of Pepys's daily life has no equivalent today. Sometimes it began in the dawn not with breakfast but playing his flageolet while his wife read to him from one of the many books he had already accumulated. This relaxed opening characterised the greater part of the day. A draught of ale at the Harp and Ball replaced breakfast while his wife went about her 'womanly chores'.[4] Proceeding to the office he might find himself busy making Exchequer payments or — much more likely — without any work of consequence, whereupon he adjourned to the Harp & Ball to drink and gossip or went off to St James's Park to saunter among the pretty girls and prostitutes. Work, social life, home and office, all frequently had no clearcut distinction and it was not unusual for him to go to the theatre in the afternoon and work later at night. Normally, Elizabeth remained cut off from his working routine and Pepys ate a relatively frugal lunch at a tavern with friends. According to the state of his finances he might be reduced to a simple 'dish of pease porridge and nothing else', but more likely it was a piece of chicken or beef from Wilkinson's cook shop. As he grew richer he sometimes had friends home for a full-scale dinner, but for the moment his purse put restrictions on his appetite. The lack of strict office hours and the degree of independence he enjoyed were remarkable for a humble clerk in the Navy. Yet the whole way of life in the seventeenth century was different. Afternoons tended to drift away playing music with friends, rowing down the Thames, dabbling in a little business or collecting Elizabeth and conducting her along Paternoster Row where fine clothes were 'mighty' expensive.[5] Sometimes such dawdling was replaced with high-powered activity when a change in policy, new economies or a rush of dismissals brought sailors crowding into his office demanding to be paid off. But this was unusual.

Streets in seventeenth-century London were unlit, policing improvised, watchmen largely inadequate and footpads free to operate with relative impunity. As a result, a great deal of social life took place at home and if Pepys ventured out at night, either his boy Will carried a lantern for him, or he hired one of the many thin and exploited link boys with flaming torches. As yet his wining and dining was limited, and frequently he used taverns for such occasions. Sometimes Elizabeth accompanied him, but there is no mention of a full social life. Pepys would make his way home through deeply rutted streets, past the cheerful house lights, still sober enough to curse the waywardness of his link boy, but very aware, on a moonlit night, of its beauty. He would listen with pleasure to snatches of bawdy songs from taverns, be very conscious of the black silhouettes of tall chimneys and crazy casements of his beloved London, and as the chimes of midnight began, hear the watchman's call: 'Take heed to your clock: beware your lock, your fire and your light and God give you good night. One o'clock – and all's well.'

Violence was a permanent background threat, not only from criminals. According to Pepys's *Occasional Papers*, butchers organised and fought against brewers, watermen fought against butchers, and family vendettas could be fatal. Retainers of French and Spanish ambassadors engaged in pitch battles on fine points of procedure, and assassinations by hired ruffians were all too familiar. The fury of hot-headed gallants led to duels. In one such duel Lady Shrewsbury, disguised as a page, held the horse of her husband's opponent, the Duke of Buckingham, and subsequently became the mistress of the man who made her a widow. The *Occasional Papers* place great emphasis on these highlights. The general picture was violent but not nearly so spectacular.

In contrast, as we have seen, religious beliefs were carefully structured. They included the conviction that the earth was the centre of the Universe, that the Bible satisfactorily explained the origins of the world, that an irreducible distinction remained between soul and body, and that life after death was a near certainty. Religion and politics were inextricably interwoven and the state had a duty to enforce and preserve religious belief. As Conrad Russell put it in *The Causes of the English Civil War*, religion was the 'basis of political obligations, family integrity and private morality'. The populace mediated its view of historic events through religious persuasions, as did Pepys.

He no longer declared Sunday a dull day and his formal church-going which took place morning and afternoon was now both a form of worship and theatre. Commonly, comparisons were made between different preachers, and Pepys like many others would drop in on several sermons in one morning to take the taste of the preachers.[6] His religious feelings were ambivalent. Never given to religious fervour or even to regular prayers, he frequently thanked God for His beneficence when things were going well, but did not believe that the rule of the angels had brought about a better way of life. Disillusioned by the spiritual zealotry of their parents, Pepys's generation had come to suspect their pious rhetoric as a cover for the exploiters, profiteers and social manipulators. One such manipulator, George Downing, now broke in to add refinement to Pepys's professional life in the summer of 1658.

It was customary in the seventeenth century for senior civil servants to hire and pay assistants who relieved the tedium of their day-to-day transactions. This was common practice in the Court of the Exchequer where Downing worked. It was dominated in those days by a number of barons wearing the insignia of state overseeing a huge chequer-covered table in Westminster Hall, backed up by a mass of minor clerks in the Exchequer Office in Old Palace Yard. Through these offices poured the flood of taxes and revenue due to the state from its many different departments. Each payment was inscribed with a quill pen in elaborate books and the amount reproduced on slips of paper which were sucked into a pipe and passed down to the Tally Court. There, two wooden tallies were granted for each amount paid, one tally being returned to the payer as a receipt.[7] A pushing young careerist, George Downing now employed Pepys as his clerk and paid him the quite generous annual salary of £50. The job entailed carrying and receiving cash from state departments, checking over each bag and paying creditors. It was fraught with hazards unrelieved by the rough manner of his employer, who was not above personal abuse in the four-letter words of the day. Somewhat frightened by Downing, Pepys was discomfited when he made extravagant demands on him in the middle of Pepys's dinner, expecting messages to be delivered at once. Downing came to his office on one occasion and 'asked me whether I did not think that Mr Hawley could perform the work of the office alone'.[8] By implication Pepys was easily expendable. Instead of expressing anger he received the insult 'stoically'. He was to remain in this post where he suffered constant harassment at the hands of Mr Downing[9] until his affairs were transformed by his cousin Montagu in 1656.

In September 1658 Cromwell, the great Protector, died, and Pepys watched with dismay the strife between corrupt politicians and pious generals, fighting to secure power, preference and plunder. In 1659 an unofficial army, unpaid, unprincipled and completely in the grip of its commanders, forcibly removed the Parliament of Richard Cromwell, son of Oliver, and restored the Rump of fifty MPs who remained from the once national Parliament of five hundred.[9] When the Rump cashiered Lambert, one of the most powerful army leaders, and replaced him with Fleetwood supported by six republican commissioners, Lambert promptly marched his troops into Westminster and barred the Rump from their own House. History had briefly and sharply repeated itself with some minor differences. Before Richard Cromwell's removal, Edward Montagu had been ordered to sea in command of the fleet to keep the Dutch under surveillance and attempt a reconciliation between the Swedes and Danes. Anchored in Plymouth Sound on Thursday 26 May 1659 there came alongside Montagu's flagship, the *Naseby*, the ketch *Hind* carrying Samuel Pepys and a packet from the Committee of Public Safety.[10] Montagu took the shattering news of the new Protector's overthrow with relative calm but there is no record of his conversation with Pepys. Montagu must have been aware that his cousin had already drunk many a toast to the royal family in the company of sympathetic clerks, but Pepys was kept ignorant of Montagu's clandestine correspondence with the exiled King.

The republicans next set in motion orders which were to override Montagu's authority and threaten his personal security. In furious reaction Montagu decided to disobey instructions and bring the whole fleet into harbour, only to confront the collapse of Sir George Booth's royalist rising. The exiled Charles in Calais refused to be too depressed by Booth's failure and immediately hurried to Bidussoa where a diplomatic congress was about to negotiate a peace between Spain and

France. He had high expectations that he could generate diplomatic, if not military, support for his long-planned restoration. Instead, he found a hardly concealed indifference. France and Spain were busy composing their differences with scant regard for what remained a peripheral issue – the restoration of the monarchy under the future Charles II.

Back in England republican forces quickly made themselves felt and three commissioners were sent to board Montagu's flagship. Against this background Montagu was brought before a Council of State and found himself forced to make a very cautious, uncommitted statement. The threat of arrest diminished and Montagu retired to his much loved haven, Hinchingbrooke. Pepys, among others, continued to play the intermediary, feeding Montagu with carefully prepared reports of political and military events in London.[11] His own position was now precarious, the constant exchange of power rendering the clerks of Whitehall and Westminster very insecure.

Thoughts were now stirring at the back of Pepys's mind which increased his royal sympathies month by month.[12] Rich material came readily to his pen with Milton and Harrington pouring out tracts in favour of republicanism, while the royalists and Presbyterians formed an alliance. In December 1659 he wrote to Montagu:

Yesterday's fray in London will most likely make a great noise in the country . . . This meeting of youth was interpreted as a forerunner of an insurrection and to prevent that the souldiers were all (horse foot) drawn into this citty . . . Shopps throughout London were shut up, the souldiers as they marcht were hooted . . . and where any stragled from the whole body the boys flung stones, tiles, turnips . . . many souldiers wer hurt with stones and one I see was very neere having his braines knocked out . . . the souldiers let fly theyr muskets and killed in several places . . .[13]

The scene was now set for one of the greatest ventures in the history of English literature. Pepys began with the limited ambition to record his day-to-day personal life but slowly became involved with the groundswell of British history. He was in a unique position to record the political gossip of the day. He had access to the government offices, parliamentary committees and the palace itself. He met every type of person, from soldiers, sailors, booksellers, shopkeepers, merchants and city men, to lords, dons and royalty itself. As Latham put it, 'Thanks to his gift for hobnobbing he came near to hearing the talk of the whole town.'[14] The civil service was limited and even its lesser members were familiar with the intricacies of policy which enabled them to reveal the secrets of confidential committees.[15] Pepys's pleasing personality and insatiable curiosity made him the natural receptacle for such confidences.[16]

Close on twenty-seven when he began the Diary, Pepys simultaneously filled the roles of clerk in the Exchequer and factotum to his cousin Edward Montagu. The first entries set the tone for several volumes which followed. Events spring to life on the page with the immediacy of a man sitting beside you reporting them as they happen for your private ear. Clearly, Pepys felt that his day-to-day activities deserved some permanent record or he would never have written the Diary, but deeper forces were at work. What precisely precipitated him into a daily chore, which in all its accumulated complexity represented years of disciplined and sometimes agonised work, we shall never know. Bryant points out that he had always had a strong feeling for history and 'loved to read the old chronicles ... The sad history of Queen Elizabeth's youth had haunted him almost in his cradle and throughout his life.'[17]

Diaries offer the opportunity to make transient events permanent. They are also repositories for secret lives not fit for public consumption. No better way of assuaging guilt exists than scribbling down passionate admissions to an unknown recipient who resembles oneself. The diary becomes a completely trusted confidant. Pepys may or may not have experienced these mixed motives.

What we know with much more certainty is that on 1 January 1659, in the dead of winter, he first put pen to paper with the words:

Blessed be to God, at the end of the last year I was in very good health without any sense of my old pain, but upon taking cold I lived in Axe Yard having my wife and servant and Jane no more in family than us three ... My wife after the abscence of her terms for seven weeks gave me hopes of her being with child but on the last day of the year she hath them again.

In the thousand and one entries which followed, private affairs were quickly invaded by public events and so it was with the first entry. It is the unique achievement of the Diary that it simultaneously evokes the social and political atmosphere of the time.

The condition of the state was thus. Viz the Rump after being disolved by my Lord Lambert was lately returned to sit again. The officers of the Army all forced to yield. Lawson lie[s] still in the river and Monck is with his Army in Scotland. Only my Lord Lambert is not yet come into the Parliament: nor is it expected that he will without being forced to it.

The new Common Council of the City doth speak very high to

twenty-two of the old secluded Members having been at the House
door last week to demand entrance : but it was denied them and it
is believed that they nor the people will not be satisfied till the House
be filled. My own private condition very handsome : and esteemed rich
but endeed very poor . . .[18]

Cloaked in the secrecy of a popular brand of shorthand every other
entry laid bare his personal life in a rich mixture of history and confession.[19]

Within a few weeks, Monck's army from Scotland had entered
London and Pepys was impressed by its discipline as the soldiers
paraded with bands and banners down Whitehall. Members of the
Rump also watched the parade with enthusiasm since they saw Monck
as a strong counterweight to the resurgence of royalism and an answer
to the power of Lambert. On 9 February 1660 Monck was ordered
to arrest those who had broken the Rump's authority and to press
home his victory with all means at his disposal.[20] Monck wrote a
letter to the Speaker ordering him to readmit the excluded Members
of the Commons. Pepys described its reception: 'At noon I walked
in the Hall where I heard the news of a letter from Monck, who
was now gone into the city again and did resolve to stand for the
sudden filling up of the House and it was very strange how the
countenance of men in the Hall was all changed with joy in half
an hour's time.'[21] Recreation of the scene springs to life when Pepys
turns to people in the streets:

And endeed I saw many people give the soldiers drink and money and
all along in the street cried 'God bless them'. In Cheapside there was
a great many bonfires and Bow Bells and all the bells in all the churches
as we went home were a-ringing . . . But the common joy that was
everywhere to be seen! The number of bonfires there being fourteen
between St Dunstan's and Temple Bar. And at the Strand Bridge I could
at one view tell thirty-one fires. In King Street seven or eight: and
all along burning and roasting and drinking for rumps – there being
rumps tied upon sticks and carried up and down. The butchers at the
May pole in the Strand rang a peal with their knifes when they were
going to sacrifice their rump . . . Indeed it was past imagination both
the greatness and the suddenness of it. At one end of the street you
would think there was a whole lane of fire and so hot that we were
fain to keep still on the further side merely for the heat.[22]

Montagu was duly re-established as colonel of his regiment, elected
to the State Council and appointed Commissioner of the Admiralty.
However, Montagu's implacable secrecy made it impossible to determine whether he supported the King or, as some said, desired to

resurrect Richard Cromwell. Despite his liaison with Montagu, Pepys himself remained baffled and uneasy because of his own growing royalist inclinations. There now occurred an inexplicable mistake in political manœuvring – indeed commonplace courtesy. Shrewd, perceptive and ambitious, the young Pepys could not have failed to realise that pleasing his patron was a prerequisite for the furtherance of his career. Yet when an opportunity occurred to combine a visit to Montagu with seeing his brother 'settled in' at Cambridge, he fulfilled the minor obligation and ignored the major.

Perhaps his somewhat bibulous friend James Pearse was responsible. Pearse combined his surgical skills with a network of social connections which later proved invaluable to Pepys, and their lifelong friendship really began when Pearse suggested accompanying Pepys to Cambridge where he was due to rejoin his regiment. Pepys embraced the idea enthusiastically and they left London on 24 February. 'I rose very early: and taking horse at Scotland Yard ... I rode to Mr Pearse's ... and in a quarter of an hour leaving his wife in bed (with whom Mr Lucy methought was very free as she lay) ... we both mounted and so set forth about seven o'clock and the way was very foul.'[23]

Travel always excited Pepys and in those days a trip to Cambridge from London was full of hazards beyond the mud and rain which persisted all day. They reached Puckeridge, where they stopped to drink, eat mutton and revive their spirits. Expecting to complete the journey in a day, they were forced to stop at an inn as night came down because their horses were exhausted. A merry evening followed with cards, drink and reminiscence. The next morning there was another divergence. Pearse decided to head straight for Hinchingbrooke 'to speak with my Lord' but Pepys inexplicably waited until the following morning before setting out.[24] He arrived at the Faulcon in Cambridge at eight o'clock the following evening where his father and brother were waiting. Since he was carrying news hot-foot to his patron it would have seemed imperative for Pepys to proceed at last direct to Hinchingbrooke, but even now he multiplied the delays. The following day was a Sunday and, taking a long walk with his father, he dined in the chambers of a certain Widdrington, a fellow of Christ's College. Clearly, there were occasions when the conviviality of his earlier Cambridge days broke into his new discipline. It was an odd time to choose with Montagu heading for those high places from which he could dispense elaborate patronage. One drinking session followed another in Cambridge and Pepys was highly amused to be entertained to 'some alcoholic excess' by members of the very governing body of Magdalene who long ago had reprimanded him for just such indulgences. Still he made no attempt to continue his journey but sitting before the fire in Mr Widdrington's chamber he suddenly received a message from Pearse which said that Montagu was already back in London.[25] Pepys commented with considerable understatement that he 'was a little put to a stand'. His discomposure quickly surrendered to another bout of drinking, but nothing seemed to blunt his capacity to recall events for his beloved Diary. He remembered the repeated toasts to the King, the number and kind of dinners, and the names of those he met. In particular, he remembered: 'I stayed up a little while playing the fool with the lass of the house.'[26] What in ordinary mortals would have led to a severe hangover, found Pepys already on horseback at four the next morning heading fast back to London.

There followed the momentous meeting with Montagu who told him that he would use 'all his own and the interest of his friends . . .' for Pepys's benefit.[27] Montagu 'asked me whether I could without too much inconvenience go to sea as his secretary . . . He also began to talk of things of state and told me that he should now want one in that capacity at sea that he might trust . . .'[28]

Within twenty-four hours Pepys was carefully exploring the possibilities of the new job in commercial detail. In these early days he always had an eye to the main chance and money loomed large in his calculations. 'This noon I met with Captain Hollond at the Dog tavern with whom I advised how to make some advantage of My Lord's going to sea, which he told me might be by having of five or six servants entered on board and I to give them what wages I pleased and so their pay to be mine.'[29] It was straightforward fraud but in his day common practice to which naval administrators turned a blind eye. Like all ambitious young men in the rush and stress of establishing themselves, Pepys followed his colleagues. Excitement at the new possibilities before him set him drinking harder than ever and led to insomnia. Fresh news about the arrival of John Creed might also have been responsible, because he learned that Creed – whose family had far better naval connections than Pepys's – was about to be made Montagu's secretary at the Sound. This was a different appointment but Pepys envied Creed's negotiating craftiness and felt that his cynicism gave him an unfair edge. Pepys saw Creed as a man to be watched and confided his anxiety to his Diary.[30]

On his first day at the Navy Office in Seething Lane he was received by one of the gods of naval bureaucracy, Thomas Hayter, who carried

Pepys off to breakfast at the Sun. Even deeper satisfactions were drawn from becoming an employer when he hired John Burr as his clerk and an errand boy Eliezer. Making his way through a mass of accumulated tasks and papers Pepys found himself respected if not openly courted by minor officials previously oblivious of his existence. Almost at once he recommended a person to become a preacher on one of Montagu's ships and received half a piece from him in exchange.

He still had the problem of his part-time job as secretary to the diplomat George Downing. Following Montagu's advice on 9 March 1660 Pepys wrote to Downing suggesting that a Mr Moore might carry on his work in the Exchequer Office if he offered him £20 of his £50 salary.[31] As he wrote in the Diary: 'All night troubled in my thoughts how to order my business upon this great change with me and I could not sleep: and being over-heated with drink I made a promise next morning to drink no strong drink this week for I find that it makes me sweat in bed and puts me quite out of order.'

The Diary had now become an almost daily necessity, despite the abrupt change in his way of life. History was being made by his developing network of connections and he recorded one event after another, sometimes with an excitement which belongs to the novelist. He made selections, he married events to his personal life, he combined telling detail with an eye for colour and sometimes embroidery. Perhaps the fascination of the Diary depends on this ability to combine skills normally attributed to a novelist with a concern for factual truth-telling. There is no means of verifying many of his statements, but the Diary carries the 'ring' of truth, page after page. One technical advance facilitated the physical labour of his daily chore – Shelton's Tachygraphy. This book had already sold many editions and Pepys immortalised its use, converting his manuscripts into attractive tapestries.

Pepys was now busy carrying out an instruction from Montagu which insisted on the 'utmost care in framing commissions necessary for his Vice and Rear Admirals'.[32] This became imperative because Montagu was converting the fleet by degrees to the cause of Charles II and conveying secretly to Pepys the names of those officers on whom he could rely.[33] Meanwhile, the problem of Elizabeth became acute. With scant education, less money and no means of occupying her time, she was threatened by a painful vacuum if he went to sea and even her beauty became a disadvantage when left alone in a London full of 'male marauders'. That was the view of her jealous husband while he considered what 'to do with her'. Apparently he first consulted Montagu about his problem, and then his father, before he said a word to Elizabeth — although in truth it is possible that a number of conversations have escaped record. Anxious to quell his own jealous worries, Pepys treated Elizabeth like a chattel or child and she responded with a petty irritability which he found annoying. He recorded in his Diary: 'In the morning [I] went to my father whom I took in his cutting house and there I told him my resolution to go to sea with my Lord and consulted with him how to dispose of my wife.'[34]

Two nights later a head cold and worry about his departure caused a recurrence of insomnia. 'This day the wench rose at two in the morning to wash, and my wife and I lay talking a great while: I by reason of my cold could not tell how to sleep ... Then to the White Horse in King Street where I got Mr Biddles's horse to ride to Huntsmore to Mr Bowyers: where I found him and all well and willing to have my wife come and board with them while I was at sea.'[35] Commercial transactions continued up to the last minute. 'Then to my Lord's lodging where I found Captain Williamson and gave him his commission to the Captain of the *Harp* and he gave me a piece of gold and 20s in silver.'[36] Courted, wined and dined, with one fee after another slipped into his hand, a world of relative riches was opening up for Pepys.

Walking in Westminster Hall the following day he heard that Parliament had dissolved itself. This would lead to the first free general election for many years. The talk centred around the exiled King and what was once whispered became openly spoken. It gave added zest to his own activities. 'All the discourse nowaday is that the King will come again: and for all I see it is the wishes of all and all do believe it will be so. ... My mind is still much troubled for my poor wife but I hope that this undertaking will be worth my pains.'[37] Pepys now packed his belongings in a sea chest, paid the rent on his house and his debts and began to say farewell to his friends and relations. On 18 March he rose early to visit the barber in Palace Yard and 'afterwards drank with him a cup or two of ale and did begin to hire his man to go with [me] to sea'.[38] 'Sadly and solemnly' Pepys spent his last night with his wife and recorded: 'This morning bad adieu in bed to the company of my wife. We rose and I gave my wife some money to serve her for a time and what papers of consequence I had.'[39] The papers included his sealed will. Finally, he took Elizabeth by coach to the Chequer in Holborn and after some drinks said a last farewell.

Chapter 4

A voyage to King Charles

He returned to a house where all the furniture had been piled into the dining room, a depressing experience which drove him to stay with Mrs Crisp, a neighbour in Axe Yard. There he sat late talking with the family and was given the best bedroom shared with Laud, Mrs Crisp's son.[1]

A dramatic storm intervened to prevent his embarkation and flood Axe Yard, Westminster and King Street, where boats became necessary to negotiate the streets. Never a man to waste time once set on a course of action, Pepys continued to work and received yet another pay-off when he presented Captain Williamson with a commission to command the *Harp*. The gold piece made him reflect 'how these people do now promise me anything: one a rapier, the other a vessel of wine or a gun ... I pray God keep me from being proud or too much lifted up thereby.'[2] By late March the weather had improved and he was very busy with the complicated papers passed down to him by Montagu, covering the movement of a large fleet.

Administrative work increased and Pepys became privy to the negotiations with Charles which Montagu continued to conduct behind the scenes. On the evening of 23 March Pepys bade farewell to his mother and father, an occasion made sad by his fear that his mother – sick with a bad cold – might not be alive on his return. Staying at Mrs Crisp's for the night he found that she had prepared a sumptuous supper and they talked until late. When it came to the final parting Mrs Crisp was moved by his going. Clad in his new riding clothes and stockings, resplendent with a clumsily managed sword, Pepys said a final farewell to a group of friends who showered him with presents.[3] Among them was a man called Shelston, later to apply to Pepys for a job, who did not miss this occasion to cultivate him, even inviting him – dangerously – to meet his wife, 'a very pretty woman'. Pepys then proceeded to the Tower where Montagu awaited him in his barge. Together they headed for Long Reach where the *Swiftsure* lay at anchor. 'As soon as my Lord [was] on board the guns went off bravely from the little ships: and a . . . while after comes Vice Admiral Lawson and seemed very respectful to My Lord.'[4]

Apprehensive of sea sickness on the first day, Pepys was much concerned with the weather but it remained fine. Immediately he plunged into work with an application and thoroughness characteristic of the remainder of his professional life. There were orders to be written for ships going to sea and careful memoranda intended to stop all dangerous persons liable to interfere with Montagu's mission. He was a short man (there is some dispute about Pepys's height but taking an average from the evidence he must have been some 5′5″) yet the cabin was so small it did not easily accommodate him. 'After that to bed in my cabin which was but short: however I made shift with it and slept very well: and the weather being good I was not sick at all.'[5] This cabin he finally noted with satisfaction 'was the best . . . that belonged to My Lord'.

The crew and captain showed him – to his surprise – great respect and in the big dining cabin at meal times he took precedence after Captain Cuttance over everyone.[6] They lay at Long Reach for three days and Pepys did not much like the river tide slapping against the hull, nor did he make allowance for the sudden movement of the ship which upset the beer carried by Eliezer, the boy, over his papers. He promptly boxed his ears. Twenty-four hours after Pepys's arrival, Creed, his rival and predecessor as Sea Secretary, came aboard and promptly signalled his superiority by dining 'very boldly with my Lord'. The gesture collapsed into confusion when they discovered that no bed remained unoccupied and he had to go ashore again. By Tuesday 27 March they were proceeding down the river in the *Hope* where the exchange of gun salutes 'broke all my windows in my cabin and broke off the iron bar that was upon it to keep anybody from creeping in at the scuttle'.[7] When they touched Gravesend his clerk Burr went ashore without authority and left Pepys to cope with the mounting pressure of orders and letters. By 2 April they had all re-embarked on the flagship *Naseby* and Creed took the precaution of putting his possessions aboard before he followed them in person. This upset Montagu's personal steward, who promptly ordered him ashore again.

Things were certainly going well for Pepys. He was climbing the naval ladder more swiftly than he had realised. His new cabin on board the *Naseby* was no bigger than his previous one but it had the luxury of two windows, one looking out on the deck, the other out to sea. On 5 April Pepys, working intensively, heard the rattle of rigging as the sails were hoisted and he watched from his sea window as the river banks began to slip away. The weather remained pleasant and only one serious inconvenience threatened Pepys. Burr, his clerk − overstaying his leave once again − had been left behind and now Pepys faced a mountain of work alone. The following day another complication arose to reduce the excitement of these first hours at sea. 'This morning, came my brother-in-law Balty [Balthazar St Michel, Elizabeth's brother] to see me and to desire to be ... with me as a *reformado*, which did much trouble me.'[8]

Straight out of Dickens − as Ollard remarks − Balty was to become a thorn in Pepys's flesh which quickly rendered his family obligations painful. Disguising his need to find absolutely any kind of employment, Balty arrived on the *Naseby* full of his usual pretensions, indicating that he must have a job consonant with his standing as a gentleman. Combining the implacable cheerfulness of Mr Micawber with a verbose ability to conceal his true motives, Balty began to wheedle and whine his way into Pepys's life, one moment full of strutting over-confidence, the next time pleading relative pulling out all the family stops. At this first meeting Balty stayed to dinner and Pepys recorded: 'My Lord used him very civilly ... After dinner ... I spoke to my Lord and he promised me a letter to Captain Stokes for him.'[9] The moon came up that evening and Pepys spent it walking the quarterdeck learning sea commands from Captain Cuttance. It was his first lesson in a skill that was to prove indispensable. 'And so down to supper and to bed − having an hour before put Balty into Burr's cabin, he being out of the ship.'

The following morning he looked out of his window to see they were well out to sea but shortly afterwards they were among the sands and forced to anchor again.[10] While at anchor, Pepys suffered his first attack of sea sickness. 'I began to be dizzy and squeamish.' Despite the symptoms, he happily ate his way through some special oysters sent by Montagu, and then found himself driven on deck 'to keep myself from being sick'.[11]

At noon they set sail again and now he familiarised himself with distinguishing between ships by their masts, sails and rigging. They overtook two merchantmen and Pepys − missing Elizabeth − used a telescope to pick out details including 'the women on board being pretty handsome'.[12] The landlubber still had not quite adapted to the sea, and that afternoon 'I went to bed being somewhat ill again.'[13]

By 9 April they had anchored at the heart of the English fleet off Deal; 'Great was the shot of guns from the castles and ships and our answers that I never heard yet so great a rattling of guns. Nor could we see one another on board for the smoke that was among us nor one ship from another.'[14]

It was at this juncture that a change occurred in Pepys's relations with Montagu. A fit of melancholy drove Pepys to play his viol 'all alone in my cabin'.[15] The dining room must have been within earshot of Pepys's cabin because Montagu, eating a meal, heard the music and immediately invited Pepys to join him. They stayed talking until very late and it was the beginning of closer relations which presently became professionally intimate.

A near gale blew up the next day and Pepys records with implicit pride that a certain gentleman was forced to retire whereas he remained unaffected. Anxiety about his wife had now become pervasive and that afternoon a number of letters arrived and transformed his mood. Two came from Elizabeth, but they were not – unfortunately – preserved. That Pepys loved Elizabeth is unquestionable; that his private life revolved around her certain; moreover, the letters were not just chit-chat. He recorded some of her news in his Diary: 'Things go ever further towards a King.'[16] Yet he preserved other letters and not hers.

That evening he and Montagu shared their first professional intimacies: 'In the evening My Lord and I had a great deal of discourse about ... several captains of the fleet ... his mind clear to bring in the King.'[17] According to Montagu's biographer, Harris, frequent messages were passing between Montagu and King Charles now based at Breda. As early as January the King had sent a letter which announced his intention of 'making another attempt [to land in England] and he hoped the Admiral would do his part'.[18] Montagu's reassurance quickly followed. The humble Exchequer clerk's perspectives were widening in all directions. It put him on equal talking terms with famous sea captains, lords who were organising the restoration of royalty and the secret diplomacy of Charles II himself.

The April entries in his Diary are alive with enjoyment of sea life, excitement at taking part in history-in-the-making and the simple zest for living which made vivid so much of his writing. At sea he was able to talk casually to men like Sir John Narborough, make music with Lord Montagu, listen to messages relayed from royalty itself, while distinguished men in need of passports sought his aid, and ambitious young lieutenants cultivated his company. Even the absence of Elizabeth was secondary in the wonderful world into which he had been transported. Not that he distanced himself from the ordinary seamen. It was customary for Montagu, Cuttance and Creed to join in the fun of ninepins after dinner. Pepys's first attempt at the game won him half a crown, but daily thereafter he lost money – sometimes as much as nine shillings – no small amount given that he still possessed only £40.

Music was his way of relaxing and before he slept he sometimes turned to his violin or psalm-singing. Creed had become an accepted companion and sometimes joined him while he played. Pepys still regarded him as a crafty rogue who had won the ear of Montagu and now, to all intents and purposes, was Secretary and Treasurer of the English fleet, but his learning was married to a ready wit and his conversation was stimulating. A second person who joined them in psalm-singing was the boy Will Howe, constantly in attendance on Montagu, gifted with an ear for music and full of high spirits to which Pepys never failed to respond. These late night sessions reached a high point one evening when Montagu heard their playing and invited them to his cabin. Producing his own instruments, he joined them in 'a set of locks, two trebles and bass' and they ended up singing a now popular Rump song to the tune of 'Greensleeves'.

Heaven bless the King with his two brave brothers
From rumps and Lords of the House called others
And hand these rumping sons of their mothers
Which nobody can deny.[19]

It was during these sessions that Pepys first encountered Will Hewer, the awkward nephew of Robert Blackborne and then Secretary to the Admiralty Committee. Shy, reserved and full of gangling adolescence, he none the less caught Pepys's attention at a time when he was looking for a boy assistant. This somewhat unprepossessing person was destined to become Pepys's right hand man and close friend.

Relatively unimportant events were suddenly overwhelmed aboard the *Naseby* by dramatic news from London. Montagu had by now assured the loyalty of the Navy to the King's cause which made it possible for him to commit himself to what became known as the Breda Declaration. The whole movement towards monarchy depended on the form of contract which the King had to offer the nation, and on 4 April that form became clear. The Breda Declaration gave an amnesty to those who had fought against him, allowed complete liberty of conscience and – vital for the reliability of his forces – agreed to immediate payment of long outstanding arrears to the

Army. The Declaration was read to a bareheaded House of Commons who solemnly decided that the monarchy should be restored.

Pepys's business had steadily mounted in the few days before the declaration as he issued passes to the increasing number of tardy royalists who had cunningly held their hand until the last moment. He was literally authorising their right to belong to the new regime and his popularity intensified. On 2 May he recorded in his Diary: 'Comes Dunne from London with letters that tell us the welcome news of the Parliament's votes yesterday, which will be remembered for the happiest May-day that hath been many a year to England.'[20] On the following day Montagu summoned the first council of war, where the Admiral's secretary read Charles's Declaration aloud to the assembled captains. Adroitly manipulative, Pepys appeared to 'draw up' a royal resolution which had in fact been dictated previously by Montagu. Its reception was less warm among those captains who feared for their jobs than among the seamen who anticipated – correctly – nights of drunken celebration. As for Pepys, it quickly became one of the most memorable days in his life as he moved from ship to ship, reading the royal Declaration, received with so much cheering, singing, pomp and ceremony that he might almost have been royalty himself.

In the evening as I was going on board the *Vice Admiral*, the General begun to fire his guns which he did all that had in the ship; and so did all the rest of the commanders which was very gallant and to hear the bullets go hissing over our heads . . . this done and finished my Proclamation I returned to the *Naseby* where My Lord was much pleased to hear how all the fleet took it.

In what Pepys described as a 'transport of joy' Montagu now capped his evening by showing him the private correspondence between himself and the King couched in terms of common friends. At three o'clock the next morning Pepys was hard at work and did not fail to add his name to all copies of the council's resolution in case his part should be overlooked. This was unlikely because that afternoon Montagu consulted him, for the first time, about a letter he was writing to the King. Montagu's reliance on Pepys's views and advice increased from that date. In the Hague the King had re-established his court with everyone richly dressed and ceremony observed to the letter while he awaited the arrival of the *Naseby*.[21]

The fleet sailed from the South Downs on 11 May and, without waiting for the commissioners, pressed on from Dover bound for Holland. Burr once more infuriated Pepys by going ashore the night before they sailed but so humbled himself on his return with elaborate apologies that Pepys decided not to dismiss him.

On the morning of the 14th, '... when I waked and rose I saw myself ... close by the shore which afterwards I was told to be the Dutch shore.'[22] His first reactions were hostile: 'Some nasty Dutchmen came on board to proffer their boats ... to get money by us.' None the less, eager to be ashore Pepys took an early boat and was soundly washed by the high seas. This did not prevent him joining Mr Creed to take a coach in the 'forepart' of which there were two pretty ladies, both 'very fashionable with black patches'. They 'sang very merrily all the way and that very well'.[23] Two young men accompanied the ladies and when they all fell to kissing, Pepys was inspired to play his flageolet.

Returning to the *Naseby* the following day he discovered that his old tutor, Samuel Morland, and Downing, his ex-employer, had come aboard, both in some degree of disgrace. Morland had been knighted for services which included being a double agent and Downing was suspected of disloyalty to his friends. Both received short shrift from Montagu and his officers. A man of honour could legitimately change sides out of political or spiritual conviction but not stoop to playing the spy or betraying friends. Another distinguished new arrival, Peter Pett, Commissioner of Chatham dockyard was busy making arrangements for the King's reception, unaware, like Pepys, that they were destined to rival each other in many a future project.

There was a second visit ashore when Pepys chaperoned Montagu's young son Edward to show him the sights. Full of exhilaration Pepys threw caution to the winds and set off on three days' drinking and merry-making during which he twice lost touch with the boy. Edward Montagu wandered away with another party and Pepys, in pursuit, at last overtook him. On the second occasion, the boy simply disappeared and must have been missing all night. According to the Diary it was not until the next day that Pepys stumbled on him landing from the Leiden boat. It is not difficult to imagine Pepys's state of mind when the son of the man in whose hands his whole future lay vanished while in his charge. The Diary entry for 19 May revealed the real villain to have been his old friend Pearse the surgeon. He had taken the boy off without saying a word to Pepys, '... at which I was very angry with Pierce and shall not be friends, I believe, a good while'.[24]

The merry-making seems to have limited his cultural interests and he visited the great Dutch houses in The Hague full of old masters without recording their names or his reactions. The man soon to become a patron of the arts was more interested in the acoustic qualities of the great houses which he tested out by playing the flageolet. His companions from the ship included Will Howe, the steward of Hinchingbrooke, and an acquaintance from his Cambridge days. Together they set off, again with Montagu's son, on yet another burst of roistering to Lansdune: 'We went into a little drinking house where there was a great many Dutch boores eating of fish in a boorish manner ... there was an exceeding pretty lass and I right for the sport; but it being Saturday we could not have much of her company.'[25] In the next twenty-four hours the weather was too rough to re-embark on the *Naseby*, and this led to further duly recorded temptations. Already high on liquor and forced to stay another night ashore, Pepys 'went to lie down in a chamber in the house where in another bed there was a pretty Dutchwoman in bed alone; but though I had a month's-mind to her I had not the boldness to go to her'. Mixing the sexes in the same bedroom seemed socially acceptable because, when they rose in the morning, 'I ... walked up and down the chamber and saw her dress herself after the Dutch dress ...'[26]

Pepys at last reached his cabin on the *Naseby* with such a hangover that he slept for twenty-four hours and woke in confusion – 'to piss' – believing the dawn to be the sunset. By the 20th he expected 'every day to have the King and the Duke on board' and at last the climax came. On Wednesday 23 May he looked out on a scene which he never forgot. Covering every foot of land was a great concourse of people numbering over one hundred thousand, with the sea no less crowded by innumerable craft of every kind. About ten o'clock the crowd fell back to allow the carriages carrying King Charles and his retinue to pass. A small barque, decorated with garlands and gorgeous tapestries, was waiting at the quayside. Amid the rattle of gunfire and the blare of trumpets Charles stepped with great care aboard the barque to be received by Admiral Montagu, with seamen cheering wildly, throwing their caps and even their waistcoats and doublets into the air.[27] It was the first meeting between the two men who had conspired for months, and the first meeting between the King and his subjects. 'Montagu saw a tall, dark man five years his junior who kissed the Admiral affectionately ... and overwhelmed him with compliments and thanks. The kiss was an act of oblivion. In a single moment the Civil War was forgiven.'[28]

Pepys revelled in the scene and within minutes was directly involved. 'I in their coming kissed the King's, Queen's and Princesses' hands.' A roar of guns re-emphasised the occasion, after which the

King re-named the *Naseby* – *Charles* – to Montagu's great pleasure. The ship was now grossly overcrowded and Pepys quite content to share the carpenter's cabin with a knowledgeable physician called Dr Clarke. Nothing could reduce the honour of moving on equal terms with so many distinguished people, carrying a document into the King's own cabin and watching the royal hand scrawl its signature.

On the previous day, 22 May, the Duke of York, the Duke of Gloucester, Montagu and Sir William Coventry had been brought together on the quarterdeck, concentrating the administrative intelligence of naval affairs for the next thirty years. For the moment they were concerned with alloting the role of every ship in the fleet's return to London. Pepys's fortunes over the next twenty years were inseparably tied to these men, with Sir William Coventry becoming the dominating influence.

Coventry epitomised the clever, well-bred public servant whose high-minded dedication was enlivened by wit and learning. Pepys was alone on the quarterdeck in coming from humble origins, in an age when royalty still carried echoes of divinity and aristocrats alone were at home in such company. It was a strain for him to strike the right balance. Not only must he adopt an acceptable persona, he had also to empathise with widely different types. An important test now quickly arose, according to the Diary, on 23 May. When all the preliminaries were over and they set sail for England, Pepys had to accompany the King as he paced up and down the quarterdeck describing the days when the troops were hot-foot to arrest him as he made his escape from England. 'It made me ready to weep to hear the stories that he told,' Pepys wrote.[29] The King later dictated an enlarged account of his adventures to Pepys, who recorded it in shorthand. For the moment the story was vivid in the eyes of Pepys. He envisaged the monarch clad in a worn green coat and a pair of country breeches travelling for four days and nights and frequently up to his knees in mud as he sought to shake off the troops hounding his every step. Once, when his feet were blistered from the unaccustomed country shoes, he could scarcely stir but had to run – desperately – away from a pursuing miller who thought he belonged to a gang of rogues. Every possible complication arose in his scramble from secret bedroom to priest hole, from farmer's attic to cellar, until one set of servants in a house of refuge swore he was a Roundhead and forced him to drink a toast – to himself![30] As the story unfolded it fascinated Pepys. He concluded his Diary entry for Thursday the 24th: 'In the evening I went up to my Lord to write letters for England ... Under sail all night and most glorious weather.' As they approached England the Duke of York spoke personally to Pepys, addressing him by name and promising his future favour.

On 28 May they came within sight of land before night fell, and the following day everyone was awake 'full of expectancy'. The King rejected the *Brigantine* which had been made ready for him and travelled instead in Montagu's barge with the two dukes. A great crowd of people on foot and horseback welcomed him as he stood under the specially arranged canopy.[31] Pepys observed: 'The shouting and joy expressed by all is past imagination.' While the King proceeded to Canterbury, Montagu and Pepys returned to the ship and in the Admiral's cabin Montagu said to Pepys, 'Given a little patience we will rise together.' In the meantime he would give Pepys 'all the good jobs' he could.[32] Nothing suited Pepys better. He recorded in the Diary: 'My Lord almost transported with joy that he hath done all this without any least blur and obstruction in the world that would give an offence to any.'[33]

The next morning the post brought news of an earldom conferred on Montagu, and the even more distinguished offer of the Garter. Ten drawn-out days followed as they waited on board ship for the King to summon Montagu to London. For Pepys, excitement at his future prospects was matched with anxiety in case luck or misfortune should even now intervene. Already he had learnt that luck was a great force in life which could cruelly distort human objectives.

A recurrence of his urinary trouble broke in to increase his anxiety. He recorded on 28 May: 'This night I had a strange dream of be-pissing myself which I really did: and having kicked the clothes off I got cold and found myself all muck-wet ... and had a great deal of pain making water which made me very melancholy.'[34] The following day: 'My pain was gone again that I had yesterday, blessed be God.'[35] Excluded from the Diary for many days, Elizabeth was now remembered fondly. 'I find myself in all things well as to body and mind but only for the absence of my wife.'[36] She had written to him saying how much she missed him, and Pepys had replied that for the moment they must remain content.

On 7 June the King at last summoned Montagu to London and Pepys rode off on horseback – alone it seemed – to reach Canterbury in time for dinner. He then went on via Chatham and Rochester to reach Gravesend a very weary man. The sight of a handsome wench, 'the first that I have seen a great while', revived his spirits and he stayed up far into the night drinking heavily with a friendly captain.

The whole *entourage* embarked next morning on a convoy of small boats which arrived at Temple stairs at twelve o'clock. It was three months since he had seen Elizabeth but Montagu took precedence over his wife and Pepys spent the remainder of the day in attendance on him. He came to Whitehall late in the afternoon and was now within easy reach of Elizabeth but instead of hurrying to spend the night with her he decided to stay at his father's house. The next day was Sunday and in the morning he again visited Montagu before proceeding to church on his own. Given his undoubted devotion to his wife, such movements were perhaps unexpected, although this was a pattern which persisted for many years. Moreover, instead of at last proceeding to Elizabeth in the privacy of their home, he summoned her to his father's house where they ate dinner together. Afterwards, they took a walk in Lincoln's Inn, but the Diary records neither what was said nor any great joy at their reunion.

The summer of 1660 saw half of England flocking to the capital in search of favours from the newly arrived monarch, and Pepys was in danger of being overtaken by numerous rivals but for his special relationship with Montagu. Bryant believed that Pepys overplayed his hand by dancing too close attendance on Montagu, but Pepys found court rituals 'infinite tedious'. Much remained in the balance over the next few days. Promises had been made, Montagu elevated and the Duke of York's patronage offered, but nothing of real substance had emerged. While he waited he did not hesitate to become involved in minor business deals by which he made as little as £5 for a lot of trouble. Then came the appointment of Montagu as Master of the Great Wardrobe, one of the most lucrative and important of the household offices. Montagu's career was entering a new and vital phase yet still no concrete offer came to Pepys, who consoled himself with the pleasure of returning at last to his 'little house in Axe Yard' and his beloved Elizabeth. Almost at once she was forced to go back to Buckingham to collect her personal possessions and Pepys found the nights very lonely. And then on 18 June Pepys returned 'to my Lord's lodgings, where he told me that he did look after the place of ... Clerk of the Acts for me'.[37] It was one of four senior administrative posts in the Navy, and the only one open to a man of such humble origins. Aware that the appointment might have rich possibilities, Pepys could not immediately believe that it would materialise. On 23 June he went to a dinner party accompanied by Montagu and now Montagu confirmed that the job was his: 'At which I was glad.'[38]

This seemed to be a low-key reaction to a piece of luck that was to transform his life. By the following day he responded differently, and his mind was 'full of thoughts for my place as Clerk of the Acts'.[39] He moved at once to reaffirm his appointment, talking to Sir William Coventry, closely attending Montagu and negotiating with Mr Turner of the Navy Office who frankly admitted that he coveted the job. Pepys suffered a temporary setback which might have produced alarm in him although none appears in the Diary. Lady Monck wrote to Montagu claiming that she had promised the Clerkship 'elsewhere' and could not retract her undertaking. Married to General Monck, she did not hesitate to accept bribes for jobs in the Navy which were not within her patronage. Montagu blandly replied that General Monck would take it very ill if he began naming candidates for officers in the Army. There was no reply from Lady Monck.

No sooner had one possible complication been overcome than another appeared. He met and came to terms with Turner his rival, already established in the Navy Office, only to be confronted by a merchant who offered him the very large sum of £500 to withdraw his candidature.[40] Resorting — unusually — to prayer for guidance, he decided to refuse the offer, but yet another threat then appeared. The bush telegraph warned him 'that Mr Barlow my predecessor as Clerk of the Acts is yet alive and coming up to town to look after his place'. Pepys reacted with understatement: '[it] made my heart sad a little'.[41] The jungle of freewheelers in public administration who openly extorted bribes and fees for public offices regarded the Clerk of the Acts as a superb prize to be bargained over until the last drop of dues had been extracted. Pepys was subjected to one hazard after another until Montagu urged him to 'secure his patent', the last stage in the appointment process. Pepys drew his attention to the new threat of his predecessor, Mr Barlow, and the faithful Montagu reassured him that he would 'do all that could be done to keep him out'. Pepys then dashed in a frenzy up and down Chancery Lane desperate to have his warrant converted into a bill and his bill a patent.[42] One lawyer, Mr Beale in Chancery Lane, was recommended as expeditious but pleaded that business momentarily overwhelmed him. Pre-empting the privileges which were so tantalisingly offered and withdrawn, Pepys now encountered a man who wanted to buy an ordinary clerk's place and, without hesitation or authority, Samuel asked £100 for the position. Clearly, he was an apt pupil in one aspect of the job he craved. Simultaneously, he fought off yet another rival, drove fresh bargains with corrupt competitors and was greatly relieved to learn that Barlow's ill health now disinclined him to re-enter the service. Finally, in desperation, at eleven o'clock one night he persuaded a Chancery clerk, Mr Spong, to 'come to my Lord's lodgings, where I got him to take my bill to write it himself . . . against tomorrow morning'.[43] A very accommodating Mr Spong was still working on the document in his nightgown when Pepys called to collect it. Pepys literally ran with it to Mr Beale who required the 'timely production of two gold pieces' before he gave it proper attention. Superstition notwithstanding, on the dreaded 13 July the patent was at last signed and sealed by the Lord Chancellor. Pepys rushed from Mr Beale's office to the coach outside where his wife was waiting, and there he 'presented her with my patent at which she was overjoyed'.[44] The last entry for 13 July read: 'To bed with the greatest quiet of mind that I have had a great while, having eaten nothing but a bit of bread and cheese at Lilly's today . . .'[45] Pepys now joined the happy band of Naval administrators who could, when it suited them, exploit their fellows for commercial gain while giving dedicated service to King and country.

With great pride he showed Elizabeth their new house overlooking the gardens and courtyards of the Commonwealth Navy Office. Built of warm ochre brick it had nine rooms with all the 'necessary appurtances'. Pepys wasted no time in taking possession. He arranged for a door to be made in the leads (or roof) which would enable Elizabeth to sit with him on a summer evening looking out over London.[46] Torrential rain delayed the delivery of their goods and chattels, but by 17 July they followed the baggage in a hackney coach and slept for the first time in their grand new home. Servants proliferated in many seventeenth-century households and they began to multiply in Pepys's. First came the boy Will to help out when the maid Jane was taken ill. July saw the other Will, nephew to Robert Blackborne[47] arrive in the mixed role of personal attendant, clerk and general factotum. Initially, his behaviour was erratic, with late-night drinking and a failure to bolt doors, but this marked the beginning of a relationship which slowly developed and lasted until Pepys's death.[48]

Still regarded as something of a sinecure, Pepys's job as Clerk of the Acts gave him little trouble in his first few months. Twice a week when the Navy Board met he was expected to prepare its agenda and record its proceedings.[49] A residue of his duties for Montagu included corresponding with ships at sea, but both undertakings left plenty of time for private deals. A certain Mr Mann offered him the huge sum of £1,000 for the Clerkship and for a time he was tempted, but he turned it down on the not entirely objective advice from Montagu, who wanted him to keep the job.

Special privileges accompanied commercial gain. The vicar of nearby St Olave's church offered Pepys and a Commissioner of the Navy Board, Sir William Penn the pew with the highest ranking, and Pepys sat there on two following Sundays, thanking God for his good fortune. Most human beings surrender to hypocrisy at some time in their lives and Pepys easily accommodated a major concession. Alongside solemn prayers – 'May I justify my good fortune, O Lord' – he took advantage of his still owning two houses to deceive his wife on the first of many occasions. Before he completed the sale of his Axe Yard house to a wine seller called Dalton for £41 he went to a farewell party given by his neighbour, 'old Mrs Crisp'. Present at the party was a good-looking aunt, Mrs Crisp's daughter – Diana – and as the merry-making mounted she flirted with him in such a manner that he 'doubted her virtue'. Whether by accident or as a precaution, he had already sent Will Hewer home to tell his wife that he would not return that night because Montagu was going out early in the morning.[50] Three days later Pepys revisited his old house, Diana passed down the street and he immediately seized the opportunity. He 'took [her] into my house upstairs and there did dally with her a great while and find that ... *nulla puella negat* [let no girl say no]'.[51] Completely unaware of what had happened, on the following day Elizabeth was the recipient of an expensive pearl necklace, a gesture which she might have interpreted as spontaneous generosity.

Chapter 5

Clerk of the Acts

Since the members of the Navy Board were older, tougher and altogether more sophisticated in naval matters than Pepys, a certain uneasiness might have characterised his early attendance. Instead, according to the Diary, whenever he felt out of his depth he managed to conceal it. From the outset he observed the Board going about its business without intervening, listened with great care and made notes, elaborated by entries in the Diary. Quick to learn, memorise and turn experience to useful purpose, there remained one aspect of his relations with his grand masters in which his skills matched theirs. He understood the uses of conviviality. Many a time Sir George Carteret, Treasurer, Sir William Batten, Surveyor, and Sir Robert Slyngsbie, Comptroller, returned from the tavern with Pepys, sharing the mutual support which a gentleman needed in his cups. Before Pepys's fascinated eyes now unravelled the duties which distinguished the work of the Navy Board (the 'tarpaulins') and the Lord High Admiral (the 'gentlemen'). The Navy Board dealt with the down-to-earth realities of naval requirements from ships, masts, sails, anchors, cordage and flags to boatswains, gunners, pursers, cooks and carpenters. The Lord High Admiral administered the best use to which the Navy could be put as a fighting or political instrument. In fact the basic daily concerns of the Navy were not Pepys's affair. He concentrated on recruitment, officer appointments, discipline and tactical advice. James, Duke of York and Lord High Admiral, combined administrative intelligence with tactical skills, but the range of his responsibilities was too great for one man. Indeed, since his day his functions have been undertaken by a Commission of Lords of the Admiralty. When Pepys joined the Board, the Duke of York was already accustomed to consult its well informed and co-operative members. Moreover, Sir William Coventry, as secretary to the Duke of York and a member of the Navy Board, bridged their very different functions. The Diary reflects a sustained respect and admiration for Sir William Coventry, even though not all his colleagues shared Pepys's view.[1]

Pepys found Coventry highly sympathetic and was made privy to policy decisions which were not strictly within his competence. These were the very early beginnings of his widening interests in the Navy which would enabled Pepys, before long, to influence its destinies in a manner far beyond the range of a clerk of the Board. Coventry was a high-minded public servant, incisive in action, witty in conversation and principled enough to be concerned by the increasing corruption in naval affairs. Very early in their acquaintance Pepys wrote: 'By and by comes Mr Coventry and he and I alone sat at the Office all morning upon business . . . having good discourse . . . I find him the most ingenuous person I ever found in my life. And am happy in his acquaintance and my interest in him.'[2] Later he developed this opinion: 'Thence to St James's to Mr Coventry, and there stayed talking privately with him in his chamber . . . I think [him] my most true friend in all things that are fair. He tells me freely his mind of every man and in everything.'[3]

The respect, according to the Diary, was mutual. Coventry told Montagu, now Lord Sandwich, that Pepys 'was indeed the life of this Office and much more to my commendation'.[4] Despite reciprocal appreciation, Coventry found his integrity endangered by the underlying network of corruption. A man committed to the abolition of the sale of places and all the perquisites which pervaded the Navy, he none the less continued to accept such rewards himself. Coventry remained a man of vision who clearly conceptualised a large and permanent Navy for England. Pepys took his inspiration from that vision but did not at this stage share Coventry's desire to sweep away graft – not that Pepys's position was straightforward. Incapable of freeing himself completely from his Puritan upbringing, his conscience struggled to discriminate between different shades of corruption. He was young, avid, ambitious, and the taste of easy money was not merely tempting, it became irresistible. The conflict remained. Accepting money for goods which had never existed, or payment for seamen whose names were pure invention was for him the unacceptable face of Navy practice. However, forty gold pieces slipped under the counter in a glove did not outrage Pepys if the gift accompanied the supply of better and cheaper ships' rigging. As Ollard put it: 'Treachery, disloyalty, cringing were unthinkable. But everything else was relative and therefore, up to a point, negotiable.'[5]

Pepys's portraits of his colleagues on the Navy Board were dashed down after meetings, discussions or quarrels with all the emotional power of the immediate moment. That is what makes them so readable, although possibly not altogether reliable. The second Commissioner on the Navy Board, Sir William Penn, was a man of altogether different calibre from Coventry. If Pepys's view of Penn was to fluctuate over the years, he and Coventry both became his fellow-revellers on many a social occasion at the outset. The Diary for 8 September records Penn sending for Pepys to share a glass of wine with him. 'I find him to be a very sociable man and an able man ...' There followed a crucial additional qualification which later he was to develop, ... and very cunning'.[6] The *Dictionary of National Biography* describes Penn as 'A mild-spoken man, fair-haired, of a comely round visage'.[7] Still developing his musical skills, Pepys was pleased to find Penn capable of bursting into song, enlivened occasionally by bawdry.

The third member of the Navy Board, Sir William Batten, the Surveyor, was also highly sociable, frequenting taverns, and, in particular, the Dolphin in Seething Lane. Different from Penn, Batten was a real man of the sea. Seamanship ran in his family and his father qualified for the title master which was reckoned a cut above captain. Carteret (Treasurer of the Navy) and Slyngsbie (Comptroller) were gentlemen who had become sea officers without Penn's seamanship. Batten, according to Pepys, could never aspire to being a gentleman and remained inescapably a tarpaulin. Penn and Batten were admirals whose position and wealth enabled one to preserve an Irish estate and the other a country house at Walthamstow. They were rich and privileged beyond Pepys's means. Normally, his leisure associates were men of his own origin or drawn perhaps from neighbours in Axe Yard or Whitehall. Instead he now found himself – to his delight – hobnobbing with Penn and Batten in many a drinking session. The hierarchy in the Navy was closely observed and rank usually decided what company admirals, captains, ratings and clerks kept, but Pepys broke the rules. Good-natured, talkative and vividly alive Pepys's wide-ranging interests combined to make him delightful company.[8] Thus he was acceptable to those distinguished men whose daily encounters frequently brought them in touch with the dullest civil servants. It would be surprising if they remained unaware that this newcomer among them had talents which could be turned to good purpose and perhaps personal profit. References in the Diary to Penn and Batten grow: 'At Sir W. Batten['s] with Sir W. Penn we drank our morning draught and from thence for an hour in the Office and dispatch a little business.'

In his first year at the Navy Office heavy drinking threatened to become a danger to Pepys. Impoverishment as a young Clerk had not prevented the occasional drunken indulgence as we have seen, but now he had more money and tried to drink as the admirals drank, until his unaccustomed stomach rebelled. There were even times when he vomited a breakfast of pickled onions. The Diary resounds in self criticism – 'last night's drinking was my great folly' – and on one occasion Pepys was forced to summon help in the middle of the night: 'I was very ill ... and so I was forced to call the maid (who pleased my wife and I in her running up and down so innocently in her smock) and vomited in the basin.'[9] Calling a maid out of bed in such circumstances seemed the ultimate humiliation, but poor Jane was accustomed to every kind of service at any time of night.

Eventually he was invited to Batten's country home at Walthamstow and tasted the luxury of Batten's way of life. Riding home with Penn, two 'insolent country fellows' deliberately broke across Batten's path, whereupon – according to Pepys – he knocked them down. Pepys expressed distaste rather than scepticism. Professionally, socially and now spiritually he was assimilated into the lives of grand new colleagues. 'In the afternoon to our own church and my wife with me (the first time that she and my Lady Batten came to sit in our new pew): and after sermon my Lady took us home and there we supped with her and Sir W.Batten and Penn and were much made of – the first time that ever my wife was there.'[10] Pepys makes no comment about his wife's ability to cope with distinguished company but it must have put a strain on her limited resources, unless her beauty redeemed her in any company. By 26 November, whatever her gaucheries, an event took place which confirmed her new social standing. Pepys returned home that evening to learn that 'my Lady Batten hath given my wife a visit (the first that she ever made her) which pleased me exceedingly.'[11] In our eyes Pepys cannot escape the charge of snobbery. He kept his servants at a considerable distance behind his own pew and was careful of the company he kept in public places. Ruthless expediency characterised his choice of professional company, as when Commissioner Pett was thought to be losing his place in the pecking order and Pepys avoided him. However, such behaviour was enshrined in the values of the day.

By 24 January he had taken yet another step in his career, becoming a Justice of the Peace without the slightest knowledge of the skills required. His life was now busy in all directions. He spent one night dining with the admirals, the next night in the company of a Duchess followed by a state dinner at the Tower, and an evening in the Dolphin where he kissed a pretty lady only to discover that she was the wife of Batten's son. Business life offered similar satisfactions as he sat alone with Penn answering petitions. One day a Mr Jessop arrived. Once a man of 'great estate and good report' he now came cap in hand asking for favours from Pepys.[12] Unaware of the dizzy heights he was to climb, Pepys felt that he had indeed arrived. All that winter it seemed to him that a miracle had placed him where he was and he must behave with appropriate dignity. From the Diary it appears that he would have been happy to remain in such a splendid position as Clerk of the Acts for the rest of his life.

His importance was dramatically reaffirmed early in January when Thomas Venner, a rebellious Fifth Monarchist, stirred the whole city to near panic. Sixty men led by Venner held a conference at their meeting house near Coleman Street on 6 January and decided to take up arms and conquer the world in the name of Christ the King. They launched their attack the following day and indiscriminately killed six men, striking terror in the heart of London. On the 9th Pepys awoke 'in the morning about six o'clock to the sound of people running up and down ...' They said 'that the fanatiques were up in armes in the city and so I rose and went forth where in the streets I find everybody in arms at the doors; so I returned (though with no good courage at all, but that I might not seem afeared) and got my sword and pistol which however I have no powder to charge ...'[13] The city had ground to a standstill with the shops shut, trained bands roaming the streets searching 'for the rogues', and rumours that a dozen people at least were now dead. Wonderfully frank about his inadequacies, Pepys faced the situation with characteristic self-sufficiency: 'Seeing the city in this condition, the shops shut and all things in trouble, I went home and sat.'[14] Later that night he turned to his lute until midnight, 'there being strict guards all night in the city'.

The government took the incident much more seriously than Pepys, having miscalculated the number of malcontents and fearing their power to take over the naval arsenals. The Comptroller, Slyngsbie, and the Clerk of the Acts were sent post-haste to Deptford, where they arranged to provide armed guards for all naval institutions. Travelling to Deptford, Pepys was treated with reverence by dockyard officials. On the Sunday night after their arrival an alarm sounded and Pepys crawled out of bed with Slyngsbie to distribute hand-picked guards whose ferocious patriotism threatened to frighten their employers. Slyngsbie enjoyed Pepys's company on this trip and went out of his way to co-operate with him. Slyngsbie, coming from an old naval family, quickly won Pepys's respect as a man of integrity with something akin to a natural nobility. Socially they would meet in the Mitre tavern to discuss cultural and intellectual subjects rarely touched upon by Pepys's other associates, and professionally he went out of his way to interest Pepys in wider theoretical questions about the Navy's future. 'The office done I went with the Comptroller to the coffee house . . . I seem to be fond of him.'[15]

Overwhelmed as he might be by his new status, already a glimmering of ambition was disturbing his contentment. The growing intensity of his devotion to duty was dampened somewhat when he brought to Sir William Batten's house a rough proposition for saving on naval expenditure and found Penn and he so engrossed in playing cards that they could not be interrupted. There is some disagreement about Pepys's precise duties in these early days at the Navy Office where lesser clerks and dockyard officials collaborated to convey the Board's instructions. Paying off ships, selling surplus vessels and stores also fell within his province. One major problem immediately became evident to him : the very complex one of manning the Navy. Ordinary ratings were at this time very sceptical of their indirect dealings with the Navy Board. Unemployment was rife and the threat of starvation for some people was very real, but even those twin pressures failed to produce enough recruits for the simple reason that seamen were afraid they would never be paid. Penn, Batten, Coventry and Carteret all fulfilled double roles as MPs and members of the Board, and it was part of Pepys's job to brief them on the essential facts necessary to underpin their constant appeals for more men and money. They, in turn, were pressured by large numbers of seamen who, when ships were paid off, failed to receive their wages. Time and again there was insufficient money to meet the Board's debts and the custom developed of issuing tickets which theoretically were redeemable at the Navy Office. Simultaneously, the con-men of the day moved in to buy up the tickets at cut rates and later sell them at large profits. Ignorant seamen found themselves victimised on all sides and, driven by a fierce belief in their rights, sometimes attacked local officials or besieged their offices. However, seaman were a small part of the Navy's financial problems, and unscrupulous administrators could always arrange to prolong their voyages. Keeping a distance between themselves and the merchants selling essential supplies to the Navy and dockyard workers was far harder for the Board. Merchants could refuse to continue supplies until debts were settled and workers could simply stop their labour and bring the dockyards to a standstill.

John Holland's *Two Discourses on the Navy* gives us an illuminating account of the abuses of the Navy.[16] 'Such hath been the indulgence of past times that men that never knew the Navy ... have been commended to their places by and upon certificates from officers.'[17] Yet Holland printed one set of precepts and personally recommended another. On 8 March 1660 Pepys wrote: 'This noon I met with Captain Holland at the Dog tavern with whom I advised how to make some advantage ... which he told me might be by having of five or six servants entered on board, and I give them what wages I pleased and so their pay to be mine.'[18] Such corruption was inexcusable. Holland's reputation was to some extent redeemed when he later wrote a defence of seamen's delinquency. 'How is it possible for a boatswain, having a wife and three, four or five children depending upon his labour, to maintain himself and them on 20l per annum ...',[19] 'without clenching',[20] 'changing, selling ... and purloining of His Majesty's cordage and other stores committed to his trust?'[21]

There were many forms of corruption. Pepys quickly discovered that responsibility for powder, shot and victualling was split between many bodies to the confusion of administration and the incitement of further malpractice. An order issued by one department might need agreement from several others and each exchange of memos introduced fresh possibilities of graft. Anxious to disentangle the complexities, Pepys began to probe behind the scenes with a mind which not merely observed and recorded but automatically sought to reform deficiencies. His keen commercial sense, very aware of the crime of waste, was matched by a detached – perhaps even aesthetic – desire to impose order. This 'aesthetic' quality has been seen as central to Pepys, but order itself is not necessarily aesthetic. Pepys's Puritan sense would have seen order as a necessity and this had nothing to do with art. Expressing his new concerns, Pepys wrote to Coventry on 22 August 1662: 'Would to God you could for a while spare two afternoons a week for general debates ... ye many old rates to be enquired into tickets ... regulating ye shopsellers' practices with forty more scandalous errors.'[22]

Pepys's deepening experience of naval affairs coincided with developments in his domestic life. First he decided to transform his house and convert it into a dwelling worthy of his new status. So enthusiastically did he set the labourers working that the carpenters, plasterers and painters were given free access to the whole house until poor Elizabeth Pepys carried her bed from one room to another to escape their tramplings. Casual as ever in his early professional life, Pepys would take several days away from the office to supervise the workmen. Nor was he above joining their company in the evening to share his liquor and sit exchanging drolleries. There followed what seemed a minor annoyance. He returned home one evening to find that Mrs Davis, wife to the Navy Commissioner, had come to lodge next door and 'locked up the leads door from me which put me into so great a disquiet that I went to bed and could not sleep until morning'.[23] The following day he went to see *The Tamer Tamed*.[24] It was intended to relieve his anxiety but failed to do so. The anxiety continued and spread over three entries in the Diary, reaching a new intensity when he discovered that someone had broken open the bolt of the door which gave upon his leads.[25] Worse complications arose when sewage from his neighbour's cellar broke into his own as he discovered to his cost one morning. Heated altercations with his neighbour led to a quick clearance but by the end of the month his mood was still gloomy. 'This month I conclude with my mind very heavy for the loss of the leads – as also for the greatnesse of my late experiences. In so much I do not think I have above 150l clear money in the world ...'[26] The loss of the leads meant that he could not walk on the roof on a summer evening and his alleged impecuniousness was probably due to elaborate house renovations. During the summer his wife's menstrual troubles prevented intercourse for a fortnight[27] 'which is a pain to me'.[28]

Economic insecurity is commonplace but Pepys's preoccupation with money was particular. One October evening he sat up very late poring over one sum of money after another, examining its amount and origin minutely. The discovery, for instance, that Lord Sandwich owed him £80 was 'a good sight and I bless God for it'. God and Mammon were frequently associated in the mind of Pepys. Constantly he attributes the accumulation of small sums of capital to divine benevolence. The sums were always recorded in meticulous detail: £23.14.9d from Major Hart, £11.5s from Creed and £87.10s as three months' salary. Money of course was a measure of status and the slow growth of his capital began to give him reassurance. This was reaffirmed when all the renovations to his home were at last complete. On Christmas day 1660 he recorded: 'In the morning very much pleased to see my house once more clear of the workmen ... and indeed it is so far better than it was that I do not repent of my trouble.'[29]

The spectacular event late in April 1661 was the King's Coronation. It might have produced a flowering of Pepys's talent as a writer which unfolded the scene step by step in all its glittering reality, but he retreated into relatively commonplace language. 'And got to the Abbey ... with much ado ... did get up into a great scaffold across the north end of the Abbey ... where with a great deal of patience sat from past four till eleven ... And a pleasure ... to see the Abbey raised in the middle all covered with red and a throne and footstoole.'[30] There were scores of musicians in red, bishops in cloth of gold, the massed nobility brilliantly robed and many beautiful women in all their finery such that Pepys had difficulty removing his eyes to the proper object of their appraisal. Suddenly, the whole scene fell quiet as His Majesty approached. 'The King in his robes, bare-headed which was very fine. And after all had placed themselves – there was a sermon and the service. And then in the quire at the high altar he passed all the ceremonies of the Coronacion – which to my very great grief I and most in the Abbey could not see.'[31] Exploiting every device of pomp and circumstance, the ceremony moved to its climax when 'the crowne being put upon his head a great shout began'. There followed a general pardon read by the Lord Chancellor while medals of silver were flung amongst the throng. The roar of acclaim rose again, overwhelming all words and music. Suddenly, Pepys had 'so great a list to pisse' that he was forced to leave the Abbey before the completion of the ceremonies. Poor Elizabeth had no part in all this. Perhaps, climbing scaffolding was unladylike; perhaps Pepys's invitation excluded her. Whatever the cause, he now went in search of her in Westminster Hall. 'All the way' it was 'within rayles and 10,000 people covered with blue cloth and scaffolds ... Into the Hall I got – where it was very fine with hangings ... one upon another, full of brave ladies. And my wife in one little one on the right hand.'[32]

At last it was all over. Excitement gave place to exhaustion as Pepys dropped his fine company to retire to his old friends in Axe Yard. 'In which at the further end there was three great bon-fires and a great many gallants, men and women: and they laid hold of us and would have us drink the King's health upon our knee ... and I wondered to see how the ladies did tipple.' A second bout of drinking in a wine cellar proved disastrous. 'We drank the King's health and nothing else till one gentleman fell down stark drunk.'

Pepys was no sooner abed that night than his head began to swim and he woke in the morning to find himself 'wet with my spewing'.[33] Because of 'last night's drink which I am sorry for' his head was in a sad state. Venturing out into the light of day he was surprised to find in what respect his old neighbours now held him. 'I began to know how to receive so much reverence which at the beginning I could not tell how to do.' There is a curious anomaly in Pepys's writing. Sometimes, he invested personal incidents with wonderful colour and life which was missing from his description of events like the Coronation. That same summer, for instance, he witnessed the leap of a possible suicide and brought it painfully to life in all its comic-tragedy. Discussing with a certain Captain Ferrars whether he should go to sea the captain suddenly 'grew so mad with joy that he fell a-dancing and leaping like a madman'. The balcony window was open and Ferrars went to the rail and offered to leap over. 'What', he asked Pepys, 'if he should leap over' there and then. 'I told him I would give him 40l if he did not ...' Pepys then shut the balcony door but Ferrars reopened it and 'with a vault leaps down into the garden – the greatest and most desperate frolic that ever I saw in my life. I run to see what was become of him and we find him crawled upon his knees – but could not rise. So we ... dragged him to the bench where he looked like a dead man and could not stir. And though he had broke nothing yet the pain in his back was such as he could not endure.'[34]

The day following the Coronation was a Sunday but he no longer dined every Sabbath with his ageing parents although he remained in touch with family affairs. His brother Tom had been forbidden entry to the home in Axe Yard because of 'his lying out of doors ... a day and a night' but, after chastising Tom, Pepys persuaded his father to re-admit him.[35] Then an absurd quarrel blew up between his father and mother over his father's devotion to a maid who aroused misplaced jealousy in his mother and Pepys was driven to use 'high words' against a mother he now regarded as very fractious. It does not seem to have been very effective, for it left 'them in the same discontent'.[36] Later he recorded: 'My mother is now grown so pettish that I know not how my father is able to bear with it.'[37]

Uncle Robert of Brampton died on 6 July and Pepys rode post-haste the sixty miles to Brampton where his father and Aunt Annie waited with the body already beginning to smell in the house. Pepys had deliberately cultivated relations with his uncle before he died but they had gradually deteriorated. Now the will revealed that the majority of the real estate was to go to his father with only the remainder to Pepys. Complications arose over some 'lost surrenders' of £146 and Sir Robert Bernard, the lawyer, finally pronounced that the money due should go to Uncle Thomas not Pepys.[38] Two weeks' negotiations left him annoyed with a manipulative aunt and hypocritical lawyers, and the fear that his brother Tom was not capable of sustaining his father's tailoring business. Returning home on 22 July he took up his Office duties the next day and was pleased to talk once more with congenial spirits deliberately 'putting it about' that he had inherited no less than £200 a year.

By 24 July domestic affairs again disturbed his professional satisfaction with his sister Pall in bad odour for her untidiness and Will Hewer losing Pepys's favourite silver tankard.[39] When the legal fees had been paid his parents were left with little more than £100 a year to live on, complicated by the fact that his father John's liabilities practically matched his assets.[40] Then came the sad business of arranging the removal of his father to Brampton where he would in future live. Relations with his sister Pall slowly deteriorated until he had to tell her that she too must leave his household. This led to another scene as he helped his mother and sister into a country cart which would carry them to Brampton. Despite her floods of tears and belated cries of penitence, Pepys insisted that Pall must leave. Both women made a great fuss about going.

Pepys sought consolation from his troubles in the theatre and drink. The small glittering box which encompassed the world in miniature, the huge candles flickering over the richly dressed actresses, the whores and orange-sellers, these were the stuff of an alternative way of life where plays like *The Changeling* and *The Bondsman* delighted him.[41] It all came fresh and sparkling after the closed world of Puritan England. Theatres were first reopened on 9 July 1660 when the King issued an order for a royal warrant giving Sir William Davenant and Thomas Killigrew the exclusive right to establish companies.

Excitement from the theatre sometimes ran over into intoxication in the tavern. Theatre-going dissipated time but left him elated. Drink dissipated time, created good conversation and good fellowship, but left him with appalling hangovers. Again and again he vowed to stop drinking and repeated the offence the following day. On 26 July he wrote: 'Having the beginning of this week made a vowe to myself to drink no wine ... (finding it to unfit me to look after business) and this day breaking it against my will I am much troubled for it but I hope God will forgive me.'[42] By August of the same year another problem had resurfaced threateningly – money. His heavy drinking, family complications and attempts to keep up with the luxurious life of Batten and Penn led to the following entry: 'No money comes in so that I have been forced to borrow a great deal ... for my own expenses and to furnish my father ... I have some trouble about my brother Tom who is now left to keep my father's trade...'[43]

As ever personal troubles were quickly qualified by public ones. The court, he wrote, was given over to swearing, drinking and whoring, the clergy 'so high' all people protested, and benevolence so little it had led to discontentment everywhere. In short, he saw no satisfaction anywhere in any sort of people.[44] Even his staff in the Admiralty Office were quiet 'only for lack of money' which meant that 'all things go to wrack'.

That summer saw a dramatic change in Lord Sandwich's fortunes when he was ordered to overcome the Barbary Corsairs in the Mediterranean, call at the English colony at Tangier and return with the new Queen of England. Making all the necessary arrangements threw Pepys into a flurry of work. Still relatively impoverished, on the day Lord Sandwich departed Pepys managed to face his coat with white material torn from his wife's petticoats and set out to join Lord Sandwich with some pretence at the necessary elegance. At Deptford in high spirits they went aboard a Dutch yacht. As he disembarked again, 'My Lord did give five guns ... which was the greatest respect my Lord could do me and of which was not a little proud.'[45]

Chapter 6

Battles with the Navy Board

In the autumn of 1661 came news that his closest friend in the Navy Office, the Comptroller Slyngsbie, was seriously ill. Slyngsbie had cultivated Pepys's company, inviting him to his house in Lune Street, drinking with him in the Mitre and sharing his love of poetry. Cast in finer mould than Penn or Batten, Slyngsbie had endeared himself to Pepys beyond Pepys's professional relationship with Penn and Batten. Now, to Pepys's great distress, within forty-eight hours, he no longer recognised anyone and could not speak. Death followed quickly and led Pepys into so 'great trouble of mind' that he could not sleep. After Slyngsbie's death he was thrown far more into the company of Sir William Penn and Sir William Batten and increasingly found himself making comparisons between them.

Life for Sir William Penn and Batten on the Navy Board was aristocratic and relaxed. An average day's work frequently ended by midday, whereupon they retired to dine and drink at their favourite taverns. What better way of enlivening their company than by inviting young Pepys, who added to proper respect, vivacious conversation and an appreciation of their bawdry. However, Pepys's respect was wearing thin and his pocket empty. He saw limitations in these grand gentlemen who had at first so intimidated him. It remained necessary for him to 'keep in with them'. He regretted an age which required such expediency but practised it with considerable skill. Unexpectedly, it was Elizabeth who first sparked off Pepys's real disagreement with Sir William Batten. She resented Lady Batten's imperious manners and refused to play a humble role. The battle for precedence was taken up by their rival maids, extended into rights over pew seats, expressed at dinner parties and brought to a special pitch of satisfaction for Elizabeth when rumour had it that Lady Batten had once been the mistress to a rich man who left her his estate.[1] Pepys could not resist recording; 'And indeed I do believe that this story is too true.' Coming from a man with his record, it was a little out of place. Later a throwaway joke was misunderstood by Penn when Pepys remarked on Penn's pleasure at the company of the pretty maid in the Three Tuns tavern.[2] Their differences deepened when both Penn and Batten agreed that they were not a committee without their little register, meaning Pepys, at which 'I take ... some dudgeon and see clearly that I must keep a little distance with them ... or else I shall never keep myself up with them.'[3] Once desirable and enjoyable, their company became less so in his struggle to maintain equality. One particular occasion shows just how difficult he some-times found this. The Duke of York summoned his Navy officers to seek their advice on a piece of naval etiquette which, trivial in itself, had long been respected. The time-honoured salute to the English flag by foreign navies was generally recognised but difficult to enforce. Pepys found himself in some confusion because he knew nothing about the subject but his ability to dissemble came to his aid. He simply invented the story that he 'had heard Mr Selden often say that ... in Henry VII's time he did give commissions to make the King of Denmark's ships to strike him [dip their flags] in the Baltique'.

Breaking all his freshly established vows, he left the meeting to surrender once more to the theatre 'but it was so full that we could hardly get any room ... I to the 18d places and saw *Love At First Sight*.'[4] Another play, *Father's Owne Son*, occupied yet another after-noon and he commented: 'I went home by coach with my mind very heavy for this my expenseful life: which will undo me I fear after all my hopes ... for now I am coming to lay out a great deal of money in clothes upon my wife I must forbear other expenses.'[5] It was his ignorance about the Duke's demand for advice on flag salutation which led Pepys to buy *Mare Clausum*, a book which set him on new speculative paths.[6] 'At the Office all afternoon and at night home to read *Mare Clausum*.' The book inspired enquiries about the intrinsic nature of navies and coloured much of his thinking for years to come.[7]

Early in December came a long letter from the Lord High Admiral, the Duke of York, to the principal officers and commissioners of the Navy. It began: 'I have long deferred the sending to you a book concerning the duty of the several officers belonging to His Majesty's Navy ... I was informed that its present want of money had so har-dened and emboldened many persons in their negligence and abuses that there was little hope of amendment ... I thought it better to delay publishing ... rules until the want ... were removed ...'[8]

The letter then laid down principles which included checking for competitive prices and forbade any Naval Board employee from dealing in merchandise for the service.

I must likewise recommend to you the examining of His Majesty's yards, which I am informed is in some of them rather fit for a hospital than the King's service ... I [also] require you as often as ships return from any voyage and are paid off to make a strict enquiry by the commanders and masters of the ability and behaviour of all the standing officers during the voyage.[9]

The letter ran on in mandarin English admonishing and correcting until it had established a new code of naval conduct which Pepys found very sympathetic. Such instructions were issued at the beginning of each Lord High Admiral's term of office but the Duke of York's instructions remained substantially in force until Nelson's day.[10] On the day after, the Board met to read over the Duke's letter. Pepys's Diary entry for 5 February opened with the words: '... early at the office; Sir G. Carteret, the two Sir Wms and myself all alone reading over the Duke's instructions ... whereof we read as much as concerns our owne duties and left the other officers for another time. I did move several things for my purpose and did ease my mind.' He then promptly went off to dinner with Sir William Penn, before proceeding once more to the theatre to see *Rule a Wife*.[11]

None the less the Duke's message and Pepys's growing awareness of his own powers did at last coincide to revolutionise his attitude to the Navy. He began a new practice, rising sometimes by candlelight, hurrying to the Office and staying beyond the usual hours. Expeditions were made to depots at Woolwich and Deptford to check working practices and the accounts of the Treasurer's Office were scrutinised for swindling. General principles were translated into personal examples. On 8 March with Sir William Penn and an alderman of the city he cross-examined a certain Colonel Appesley who was accused of counterfeiting bills. 'We stayed about this business at the Office till ten at night and at last did send him with a constable to the courtes. And did give warrants for the seizing of a complice of his ...'[12] Although officers of the Navy Board were simultaneously justices of the peace, their jurisdiction covered Middlesex but not the city. Hence the presence of the city alderman. Later Sir Richard Ford was exposed for supplying a special brand of old hemp skilfully disguised as new. Pepys went to Woolwich to compare different hemps and, seething with anger, came back, to present his findings to the Board, which reluctantly stopped payment of Sir Richard's bill. 'I ... have got Sir Ford to be my enemy by it: but I care not for it is my duty.'[13] Pepys's growing disillusionment with Penn and Batten hardened into open criticism. Aware in some detail of their corruption, he no longer allowed them to lord it over him. Indeed, when Batten tried to snub him on one occasion he was amazed to find the upstart little Clerk criticising him bluntly to his face. 'Being provoked by some impertinence of Sir W. Batten's I called him an "unreasonable man". At which he was very angry ...'[14] By June he had also fallen out with Sir William Penn: 'Whatever the matter is he doth much fawn upon me and I perceive would not fall out with me ... but I shall never be deceived again by him, but do hate him and his traitorous tricks with all my heart.'[15] So now a new wind was blowing through official naval circles and – remarkably – it all had its source in the indefatigable, newly principled and alarmingly determined Samuel Pepys. The Treasury Office, the victuallers and merchants all became aware that some mysterious presence was haunting their activities and reviving principles long laughed out of court. The shipbuilders, the captains and pursers all felt that presence and, although the widespread corruption could not be overcome by a single man, consciences began to stir among hardened sinners.

Pepys's new life did not entirely exclude pleasure. 'But hard to consider how my natural desire is to pleasure which God be praised that he hath given me the power by my late oaths to curb ...' he wrote, closing with an endearing surrender to reality: ' ... and will do again after two or three plays more.'[16] Dedication to extracting pleasure from life remained ineradicable and sometimes took a ghoulish form. On 14 June Pepys made his way to a specially booked room on Tower Hill to witness the execution of Sir Henry Vane.[17] He brilliantly evokes time, place and atmosphere in the Diary. A very great crowd of people around the scaffold interfered with his view but he listened to Sir Henry Vane's long speech, interrupted many times by the sheriff who tried 'to take his paper out of his hand but he would not let go'. 'Trumpets were brought under the scaffold,' and repeatedly blared 'that he ought not be heard'. Sir Henry Vane continued to speak at great length, recounting his life and beliefs until once more silenced by the sheriff. There was a blister on his neck, said Vane, which he asked them not to hurt. 'Then he prayed and so fitted himself and received the blow.' Pepys was disappointed not to witness the final moment: 'the scaffold was so crowded that we could not see it done.'[18]

From now on throughout the Diary Sir William Penn is variously referred to as a rogue, a knave, a poor speaker, lazy and corrupt. Indeed, the torrent of criticism is overplayed. Pepys was hardly in a position from his past record to talk about corruption and he did not himself escape the further charge of meanness which he next levelled at Penn. He watched carefully every penny, rubbed his hands when he had saved another £50 and constantly thanked God for his slowly accumulating capital. If it remains true that Penn had a distinguished array of shortcomings, he also contributed to the slow revolution in the British Navy. It was a fact conveniently overlooked by Pepys.

Ollard gives one explanation for what slowly became Pepys's unrelenting dislike, if not hatred for these two men: the jealousy of rivalry. Sandwich, who had put Pepys on the Board was once General-at-Sea under Cromwell and had not reneged until 1659. Penn, also at one time was General-at-Sea and more distinguished than Sandwich, had become a royalist earlier. 'Penn was therefore a potential rival to Sandwich and thus at one remove to Pepys.'[19] The rivalry interlocked three ways. Pepys easily won the good opinion of Coventry but Coventry in turn was not a devotee of Sandwich. He claimed prior loyalty to the King since he had fought as a royalist in the Civil War and clashed with Clarendon who shared political friendship with Sandwich. These rivalries produced uneasiness in Pepys and drove him to attack his competitors.

Meanwhile, Pepys's actively collaborative relationship with Sir William Coventry developed. Instead of theorising about reforms of practice they continued to make personal surveys of dockyards and ports. On one occasion they surprised a truant captain who should already have left for sea. On another their totally unexpected arrival at Woolwich found many ships in a sad state of confusion.[20] A touch of pleasure appears in the Diary about these activities and pleasure becomes glee when they expose the shortcomings of pursers, boatswains and clerks. Pepys's admiration for Coventry recurs in the Diary: 'I think [Coventry] my most true friend in all things that are fair. He tells me freely his mind of every man and in everything.'[21]

As his probings into naval practice deepened Pepys found a knowledge of mathematics necessary and hired a discharged mate, Mr Cooper, to teach him multiplication. He would rise at night by candlelight and repeat his tables by rote until he had mastered them. Mr Cooper also explained some of the mysteries of ship design and was rewarded for his trouble by becoming master of the naval reserve. Once again the exercise of his new powers pleased Pepys. With

Hollond's discourses, which he had recently discovered, he broadened his naval knowledge even further. 'Amongst other inconveniences these are not to be passed over with silence ... First that no man (though otherwise never so able) be employed that hath another duty or place to attend upon at the same time.'[22] Pepys seems to have become obsessive about his responsibilities, when he descended to spying on his clerks in the office next to his by boring a hole in the wainscotting. There is, indeed, a point at this period in his development where he became almost neurotic. Certainly, his behaviour, if not his character, had changed. Where before he avoided too much contact with old friends and members of the family, now he recognised he had been a snob. If he found it hard to take the oafishness, unreliability and sheer stupidity of some of his relatives, he remained loyal to them and was prepared to assist them whenever possible. His mother, father, sister and his two brothers, were all at different times helped financially and otherwise by Pepys. Nor did his new life interfere with occasional visits to their homes. For a man so financially prudent he was then surprisingly indulgent when he commissioned a portrait of his father and wrote: 'Here I find my father's picture begun; and so much to my content that it joys my very heart to think that I should have his picture so well done – who besides that he is my father and a man that loves me and hath ever done so – is also at this day one of the most careful and innocent men in the world.'[23]

His relationship with his Aunt Jane was still ambiguous: 'My aunt ... has been here today ... I do condemn myself mightily for my pride and contempt of my aunt and kindred that are not so high as myself that I have not seen her all this while ...'[24] Tom, his brother, only a year younger than Samuel, remained a perennial problem. When John Pepys retired to live on the small estate left by Uncle Robert at Brampton, Tom, as we have seen, was left to keep the tailoring business going, which he did with diminishing success. Samuel tried to find him a wife with a dowry to buttress the dwindling business. He went 'to see a gentlewoman for a wife for Tom ... worth 500l, of good education: her name Hobell and lives near Banbury; demands 40l per annum joynter'.[25] By the autumn of 1663 the tailoring business was failing fast and suddenly Tom fell sick with a mysterious illness which found Pepys in an embarrassing situation.[26] The sequence of events in the Diary show his distress which 'multiplied mightily' when rumour suggested that his brother might have the pox. 'A ... boy [arrived] ... with a note to me to tell me that my brother Tom was so ill as they feared he could

not long live and that it would befit I should come and see him.'[27]
When he called, a friend of his brother's wished to speak with him
alone and told him, to Pepys's horror, that Tom was not only deadly
ill but did in fact have the pox. Worse was to follow. Rumours
circulated that his brother was homosexual and this threw Pepys
into fresh distress. His visits to his brother now became – partly
– the desire to redeem Tom's reputation with Pepys's own impeccable
presence. Pepys was greatly relieved when Dr Wiverley searched
his brother's mouth, found no sores and declared him free of the
pox. Whatever the truth, it was Pepys's reaction to his death which
revealed the compassion he could still feel for a brother he disliked.
The death scene in the Diary is an example of Pepys's power to
evoke time, place, mood and person. 'I once begun to tell him something of his condition and asked him whither he thought he should
go. He in distracted manner answered me: "Why whither should
I go? there are but two ways. If I go the bad way I must give God
thanks for it. And if I go the other way I must give God the more
thanks for it . . ."' The next day Pepys

went up and found the nurse holding his eyes shut; and he, poor wretch,
lying with his chops fallen, a most sad sight and that which put me
into a present very great transport of grief and cries . . . I had no mind
to see him die as we thought he presently would . . . And so this was
the end of my poor brother continuing to talk idle and his lips working
even to his last . . . and at last his breath broke out bringing a flood
of phlegm and stuff out with it and so he died . . .

He went home grimly to his wife and lay very close to her, 'being
[so] full of disorder and grief for my brother that I could not sleep'.[28]

His grief quickly gave way to realism. First there was the grave-
digger who for an extra 6d would 'jostle together' the not-quite-
rotten corpses to make more room for his brother. Then there was
a ruthless, but honest, change of mood when Pepys reflected that
the world made nothing of the memory of a man an hour after
he is dead. 'And indeed I must blame myself; for through the sight
of him dead and dying I had real grief . . . while he was in my sight,
yet presently after and ever since I have had very little grief
indeed . . .'[29]

At the heart of family disturbances Elizabeth, his wife, was herself
becoming discontented as early as the summer of 1662. Quarrels
recurred between Pepys and Elizabeth as they would with any couple,
mollified in most instances by a basic affection. On 24 October 1662
he reported that they were 'more and more a very happy couple,

blessed be to God'. Once he hurried away from dinner with Sir Anthony Deane, a shipwright, because Elizabeth languished alone at home. A spectacular quarrel on another occasion drove him out of the house on a pitch black rainy night, but she did not hesitate to chase after him and bring him back. Toothache rarely occurs in the Diary but when it attacked Elizabeth her face 'swelled miserably' and he sat up half the night sympathising with her. Yet Elizabeth's behaviour in the house was hardly exemplary. She seemed to make a cult of untidiness, extravagance came naturally to her, and she had considerable skill in exacerbating servants. While at Brampton, she had quarrelled fiercely with Wayneman and their new servant Sarah. When they all returned home again Pepys found the atmosphere intolerable because he loved of an evening to sit cheek by jowl with his servants in the kitchen, making merry. Bryant points to a deeper cause for Elizabeth's discontent. Pepys lived on the fringes of high society but was not concerned at this stage with social-climbing. Indeed, his new immersion in work make him indifferent to the very company which his wife now sought. She desired to live the life of the fine lady attending dinners and plays, wearing expensive clothes and longed to engage a gentlewoman in place of clumsy Sarah. In her wilder moments she even coveted the kind of adorers common to court life. It all began to irritate Pepys, but his mood fluctuated enormously. On 2 November 1662 he lay long in bed with Elizabeth and wrote: 'I never had greater content, blessed be to God! than now ...'[30] By 13 November he woke in the morning to begin: 'Our discontent again and sorely angered my wife ... I to my office and there sat all the morning and dined with discontent with my wife at noon.'[31] Elizabeth left the dinner table to return home and scribble her husband a letter which threw Pepys 'in a quandary what to do, whether to read it or not'.

Dramatically, he decided that he would do neither but 'burn it before her face that I may put a stop to more of this nature'. Returning home to supper he found Elizabeth sullen and uncommunicative, 'so went to bed ... without speaking one word to her'. Matters were reconciled in the next few days, but an experiment with a new gentlewoman, Winifred Gosnell, proved unfortunate. Within a week she left seeking a career on the stage, while Sarah had gone weeping into the darkness. A new cook, Susan, arrived, and Jane was promoted to chambermaid. Still dissatisfied, Elizabeth continued to press for yet another gentlewoman companion and Mr Ashwell's daughter Mary, fresh from finishing school, joined the household in March 1663 with all the appearance of quiet modesty. 'I hope well and pray God she may please us – which though it cost me something yet will give me much content.'[32] Mary revealed behind her modest mask what Pepys referred to as a 'merry jade',[33] and her zestful enjoyment of life seemed to infect Pepys. He found himself relaxing his austere regime to play the fiddle, walk beside the river and – the final heresy – return once more to the theatre. He quickly pulled himself together again but now Mary – whose flower-like presence and graceful carriage eclipsed Elizabeth – infected Elizabeth with new ambitions. Searching for compensation, Pepys persuaded his wife to take dancing lessons with dangerous results. How he came to select a 'pretty neat black man' is difficult to determine, but Pembleton was married and at first behaved impeccably. On 15 May an exhaustive entry in the Diary reveals that he had come home to find 'it almost night and my wife and the dancing master alone *above*, not dancing but talking' (my emphasis).[34] Did 'above' mean in a bedroom? Whatever the answer it threw Pepys into a paroxysm of jealousy. 'Now so deadly full of jealousy I am that my heart and head did so cast about and fret that I could not do any business ... but went out to my office: and anon late home again and ready to chide at everything.' Tossing sleeplessly, his wife enquired what was wrong, at which he made the excuse that he had bad news from the Duke. Humiliation followed close at the heels of jealousy and now he found himself driven to 'see whether my wife did wear drawers today as she used to do and other things to raise my suspicion of her'.[35] Matters were worse the following day. After dinner Pembleton called again for another lesson and Pepys walked up and down his chamber, 'listening to hear whether they danced or no or what they did'. This, despite the fact that he knew Ashwell, the maid, to be in the same room with them.

Recovering something of his balance, he became newly introspective. Not only was his jealousy exaggerated but he himself 'upon a small temptation' could be 'false to her and therefore ought not to expect more justice from her'. He ended the Diary entry: 'God pardon both my sin and my folly.'[36] Less than six months before there had been reason for this upsurge of guilt. Visiting Lord Sandwich he found nobody at home but Sarah. 'I went up to her and played and talked with her and God forgive me did feel her: which I am ashamed of, but I did no more though I had so much a mind to it that I spent in my breeches.'[37] Pembleton continued to give dancing lessons, and Pepys's jealousy fed on itself. If he did not discover Pembleton sneaking secretly away from the house on one occasion or another, he sometimes caught them walking hand in hand. In church one Sunday Pepys understood what might have been an admiring glance from Pembleton for Elizabeth to be a leer of lust. Once his wife openly mocked him in front of Pembleton and suddenly he was in fear of losing his 'command over her'. Elizabeth was not slow to exploit his obvious attraction to Ashwell. Whenever his complaints about Pembleton became too troublesome she threw her name in his face and challenged him to explain his obvious delight in her company. It was a power game which neither of them won, despite Pepys's wilful belief in his own innocence. The climax came on 7 September: 'I know not at this very moment that I now write this almost what either I write or am doing nor how to carry myself to my wife ... being unwilling to speak of it to her for making of any breach ... nor let it pass for fear of continuing to offend me and the matter grow worse.'[38] His jealousy now made a 'very hell' in his mind and he asked God to remove it 'or I shall be very unhappy'. In place of God removing his jealousy, Pepys decided to remove Elizabeth. She did not resist him when he suggested that she go into the country for a while, which is a measure of how misplaced his jealousy had been. The final hours were agonising. Pembleton arrived to give his farewell lesson, Pepys shadowed his wife about the house and the next morning lay abed to be sure his wife put on her drawers before leaving. Then, at last, he was free to settle down to his professional life once more, abhor drink and stiffen his vows of abstinence as if in thanks for his deliverance.

A short time afterwards he was to begin a relationship with another woman far more abandoned than Elizabeth's innocent flirtations. There were several preliminaries. His brief commitment to abstinence broke down imaginatively when he fell into the habit of staying in bed late and allowing his thoughts riotous freedom with women casually met or conjured out of the air. On one occasion at least he did 'use himself'. Then came a new dalliance at court where Mrs Castlemaine, the King's ex-mistress, looked 'mighty out of humour'. Leaving court one fine day he proceeded to Westminster Hall where he knew those of easy virtue rubbed shoulders with acquaintances of earlier years, and especially one called Betty Lane. He did not miss the chance to 'towse her and feel her all over', so much so that a lad called in at the window: 'Sir, why do you kiss the gentlewoman so?'[39] Such adventures remained for these few weeks within limits, but he never missed an opportunity for the odd kiss, caress or fumble. Except perhaps at that high moment of imaginative splendour one night, when the Queen herself surrendered to his wishes and the gallows loomed over his bed with the threat of high treason.

Chapter 7

Sexual adventures

The record of Pepys's sex life is variously regarded with embarrassment, condemnation or toleration. No one has viewed his indulgences as the natural efflorescence of a man who thoroughly enjoyed the physical pleasure of straight, uncomplicated sex. Bryant dealt with it uneasily and Ollard elegantly analysed the Lawrentian and mystical approach without committing himself to either. Perhaps disdainfully, neither Ollard nor Bryant translated the mish-mash of Latin-Spanish-English in which Pepys cloaked the clinical detail of his sex life.

He clearly loved and was devoted to his wife. Her menstrual problems must have complicated their sex life and the lack of children frustrated him. Certainly, an air of furtiveness surrounded many of his adventures, and the mores of the day subjected him to disapproval. Craving the indulgence of every sexual arousal he was frequently forced to snatch his pleasures illicitly under almost sordid conditions. He had no philosophy of sex. He simply enjoyed it and would have forgotten about it but for the guilt which shrouded a society condoning the most elaborate sexual charades at court. And not only at court. At the beginning of July 1663 Pepys recorded that Sir Charles Sydly had one day appeared naked in open daylight on a balcony,

acting all postures of lust and buggery that could be imagined . . . saying
that here he hath to sell such a powder as should make all the cunts
in town run after him . . . And that being done he took a glass of wine,
washed his prick in it and then drank it off: and then took another
and drank the King's health.[1]

Buggery seemed to Pepys to have become almost as common amongst the English gallants as it was in Italy but – blessed be to God – 'I do not to this day know what is the meaning of this sin nor which is the agent or which the patient.'[2] Since his wife could not read Latin or Spanish they seemed the natural cloak for his deviations, but why trouble to record them at all? A kind of self-destructive dedication to truth runs through the Diary which is also a confessional. He is hell-bent to get it all down on paper. Why? As we have seen, in the Diary he had a completely reliable confidant. It also made possible the expiation of guilt at one remove. Familiar as he was with earlier diaries, it would be remarkable if Pepys did not intend posterity to enjoy his. Extraordinarily, his wife seems never to have discovered this other elaborate, many-volumed self who could have explained so much to her, but how did he manage to conceal it? There is no answer.

Certainly he ran grave risks, but re-reading his entries must have yielded the preservation of erotic thrills otherwise doomed to the uncertain power of memory. Pepys could not escape the charge that he exploited the women who surrendered to his wishes. For those who enjoyed his attentions there was no problem, but not all did. He seems rarely, if ever, to have paid for sex. Becky Allen, Betty Howlett and many a serving maid flicker across his pages seldom protesting at the liberties he takes, but we have no independent record from the women themselves.

He first met Betty Lane on 5 August 1663. Later they made an assignation at the Parliament stairs which led down to a boat.[3] Instead of reserving rooms, lovers sometimes rented boats. Eagerly on his way to keep the appointment, who should meet him but Lord Sandwich's wife. After an embarrassing pause he was forced to acknowledge her – 'to see whether she would take notice of it or no'. Accustomed to the ways of the court, clearly such a minor dalliance would have meant little to Lady Sandwich, even if she suspected what he was about. Pepys duly met and tried to seduce Betty Lane, but his efforts went awry, and for all he 'did so towse and handle her' he could 'get nothing more from her though I was very near it'.[4] Bryant indicates that he was greatly distressed at this episode – his wife being still away with Ashwell in the country – but the evidence is slender. Afterwards he simply regretted being so sweaty that it necessitated returning home by coach rather than by boat. A letter awaited him from his wife describing a quarrel with Ashwell, when Elizabeth struck her and Ashwell hit back, causing a 'great stir'. It disturbed Pepys, who wondered whether he would ever get 'his wife's head down again' when she returned home.

A new amour remained in his memory far into life. One day Mrs Bagwell came to his office on an errand. She at once struck him as unusually pretty. Deliberately, he engineered a visit to the Deptford Yard where Mrs Bagwell's husband worked in order to meet her again and 'enter upon an acquaintance' with her. Allegedly, the encounter was not for Pepys's benefit alone. Mr Bagwell wished to leave his present ship for a better one and here visiting him – in all his grandeur – was a man with the power to affect that change. Their second meeting was accidental. Early in August Pepys recorded: 'So [he] walked back again and on my way young Bagwell and his wife waylaid me to desire my favour about getting him a better job which I shall pretend to be willing to do for them, but my mind is to know his wife a little better ...'[5] Some days later, conscience-stricken, he resolved to do her husband a courtesy, 'for I think he is a man that deserves well'. However, the summer drifted to a close without any sign of the preferment for Mr Bagwell or success with Mrs Bagwell. The remainder of the year and early 1664 saw Pepys dallying elsewhere with Mrs Bagwell still an unrealised prey in waiting. There were fugitive rendezvous with Jane Welsh, the barber's assistant, Betty Martin, a linen draper and the occasional flower girl. Indulgence ran counter to the constant renewal of his vows of abstinence from plays, drink and illicit sex, but sex above all proved irresistible. And then one day there was a nasty shock from Betty. She thought she might be pregnant. Coldbloodedly, he vowed never to sleep with her again until she had married. The sacred vows of marriage were expected to accommodate and mask the results of Pepys's lust. Unexpectedly, Betty turned down a number of suitors but at last surrendered to one no less simple and oafish than his rivals. Pepys now had an alibi for all possible consequences and wrote: 'I must have a bout with her very shortly to see how she finds marriage.' Post-haste he followed up the resolution, finding Betty completely willing in everything he desired. Moreover, within two days, ignoring the prostitutes clustering around Seething Lane, Pepys repeated the experience with relish.

It was the exploitative element which made Pepys's behaviour unpleasant. He reserved his lust for lower-class women who saw him as a grand person with money to spend on wine, food and entertainment. Upper-class women were in a different, more romantic category. Jane Welsh was an exception among these working-class women. She tormented him as much as he tormented her, constantly standing him up and denying anything beyond a tumult of kisses. He was driven back to her again and again, and his relationship with her in the winter of 1663 coincided with a new concern for his dress and appearance. He bought a black suit trimmed with scarlet ribbon and a brilliantly lined velvet cloak, completing his transformation – dangerously – with one of the new-fangled periwigs. The

wig cost him many anxious hours. He felt that his friends and colleagues would see it as pretentious, but the only comment he recorded
was the Duke of York's, who found him so transformed he did
not recognise him. His last meeting with Jane Welsh was cold if
not detached, but he recorded 'a strange slavery that I stand in to
beauty that I value nothing near it'. An appreciation of beauty for
beauty's sake was certainly part of Pepys's character.

During this imbroglio his attraction to Mrs Bagwell persisted and
their relationship moved slowly towards consummation. Pepys was
able to deceive Mr Bagwell with remarkable panache, as when he
calmly ate an elaborate dinner with both husband and wife at their
home and simultaneously made dates with his wife. By the autumn
of 1664 he launched a direct assault on the prize.

Meeting Bagwell's wife at the Office before I went home, I took her
into the Office and there kissed her only. She rebuked me for doing
it: saying that did I do so much to many bodies else it would be a
stain to me. But I do not see but she takes it well enough.[6]

By late October he was still in close pursuit: 'Then I to my office
where I took in with me Bagwell's wife.'[7] His emotional detachment
can be measured by the lack of any reference to her Christian
name. 'There I caressed her and find her every day more and more
coming with good words and promise of getting her husband a place
which I will do.' He continued to dangle the bait before her
eyes, and his delay in promoting Bagwell from the fifth-rate
Dauphin to the fourth-rate *Providence* remained inexcusable since
the threat of war with the Dutch increased the demand for naval
carpenters.

Early in November something happened which might have dampened the enthusiasm of any man but Pepys. Leaving the Exchange
at noon, he met by appointment Mrs Bagwell. 'She followed me
into Moorfields and there into a drinking house – and all alone we
eat and drank together.' Private rooms were available at a price.
'I did make some offer [was it promotion for her husband?], did
not receive any compliance in her ... but very modestly she denied
me; which I was glad to see and shall value her the better for it
– and I hope never tempt her to any evil any more.'[8] It was a pious
hope. Two days later in the same 'blind alehouse' with 'many hard
looks and sighs the poor wretch did give me and I think verily was
troubled at what I did; but at last, after many protestings by degrees
I did arrive at what I would with great pleasure'.[9] Now his audacity
knew no bounds. After an abortive meeting on 19 December, the

following day he calmly joined Bagwell and his wife at dinner – a very good one, he recorded – and then found some excuse to send Bagwell packing before settling down to seduce his wife in her own home.[10] Alone *'avec elle je tentoy a faire ce que je voudrais, et contre sa force je la faisoy, bien que pas a mon contentment* [alone with her I tried what I wished and against her will I "had" her but not to my satisfaction].'

For three long years the affair continued, with Pepys occasionally reflecting hypocritically on the virtue of married women: 'Strange to see how a woman notwithstanding her greatest pretences of love *a son mari* and religion may be *vaincue.*'[11] He now made one resolution after another.

So I back again and to my office where I did with great content [make] a vow to mind my business and *laisser aller les femmes* for a month; and am with all my heart glad to find myself able to come to so good a resolution that thereby I may follow my business.[12]

The vow was no sooner made than broken. By now Mrs Bagwell was a very willing partner and sometimes voluntarily presented herself at his office after dinner for 'further dalliance'. Alas, satiation began to take its toll. Within a year he was losing interest in her and there came an evening when open revulsion replaced his lust. It was a spectacular evening because before he encountered Mrs Bagwell he had already met and made love to Betty Martin. 'Thence to Martin and there did *tout ce que je voudrais avec* her ... so ... back home ... and then I found occasion to return in the dark and to Bagwell ... did do all that I desired.'[13] The aftermath was depressing. Guilt and distaste gave way to hatred. Then, remarkably, Pepys turned to chiding – indeed openly criticising – Lord Sandwich for behaviour closely similar to his own.

It all began when Sandwich fell ill in the spring of 1662 and, in order to convalesce, he rented a house in the riverside village of Chelsea. There he began an affair with Betty, one of the daughters of Mrs Becke. Pepys heard of this through Will Howe, now Sandwich's servant and muster master. The Diary records: 'I find that my Lord doth dote upon [her] so that he spends his time and money on her. He [Will Howe] tells me she is a woman of a very bad fame and very impudent and hath told my Lord so.'[14] The reference to money was especially pertinent because Lord Sandwich owed Pepys £700 as well as being heavily in debt elsewhere. Once again morality merged with practical convenience when Pepys's conscience stirred. Expediency checked the immediate expression of his disapproval. Hesitating to comment on the morals of an aristocrat Pepys felt it would be wiser to await the spontaneous birth of guilt in Sandwich. This had some ironic repercussions. Rumours now multiplied. Edward Pickering, Lord Sandwich's servant, considered by Pepys to be a fool and a coxcomb, enlarged to Pepys the gossip against Lord Sandwich. Pepys walked with him one evening for three or four hours,

he telling me the whole business of my Lord's folly . . . of all which
I am ashamed to see my Lord so grossly play the beast and fool to
the flinging off of all honour . . . and only will have his private lust
undisturbed with this common whore – his sitting up night after night
alone, suffering nobody to come to them and all the day too . . . playing
on his lute under her window and forty other poor sordid things: which
I am grieved to hear but believe it to no purpose for me to meddle
with.[15]

Pepys's hypocrisy deepens with every word he writes. On the very evening he gossiped with Pickering it was his original intention to pick up Betty Lane in Westminster Hall to commit the very sin of which he complained. He has the decency to exclaim in the Diary 'God forgive me', but makes absolutely no connection between himself and Sandwich. It should also be said that Sandwich was merely reproducing the accepted dalliance of the court and did at least add a touch of romance by playing his lute beneath Miss Becke's window.

Blind to its implications, indignation mounted in Pepys to the point where something had to be done about Lord Sandwich. He resolved to steel himself to the sticking point and speak directly to him. Simultaneously, physical retribution attacked him, as caressing Betty Lane beneath a draughty tavern window he was suddenly smitten with pains in the head and ear and resolved never to touch her again. For once the Diary even referred to the pain that he was giving his wife. It grieved his heart to 'see that I should abuse so good a wretch'.[16]

According to Sandwich's biographer, much of Pepys's information was false and his mind poisoned by gossip. Becke was no slut or common strumpet.[17] It suited Pepys's indignation better to believe what he heard. Whatever the truth, at last on the evening of 12 November 1663 Pepys's resolution hardened and he took a coach to Chelsea fully intending to warn Lord Sandwich. Confronted with His Lordship his courage failed him, which is not surprising. Like many a critic before him, what he could not face up to doing personally he now put on paper.

That evening he wrote a letter to Sandwich which began: 'I do hope that neither the manner nor the matter of this advice will be condemned by Your Lordship ...'[18] The letter repeated the gossip about the

> bad report of the house wherein Your Lordship ... continues to
> sojourne. And by name having charged one of the daughters for a
> courtizan, alleging both places and persons where and with whom she
> hath been too well known ... Lastly (My Lord) I find a general coldness
> in all persons towards Your Lordship; such as from my first dependence
> on you I never yet knew ... I rest confident of Your Lordship's just
> construction of my dutiful intents herein and in all humility take leave.

Pepys's resolution wavered once more before sending the letter and he decided to discuss it with Sandwich's lawyer and man of business, Henry Moore. He was all for delivering the letter at once, assuring Pepys that 'it could but endear me to My Lord'. So the fatal letter was sent.[19] The next four days Pepys's anxiety mounted, but he was unable to approach Sandwich. When at last he confronted him he was first pleased to find with what grace His Lordship received the letter and then cornered when Sandwich demanded the source of his information. Forced to admit the names of Pearse the surgeon, Pickering the servant and some maidservants, Pepys then made the mistake of claiming that no one else knew of his protest. 'Except one,' came the immediate riposte from Sandwich, meaning Moore. Sandwich then defended the Beckes: 'and the young gentlewoman, for whose reproach he was sorry'.[20] This double attack reduced Pepys to tears and he left His Lordship with 'no medium between My Lord's taking it very well or very ill'.[21] Many sleepless nights followed but in the end Sandwich overcame any initial ill feeling and assimilated the letter with goodwill. During the whole episode Pepys can be seen as displacing his own guilt on to Sandwich, thus punishing himself at one remove. As a victim of unconscious motives he did not escape the charge of hypocrisy.

Meanwhile, Pepys's domestic situation had undergone one upheaval after another. After the quarrel between Ashwell and Elizabeth which led to an exchange of blows, Ashwell decided to leave, and on 25 August swept out of the household in the full flower of abuse. Hannah, the cookmaid, also left in a considerable huff. Susan the cook and Goody Taylor the daily reappeared but not for long, to be followed by the lice-ridden Jinny who was no sooner cleaned and re-dressed that she ran away. Pepys did not hesitate to have her arrested and whipped, a fashionable enough reaction in his day, but undermining the picture of a man whose compassion rose above current values. Elizabeth lived in confusion during these upheavals, neglected her duties, became even more untidy and constantly craved her old pleasures. Pepys reflected that he must renew his efforts to 'break in his wife', as Bryant put it. None the less, he made one concession. Pembleton temporarily reappeared to please Elizabeth and put Pepys into a cold sweat, but no serious consequences materialised.

Many revealing personal vignettes ran through the latter part of 1663. His bowels gave him great trouble in October and he decided to lay down a set of Rules For My Health which set out explicit instructions on different methods of 'shitting'. 'And so rose in the morning in perfect good ease but only strain I put myself to shit, more than I needed.'[22] In October it seemed that Elizabeth might have a vaginal infection. 'She hath also a pain in the place she used to have swellings in.' He worried in case the 'matter that I give her ... causes it: it never coming but after my having been with her.'[23] Despite his promiscuity Pepys showed little concern for venereal disease until his wife revealed her symptoms. If either one of them had contracted syphilis the symptoms would have caused him much greater alarm and would certainly have been included in the Diary. Gonorrhoea can be almost symptomless but would eventually have taken its toll. Anxiety recurred the following month. A Mr Hollyard, probably a physician, came to visit Elizabeth, and together the two men examined 'her parts' and found symptoms which would be 'painful in the tending'. Pepys felt that he could not carry out the doctor's treatment without the help of a nurse, but Elizabeth refused to have one for fear she would gossip about her complaint, 'though it be nothing but what is very honest'.[24] By 16 November 1663 the swelling had subsided and left a crater 'near three inches deep' which Mr Hollyard thought would necessitate surgery with Pepys present to help control his wife. 'My heart will not serve for me to see it done and yet she will not have anyone else.' Finally they decided to treat her symptoms with a fomentation which the maid could apply on the understanding that she was treating piles. According to the *Occasional Papers* she had experienced an abscess in the vulva which developed into an ischio-rectal abscess and then a fistula. Pepys was delighted when the condition improved and remarked that he could not bear having his wife cut before his face.

In the same month a drunk threatened his wife in the coach while Pepys was shopping. The coachman became involved in a minor struggle with the man and Pepys joined in the fray, giving 'him a good cuff or two on the chops. Seeing him *not* oppose me I did give him another' (my italics).[25]

In February 1663 the extraordinary intervention of the bailiff turned into a comic opera.[26] 'Towards noon there comes a man ... as if upon ordinary business and shows me a writ from the Exchequer called a commission of rebellion and tells me that I am his prisoner.' As Pepys puts it, he was 'struck to the heart' to think that even 'in the middle of the King's business' he could be so threatened. The bailiffs were the most 'rake-ashamed rogues' he ever saw in his life and he warned them to have a care. Sir John Mennes hurried off to court at once to see 'what could be done' and discovered the cause of the intrusion.

The previous winter Pepys had committed to prison a man called Fielde who used 'ill words' in the Navy Office one day, and now a writ had been issued to 'secure the appearance of the defendant'.[27] Pepys's solicitor was summoned and said that he would satisfy the fees of the court which should end the business. Pepys decided to remain house-bound, but presently five threatening gentleman arrived to ask what else he proposed doing. 'I told them stay till I heard from the King or my Lord Chief Baron.'[28] The men then extracted a promise that he would remain in the house while they went to refresh themselves. Before Pepys could dine the bailiffs were back again demanding satisfaction, but Pepys concealed himself and listened − amused − to their irritated inquiries. Then Sir William Batten's servant Mingo came knocking gently on the parlour window to tell Pepys that his Master and Lady would have him come to their house for refuge, 'which I could not do'. However, by the use of ladders he climbed over the palings between the yards and entered their house where he found them 'much concerned for me'. They then played cat and mouse with the bailiffs who had now been joined by two constables. Pepys went up to the top of Batten's house and through one window joked with his wife standing at her bedroom window. Sir John Mennes returned to say that he had achieved nothing and Pepys began to wonder how this ridiculous affair would end. Next a Captain Grove − inexplicably − came to his rescue, but when he challenged the bailiffs he was forced to draw his sword.[29] The threat of violence was real and the sword did indeed prick the breast of one of the bailiffs. Everything was at last resolved when Pepys's clerk hurried back with a release from the attorney, providing Pepys paid the fees of the commission. The prolonged farce left him reflecting on bureaucracy and its confusions. The confusions multiply when we find Pepys in unscrupulous mood giving Coventry advice on the best way to avoid paying a debt – honestly![30]

By the end of the year domestic life had settled down more satisfactorily. Whether Elizabeth shared this new contentment is doubtful. She was reduced to taking lessons in arithmetic from her husband; making marmalade; sighing for her dancing lessons; and so craving a child that she imaginatively induced a pregnancy. There is no detailed record of his discontentment with Elizabeth's barrenness but it must have put considerable strain on her if he made her 'guilt' clear. She also displeased him by gossiping about his family at the most inappropriate moments. Sensuality frequently reconciled these irritations, when he 'Lay long caressing my wife and talking.' She told him sad stories of '... the sluttish manner that my father and mother and Pall live in the country which troubles me mightily and I must seek to remedy'.[31] Pepys's meanness persisted and Elizabeth hardly dare buy herself a piece of lace for her gown, or a twenty-five-shilling pendant, without suffering censure. In a moment of anger Pepys pulled his wife by the nose.[32] Matters improved when Susan, the new maid, turned out to be an 'admirable slut'; the new cook Jane proved very efficient; and a new companion for Elizabeth named Bess Mercer revealed unexpected musical talents. By the end of the month he recorded 'waked about one o'clock in the morning to piss (having gone so soon overnight to bed) and then my wife being waked rang her bell and the maids rose and went to washing ...'[33] The picture of a sleepless mistress summoning her servants at one in the morning to take domestic advantage of her husband's insomnia makes incredible reading today.

Chapter 8

First Dutch War and the plague

Early in October 1663 Pepys met Mr Cutler, a supplier of hemp and tar to the Navy, who warned him of the great likelihood of war with Holland. 'I hope we shall be in good condition before it breaks out.' A visit to his cousin Roger Pepys convinced Pepys that Parliament was determined to 'throw down Popery'. A bill to this effect had just reached the committee stage, to be followed by an address to both houses concerning the expulsion of priests and Jesuits. As war became more likely Pepys did not spare himself from rising early and working late at the Office. His letters to Commissioner Pett and Sir William Coventry concerning the best kind of naval equipment multiplied and revealed a remarkable understanding of technical details.[1]

Sandwich went off to command the fleet which somewhat discomposed Pepys who feared in the event of his death that the £700 owed to him would also disappear. When the Duke of York announced his intention of joining the fleet the whole nation became aware of threatened war and turned its attention to the Navy, the vital bulwark of defence. While large numbers of ships, men and supplies were being moved into position and problems growing in the process, Pepys the tailor's son was slowly elevated to the centre of intelligence if not power. Batten was said to be too far gone in corruption to be trusted; Coventry and Penn had left with the Duke of York to join the fleet; and Pepys became the focus of an administrative machine indispensable in the conduct of any war. He had never fired a gun or raised a sail; his sea-faring experience was negligible; and his knowledge of battle tactics limited. Yet the Navy would have fallen into confusion but for this man working furiously at his desk day and sometimes night.

A long letter went to Sir George Carteret in November 1663 elaborately analysing the value of different masts.[2] In early skirmishes with the Dutch an English ship loaded with masts was seized by the Dutch Navy on 14 November 1664. The following day all Pepys's professional commitments were blown to the winds when he retreated at dinner time to the alehouse where his previous assignations with Mrs Bagwell had been so successful. In the midst of overwhelming work he found time to indulge himself with her even if the 'poor wretch' gave him many 'hard looks'. On 21 November he wrote in the Diary: 'I to the Change and there stayed long doing business. And this day for certain news has come that Teddiman hath brought in 18 or 20 Dutchmen, merchants, their Bordeaux fleet and two men-of-war to Portsmouth.'[3] According to Pepys the war had begun, but it was not declared until 22 February 1665.

The last weeks of 1664 were full of strain and trouble. Overwork created insomnia; stress gave him agonising wind; and driven by a trivial misdemeanour one night he demanded that Elizabeth sack the easy-going Bess. She snapped back at him and he promptly hit her so hard over the left eye that she cried out in pain. The following day an embarrassed Pepys confronted his wife whose eye was blackened. Very 'vexed at heart' he did nothing to help her and left his wife to apply the necessary poultice. Explosions of small-scale domestic violence distressed Pepys but he could not escape them. Hewer enraged him on another occasion by failing to keep an appointment and he struck out at him. Why Hewer tolerated a number of such indignities is puzzling, for he was a man of means and could easily have set up on his own. However, he had by now become Pepys's confidant and Pepys was beginning to look upon him as the son which his wife had failed to give him.

By the end of 1664, according to the Diary, the whole atmosphere had changed. His last entry was full of satisfaction. 'As soon as ever the clock struck one I kissed my wife in the kitchen by the fireside wishing her a merry New Year.'[4] The year ended with great joy for Pepys, 'not only from my having made so good a year of profit as having spend 420l and laid up 540l.' His credit privately and publicly had grown and he was – he thought – held in high esteem by everybody. Certainly he had the confidence of the Duke of York; Coventry reciprocated his friendship; and distinguished men in the city and Royal Society respected him.

Pepys's opposition to the war expressed itself in many ways. He was patriotic and anxious for England to settle the score with the Dutch but his realistic appraisal of the state of the Navy did not encourage him. Finances were inadequate, vital stores in short supply and morale low. How could it be otherwise if we accept Pepys's picture of dockyard workers unable to eat because they had not been paid? Widows were dying in the streets from hunger and sea-men's families were reduced to street-begging and worse. It was ironic that as the Navy suffered under such pressures Pepys's private wealth increased and he could not have been unaware of the paradox.

The incident which led to a declaration of war was the attack launched by Robert Holmes on the West African possessions of the Dutch East India Company. Without what the Dutch regarded as reasonable provocation, in the summer of 1664 Holmes fired on the Dutch forts and immediately the Dutch ambassador in London lodged a protest. The vessels which launched the attack were not directly part of the British Navy but privately rented to the Royal African Company. Under this cover the attack could be seen as piratical and nothing to do with the British Government. Such cover was blown when it became known that the King himself and the Duke of York held financial interests in the Company. Contradictory reports were pouring in on all sides and Pepys wrote to Sandwich as early as December 1664:

Yesterday came all the news we have long expected from Guinny of
De Ruyter's retaking all the Dutch had lost and that in the most
advantageous circumstances to themselves they could have wished . . .
First to possessing themselves of all our wealth . . . to the utter ruin
of our company's stock . . . Next to the foulest reproach of cowardice
that has ever been found due to so many English ships we had
there under the protection of two forts, there being not the least show
of opposition made by us but all (and more than was asked) calmly
surrendered to them.[5]

Holmes's attack on the Dutch could not escape unpunished if England was to save face. Dutch fury was temporarily placated when it became clear that Holmes would, on his return, be committed to the Tower, but the Dutch ambassador quickly unmasked this as a piece of easy expedience. He clearly understood that behind these skirmishes they were not fighting for minor honours but, at root, world trade. Captain Cooke, a director of the Royal African Company, put it succinctly to Pepys: 'The trade of the world is too little for us two, therefore one must down.'[6] Primitive economics had not yet derived the princi-ple of expanding world trade as an alternative to the imposition of trade routes. Deeper still there was a political need to heal the rifts of the Civil War by creating a threatening external enemy. Pepys was not against imprisoning Holmes in the Tower. He had already experienced a gruelling exchange with him over his former protégé and mathematics teacher, Cooper.

Recommended by Pepys, Cooper had became master of a fourth-rate ship which operated off Tangier. Cooper returned with a very bad reputation for drinking while in command, ignorance of sea-faring law and mutineering.[7] Holmes appeared before the Navy Board to defend him but Pepys demanded Cooper's discharge. The hot-headed Holmes would have none of it and made his views plain with such insolence that Pepys rounded on him. 'We fell from one word to another that ... came to very high term such as troubled me.'[8] Holmes said that it was lucky Pepys had made his criticisms under the privilege of the Navy Board, clearly hinting at the duel which might have followed in other circumstances. Sir William Batten, Penn, Sir John Mennes and Sir George Carteret were all behind Pepys but that was of no avail in the heated atmosphere which threatened to point Holmes's rapier at Pepys's throat. The following day was a Sunday, and Pepys 'could not get yesterday's quarrel' out of his mind. On the Monday he made his way with trepidation to the Board but he did not see Holmes until later the same evening. They met on Sandwich's doorstep. Holmes made to turn away but Pepys confronted him. An exchange of civilities ensued in which – according to Pepys – Holmes 'did as good as desire excuse for the high words that did pass in his heat'. Pepys won the moral and lost the professional battle. Three years later a fierce encounter with the Dutch drove the flagship *Royal Prince* aground on Galloper sand, where the Dutch captured and burnt her. The man responsible for her navigation was Richard Cooper.[9]

In April 1665 anticlimax followed. Largely due to Pepys's efforts the fleet which assembled at Gunfleet in April 1665 was the largest in British naval history, totalling one hundred and three men-of-war with an elaborate array of attendant fireships. On board the flagship were Penn as Captain General, the Duke of York and Sir William Coventry. They set sail on 21 April for the Dutch coast hoping to draw out the Dutch fleet. Three weeks later the supply of beer for the sailors ran out, protests arose and a wise Captain General was forced to surrender to the superior force of alcohol. All previous studies of Pepys have showered praise on him for getting the fleet to sea properly equipped, but someone seems to have outwitted him. Pepys had in fact done a sharp deal with the Plymouth merchant Timothy Alsop, whereby he would receive a percentage amounting to £150 a year if they won the contract at three shillings and a penny halfpenny, or £300 at the increased price of three shillings and two pence. This contradicts the idea of Pepys cutting the costs of the Navy by driving hard bargains. On the contrary, the more expensive the bargain he struck the better were his perquisites. Details of the deal with Gauden the Navy victualler are not available, but the lack of beer when searching for the enemy seriously interrupted naval manœuvres. Pepys frantically plunged in once more to re-equip the fleet: 'so to my office where busy all the afternoon till late; and then home to bed being much troubled in mind for several things. First for the condition of the fleet for lack of provisions ... the blame this Office lies under and the shame they deserve to have brought upon them for the ships not being gone out of the river.'[10]

An enlarged fleet of one hundred and nine warships, twenty-eight fireships and twenty-one thousand men did at last set sail from Gun-fleet on 30 May 1665 with Pepys committing their good fortune to the care of the Almighty. As if in reaction from overpowering work, the following day he put on his 'new silk camelott suit, the best that ever I wore in my life', and proceeded by coach to Westminster Hall, 'where I took the fairest flower and by coach to Tothill Fields ... till it was dark. I light and in with the fairest flower to eat cake and there did do as much as was safe with my flower ...'[11] Returning home to write letters he finished very few because his pleasure with his flower made him 'forget everything that is'. The great fleet had been newly launched, the fate of the nation hung in the balance, but both were swept aside in his sexual passion.[12] By 1 June the rival navies were within firing distance of each other, and the English, having the advantage of the weather, went into the attack. Since they were only fourteen miles off Lowestoft, the sound of battle carried, and sometimes penetrated beyond Suffolk and Essex into the heart of London. Dryden, whom Pepys had known at Cambridge, recorded: 'Everyone went following the sound as his fancy led him; and leaving the town almost empty some took towards the park.'[13] The echo of guns created excitement and uneasiness in Pepys. He was particularly anxious for his cousin, the Duke of York and Coventry who were now under threat of mutilation and death. All his future hopes were bound up in these men and his fate inextricably connected to that of England. Briefly, his attention was distracted by his clerk Hayter, who broke some obscure technical regulation and found himself incarcerated in the Gatehouse.[14] 'At noon ... upon entering recognizances ... for his appearance ... he was released.'[15]

These May days were oppressively hot – hotter than any May Pepys could remember – and rumour ran rife. Letters coming in from the coast spoke of the battle drifting towards Holland, but others said the sound of gunfire was more distinct in England. Nerves were razor sharp, sleep not easy and a sudden rumour that Lord Sandwich had been killed devastating. Elizabeth went off with the servants to seek the cool of the river, and Pepys was left in the heart of the city to face the terrible appearance of red crosses on three houses in Drury Lane announcing the arrival of the plague in London. 'Lord have mercy on us' was inscribed beneath each of the crosses. Pepys, like many people, believed that chewing tobacco reduced the smell and apprehension, even if it did not fully repel the plague. He spent the next day chewing industriously.

Then the great news came. Pepys was attending a meeting at the Lord Treasurer's with a number of bankers when Bob May, Keeper of the Privy Purse to the King, arrived from the Duke of York to announce: 'We have totally routed the Dutch. The Duke ... the Prince, My Lord Sandwich and Coventry are all well, which did put me into such a joy that I forgot almost all other thoughts.'[16] The weather had favoured the English and on the morning of 3 June they attacked, sailing southeast with Coventry in the van, the Duke at the centre and Sandwich in the rear.[17] 'Not one of either side was out of play at this first encounter. The calm sea gave a chance for good shooting but no great harm was done.'[18] Accounts of the second stage of the battle varied, but an order from His Royal Highness broke the original formations of the English squadrons and the action began to assume the character of a mêlée.[19] Suddenly, Sandwich was able to break through the Dutch line, causing chaos. The enemy became disordered and a fireship was sent plunging into their midst. There was a moment when the Duke of York's life was in danger. According to one report a round of chain shot killed three of the crew of the *Royal Charles* and the victims were so near His Grace that they sprinkled him with their blood and brains. By the evening the end was near with the whole Dutch fleet 'but one large blaze'.[20] As night came down twenty-four ships were destroyed and the Dutch High Admiral Opdam killed when his flagship blew up.[21] Estimates of Dutch losses varied from eight to ten thousand men, with the English figure put at seven hundred, but the statistics were shaky. Pepys wrote: 'A great victory, never known in the world. They all fled: some forty-three got into Texell ... and we in pursuit of the rest.'[22] Pepys, alive with the spirit of victory, hurried off to the Cockpit where he joined the Duke of Albemarle, no less overwhelmed with national pride and joy. Impatient with protocol, when a letter arrived from Coventry addressed to the Duke of Albemarle, he simply flung it at Pepys unopened.[23] Pepys was suitably shocked and later made a careful copy of the letter giving details of the victory. Meanwhile, he went off with Lady Penn and others to build a great bonfire at the gate of her house. One worry persisted at the back of his mind. 'I hear nothing said or done by My Lord Sandwich'. In fact, that very day the King wrote a letter of thanks to Sandwich which Pepys discovered later.[24] Whether Sandwich broke the Dutch line remains in dispute. Two accounts of the battle credit Sandwich with the vital manœuvre, but one was written by Sandwich's Captain Cuttance at a time when Sandwich expressed deep disappointment with the current reports of his performance.[25] Harris in his biography of Sandwich concludes that Sandwich divided the enemy but breaking the line was an accident, not a tactical design.[26]

The plague now became very real in Pepys's life. He first began to take serious precautions on 8 June when his wife and mother were dining with Mr Joyce and he warned them to 'go round by the Half Moone to his house because of the plague'.[27] Later in the same month he recorded that going home by hackney coach 'is become a very dangerous passage nowadays, the sickness increasing mightily'. By July he complained that the town had emptied of people to such an extent that there was not a single person in the Spring Gardens. 'While I was there a poor woman came to scold ... the master of the house that a kinswoman ... was newly dead of the plague.'[28] After a day of dalliance on 27 July when he was able 'to kiss and spend some time with the ladies' he came home to 'meet the weekly bill' of one thousand seven hundred dead of the plague. His officers now seriously considered moving their activities out to Deptford, which perplexed Pepys who still refused to retreat as the plague progressed. On 15 August 1665 the King ordered the Navy Commissioners to move their offices from Westminster to rooms in the manor house at Greenwich.[29] A letter from Pepys to Carteret quickly followed which said that Sir John Mennes has 'since otherwise advised and will not have the office kept at his lodging'.[30]

From the beginning of July the streets of London had been crowded with handcarts, coaches and waggons leaving London loaded with household goods heading for the country. When Pepys's mother came to London he promptly packed her off back to Brampton and simultaneously arranged to lodge his wife with William Sheldon, the Clerk of the Cheque, at Woolwich. The maids, Mary and Bess, accompanied her, leaving Susan and Alice to service the Seething Lane house. Most of the court had already left London and Coventry next decided to go, which left 'old Albemarle serenely behind at the Cockpit'.[31] Pepys has been praised for his courage in remaining within the stricken city and he certainly outfaced alarming hazards, but his motives appear ambiguous when seen in the light of some of his activities. Whether he had engineered a period free from family surveillance or whether under the shadow of the plague he became more aware of the brevity of human life, he now indulged one pleasure after another. He shut his office even before darkness fell and went off to enjoy the full burgeoning of perfect summer days in Vauxhall Gardens. Hiring a coach, he drove to Hampstead Heath with Mary, the girl from the Harp and Ball, and 'had what pleasure almost I would with her'.[32] He also found time to fit in a visit to Mrs Bagwell.

On 10 August he recorded the strange story of alderman Bences who stumbled at night over a corpse in the street, went home to tell his wife and she, being with child, fell into such a fright that she was taken sick 'and died of the plague'.[33] From other evidence Pepys concluded that 'not a word of all this is true'. On 30 August he went for a walk towards Moorfields to see whether he could actually see any corpses being transported to the graves. 'God forgive my presumption.'[34] He remarked how everybody's looks and discourse in the street was of death from the plague, with few people promenading and the town 'like a place distressed – and forsaken'. He returned home to take consolation in counting up his money and finding himself 'yet in the much best condition that ever I was in . . . worth 2180l and odd'.

Although his fears steadily mount in the Diary, he shows no signs of retreating from a city which had emptied to the point where the most important areas of commerce were almost bereft of business. By September he was writing: 'Up and put on my coloured silk suit, very fine and my new periwig bought a good while since but durst not wear it because the plague was in Westminster when I bought it.'[35] By October he had encountered so many corpses that his sensibilities were numbed and when one evening he 'came close by the bearers with a dead corpse' he reflected in the Diary: 'But hard to see what custom is, that I am come almost to [think] nothing of it.'[36] Another entry re-emphasised the growing indifferences of many people when a dead body was left out all night, 'the disease making us more cruel to one another than we are [to] dogs'.[37] On the same night sex with Elizabeth blotted out the plague. Pepys has been praised for his descriptive powers in the Diary which are said to evoke time, place and person with such immediacy that the reader relives the events in all their reality. Evocative though his plague entries are, they do not live up to this view. Indeed not the Diary but some of his letters bring the plague alive more effectively. He wrote to Lady Carteret that autumn:

the absence of the court and emptiness of the city takes away all occasion of news ... I have stayed in the city till above seven thousand four hundred died in one week and of them about six thousand of the plague, and little noise heard day and night but tolling bells till I could walk Lumber [Lombard] Street and not meet twenty persons from one end to the other and not fifty upon the Exchange; till whole families (ten and twelve together) have been swept away; till my very physician Dr Burnet who undertook to secure me against any infections (having survived a month of his own having been shut up) died himself of the plague; till the nights (though much lengthened) are grown too short to conceal the burials of those that died the day before ... lastly, till I could find neither meat nor drink safe, the butcheries being everywhere visited, my brewer's house shut up and my baker with his whole family dead of the plague.[38]

But Pepys – 'your poor servant' – remained unscathed and, plague or no plague, found time to revisit Mrs Bagwell on his way to meet his wife. Afterwards, driven by guilt, he showered presents on Elizabeth and forgot the rumours from the maids that she herself was 'gadding about'. Elizabeth's pleasures had developed from socialising and dancing to painting, which, on the day of his Bagwell visit, he went out of his way to admire.

An enlivening episode now occurred which cast Pepys in the unusual role of respectable liaison agent. Lord Sandwich desired to marry his daughter to Sir George Carteret's eldest son, a piece of matchmaking approved by both the King and Duke of York. Custom required that an intermediary move between Sandwich and Carteret and the choice automatically fell on Pepys. He was delighted to negotiate a satisfactory settlement because it strengthened the relationship between his two powerful allies.[39] 'I am mightily contented that I have the good fortune to be so instrumental and I think it will be of good use to me.' His liaison brought him into fresh social prominence and he found himself indulging in merry discussions with Carteret about that unfathomable mystery, marriage. A weekend at the country house of Lord Sandwich's sister followed where the bridal pair held parties which – briefly – drove out all thought of war and the plague, to Pepys's delight.[40] The mood passed quickly.

Within a few days Britain's relations with Holland and Denmark once more interrupted his personal preoccupations. The lull which followed the engagement at Lowestoft had enabled both sides to refit their ships and rethink their strategies. The English display of cunning tactics had driven the enemy back into harbour but the command of the sea was merely in abeyance.[41] Once more Pepys plunged into the multifarious business of re-equipping and manning the fleet against dwindling funds and a background clamour which led to the ropemakers discharging themselves for lack of pay, while Pepys was forced to take action against a strike among unpaid dockyard workers. The plague had thrown the whole economy into confusion, with trade diminished and taxes uncollected, which deepened the Navy's debts. As a result, by September the Navy Board was pre-occupied with one subject alone – money. As Pepys left the Office at Greenwich one day he was threatened with physical violence by a hostile crowd of 'poor seamen that are starving ... for lack of money'.[42] He tried to talk to them but it was to no avail and a little scattered largesse did no good. Matters grew worse by November when Sir William Batten had his cloak torn from his back and his servant assaulted by demonstrating sailors.[43] The very same day Pepys was 'much troubled to have one hundred seamen ... cursing us and breaking the glass windows. [They] swear they will pull the house down on Tuesday next.'[44] There was a charitable fund, The Chatham Chest for Stricken Sailors, in which Pepys took considerable interest, but it was totally inadequate to meet their needs.

Politically, another question had come to dominate all others – who should command the fleet when it did set sail. In accordance with the custom of the time, the most obvious choice would have been the Duke of York, but his near-death at Lowestoft, and the need to secure the succession to the throne, made his appointment too danger-ous. The King's Council debated which of the two alternatives – Sandwich, Vice Admiral of England, or Prince Rupert, Admiral of the Squadron – would serve their purposes. A joint command was proposed as a compromise, but when Prince Rupert insisted on unac-ceptable terms the King stood out against him and summoned Sand-wich to his cabin and '... expressed more value for me than I deserve, God knows, and told me I should be sure either to command jointly with the Prince or be trusted alone with the whole affair'.[45] Both the Duke of York and Coventry regarded Prince Rupert's possible succession hazardous and Sandwich revealed to Pepys that they fre-quently laughed behind his back. In the event, the Duke of York set off for the north to repel any possible Dutch landing; Prince Rupert was left floating in a vacuum; Albemarle stayed in London; and

Sandwich was given joint command with Penn. It was the perfect realignment of all Pepys's interests and loyalties. Unfortunately, they were no sooner brought together than division threatened. When news came through in July 1665 of heavily laden Dutch convoys emerging from the Indies homeward bound, Sandwich persuaded Penn to intercept, board and take them as prizes. A conspiracy to make this manœuvre possible at little cost was arranged between the English ambassador in Copenhagen and the King of Denmark.[46] According to Sandwich, the English ambassador indicated that the King of Denmark was ready to do a deal breaking his treaties with Holland at a time advantageous to Sandwich's expedition. Although instructions for attack upon the convoys were made out in Penn's name he was ordered to surrender the command to Sandwich as soon as Sandwich joined the fleet.[47] Cautious as ever, Sandwich checked back with Coventry, received confirmation and was left in absolute control of the campaign. It turned out to be disastrous.[48] The ambassador's words were not matched by the King of Denmark's actions. None of his commanders at Bergen were informed of the conspiracy and when Sandwich detached a squadron under Sir Thomas Tiddeman to attack the ships sheltering under the Dutch forts, they opened fire on the English. Within a few hours the English were forced to retire with severe casualties, including the death of Sandwich's cousin. 'Three hundred guns were trained upon our vessels and supported the fire of the Dutch . . . For three hours Tiddeman was exposed to an attack twice as fierce as he expected. At length he withdrew.'[49] Pepys was dismayed to find the responsibility for the fiasco placed squarely on Sandwich's shoulders. The fleet was now forced back to England, partly to repair the damage, and partly for lack of supplies. Once again, despite Pepys's efforts, the goods supplied fell short of the quantities agreed in his contracts.

Something immediate and spectacular was required to recover Sandwich's reputation and Pepys brought all his powers to bear on re-equipping the fleet yet again in record time. It was no simple matter. The whole system of victualling the fleet, despite Pepys's work, was still inadequate. A single contractor had responsibility for keeping the fleet supplied and 'if he died all would have stood still'. Pepys wrote to His Lordship: 'I am grieved at the heart to see Your Lordship in this strait which shall be eased as far as any payne of mine will stand insteade.'[50] When the fleet set sail once more towards the end of August it was supposed to be fully manned, provisioned and equipped for ten to fifteen days' operations. Whether because of Sandwich's rush to get to sea again or of Pepys's inadequacy, the results were unsatisfactory. 'The liquour allowance was one half and certain vessels were ill fitted.'[51] Since liquor seemed indispensable to the fighting spirit and sailors liable to 'rebel' without it, this was an inauspicious start. Intelligence relayed to Sandwich indicated that a number of Dutchmen overdue from the Mediterranean were carrying silks, spices and one hundred and twenty tons of solid gold.[52] It was a glittering prize. Initially, they were under the protection of the Dutch fleet, but rough weather intervened to break up its formations and a number of East Indiamen drifted away, rolling helplessly in very rough seas.[53] On the morning of 3 September the English bore down upon the quarry then heading for Texel. The pursuit lasted all day but the heavily laden merchantmen were no match for the English warships and they quickly boarded and took control of two big East Indiamen. The final haul included two other large merchant ships, four men-of-war and one thousand three hundred prisoners.[54] The British fleet did not escape completely unscathed, losing the *Hector*, a fifth-rate ship with eighty men aboard.

Six days later excitement ran high again with eighteen enemy sails sighted and attacked. 'Four men-of-war were taken, one of seventy guns; some merchantmen, their victuals, ammunition and one thousand prisoners; a glorious but cumbersome amount ...' As Clarendon put it, the prisoners had 'to be clothed and fed and did us more harm ashore than afloat'.[55] What at first seemed an unadulterated triumph threatened to turn sour once more for Sandwich. Pepys followed these events with avid interest. While the fleet remained at sea and the chase was still on, his spirits were effervescent but occasionally dampened by the steadily emptying coffers of the Navy. A strike by carpenters at Woolwich dockyard was symptomatic of a mood engendered by huge debts outstanding to suppliers and seamen alike.

The plague constantly pressed in to overshadow public interest in these affairs. In September 1665 Pepys recorded: 'Up by five of the clock mighty full of an ague but was obliged to go ... and there sent for the weekly bill and find 8,252 dead in all and of them 6,978 of the plague – which is a most dreadful number.'[56] On 9 September he makes the simple statement in the Diary: 'Up and walked to Greenwich' which was no small walk. Later, after talking to Captain Cocke the hemp merchant, he recorded they were 'full of discourse of the neglect of our musters, the great officers of state about all businesses and especially that of money – having now some thousand prisoners kept to no purpose at a great charge'. This especially concerned Captain Cocke who was Commissioner for the Sick and

Wounded and Prisoners of War. Pepys quoted Cocke: 'My Lord Treasurer has his ease and lets things go as they will; if he can have his 8,000l per annum, and a game at lombre he is well. My Lord Chancellor ... minds getting of money and nothing else; and my Lord Ashley will rob the devil and the altar but he will get money if it be to be got.'[57] Pepys disputed these charges but according to Baxter,[58] the Treasurer (Carteret) had overcome the tiresome business of piecemeal fees by accepting a yearly salary in lieu, a move which gave respectability to devious practices.

The next day was Sunday and Pepys walked from Cocke's house at Greenwich to visit his wife still safe from the plague at Woolwich. While he was talking to her about the illness of her father, a letter arrived from Coventry enclosing Sandwich's account of their success-ful sea skirmish. '[It] did put us all into such an ecstasy of joy ... in all my life I never met with so merry a two hours.'[59]

Serious trouble for Lord Sandwich followed fast on the heels of celebration. The Dutch prizes were said to be worth immense sums – £400,000 – and the temptation was too great for him. Ordinary seamen were allowed to confiscate any goods lying between the decks of prize ships, but they were forbidden to open the holds and make free with the actual cargo. The sale of ships and cargo was legally controlled by the Prize Court, which also determined how the money should be distributed. Underpaid captains and officers frequently found themselves relatively rich after a big haul and the commander in chief could be awarded very large sums.[60] On this occasion, according to Harris, the vessels were shamelessly ransacked by sailors and some flag officers, who became willing collaborators.[61] Pepys gave a more vivid account: 'They did toss and tumble our spoil and broke things in the hold to a great loss and shame to come at fine goods and did take a man that knows where the fine goods were and did this over and over again for many days, Sir W.Berkeley being the chief hand that did it, but others did the like at other times ...'[62]

Sandwich foolishly allowed a proportion of silks and spices to be assigned to the flag officers before legal warrants for their distribution arrived. Flag officers received goods valued at £2,000, while Penn and Sandwich appropriated materials later valued at £4,000. All this was strictly illegal and now a council of war on board the *Prince* decided to send the prize ships up the river to Erith where customs officers were allowed on board to nail down the hatches.[63] There were flag officers who disputed these proceedings, but Sandwich had the ear of the King and wrote to him: 'We have desired my

Lord Brouncker and Sir John Mennes to ... remain on board the East Indiamen and see the goods delivered into warehouses ...'[64] Anxious to protect his plunder against any confiscation, Sandwich went so far as to transfer some of the goods to a vessel bound for King's Lynn and put them within easy reach of his home at Hinchingbrooke. 'And thence', Pepys commented, 'we may conceive indeed the rise and fall of My Lord's misfortunes.'[65]

Suddenly assailed by fears, Sandwich wrote to Carteret, the Treasurer of the Navy, then at court with His Majesty, and received 'an assurance coupled with a warning'. When shown Sandwich's letter, Coventry commented: 'Here My Lord Sandwich has done what I durst not have done.' Carteret had suggested that Sandwich have his officers 'dispossessed of their goods'.[66] Fatally, Sandwich ignored this advice. Sandwich claimed that he had the court's approval for his conduct, but the order sent to Albemarle merely stated that 'all respect' must be 'paid to the Earl of Sandwich and his goods'.[67] The order arrived late and the outcry against Sandwich was already spreading.[68] As the spoils began to come ashore in waggonloads under semi-secret conditions, they were in such bulk that they could not escape public notice. Stories spread along the river banks of great wealth distributed by night to mysterious destinations, and even in the day 'crowds stood agape to see the riches of the East'. Seamen were busy in the streets and taverns selling their small share at bargain prices. Never at a loss in these situations, Pepys recorded how he 'went to a blind alehouse at the farther end of the town to a couple of wretched, dirty seamen who had got about 37lb. of cloves and 10lb. of nuttmeggs. And we bought them ...'[69] It was not to be expected that Pepys could long restrain himself from taking advantage of all this corrupt dealing.[70]

Accompanied by the crooked merchant Captain Cocke he then set sail on the *Bezan* to visit Lord Sandwich still on board the warship *Prince*. Arriving early in the morning he found Sandwich still in his nightshirt but willing to discourse at once on the shortcomings of naval supplies. After a respectable interval Pepys proceeded in partnership with Captain Cocke to buy from Sandwich £1,000-worth of nutmegs, cinnamon and cloves. It did not seem to worry him that the deal involved Captain Cuttance who had encouraged Sandwich's recklessness, and he did not hesitate to borrow £500 from Will Howe, now the Admiral's Deputy Treasurer, to finance his half of it.[71] Travelling back to London he disembarked at Chatham where he found Sir William Penn in bed, 'and there much talk and much dissembling of kindness from him, but he is a false rogue and I shall not trust him'. Calling at Rochester he found time for three pretty maids on the stairs leading to the tower of the castle, but when he escorted them to the top the height 'did fright me mightily and hinder me of much pleasure which I would have made'.

Although he did not know it, he was heading for trouble with his contraband. He feared first of all that Cocke would double-cross him. He then became involved in such a nest of corruption it is difficult to disentangle the interlocking strands. First, he warned Sandwich against Cocke's behaviour and persuaded the always relaxed and worldly Sandwich to sell him yet another £1,000 of illegally confiscated goods. Next he turned his attention to the discredited Cuttance and disliked Penn. Further bargains were stuck with both men which left Pepys in possession of yet more valuable merchandise. But his anxieties multiplied in proportion to his profit. How was he to protect it all from marauding officialdom already showing a searching interest in his activities? His first thought was to get the backing of Lord Sandwich, and he wrote a carefully worded order which attested that the said Mr Samuel Pepys should be allowed whenever he chose 'to dispose of his silks and spices'.[72] This was rushed to Sandwich, who signed it without any qualms. Lulled into a false sense of security Pepys's anxieties suddenly surfaced when he learnt that Custom House officers had been warned by the commissioners of prizes not to pass any goods without the King's warrant.[73] A letter to Sandwich revealed the King's displeasure in these proceedings.

I have been in very great pain . . . touching the business of these prize goods, very severe orders being issued for the seizing [of] all men's . . . accordingly even those for which Your Lordship's certificates . . . are shown. And further My Lord Brouncker has wrote me that the King and Duke do disown their order . . .[74]

There was further consultation with Cocke on 27 September. Cocke offered to buy Pepys out for a £500-share in the profits, with Pepys holding out for £600.

The day of 4 October brought good news about the diminishing plague and bad news about Cocke. 'All the town is full of Captain Cocke's being in some ill condition about prize goods, his goods being taken from him.'[75] Pepys reassured himself by simply refusing to believe it, 'for he would have wrote to me . . . about it'. Londoners living near the river were agog at the gossip about illicit dealings and on 7 October Pepys worked hard, housing – or attempting to conceal – two whole waggonloads of merchandise. In the very midst of his attempt, two customs officers appeared and proceeded to confiscate the goods 'until further decision was made'. Pepys immediately waved Lord Sandwich's transit in their faces. They were quite unimpressed. Fierce exchanges followed but nothing could dissuade the officers from locking up the goods, and leaving the key in the safe custody of the parish constable. This led to further intrigue. 'But Lord, to think how the poor constable came to me in the dark ... "Sir," says he, "I have the key and if you would have me do any service for you send for me betimes tomorrow morning." '[76] The invincible Pepys made short work of the customs officers. However, no sooner had he received his goods than they were seized again by another official. Worse followed when a second consignment of goods was confiscated opposite Greenwich church with a large and somewhat hostile crowd agape at the proceedings. A furious Pepys once more set about recovering his 'possessions'. An entry in the Diary early in October put his activities into unpleasant perspective. 'Did business but not much at the Office because of the horrible crowd and lamentable moan of the poor seamen that be starving in the streets for lack of money – which doth trouble and perplex me to the heart. And more at noon ... for then a whole hundred of them followed us – some cursing, some swearing and some praying upon us.'[77] In the middle of October Pepys wrote to Sandwich: 'What I did acquaint Your Lordship with my fear ... in my last ... I am now too much confirmed in by a multiplying seizures made upon Capt. Cocke's goods.'[78] The letter was a mish-mash of hypocritical reasoning in favour of Sandwich and Pepys retaining their plunder. It emerged that Sandwich had appealed directly to the King and Duke of York to suspend orders of seizure, 'with bad success from the Duke and a severe denial from the King'. Disquieting news then came from the court where some of the fleet commanders had complained to the King and the Duke of York who proceeded to disavow Lord Sandwich.

A much more serious threat now renewed itself. A fleet of eighty Dutch ships had been sighted off Solebay and were said to be heading – with relative impunity – straight into the bay. 'God knows what they will do to us, we having no force abroad able to oppose them ...' The resilient Pepys plunged back into work the following day, summoning the captains of all the ships in the river to confer with him. 'I think of twenty-two ships we shall make shift to set out seven.' Bad news persisted: the Pope had died, the King of France was stabbed and, much more significant to Pepys, Lord Sandwich was under heavy opprobrium. On 11 October Mr Seamour, one of the Commissioners, arrived with a man who proceeded to seize Pepys's goods and – 'he mighty imperious would have all forfeited and I know not what.'[79] Angry words were exchanged, and Pepys became heated, much to his regret because it showed him to be 'too much concerned'. Preparing to disengage himself from the whole unfortunate business, Pepys learned that the King had ordered an examination of Sandwich's spoils which the officials 'did toss and tumble and . . . broke things in the hold'.

Chapter 9

First Naval Report

Mustering ships to confront the invading Dutch fleet revealed ship after ship either to be in a sad state of repair or dangerously unseaworthy. In a letter to Coventry Pepys wrote: 'I will not rest night or day to send away what is possible ... that our fleet may be out again by times.'[1] Another letter to Coventry spoke of the number of sick and wounded from the previous campaign 'flung upon us to be fed'.[2] When he learned the state of the Navy, Albemarle, Captain General of the Kingdom, fell into a fine temper and bluntly turned his anger on Sandwich, but Sandwich was away at Oxford putting his case before the King. What had begun as a mild criticism of Sandwich's behaviour now mounted into a hue and cry which laid one charge after another at his door. Instead of crushing the Dutch fleet in September he had concentrated on bringing home the prize ships for the primary purpose of plunder.[3] Confronted with the new Dutch challenge he had simply disappeared to Oxford intent on living the country life. Nothing seemed to placate, much less satisfy, public opinion. It fell to Pepys to prepare a defence of Sandwich and the handwritten result is still kept in the Bodleian.[4]

The public outcry continued to re-echo throughout London and at last there was nothing for it but Sandwich's resignation. Remembering the many services Sandwich had rendered the country, the King appointed him ambassador extraordinary to Spain. None of this was satisfactory to Pepys, who decided that he must extricate himself from the highly compromising prize goods situation. Cocke, the supreme manipulator, had managed to regain possession of their confiscated goods and now Pepys persuaded Cocke to buy him out of his share for £500 profit. 'I am afeared we shall hereafter have trouble ... therefore I will get myself free of them as soon as I can and my money paid.'[5] It gave him 'extraordinary inward joy'. There was reason for this. He had made twenty per cent on his capital investment of £1,800 and at the end of the year his finances were riding high. His wealth had increased by £1,000, but there was no hint of compunction about its source. The £500 prize money profit was dubious enough but another £500 came from an equally tainted source. Having carefully procured for Gauden, the victualler, the contract for supplying the Tangier garrison, Pepys received a gift of £500 from him. Now as the year drew to a close, he declared with delight that he had raised his estate from 1,300l to 4,400l. Pepys's skill at rationalising his conduct was highly developed and he exclaimed: 'I have got myself greater interest I think by my *diligence*' (my italics). Integrity frequently begins where rationalisation stops but the exercise of such skills were as socially acceptable then as they are to some extent now. Predictably, Pepys turned to praise God for his good fortune.

There were other reasons why God seemed well disposed towards Pepys in the winter of 1665. The number of plague victims had diminished dramatically and the professional classes, the court and even the King himself were returning to a capital where the streets were grass-grown, houses unrepaired and even the Exchange 'unkept'. The King himself paid tribute to Pepys's courage during the epidemic and his service for the Navy with the words: 'Mr Pepys I do give you thanks for your good service all this year and I assure you I am very sensible of it.'

In the growing variety of his life, combining music, theatre, naval administration, sexual adventures and writing his Diary, another distinction now marked him out in the spring of 1665. He was invited by a handful of scientific virtuosi to become a member of the Royal Society. In their company he observed the spectacle of a hen, drunk on Florentine poison, and an aborted foetus preserved in spirits of salt. These were the days of Renaissance man when an interest in the humanities and the sciences often went hand in hand. Marjorie Nicolson has shown how Pepys's first excursions into the new science were concerned with mechanical devices. He became fascinated with instruments.[6] As early as January 1664 a technician had brought him 'an instrument made of a spiral line very pretty for all questions in arithmetic'.[7] This was probably a forerunner of the slide rule, the invention of which is attributed to William Oughtred. It was scientific mathematics which enlarged Pepys's interest in early meetings of the Royal Society and he complained about his brother's 'lack of interest' in the subject: 'I do not see that he minds optickes or mathematique nor anything else that I can find.'[8] He makes no mention of meeting Hooke or Isaac Newton in these early days, but later he was to correspond with both.

Dominating everything at the end of 1665 was the fall of Lord Sandwich, which led Pepys to reflect that a company of rogues had got away with ten times more than Sandwich without suffering the same censure. In such an atmosphere it was a tribute to 'the aristocratic powers' that they meted out such punishment as they did to Sandwich. According to Ollard, Sandwich's embezzlement was not only wrong but stupid. He had, for instance, failed to gain the *quid pro quo* so ingeniously secured by Pepys.[9] Pepys came through these dangerous waters with consummate skill and revealed a combination of compromise, cunning and concern for public welfare which had already characterised him as a survivor.

Pepys continued to concentrate on the Navy's problems. In June he wrote to Sir William Penn at the Nore : 'God send we may acquit ourselves well in the getting the fleet out again ...'[10] Three times the fleet had put to sea, successfully engaged the enemy and failed to press home victory, partly because victuals ran short at crucial moments. The pressure of straitened finances and the Navy's inability to pay debts began a crippling process which was completed by the lack of sufficient food and drink to keep the crews active in the midst of battle. At the centre of the troubles the ubiquitous Gauden came in for more than his fair share of criticism.[11] Summoned to appear before the Navy Board by Pepys, Gauden sent his chief clerk, Mr Lewes, as a substitute, and he was duly interrogated. He gave a convincing account of all his obligations and produced pursers' receipts to prove that the quantities invoiced to the Navy had been duly delivered. Intermediaries were shown to have tampered with some accounts and deliveries, but the quality of the food and drink supplied was not in question. The peacetime establishment of the Navy had multiplied twelve times in war and Gauden's ability to enlarge supplies depended on his being adequately financed. As Tedder wrote : 'The fault did not lie with him personally ; on the contrary, it is very striking to notice how in one complaint after another it is expressly stated that it is not directed against him.'[12] While Coventry was 'frantic with worry over insufficient victualling' he decided Gauden was a man 'of good words' who provided 'good victuals'.[13] All this was scribbled down one August day by Pepys in a letter to Carteret.[14] At the heart of the problem lay the Navy's refusal to meet its debts. During the previous year, of £474,000 due to Gauden for victualling only £125,000 had been paid.

As a result of Pepys's investigations and his growing reputation he took another step forward when he was appointed Surveyor General of Victualling for His Majesty's Navy, which added £300 a year to his salary.[15] Never a man to waste time, immediately he set about preparing a statement on the Navy's finances. Very detailed, it covered many aspects of expenditure and showed the current cost of the Navy to be over £1 million, which could not be met unless previous debts were first cleared. Success attended his report almost immediately. Parliament voted another £1¼ million – with one unfortunate proviso. It was to be paid in instalments of £50,000 a month – reducing the original offer to farce. The whole machinery for financing the Navy was a hopelessly outdated system of subsidies, parliamentary aids and levies which derived from the Middle Ages, and attempts at modernisation were constantly frustrated by traditional practices. This happened now. Pepys found himself driven to write letters to Coventry which allowed emotion to underpin argument. Payment of debts apart, the Chatham Chest fund for seamen in distress was still unable to meet the demands made upon it and Pepys wrote to Coventry: 'I have every week complaints from the governors that for want of money they having not received a penny since December 1663 and poor wretches are for relief forced to come crawling up hither that would break one's heart to see them.'[16] At the heart of the matter lay an inescapable truth which Pepys put forcibly to Carteret early in November. No fleet could be made ready to put to sea to confront the Dutch in the following year unless financial problems were given immediate priority. Moreover, as we have seen, forces outside the control of Pepys or Parliament were still at work to cripple one solution after another. The plague had interrupted tax-collecting and a deep reduction in trade had reduced the national income. Reorganisation of the Navy's finances might just counter both these forces.

So it was that early in January 1666 Pepys was called up at five o'clock by his own request and began dictating his distinguished report on pursery to the Office messenger Tooker. He continued 'without eating or drinking till three in the afternoon and then to my great content finished it'.[17] The report analysed in detail the defective methods then in use and was especially critical of the system in which every ship's purser was 'controlled by captain and muster masters'. This method practically enforced embezzlement and encouraged every artifice 'to find ways of charging the defects of provisions upon the King or by mutual exchange of fraudulent practices with the captains'. Pepys strongly recommended returning to the old practice, where the purser had no obligation beyond maintaining 'the ship at its full complement of men during the time for which it was victualled'. Thus any deficiencies would devolve on the purser and not the King, with the added incentive of efficient book-keeping and saving. The purser would not be forced to conspire with captains to dupe the Navy Board and the crown since he would 'reckon all unuseful men entertained for the captain's profit burdensome to him in consuming his victuals as much as they are to the King in taking up wages'. Pepys's paper ran to many pages and needed two days 'examining and fitting up' before, on 3 January, it was sent away 'by an express to Coventry'.[18]

In the meantime the incorrigible Pepys managed to relax with a little sexual diversion. Turning his mind from abstract thinking to sex came naturally to him. On the morning following his first day's dictation he was 'up by candlelight again . . . and made an end of my fair writing it'.[19] The same evening he joined Lord Brouncker to hear 'my dear Mrs Knipp' sing 'and got her upon my knee . . . and played with her breasts'. The following evening he relaxed again, singing and dancing 'and mighty merry till Mr Rolt came in whose pain of the tooth made him no company and spoilt ours'.[20]

The following days were devoted to emphasising the urgent need for his reforms with elaborately phrased memos, and throughout February and March he complained bitterly to Coventry of the delay in their realisation. 'Is it not that the frauds practicable with exposure of £435,000 . . . are not worthy of our preventing?' In the evenings after dinner, having settled his wife safely at home, he would make his way to the Swan tavern and seek out Mrs Martin. There: 'I did what I would with her.' However, Mrs Martin quickly lost her charms. When she asked him one day to lend her £5, he first demanded a security and later reflected that 'she is come to be very bad and offers anything'. Whether this meant sex in all its forms or promiscuity with other men is not clear, but he decided that it was dangerous to continue seeing her, 'nor will I . . . a good while'.[21] His capacity for introspection was outmatched by his ability to rationalise: 'Most men that do thrive with the world do forget to take pleasure during the time that they are getting their estate . . . and then it is too late for them to enjoy it with any pleasure.'[22]

Chapter 10

Second Dutch War and the Fire of London

Samuel Pepys was now a man of thirty-three verging on that uncertain condition called maturity and living life to the full in all its aspects. Described as squat, if not thickset, he made the most of his five feet five inches with an upright carriage which conveyed a touch of pride. In all his finery of silk shirt, velvet cloak, buckled shoes and wig, he had a certain distinction. His eyes were large if not luminous, his mouth deeply sensual, and he had a frank, open countenance. That he had occasional nightmares and was beset by the whole gamut of anxieties which trouble the average man is clear from the Diary and this went to the heart of him. He was the ordinary man brought to a tenth pitch and the resonance millions of readers have found in his Diary is explicable in those terms. His very family mirrored a thousand others which if not cast in quite the same mould, more or less struggled to accommodate the same conflicts and satisfactions. Many a reader has imagined sexual adventures which, if unrealised, could be indulged at one remove in Pepys's Diary. The deeper satisfactions of sex and work, music and learning, were interlaced and sometimes overwhelmed by the minutiae of everyday life which put flesh and blood on the written page and produced inescapable identification. Sleepless nights, meals engorged, women loved or casually indulged, every detail from his wife's periods to his toilet habits, were recorded with loving detail which was completely detached from bodily disgust. Here was a man full of human frailties who rose above them with his extraordinary ambition. Here was a man capable of giving his wife a black eye,[1] who recoiled from violence and identified with the woes of common seamen.[2] Surrendering to lust, he made no bones about enjoying it, but struggled to control his sexual appetites. Preaching a morality far removed from his practice, he could happily damn a colleague for the very sins he himself committed. Praising God for his beneficence when things went well, his faith in a divinity was shaky but he always ready to admire Him when his bank balance increased. Money meant social status to him as it does to most men, but he pursued its accretion with the detailed accuracy of a bank clerk and gloated over every fresh sum as a glittering prize. The steady growth of his wealth – now considerable in middle age – was matched by a growth of meanness, but he had the acumen and honesty to record the alliance in his Diary. It enshrined Pepys's 'soul' laid bare every night in a shorthand few could read, deliberately kept secret, with tortured industry, for his eye alone.

The candle gutters, it is three in the morning, outside the pitch black streets are empty and full of danger, but already a blackbird calls.[3] Inside, straining his eyes against the flickering candle flame with a quill pen scratching across the paper Pepys, exhausted after a day of 'naval battle', drink and casual sex, insists on completing the day's entry, recording in the greatest detail the doings of an extraordinary ordinary man.

Central to his home life his wife Elizabeth was treated – more so now in middle life – as a second-class citizen. He skilfully deceived her, not with grand passions or inescapable love affairs, but frequently sordid encounters. He was seldom, if ever, ambushed by love. Petty intrigues and fumblings, stealthy meetings where complete sex was the exception, seem to characterise many of his infidelities. He hardly qualified as a sexual athlete and in a sophisticated world where men were always seeking ways to escape the monotony of married life, his behaviour was not abnormal. The record of Pepys's infidelities can be read in four ways. He was a roué who rationalised the licentious indulgence of all his appetites; his sexual relations with Elizabeth had lost their fire and he was searching for variation; adultery gave an excitement he could not get by other means; if he could not quite reach aristocratic licence, he sought to produce a satisfying imitation. Several incarnations were continuously struggling to find expression, if not dominance: Pepys the born administrator, Pepys the musically minded aesthete, Pepys the avaricious materialist, Pepys the dedicated sensualist, Pepys the practising hypocrite – all indissolubly bound together by some intangible bond which was insufficient to reconcile one with another and only succeeded in putting now one, now another in the ascendant. The warm, compassionate Pepys concerned with the everyday lives of his fellows would frequently dominate all the rest. He retained a remarkable gift for reconciling the sublime with the sordid, one moment transcendent on a soft summer evening as he listened to his divine music, and the next engaged in the sexual fumblings of an adolescent.[4] Permeating everything was the genuine pleasure he took in small things – a blackbird singing, a new silk coat, the rebuilding of his backyard door – which explains his capacity to charm the ordinary reader.[5] It is impossible not to share his innocent glee at his own advancement nor feel with him the delight he felt when he first acquired the right to be called esquire. Frankness about his failings was another quality which endeared him to his friends, just as his open admission of cowardice endears him to readers of his Diary. He retained his boyish delight in ordinary things in his new maturity. 'But Lord, to see how much of my old folly and childishness hangs upon me still that I cannot forbear carrying my watch in my hand in the coach all this afternoon and see what o'clock it is one hundred times.'[6] There also persisted in Pepys a love for his wife which was about to be subjected to fresh strains. At his very centre, he was still not completely sure of himself and continued to search for those strategems which might give him total confidence. Meanwhile, he continued as Ollard put it to 'quiver with every ripple from the sea of life'.

Certainly, historic events in the outside world were about to put to the test his complex character and all the capacities he had by now acquired. Declarations of war from France and Denmark began the year 1666 ominously. The Dutch fleet was superior in men and equipment to the English fleet, which was now under the command of Prince Rupert and the Monck, Duke of Albemarle. There was every possibility that the French based at Toulon would break out of the Mediterranean and co-operate with the Dutch to confront the English – an alarming prospect to Pepys. Throughout these anxious months he and Coventry worked together even more closely and their contempt for the fleet's joint command was mutual. The French did leave Gibraltar on 8 May and Pepys waited apprehensively for any news of their appearance in the western approaches. At the very point when the English were anchoring their fleet at the mouth of the Thames, news of the French fleet entering the approaches reinforced a sense of crisis. In the event it became clear that the rumoured movements of the French were false, but for the moment strategy was based on this intelligence and Rupert was dispatched in search of the French, with sixty ships. Monck remained home-based with fifty-five ships ready to contain the Dutch fleet of eighty-four. No sooner had Rupert set sail than news came through of the Dutch putting to sea and urgent attempts were made to recall him. Three days elapsed before he received the message (Coventry had sent the order recalling Rupert by express post instead of special messenger)[7] and by then he had already reached St Helens. Monck now faced the crucial decision of whether to wait for Rupert to rejoin his force or to tackle the Dutch who were more heavily armed. He decided to risk confronting the Dutch alone, a decision with far-reaching consequences. Pepys later condemned him as had condemned Coventry, but any withdrawal to safety would have left Rupert at the mercy of the Dutch.[8] In a burst of what could only be described as audacious courage, Monck sent his fifty-five ships into the attack on De Ruyter's eighty-four. An historic four-day battle followed which Pepys followed as closely as sluggard communications made possible. In the days following Monck's attack he recorded: 'At Greenwich and into the Park and there we could hear the guns from the fleet most plainly.'[9] 'All our hopes now is that Prince Rupert with his fleet is coming back and will be with the Fleet this noon . . . and the fresh going off of guns makes us believe the same.'[10]

It was not to be. Albemarle, whose fleet was hopelessly outnumbered, fought a desperate battle. The fleet was half crippled. By the second day he was fighting at odds of two to one and slowly, inexorably driven back towards the Thames. The outcome looked a foregone conclusion until late in the afternoon of 2 June. Rupert's fleet was sighted closing in with nothing more than a light breeze slowing its progress. Quick consultations with Albemarle led to the decision to have Rupert renew the attack on the Dutch the next day. It was, in a sense, suicidal.

Back in London, contradictory reports made Pepys rejoice one day and relapse into gloom the next, but slowly it became evident that all was not well. Urgent requests arrived for soldiers to reinforce Albemarle's seamen and Pepys went to work with a will. 'But Lord, to see how the poor fellows kissed their wives and sweethearts in that simple manner at their going off and shouted and let off their guns.'[11] Whether these men were pressed or not remained unclear but Pepys was ready to condemn the practice of arresting men and forcing them to serve while still allowing its practice.[12] On 4 June came false news of a great English victory – with half the Dutch Fleet destroyed – which set the bells of victory ringing all over London. Duped himself, Pepys actually watched his neighbours give a firework display at the Navy Office gate. Soon the illusion was shattered and as the extent of the devastation became clear, even Pepys, enjoying the favours of Miss Tooke, the daughter of his neighbour, found himself suddenly depressed. Detailed news arrived when a Mr Daniel appeared 'all muffled up and his face as black as a chimney and covered with dirt, pitch and tar . . . with dirty clouts and his right eye stopped with okhum'.[13]

Pepys escorted him to the King and the full account he then gave was depressing. Using tactics derived from his military experience, where courage played a bigger role than strategy, Albemarle had lost twenty-two ships and nearly nine thousand men. It became clear that Penn, a solid tarpauliner, should have remained in command of the fleet, with his devotion to in-line fighting substituting Albemarle's individual action. He claimed, moreover, that two-thirds of the captains had been against the action but were afraid of being charged with cowardice if they said so. Actively hostile towards Penn before the battle, Pepys now openly admitted respect for his views.

The post-mortem on the strategy which followed was savage. When the full extent of the damage to the British fleet became known, Pepys did not hesitate to reiterate his low opinion of the two commanders. Albemarle replied by charging his captains with cowardice and Rupert made great play on Coventry's mistake in sending his recall by express post. Rupert had already written to the King: 'We are not supplied with provisions according to the necessity of your affairs, notwithstanding the repeated importunities we have used ... and when we send up our demands, instead of having them answered, we have accounts sent us which are prepared by Mr Pepys ...'[14] Pepys was not dismayed. United with Sir William Penn, Coventry and Sir John Harman he blamed Albemarle for deciding to fight once the fleet had been divided.[15] The disclosure that the original sighting of the French in the western approaches had been false produced an even worse atmosphere. Pepys seems to have spent the whole afternoon with Miss Tooker busily 'recovering his spirits'.[16] He might have felt less reassured had he known that Miss Tooker was infected with 'the clap', having led such a free life in the past that she shared favours with her mother's lover.[17]

Despite Rupert's complaint about supplies and Coventry's criticism of outdated tactics, Ollard describes this defeat as a victory for the quality of leadership shown by Albemarle.[18] Immediately, a clamour arose to refit the fleet once more with orders distributed in all directions. 'We have in the last action taken very much notice', one order to Sir William Coventry said, 'of the great use of fireships ... which the enemy had furnished themselves withal. We desire therefore that eight fireships be fitted for us in fourteen days.'[19]

Pepys now found it expedient to come to terms with Sir William Penn whose skill at recruiting men was acknowledged by the Prince and the Duke of Albemarle: 'Therefore I think it discretion, great and necessary discretion, to keep in with him.'[20] On 1 July he deliberately went down to Deptford with a double purpose in mind. First, knowing that Bagwell the carpenter was away at sea he hoped to re-encounter Mrs Bagwell, but his luck was out. Secondly, and clearly his primary purpose, he intended to ship away another group of pressed men. On July 2 he reported to Coventry that for two days he had worked until midnight arranging 'nothing else'.

But Lord how some poor women did cry and in my life I never did
see such natural expression of passion as I did here in some women's
bewailing themselves and running to every parcel of men that were
brought one after another to look for their husbands and wept over
every vessel that went off ... and looking after the ships as far as ever
they could by moonlight, that it grieved me to the heart to hear them.
Besides to see poor, patient, labouring men and housekeepers leaving
... wifes and families taken up on a sudden by strangers was very hard
... It is a great tyranny.[21]

This is Pepys the diarist at his most moving, but Pepys the humanist suffered a setback. He protested to the Diary, shared his compassion with Coventry, and did nothing about it.[22] Naval efficiency came first and, with England's survival in the balance, the priority could be justified.[23]

The Second Dutch War, as Tedder has called it, now followed, with the English once more in opposition to the Dutch, but this time in equal numbers using classic in-line fighting tactics. The Dutch van and centre were routed and left their rear squadron to confront the whole of the English fleet. Sir Jeremy Smith, commanding the English rear, decided to keep clear of dangerous Dutch waters on the advice of his pilot and thus allowed the Dutch to escape into harbour protected by the network of sand dunes too complicated for foreigners to negotiate. Pepys's paper on the subject graphically summed up the situation: 'The Dutch totally routed, fourteen ships taken; twenty-six burnt and sunk; two flagships taken ... Taken in all six thousand men.'[24] In Holland the naval commander De Ruyter 'came in raging against the disgrace of the retreat. "Several of my captains and particularly Tromp shall answer for it."'[25] The English view of the battle was also divided. Once more there were accusations and counter-accusations, with Holmes, who had commanded the rear division of the centre squadron, charging Smith with outright cowardice.

Their differences reached a point where there was nothing for it but to fight a duel.[26] Since Smith was Monck's favourite and Holmes Prince Rupert's it led to further complications. On 31 July came the dramatic news that the Dutch commander De Ruyter was dead, followed by a complete denial from Sir William Coventry, 'which quite dashed me again. God forgive me, I was a little sorry in my heart before lest it might give occasion of too much glory to the Duke of Albemarle.'[27] The ever-honest Pepys did not hesitate to record his partisanship. The Diary concluded July with the comment: 'Mighty well, and end this month in content of mind and body ... we having a victory over the Dutch just such as I could have wished ... enough to give us the name of conquerors and leave us masters of the sea ... without any such great matters done as should give the Duke of Albemarle ... cause to rise to his former insolence.'[28]

Matters private and public were next overshadowed by the outbreak of the Fire of London on 2 September 1666, a drama which unfolded before Pepys's fascinated eyes and tested his writing skills to the full. The fire began at the premises of Thomas Farriner, the King's butcher, whose shop stood in Pudding Lane ten doors down from Thames Street.[29] Between one and two o'clock on Sunday morning flames broke out in the bakehouse and the baker found his home full of smoke. Within an hour the flames had gathered apace, leapt from house to house and run out of control. It was Jane the maid who called Pepys at three o'clock that morning 'to tell us of a great fire they saw in the city'.[30] Being naked in bed, he rose, slipped on his nightgown and went to the window. Judging the fire to be far enough off not to concern him, he returned to bed and slept soundly. When he rose at seven the fire seemed to have retreated and he began setting things right in his closet without further concern. The maid came again shortly afterwards to tell him that according to rumours three hundred houses had burnt down and the whole of Fish Street by London Bridge was already ablaze. Suddenly anxious, Pepys made himself ready and walked to the Tower where he climbed some unnamed eminence and saw an astonishing scene. Descending hurriedly he went into the Tower to speak to the lieutenant who told him how the fire had already destroyed St Magnus' church and most of Fish Street. Walking towards the Thames, Pepys took a boat under the bridge and met with a deeply disturbing scene. 'Poor Mitchell's house ... already burned ... and the fire running further ...' Mitchell was the bookseller's son who had married one of Pepys's lovers – Betty Howlett. Also endangered by the flames was another ex-mistress Sarah, who lived on the bridge itself. His heart sank as he observed the flames and their effect upon people. 'Everybody endeavouring to remove their goods and flinging into the river or bringing them into lighters that lay off. Poor people staying in their houses as long as till the very fire touched them, and then running into boats or clambering from one pair of stairs by the waterside to another.'[31]

The northern houses on London Bridge were all ablaze and between Thames Street and the river a maze of timber-built, pitch-coated houses jostled cheek by jowl among warehouses full of tallow and oil, providing the material for a natural inferno. The prospect freshly alarmed Pepys. The wind drove the fire towards the very heart of the city but everyone was so intent on preserving household goods that they ignored the wider implications. Pepys, however, realised that the fire would lead to the total destruction of the city. He ordered the boatmen to row him to Whitehall and there without more ado proceeded 'up to the King's closet . . . where people came about me and I did give them an account that dismayed them all.'[32] Brought into the presence of the King himself he told him – unequivocally – that unless whole rows of houses were pulled down nothing could stop the fire. One entry in the Diary about the fire runs to five pages and every other paragraph brings the scene vividly alive. The King authorised Pepys to instruct the Lord Mayor to spare no houses in the path of the fire and the Duke of York offered him as many soldiers as he needed.

At last met my Lord Mayor [Sir Thomas Bludworth] in Canning Street like a man spent, with hand kercher about his neck. To the King's message he cried like a fainting woman: 'Lord what can I do. I am spent. People will not obey me. I have been pulling down houses. But the fire overtakes faster than we can do it.'[34]

Pepys returned home to play host at a pre-arranged dinner party, but all the guests were apprehensive and made the fire their excuse to leave early. Once more Pepys went out to perambulate the streets. They were 'full of nothing but people and horses and carts loaden with goods, ready to run over one another, and removing goods from one home to another'. Whether by accident or design he next met the King and the Duke of York in their barge and they repeated their instruction to 'pull down houses apace', which seemed irrelevant because the fire still out-paced the house destruction. Hopes of stopping the flames at the Three Cranes above the bridge and at Buttolph's Wharf below, were frustrated by the wind which carried the fire into the heart of the city. The wind became the chief enemy, like a giant bellows determined to re-ignite dead ashes and send the flames leaping across the fire-breaks.[34] Meeting his wife at a pre-arranged place, he took to his boat again to follow the fire and found to his dismay that it was still spreading: 'All over the Thames with one's face in the wind you were almost burned with a shower of firedrops and flakes.' When it became searing hot on the water they retreated into a little alehouse at Bankside '... and there stayed till it was dark almost and saw the fire grow: and as it grew darker, appeared more and more, and in corners and upon steeples and between churches and houses as far as we could see up the hill of the city in a most horrid malicious bloody flame not like the fine flame of an ordinary fire ...' They remained watching until the fire formed a complete awe-inspiring arch from one side of the Bridge to the other 'above a mile long'. 'It made me weep to see it. The churches, houses ... all on fire and flaming at once and a horrid noise the flames made and the cracking of houses at their ruin ...'[35]

Pepys had a rival in his pen-portraits of the fire; the remarkable John Evelyn. Their mutual observations of the fire did not bring them together but one vivid account reaffirms the other. On 7 September Evelyn drew a picture in his diary of St Paul's in ruins with its vast stonework split asunder and huge areas of lead melted and dripping into the interior. Confusion was confounded when rumours that the French and Dutch had landed led to such an 'uproar and tumult that [people] ran from their goods and taking what weapons they could come at ... could not be stopped from falling on some of those nations ... without sense or reason the clamour and peril growing so excessive as made the whole court amazed'.[36]

Back home Pepys found Tom Hayter, his Navy Office colleague, waiting with a few of the goods he had salvaged from his Fish Street home. 'I invited him to lie at my house and did receive his goods; but was deceived ... the noise coming every moment of the growth of the fire so as we were forced to begin to pack up our own goods and prepare for their removal.'[37] While the exhausted Hayter tried to sleep Pepys, Elizabeth and the maids spent the greater part of the night tramping up and down stairs carrying iron chests, bags and boxes full of money, papers and gold. Carts from Sir William Batten's home at Walthamstow arrived, servants hurried about arguing and poor Hayter found sleep impossible. High above the crackling roar of fire the moon shone steadily down on this concourse of bewildered Londoners.

Around four o'clock in the morning a retinue of carts piled high with household goods set out towards Bethnal Green and riding high atop one crazily packed vehicle Pepys wore nothing more than a nightshirt. Sir William Rider had agreed to give Pepys safe haven in his house at the Green and here Pepys surrendered his most trea-

sured possessions: money, jewellery, gold and, above all, the irreplaceable Diary. When he attempted to go back into the city he found
the roads jammed with people, carts and horses, and had to fight
his way through. The perfect summer weather with glorious sunshine
the following day seemed to make a mockery of the blazing confusion,
and Pepys's family, exhausted and sleepless, continued staggering up
and down stairs preparing the less valuable household goods for transport to the Green. They were to be loaded on to a lighter at Tower
Dock ready to be retrieved if ever this evil fire relented and allowed
the citizens of London to return to what remained of their homes.[38]

On Thursday 6 September the King himself rode out to Moorfields
to address the multitude of homeless citizens who sat, slept and stood
among what few possessions they had managed to save. 'Rich and
poor mingled together united in a common calamity which shattered
distinctions and over all the blue sky of a summer day.'[39] On this
fourth day the fire raged far north until it crossed the Fleet, consumed
the wooden houses in Salisbury Court next to Pepys's birthplace
and nearly trapped the soldiers blowing up houses on Ludgate Hill.
Presently there was no escaping the threat to the Navy Office itself.
Two distinguished naval administrators wielded spade and shovel to
dig a pit in the garden of the Navy Office to bury Batten's wine
and Pepys's papers. The same afternoon the threat of destruction
became inescapable and Pepys swiftly consulted Penn, suggesting that
they rally some hands from the naval dockyards to pull down houses
around the Office. Penn set off to summon help while the ever-
prudent Pepys remembered that by law anyone destroying his neighbour's house must bear the cost of rebuilding it. He wrote at once
to Coventry seeking the Duke's endorsement of their plan.[40] That
evening he and Elizabeth with their neighbours Mr and Mrs Turner
ate a frugal meal in the Office, '... without any napkin or anything
in a sad manner but were merry'.[41] Walking into the garden he
saw '... how horridly the sky' looked, 'all on fire in the night ...
enough to put us out of our wits; and endeed it was extremely
dreadfull – for it looks just as if it was at us and the whole heaven
on fire'. Afterwards he walked down to Tower Street and saw it
burning from Dolphin tavern to Trinity House 'with extraordinary
vehemence ... Paul's was already burned, Cheapside burning and
the fire running down the Old Bayley to Fleet Street.'[42]

Pepys wrote to his father that night but could not post the letter
because the posthouse had been destroyed. Afterwards, being so weary
and his feet so sore that he could hardly stand, he lay down in the
Office under Will Hewer's quilt. At two in the morning his wife

broke in to tell him of new cries of 'Fyre!' Fresh outbreaks had already reached Barking church which was at the bottom of their own Seething Lane. Pepys rose at once, gathered his wife and Will Hewer and headed towards a friend's boat which would take them down to the safety of Woolwich. With him – jealously guarded – he took his life savings in the form of gold.[43] Lodging his wife and Hewer with Mr Sheldon, the Clerk of the Cheque at Woolwich, he carefully locked up the gold and charged both of them 'never to leave the room without one of them in it night nor day'. Hurrying back home he expected to see his house on fire, instead of which the church at the end of the road was half burnt out, but there – miraculously – the fire had stopped. Blowing up houses in the immediate neighbourhood had saved the Office as well as Pepys's home. Tired, dirty, disillusioned, the insatiable curiosity in Pepys could not be resisted and instead of eating a meal – he had not eaten properly for three days – or throwing himself down to sleep, he promptly climbed to the top of Barking steeple and there looked down on a scene of desolation such as he had never seen before. 'Everywhere great fires ... I became afeared to stay there long ...' Hurrying down to Sir William Penn's house for the first time in seventy-two hours he allowed himself to relax long enough to eat a piece of cold meat, but almost at once he was up and busy again. Meeting two friends he walked once more into town. There they found to their dismay that the great thoroughfares of Fenchurch, Gracechurch and Lombard Streets were all reduced to ashes, with not a single building left intact.[44] The Exchange had melted away into nothing with just a bust of the founder Sir Thomas Gresham surviving in absurd isolation. On the same day Evelyn went on a similar pilgrimage with extraordinary difficulty, 'climbing over mountains of yet smoking rubbish and frequently mistaking where I was, the ground under my feete so hott as made me not only sweate but even burn the soles of my shoes ...'[45] The two men walked through similar streets but did not meet.

When it was all over, large areas of the city still reeked of burning for days, and the confused and darkened byways created a happy hunting-ground for thieves and vagabonds. Homeless men and women lurked among the ruins. Many months afterwards, whenever Pepys passed through these areas, he did so with his sword unsheathed. By the 15th he was back once more sleeping in his own bedchamber with his wife, but he could not forget the fire. He was 'much terrified in the nights with dreams of fire and falling down of houses'.[46] By the 17th he was up betimes, had shaved off a week's growth of beard and converted his neglected self into a fine newly laundered person.[47] The 18th found him still uneasy with a pain in his bladder and belly and his wife's hair beginning to fall out. By the 19th he had recovered his pictures from Deptford, set up his books again and replaced his 'many fine things'.

Chapter 11

Professional corruption and more affairs

While fire ravaged the city the political background produced an episode which did not bode well for the future. The Dutch and English fleets had been within sight of one another in the Channel early in September but the high winds which fanned the flames of the fire drove the English back to harbour and the Dutch simply slipped away home again. It was a confused time which left a sense of failure among the English and especially Pepys.[1] Once more the dreary business of lack of funds for the Navy recurred with even greater force when Pepys realised that all his arguments and appeals to the Treasury had produced no results. When Parliament met again on 21 September it was in a hostile mood. The £2 million granted to the King to conduct the Dutch War were not fully accounted for and the Hotspurs turned to Pepys for an explanation. Pepys plunged in to provide reliable figures countering the rumours of corruption and found himself embroiled in a mass of detail which required working seven days a week. On 2 October he met Sir George Carteret who told him that he must appear before a parliamentary sub-committee, which 'put me into a mighty fear and trouble, they doing it in a very ill humour methought'.[2] Neither fully fit nor even concerned, as he put it, 'to take the shame and trouble' of his Office, Pepys spent long tormented hours preparing for the ordeal. A minor alarm arose which did not soothe his nerves. Meeting Sir William Penn, Pepys surrendered his portfolio to Penn's boy for safe keeping while he went into a preliminary meeting in the committee chambers. It seemed an odd risk to take since the portfolio contained the whole of his case for the Navy's defence. Lacking total confidence in his evidence he may, of course, have wished to lose it. Whatever the reason, when he came to recover his portfolio, the boy told him that he had passed the portfolio over to the committee room doorkeeper. 'This, added to my former disquiet, made me stark mad, considering all the nakedness of the Office lay open in papers within those covers.'[3] He successfully recovered the papers at a small cost and prepared to face the committee. The preliminary exchanges were full of hazards, but Pepys quickly regained his confidence and 'did make shift to answer them better than I expected'. In the end, 'my heart eased of a great deal of fear and pain, reckoning myself to have come off with victory.'[4]

It was a hollow victory. The Commons subsequently voted £1,800,000 for war expenditure, but since that sum matched outstanding debts, there was no change in the status quo. Pepys took his case before the King at Whitehall, only to be met by an angry Prince Rupert who claimed to have brought home his ships in excellent state of repair. Undismayed, Pepys replied that he could only repeat what the surveyors had reported to him. The King now made an offer towards the outstanding debts which was derisory. He allocated £5,000 to the Navy Office, hardly sufficient to meet one of Gauden's minor bills. Frustrated and disillusioned, Pepys was acutely aware of the urgency of his case; unpaid sailors were still liable to come swarming round the Navy Office threatening violence which terrified him. One last appeal to the Navy Treasurer for payment of a relatively small debt to the broom man was met 'as if he had asked a million'.[5] Sailors on shore were rioting; sailors afloat were undisciplined; merchants were refusing to supply any more goods; and the old patriotic notion of the great and glorious Navy was in tatters. On the same day, 19 October, Pepys wrote to Sir William Penn describing his audience with the Duke of York and made it plain that the Duke could not expect 'any further service from us'.[6] In the Diary he recorded: 'Nothing but distraction and confusion – which makes me wish with all my heart that I were well and quietly settled with what little I have got at Brampton where I might live peaceably and study and pray for the good of King and Country.'[7]

Meanwhile, another personal problem arose for Pepys involving the use of one of the Navy's ships. That autumn he took over with Penn and Batten joint control of the *Flying Greyhound*, a ship which the King gave them 'on loan', and immediately a series of complications arose. They originally intended to employ her in normal trading with the Madeiras, but an unscrupulous purser, Mr Martin, and a piratical 'captain', Hogg, took command and found the temptation to prey on Dutch merchant ships irresistible. Apparently, Pepys raised no objections. He makes no mention of the moral confusion into which this should have thrown him. Here he was, dedicated to serving the highest interests of the British Navy, quietly endorsing the use of one of that Navy's ships for what no amount of rationalisation could describe as other than piracy. Captain Hogg's zeal quickly overcame his discretion and he returned to port after his first venture with several rich prizes which came under the scrutiny of the Prize Court. The Swedish resident in London was asked by the owners of the two ships seized by Hogg to fight for their recovery and he put in a strong protest, followed immediately by a hint that he was not averse to bribery. On 21 January Batten, Penn, Sir Richard Ford and Pepys descended together on the Swedish resident hoping to impress him with their combined powers, but he turned out to be a 'cunning fellow' who neither gave nor received satisfaction.[8] The three adventurers finally resorted to a £350 bribe. Pepys had already assigned a third of this interest in the *Flying Greyhound* to Sir Richard Ford, MP for Southampton, who now undertook to disentangle the confusions.

The avaricious resident rejected the £350 as trivial and the case, to Pepys's dismay, went to law. A certain Dr Walker made it clear that their 'pretence' to the prize would do them no good and gave judgment against them. More trouble arose when Hogg descended on the two ships only to discover that they were already held as prizes by a higher class of adventurer, one of whom was none other than Prince Rupert. A recognised part-time indulgence, privateering could be highly profitable, but 'embezzling' the property of a Prince, no matter where it came from, was ill-advised. Pepys now wrote a letter to the commissioners of accounts which adroitly sidestepped most of the charges.[9] Contemporary naval principles easily accommodated running one of its ships for private profit, but Pepys decided that enough was enough. He offered his interest in the enterprise to Batten for £700 and he finally paid £666.13.4d, as precise a bargain as ever was driven. But the story did not end there. Indeed, by 17 September it had taken a much more dramatic turn. On that day Batten came to Pepys in a fine rage declaring that behind their backs Penn had secretly negotiated ownership of the *Flying Greyhound* for himself. Pepys promptly went to see Penn and told him flatly what he thought in such emphatic terms that Penn at last agreed to a compromise.[10] He would try to persuade the Duke of York to give Pepys an entirely different ship. It seems never to have occurred to Pepys that it was not entirely legitimate – exchanging one ship he no longer owned for another, paid for out of the public purse. His honour was maintained when the Duke presented Pepys with the *Maybolt* already equipped under Penn's directions for a lengthy voyage. The Duke also signed a warrant proclaiming Pepys's long and valuable service to the Navy.[11] As we have seen, Pepys was not above the malpractices of his day.

By 1669, tired of trying to serve his country and alert to the dangers of too much private initiative, Pepys now spent longer evenings at home entertaining guests, playing his viol, or reading books. One evening he gave a dinner for the actors and actresses playing at the King's Theatre and brought together Lord Brouncker, Mrs Mercer the singer, a Captain Rolt, the delicious Elizabeth Knepp the actress, and none other – for Elizabeth's delight – than her old dancing master Pembleton. Mrs Knepp fell ill during the dinner and was put to bed late in the evening by Elizabeth, while Mrs Mercer held the company rapt, singing beautiful Italian songs. Pepys quietly stole upstairs, deliberately woke up Knepp, lay beside her on the bed, kissed her, caressed her breasts and brazenly stayed there singing a duet almost within earshot of his wife, 'I thinking it to be one of the merriest enjoyments I must look for in the world'.[12] A sour afterword in his Diary does, however, break the spell: 'The musicians at 30s were too expensive.'

Over the years 1666–9, as if in reaction against the doldrums of his political life, his sexual deviations grew. The names proliferate … Mrs Pearse, Mrs Knepp, Mrs Bagwell, Mrs Martin, Mrs Daniel, Doll Lane *et al.* An earlier August 1666 entry in the Diary spoke of arguing with his wife before they rose from bed about his kindness to Mr Knip (Knepp). Returning home from a party by coach with both Mrs Knepp and Elizabeth, he had sat with one hand clasped in Mrs Knepp's and the other hand about her middle. Apparently, he ignored his wife and she turned on him that night in bed showering him with abuse.[13] Troubled by her anger he did not retaliate but got up and went about his business. Elizabeth instantly rose and followed him round the house continuing her attack in which she now included his father. Still refusing to be provoked, Pepys said nothing but 'let her talk' until he was ready to go to the Office. Deliberately, he stayed away until midnight and when he returned found his wife already gone to bed in an ill humour. They rose at midday and suddenly Elizabeth seemed to think that he suspected her of being with child by another man. She had travelled back alone from a visit to Brampton with an army officer called Coleman on one occasion and Pepys commented 'God knows it never entered my head whether my father observed anything with Coleman'. The remark in the Diary is almost throwaway. The early sexual fires between them had clearly diminished, and, as Elizabeth reminded him, he had not slept with his wife for close on half a year.[14]

Moreover, Mrs Bagwell was 'only too ready' for any indulgence. As the 'offences' multiplied, none of the women involved seemed to be aware of the existence of any other and Pepys did not hesitate to sleep with two women on the same day. After dinner on 1 February 1666 he walked through heavy rain and mist from Redriffe to Deptford and there met Mrs Bagwell by appointment, where he had his way with her. She turned out to have religious scruples on that particular day, but Pepys successfully overcame them. Mr Bagwell returned home and the happy trio talked of getting him his new ship.

If the reward of a new ship was still dangled as a bait before him, he must have been a very patient man. Later the same day Pepys went by water to Billingsgate, then took a boat to Westminster where in no time he sought out Doll Lane and 'did just what he pleased with her'.[15] Without a qualm he later reported in the Diary that he was 'then home and merry with my wife'. It happened again early in June 1667. After a long talk with Sir William Coventry he first called upon the ever-ready Betty Mitchell and 'away thence ... after church to Mrs Martin's, there haze what I would with her'.[16] There was also Mrs Borrows, the pretty widow of a Navy officer whom he carried off to the park and there kissed and caressed her so passionately that he came. Sarah, once a maid at Seething Lane, had married, but that did not prevent him seducing her and her young sister, who was now the maid at the Swan. He would seduce women at any time and anywhere: once with Sarah in a coach ambling across Paddington fields, once at the Navy Office itself and, on one occasion, classic for its piquancy, in the lodgings of Mrs Martin in whose body he had not long 'empassioned'. His insatiable appetite demanded and took risks: he even dared to play with the breasts – and more – of Mrs Lowther, Sir William Penn's daughter. He would happily spend an hour with Evelyn moralising on the vices of King and court, only to hurry off to indulge himself with Doll Lane. Indeed, in that one week he went with three different women – Doll Lane, Mrs Martin and Mrs Daniel. His audacity increased in the winter of 1667. On one occasion he pretended that he had a pain in his testicle and persuaded his wife to shift sides with him in the coach so that he could better caress Betty Mitchell. 'I did hazard whatever I would with her ... And so set her at home with my mind mighty glad.' As we have seen, most of these adventures were set down in a naïve jargon of French, Latin, Spanish and English, which could rise to such felicities as: 'She would not suffer that *jo* should *poverr* my *mano* above *ses jupes* which *je* endeavoured.

[She would not permit me to put my hand up her skirts.]'[17] Misdemeanours in coaches produced several marvellous pieces of multilingual jargon: 'But to ease myself therein Betty Mitchell did sit at the same end with me and there *con sue mano* under my *manteau*, I did pull off her *cheirotheca* and did *tocar mi cosa con su mano* through my *chemise*, but yet so as to *hazer la grande cosa* – and she did let me *hazer le sin mucho trabaho* [... 'And to ease myself Betty Mitchell did sit at the same end with me and there with her hand under my coat I did pull off her muff and I did touch my thing with her hand through my shirt, but yet so as to make me do the big thing ... and she did let me do it without much difficulty.]'[18]

Bryant believed that he was in love with Jane Welsh but there is no evidence of this and even Betty Mitchell, who now dominated his promiscuous encounters, is never referred to in the language of love. When he first met her it was purely sexual: 'I had my full liberty of towsing her and doing what I would but the last thing of all.' His Puritan upbringing constantly intervened to stop him going 'the whole way' and he still could not quite conquer a latent sense of humiliation. Not that he avoided clinical detail in the Diary: '... and made her feel my thing also and put the end of it to her breast and by and by to her very belly – of which I am heartily ashamed.'[19] None the less, Betty Mitchell, like Jane, was different. When she expressed an urgent desire to marry, he even recommended himself for that role. There was also at least one direct reference to love: 'I down to the Old Swan and there to Mitchell and stayed while he and she dressed themselves: and here had a *baisser* or two of her whom I love mightily.'[20] If the body overwhelmed the mind in most of these encounters there was no questioning his response to female beauty or his capacity to experience love.

There had been a highly charged moment early in February 1667 when it looked as though Elizabeth knew about his affair with Betty.[21] In the presence of Betty's husband, on 11 February, he arranged to take Betty and Elizabeth on a shopping spree at the New Exchange. The husband's cognisance should have made it respectable but at the appointed time Elizabeth failed to appear for the simple reason that he had forgotten to invite her. Pepys and Betty went off shopping together and Pepys took Betty to a cabinet-maker where he bought her a dressing box. An hour was necessary to construct the box to her requirements and in that hour Pepys made overtures to which she would not respond. While they waited the mistress of the shop showed them the workroom and made it clear that she took Betty to be Pepys's wife. Despite the fact that Betty was swollen with pregnancy – or perhaps because of it – Pepys happily connived at this deception and they were 'very merry'. Back in the coach he immediately made renewed advances, and this time she responded and he put his '*mano* ... where I used to do but not with the same freedom as before. But now comes our trouble.' He was suddenly afraid that Betty's husband might call at his house to pick her up, and finding Elizabeth waiting there alone expose both of them. This troubled him mightily but did not disturb the worldly-wise Betty. She told him to drive her home, stopping the coach at the end of her street, which – already deeply uneasy – Pepys did. They then walked innocently to the house where Mr Mitchell increased Pepys's anxiety with the news that he had sent Betty's maid to his house to enquire her whereabouts. Pepys hurried home but had to pace up and down outside in a cold sweat – the worst he had ever experienced about his wife. While his torment was still unresolved a little woman enquiring after Betty suddenly appeared out of the darkness. The maid's arrival had been – by the greatest good luck – delayed and he now told her that her mistress was returned home. He was on the point of entering the house when another thought suddenly brought him to a halt. What if this was the maid's *second* visit to the house and Elizabeth waiting within knew all. On reflection he realised that the maid would have remarked on her second visit, and with this thought he entered the house to find, to his unspeakable relief, that all was well.[22]

His relations with his actual family had remained a muted background and, in contradistinction, revealed a man quite different from the casual lover. Here was somebody kind-hearted, loyal and with a strong sense of filial justice. 'So home', he wrote, 'and find my father come to lie at our house, and so supped and saw him, poor man, to bed, my heart never being fuller of love to him, nor admiration of his prudence ...' John Pepys expressed concern for the future of his wife now approaching senility and his son tried to put his mind at rest. He made up his father's income by £30 a year, bought him a horse and, when he came to stay, frequently prolonged his visits because he so much enjoyed his innocent company. John, the younger brother down from university, did not expect much help from Samuel since he had written a series of abusive letters about him to Tom before he died. (Pepys had uncovered these among Tom's possessions after his death.) Magnanimously overlooking them Pepys set about consulting people who might help him with his brother's preferment. When John fell ill one day it was Samuel who helped him recover, 'trembling a good while and ready to weep to see him'. As for Elizabeth's wayward brother Balty, who had redeemed his reputation as muster master in the fleet, Pepys now took great trouble to introduce him to a Mr Wren who could re-establish him in that post. As a result he soared to greater heights and finally emerged as Deputy Treasurer of the fleet.[23] Pepys's concern for his mother was not entirely straightforward. She had deteriorated rapidly in old age and on 25 March 1667 a letter came from his brother saying that his mother 'did rattle in the throat so as they did expect every moment her death'.[24] Instead of hurrying to visit her he gave priority to a supper with Sir William Penn and Elizabeth, but had to counterfeit his merriment because his heart was sad. Later he found himself much troubled in his sleep 'with dreams of ... crying by my mother's bedside laying my hand over hers ... she almost dead and dying'.[25] Two days later he received the news of her death at six o'clock. For two whole days he had known that she was dying but deliberately did not visit her because he could not face the actual spectacle of her death. When he learned her last words were 'God bless my poor Sam', he began weeping. His wife wept with him and then, recovering themselves, they realised how fortunate they had been that she had not outlived her husband, '... she being so helpless'. This expediency seemed to follow a little hastily on grief, and grief itself disappeared in a single day in the Diary. However, Pepys's distress was genuine if very short-lived.

Chapter 12

The Dutch attack London

Led by the redoubtable De Ruyter, forces were gathering in Holland by June 1667 to launch a sustained attack on England, overwhelm the inadequate defences, sweep up the Thames and threaten the very heart of London itself. There was no lack of intelligence in England about this daring plan. In May 1667 the delegates to the peace conference at Breda included from Britain a Dr Mews who had survived the struggle for priority in the diplomatic hierarchy. He wrote on 31 May: 'Certain it is that they [the Dutch] have great business in hand; and I presume will very shortly attempt to execute it.'[1] Spelling out the details he said that the fleet had left Texel on 27 May and taken on board so many soldiers that they clearly intended landing somewhere. The letter revealed the whole Breda Conference as a mask behind which the Dutch fleet was preparing to take action and had indeed already set sail. The complacency which prevailed at the English court was shared by Charles II and did have one justification. In April Louis XIV and Charles II had agreed to bring pressure on the Dutch to make peace and Louis XIV had increased the pressure by invading the Spanish Netherlands on 24 May. It was not unreasonable to assume – or so it seemed to Charles – that against such a background the Dutch would avoid further entanglement abroad.

The King now grossly overplayed his hand and wrote to the Duke of York, the Lord High Admiral, elaborating evidence that English merchant ships were safely returned to harbour and coal bunkers were full, justifying a further reduction in the numbers of men-of-war to be kept in service. Secretary of State Arlington reinforced these views, believing the preparations of the Dutch fleet to be sheer bravado. Sir William Coventry finally compounded this folly by writing to the Navy Board suggesting a cut in the complement of fireships lying off the five main ports.[2] Even when news came that the formidable Dutch fleet was approaching England, on 3 June Coventry wrote to the Navy Board: 'We hear by letters that the Dutch fleet is uncertainly abroad ... although I do not think they will make any attempt here in the river.' As an afterthought he added: 'It will be fitting that the commanders of the frigates that are in the Hope be on board to provide against anything that may happen.'[3] Coventry and Pepys both held gentlemen captains of the Navy in contempt, but worries about the Navy's 'galloping debt' and Parliament's growing hostility to the cost of unnecessary wars, turned their thoughts to domestic politics.[4] On Trinity Monday, 3 June, Pepys went down to the annual naval ceremonial at Deptford, '... and we had a good dinner of plain meat and good company at our table, among others my good friend Mr Evelyn.'[5] They talked at length about the threat of war and Pepys revealed his knowledge of Dutch and French statistics: the Dutch heading for England with eighty men-of-war and twenty fireships and the French arriving simultaneously in the Channel with twenty men-of-war and five fireships. 'We have not a ship at sea', he commented, 'to do them any hurt ... but are calling in all we can while our ambassadors are treating at Breda and the Dutch look upon them as come to beg peace and use them accordingly'.[6] Two days later he met Sir William Coventry, but instead of concentrating upon the crisis they were concerned about a mutiny aboard the ship due to convey the Portuguese ambassador to Holland. Other relative trivialities were discussed and the Diary over several days seems as much concerned with whether Pepys could lease the ground for a coach house – he now had an overpowering desire to own a coach – as with the immediate threat of war.

Busy congratulating each other, Pepys and Coventry saw the crisis through their relations with different political factions rather than as a danger overriding everything. Pepys met Coventry in his chamber and recorded in the Diary: 'He being a most excellent man and indeed with all his business hath more of his men employed upon the good of the service of the Navy than all of us that makes me ashamed of it.'[7] One fact emerges clearly. Pepys and Coventry did little to prevent or anticipate a war which threatened disaster. It is characteristic of all politically motivated actions in a time of crisis that opinions vary according to which leader or which faction is most sympathetic. Pepys was for Coventry and against Holmes, for the King and against Rupert. When Sir Robert Holmes objected to Lord Brouncker's directive to discharge officers and men from his complement, Pepys commented that his pride 'was never to be stopped'.[8] His views at this time were often much influenced by personalities rather than facts, with the result that early in June he was wrong on two major counts.

Penn wanted to strengthen the Medway defences and Rupert objected to paying off seamen. Pepys disagreed with both and came close to sneering at them. Nothing could have been more inappropriate. The Duke of York emerged as reasonably enlightened and as early as 16 December had given special orders for the defences in the river Medway to be strengthened, 'yet in reality little was done'.[9]

Meanwhile, Pepys went about his everyday business as though any threat to the nation's security was unnecessarily alarmist. Pleasant meetings with Penn were followed by 'singing and piping' with his wife, listening to Sunday sermons, and meeting both Betty Mitchell and Mrs Martin whose favours were readily forthcoming. On the evening of 9 June he took a boat upriver alone as far as Barn-elmes, wandered idly for a time and returned home to finish reading 'a merry satire called *The Visions* . . . wherein there are many very pretty things'.[10] This entry concludes with a very casual reference to finding an order for some fireships with which to 'annoy' the Dutch.

Two days before, the Dutch fleet had sailed into the King's Channel, one of the inlets of the Thames, and a council of war was held on board their flagship. Disagreements between commanders quickly became evident, although news of some twenty English merchant ships lying just below Gravesend tempted the Dutch to send in a small squadron under Van Ghent to destroy them. It was a preliminary manœuvre intended to preface a major invasion of the Thames, but it did not succeed.[11] On 10 June there were dramatic reports that the Dutch were sailing – brazenly – up the Thames and the alarm which ran through the country reached Pepys. The King ordered Prince Rupert to organise defences and sent the Duke of Albemarle to direct operations at Chatham. By 10 June the tone in Pepys's Diary had changed completely. A quickly organised meeting with Batten and Penn led to a conference with Coventry, 'who pressed all the possible for fireships'. Sir Frescheville Holles was to command the fireships, and now all three men went down to Deptford 'to pitch upon ships and set men at work; but Lord to see how backwardly things move . . .'[12] Money which Parliament had long claimed was unavailable suddenly arrived to pay the fireship crews, but Pepys had difficulty convincing the seamen that the offer was genuine. Reaching Gravesend in his search for men and ships Pepys was dismayed to find the Duke of Albemarle 'just come with a great many idle lords and gentlemen with their pistols and fooleries'. His first impression was that the Dutch had retreated down the river and left the population 'at some ease', but that quickly altered.[13] Meeting two captains, he went to a tavern to eat and learnt that people had fled the town with their goods in such numbers that there 'were scarce twelve left' to put up a defence. A quick survey of the Bulworke convinced him that it too would not survive a full frontal attack 'above half an hour'. His mission completed he set out homewards, and it becomes clear that his habit of reading high-class literature in the midst of crises was no measure of his lack of concern. The book he read that evening was unexpected: 'Mr Boyle's *Hydrostatices* ... which is a most excellent book I ever read'. Notwithstanding his anxieties, he determined to take great pains to understand Boyle and then recorded the day's events in his letter book.[14]

By the following day the crisis had intensified to the point where commissioner Pett of Chatham was 'in a very fearful stink for fear of the Dutch and desires help for God and the King and our kingdom's sake'.[15] Pett wrote a letter on the morning of the 11th admitting that Sheerness had been lost to the Dutch after no more than three hours' battle, '... which is very sad and puts us into great fears of Chatham'.[16] A letter written at one o'clock in the morning by Pepys to Coventry described the river laden with vessels full of the goods and chattels of people fleeing from the Dutch, 'such was their fright'.[17] The Duke of Albemarle, at the centre of all these activities, hurried to Chatham and spent days ranging up and down the Medway searching for men and materials. Ships had been paid off, others were in a bad state of repair, and starving seamen were unwilling to commit themselves. He reported to the House of Commons that he found 'scarce twelve of eight hundred men ... in His Majesty's yards; and these so distracted with fear that I could have little or no service from them'.[18] Pepys now hurried from one depot to another gathering fireships. At the very height of his quest he was not averse to diverting his attention to Mary Mercer met by accident near St Paul's. Back home much later, he gave his full attention to work, receiving almost every hour fresh letters from Sir William Coventry appealing for greater speed.[19] An order in council next enabled him to take any man's ship because the King considered the attack an invasion.[20]

Meanwhile, the Dutch launched two ships against the massive chain swung across the river at Chatham, the first being brought to a halt and catching fire, but the second snapping clean through.[21] The Dutch then outfaced the shore batteries and with great courage set fire to the *Royal James*, the *Royal Oak* and *Royal London*, towed away the flagship the *Royal Charles* and began converting her for use against the English.[22] Audacity could go no further. On the 12th Pepys hurried to Coventry's chamber to find him absent, but Powell his clerk told him the ill news that the Dutch had broken the chain 'which struck me to the heart'.[23] One great fear in Pepys was the threat of violence from a populace disillusioned by the failure of the Navy Office to protect its citizens. There were many precedents of mob revenge. His second fear was that the government would certainly convert the Navy into a scapegoat for its own failure to provide funds and preserve an efficient Navy. Both these worries quickly surrendered to the immediate possibility that the Dutch might launch an attack on London itself, destroying Pepys's property, possessions, prospects and perhaps even his very life. 'So God help us', Pepys cried as he took his wife and father up to Elizabeth's room, shut the door and told them the sad state of the times. 'We are like to be all undone,' he later wrote. 'I do fear some violence will be offered to this Office where all I have in the world is and resolved upon sending it away – sometimes into the country – sometimes to my father to lie in town and have the gold with him at Sarah Giles – and with resolution went to bed full of fears and fright.'[24] Given his gift for isolating the colourful anecdote, he described people bundling 'out of the city with their most precious belongings', while 'the very night the Dutch burned our ships, the King supped with his mistress Lady Castlemaine and there were all mad in hunting a poor moth.'[25] Evelyn, like Pepys, was afraid the enemy might proceed up the Thames into the heart of London and decided to 'send away my best goods, plate etc. ... for everybody were flying, none knew why or whither.'[26]

On 13 June Pepys swiftly executed his plan to save his gold. 'I resolved of my father and wife's going into the country: and at two hours' warning they did go ... with about 1,300l in gold in their night bag; pray God give them good passage and good care to hide it ... but my heart is full of fear.'[27] Attempting to withdraw £500 from the bank he found it besieged with creditors refusing to issue anything payable under twenty days. He failed to obtain his money, but Will Hewer had managed to extract £500 of his own in cash before the run on the banks reached its height. Gibson, the clerk, carried another thousand guineas in the wake of Pepys's father, travelling towards Brampton under the guise of an official messenger. Meanwhile, the Office was overwhelmed by requests for fireships, and every kind of person poured in and out, some bringing new and alarming reports. Pepys took the precaution of making a girdle containing £300 which he carried on him, 'that I may not be without something in case I should be surprised'.[28] Finally, he summoned his cousin Sarah and her husband, and passed into their hands a chest containing his writings and – most carefully guarded – his Journals. His concentration on Office work was constantly disturbed by the thought of his gold on the night coach to Brampton and the problem of what to do with his silver. Perhaps he should simply surrender it to the privy, but if Navy Office staff were arrested it would be somewhat inaccessible. Greater fears assailed him as the news steadily worsened. One after another, the charges spiralled – the Navy's incompetence was due to high treason or a Papist plot and at the very least the Office of the Ordinance had been guilty of total neglect. On the night of the 13th Pepys made his will and 'did give all I had equally between my father and my wife'.[29] Hayter and Hewer witnessed the document and he retired to bed to sleep uneasily.

Another worry nagged at the back of his mind – why had he heard nothing from his staff at Chatham? The day after he made his will, news began to arrive explaining the silence. Panic had steadily grown in Chatham, beginning with the rich who rushed their money into the country and reaching down to ordinary seamen who mutinied and deserted. Some seamen actually clamoured at the Navy Office willing to serve if only they were paid, but among them Pepys felt there were many who would just as well fight for France or Holland, so disgusted were they with the Navy Board's behaviour. As for Pett, he had decided that his time at Chatham had come and fled. In London the scene was less confused but still not reliable. Then Pepys's wife returned from Brampton with news which disturbed him even more. She and his father had buried the gold in the garden in full daylight. Anyone passing could have observed them, 'which put me into such trouble that I was almost mad about it'. He refused to eat supper with his wife, stopped talking to her and went off alone to bed very distressed.[30]

For nearly fourteen days the Dutch cruised off the mouth of the Thames before again attacking five English warships and twenty fireships, but burning some of the fireships cost De Ruyter a dozen of his own. When he retired downstream the following day he was chased by Spragge, commander of the English river force.[31] On the 25th both fleets were anchored again at the Nore almost within gunshot of each other. Pepys was awakened at three in the morning by a Mr Griffing with a letter from Coventry to Penn which revealed that the Dutch were once more 'coming up to the Nore'.[32]

Pett, the Commissioner at Chatham, next came under critical fire for failing to move the *Royal Charles* further upriver. He had also antagonised Spragge and used dock labour to carry his private goods to safety. Pepys, sensing the possibility of a scapegoat who would deflect criticisms, commented on the 'dullness' of the joint defence of Pett and Lord Brouncker against these charges. On 18 June Pett was brought to the Tower and made 'a close prisoner', which put Pepys 'into a fright lest they may do the same with us'.[33] On the 19th he was ordered to appear before the Council Board with all his papers. In impeccable order, these papers proved invaluable. Present at the preliminary hearing were all the stars including Albemarle who needed Pett as a scapegoat, and no one troubled to conceal his hostility. Sir William Coventry bore witness to the King's instructions on the safety of the Medway and Pepys gave a detailed account, supported by letters, of 'what we [the Navy Office] had done'. When summoned before the Board Pett cut a sorry figure – 'he in his old clothes and looked most sillily'.[34] What followed was not an inquiry or interrogation but the baiting of a trapped animal. Predisposed against Pett, Pepys was not an objective witness but no one else had the documentary evidence and he now made destructive use of it. Lord Arlington and Coventry were also 'very severe against Pett' and Arlington claimed that 'if he [Pett] was not guilty' then clearly the world would think that *they* were.[35] Serious examination of the case rapidly deteriorated and dissolved into laughter when Pett seemed to imply that his models of ships were more important to the country's safety than real naval ships.[36] 'I all this while showing him no respect but rather against him; for which God forgive me, for I mean no hurt to him, but only find that these lords are upon their own purgation and it is necessary that I should be so in behalf of the Office.'

Pepys emerged very uneasily from the enquiry and was glad that he met no one he knew, but rumours were rife. Some said that he had been consigned to the Tower alongside Pett, and others that he was just a pleasant hard-working cog in the bureaucratic machine who had striven to do his best. Meanwhile, diplomatic negotiations had intensified and another Coventry – Henry Coventry – representing England, left the Breda Conference to put peace terms before King Charles. News travelled slowly and both navies determined to wreak what damage they could on the other before any treaty was signed. The last engagement off the English coast, when Sir Joseph Jordan decided to attack the Dutch, ended ignominiously. A quarter of his best men deserted when summoned to action and 'the fireship crews utterly disgraced themselves; they practically refused to attack.'[37] The whole Dutch War was an inglorious episode in British history which ended when the peace treaty was signed at Breda on 21 July.[38] On 29 July Pepys committed to the Diary one of its longest entries, running to many pages. He offered to resign as victualler to the Navy and summed up the war with devastating frankness. Sir William Coventry passed on his resignation offer to the Duke of York and took the same view of the war as Pepys.[39] If his resignation was once more a pre-emptive move, his assessment of the war was all blunt honesty. 'Thus in all things: in wisdom – courage – force – knowledge of our own streams – and success, the Dutch have the best of us and do end the war with victory on their side.'[40]

Chapter 13

The affair with Deborah

Now in his thirty-fourth year Pepys was a changed man. His marriage had fallen into disarray, his lack of children still troubled him and his public life had gone awry. In his Diary he retained his confessional tone. Not given to moral introspection he found himself trying to escape from many a moral maze. He continued to move in distinguished company – the King, the Duke of York, Prince Rupert, Batten, Penn, Sandwich and Coventry – all carefully accommodated to meet the needs of his still developing career and subject to continuous reassessment as principle and strategy were uneasily balanced. Underneath everything, his inexhaustible curiosity continued, his ambition persisted and his diverse appetites clamoured for satisfaction. Nothing any longer seemed certain, but he had assimilated that fact with a pragmatism which marked many of his activities. 'I do plainly see my weakness that I am not a man able to go through trouble as other men, but that I should be a miserable man if I should meet with adversity.'[1] None of these characteristics overwhelmed the enchanting companion who made friends easily, remained loyal to those he respected and had such a zest for living that music, theatre, science and insatiable lust laced his official occasions with such variety it seemed remarkable that he could keep the whole conjuring trick in balance.

It was lust which now once more signalled near disaster. Late in September 1667 he recorded that his wine merchant William Batelier had called that day bringing a very pretty girl, Deborah Willett, as a candidate to serve Elizabeth. 'My wife says she is extraordinary handsome and inclines to have her and I am glad of it – at least that if we must have one she should be handsome.'[2] The following day, 25 September, he went to a meeting at Whitehall to discuss his paper on naval finances with Sir George Carteret, Lord Anglesey, Sir William Coventry, Lord Ashley and the King. Pepys reported that the King was dismissive: 'Why after all this discourse I now come to understand it ... that there can be nothing done ... more than is possible.'[3] Pepys left the meeting ashamed to see how lightly such matters were considered. His mind was preoccupied with the forthcoming parliamentary enquiry into the conduct of the Dutch War, but with the shattered Navy back in port there was very little active business. Partly to take his mind off the immediate future he went to the theatre, ventured into the country and engaged the fashionable pleasures of the season.

On 24 September he first met Deborah Willett who had just celebrated her seventeenth birthday, and from that day onwards she was never far from his mind.[4] She 'seems by her discourse to be grave beyond her bigness and age and exceedingly well bred as to her deportment, having been a scholar at Bow School these seven or eight years'.[5] His wife had summoned Pepys from the Office to meet Deborah and now, when he returned, he could not stop his mind 'running on this pretty girl'. Pepys was genuinely appreciative of female beauty and respected love. Both were about to trap him irremediably. Physically, Deborah had the attributes of a young Lolita, but early acquaintance revealed she had none of Lolita's tantalising reactions. Nothing could have created greater temptation than the custom of the day whereby the maid helped the master to undress before bed. In the Diary he refers to his pleasure at sharing the same bedroom with both his wife and his servant. Sometimes she lay in a truckle bed beside them, sometimes Pepys himself took the truckle bed. Male chauvinism was the reigning precept of the day, but old-fashioned chivalry would probably have dictated certain privacies. The first kiss was formal and possibly in Elizabeth's presence. Next he persuaded Deborah to comb his hair nightly by the fireside. Presently he went a little further and was so gently rebuffed that he had not the heart to press for more. This sensitivity did not survive the week. One warm August night, '*Yo* did *hazer* Deb to *car mi* thing with her hand after *yo* was in *lecto* with great pleasure. [I persuaded Deb to take my thing in her hand after I was on the couch – with great pleasure.]'[6] Already he was aware that his feeling was finer than anything he had experienced for Mrs Bagwell, although there is no mention, as yet, of love.

On 10 October Pepys went to visit his father intent on recovering his gold buried all those months ago in his garden. Waiting for darkness they took a lantern and spades and began digging but it quickly became clear that his father no longer recollected the precise location. 'Lord, what a tosse I was for some time in ... that I began heartily to sweat and be angry that they should not agree better upon the place.'[7] His fears abated as they found themselves turfing up pieces of gold with the dirt and then once more Pepys was almost out of his wits with worry. 'I perceive this earth was amongst the gold and wet, so that the bags were all rotten.' In fear that his neighbours might realise exactly what they were doing, Pepys and Will Hewer waited until midnight before they went out to find at least one hundred missing pieces. Momentarily, recovering the gold overwhelmed all other concerns, but at last it was done and once more Deborah became the centre of his thoughts. Driven perhaps by a sense of danger, he made some efforts to reawaken the old days with Elizabeth. One day he even went out of his way to buy some Scotch cakes which he and Elizabeth had always enjoyed together in the days of Axe Yard. Taking them home for supper they spent a pleasant hour in bed afterwards talking 'in harmony'.

Full of consideration for Elizabeth's trouble with a tooth abscess, and carefully controlling his reactions to Deborah, the early days of December passed without disruption. By the end of December everything had changed, but not because of Deborah. On 30 December, after a day of mixed business, he went to see the play *Love's Cruelty*, a tragedy by James Shirley. After the first act a messenger told him that Mrs Pearse, whose beauty he admired, and Mrs Knepp the actress 'did dine at my house today and I was desired to come home'. Hurrying back he found that both ladies had just left and after 'a very little stay with my wife' he took coach and returned again to the playhouse. Apparently, he preferred the company of Mrs Pearse and Knepp to that of his wife, and had gone back to 'sit out the play' with them. What possessed him to reveal these facts to his wife on returning home is difficult to understand. Knowing Elizabeth's jealousy he must have realised what havoc it would certainly cause. 'She was made as a devil and nothing but ill words between us all the evening while we sat at cards – Will Hewer and the girl by – even to gross words.'[8] The quarrel subsided into silence 'and so to supper and bed without one word to another.'[9]

Elizabeth may have been upset by the incident in itself, or she may have sensed or even known of Pepys's feelings for Deborah. Certainly, he had been uncommonly – and perhaps suspiciously – attentive of late. All that summer he had gone out of his way to please his wife, having her portrait painted, redecorating the house and hinting that he was about to buy a coach. Between 1 January and 31 August 1668 Pepys visited the theatre no less than seventy-three times, on forty occasions accompanied by Elizabeth and on thirty-two with Deborah in attendance. The theatre frequently absorbed the tensions between them, and Mrs Pepys was not averse to slipping away for a lone visit. She did not think the ambience dangerous or immoral. Indeed, she enjoyed the spectacle of noblemen, courtiers and courtesans in the pit and boxes vying with the sharpers, whores and orange-sellers. And then on Sunday 24 October everything changed. The family spent the day enjoying their new surroundings until – with Elizabeth out of the room – Pepys asked Deborah to comb his hair as was the custom. Elizabeth suddenly returned to the room to find him 'embracing the girl *con* my hand *sub su* coats; and indeed I was with my *main* in her cunny'. This occasioned him the 'greatest sorrow ... that I ever knew in this world'.[10] Pepys and Deborah were completely at a loss, and his endeavours to 'put off' Elizabeth simply left her mute with anger. As she recovered her voice, she 'grew quite out of order' and Pepys – not knowing 'how much she saw' – hardly said a word. Silently they went at last to bed, but neither could sleep and at two in the morning Elizabeth woke and suddenly announced that she was a secret Roman Catholic who had received the sacrament. This was a lie and obviously meant to punish Pepys since having a Roman Catholic wife was very dangerous. The atmosphere in the upstairs bedroom on Seething Lane thickened and Elizabeth dredged up a whole chain of complaints far beyond Deborah. It is unlikely that she knew that Pepys's insatiable appetite had, in fact, driven him not only to reopen relations with Mrs Bagwell, and to frequently indulge Mrs Martin, Pearse and Knepp, but also to prowl the streets hopeful of finding yet more women of easy virtue. There, of course, he differed from Boswell. Some see Pepys as a cult figure whose career and talents have been exaggerated beyond his means leaving only a self-intoxicated equivalent of Boswell without the clap. Paying for sex, like Boswell, was in his case unnecessary because a flow of relaxed ladies satisfied his needs. He may even have thought keeping his own lust aflame would rekindle his sexual life with Elizabeth.

Choking with tears Elizabeth returned to the attack on Deborah, claiming that he preferred this 'sorry girl' to her, which – sexually – he did. Pepys now summoned all his charm to promise future respect for his wife, declared his continuing love for her, 'forswore any hurt' and at last she slipped into sleep. Pepys himself slept very badly and the next morning struggled down to Whitehall, his mind more troubled for Deborah than Elizabeth, 'my [wife] telling me that she would turn her out of door'.[11] He spent part of the day with Lord Sandwich who tried to persuade Pepys that his – Sandwich's

– reputation stood well with the King, which Pepys doubted. Back home he found his wife and Deborah moving around in silence and quickly went to bed only to be awakened at midnight when Elizabeth 'fell foul' of him again. This time she said she had seen him hug and kiss Deborah. Pepys admitted the embrace and denied the kiss, completely sidestepping his much more brazen intrusion. He then poured out protestations of true love laced with undertakings never to see the Knepps or Pearses of this world again, finally claiming that his embrace of Deborah was a mere indiscretion with 'no harm in it'.[12] A temporary lull was quickly broken. The following night, towards bedtime, his wife 'began to be in a mighty rage from some new matter', and spent the rest of the night ranting at him 'in most high terms'.[13]

At the height of her tirade she threatened to publish his shame to the world and, seeing his alarm, realised – perhaps for the first time – the power she had over him. She then lit a candle in the chimney which must have given dramatic effect to her continued accusations. Once again Pepys exercised all his skills to win her over and at last she quietened and fell asleep. They rose the next morning in uneasy peace. Pepys remained silent about Deborah's complicity in their embrace but could not face sacking her because his desire was as strong as ever. Elizabeth seemed full of kindness the next day, unaware that Pepys had already broken all his undertakings by writing a note to Deborah telling her exactly how much he had admitted to his wife, for fear that Deborah might tell Elizabeth the whole truth. Having delivered the note he was scared that it might fall into his wife's hands and was very relieved when he learnt that Deborah had burnt it. Jealousy apart, there were powerful reasons why Elizabeth should be disturbed by what had happened. As yet unknown to Pepys she had been subjected to serious solicitations by Lord Sandwich who used an intermediary as was customary. His master of horse, Captain Ferrars, played the role without much success. Lord Hinchingbrooke also upset Elizabeth by dancing close attention on her.[14] Apparently, there were other advances but Elizabeth, who was deeply loyal, rejected them all.

The peace restored to Seething Lane was temporary and full of tensions. Pepys worried, 'lest he should ruin' Deborah but a terrible frustration fought with his sense of shame and set Pepys at odds with himself. The obvious solution was to dismiss Deborah, but the thought dismayed him. 'Yet I must bring my mind to give way to it.'[15] So he sat through those soft autumn evenings with his wife, careful his eyes did not stray to observe Deborah. On several occasions he could not prevent himself, and once produced tears in Deborah's eyes. Whether her tears represented reciprocal feelings for Pepys or simple distress at the situation, it is impossible to know. Their daily routine now changed in one vital respect. Elizabeth took over Deborah's role in dressing her husband in the mornings, which was hardly surprising. Pepys frequently slept naked and if in the mornings Deborah encountered him in that state, Pepys, torn between the knowledge that Deborah must go and his irresistible desire to share her company, found himself unable to resist smiling at her. Beneath his emotional reactions there persisted a much more primitive desire: 'I have a great mind for to have the maidenhead of this girl.'

A series of crises marked the unfolding love affair with Deborah. On one occasion, when under ceaseless pressure from Elizabeth, Deborah suddenly broke down and poured out the truth about the hair-dressing incident. At first shocked into silence, Elizabeth refused to accept Deborah at their table and insisted on Pepys's eating dinner alone with her in her room.[16] And then once more, in the middle of the night, all hell broke loose: 'She wakes me and cries out that she would never sleep more and so kept raving till past midnight that made me cry and weep heartily ... for her.'[17] This time there was only one solution. He personally must dismiss Deborah. He shrank from the prospect and again could not sleep for worry. The following day his wife again refused to dine with Deborah and Pepys sat talking with her trying to bring himself to the sticking point.[18] He failed and that night his wife suddenly reared up in bed 'with expressions of affright and madness as one frantic'. He reconstructs the scene vividly in the Diary. The moon poured into the room almost as if it were daylight and in that radiance he himself burst into tears while his wife mixed ravings with reproaches and insisted that the girl *must go*. There was only one means of bringing her to her senses. He must make a solemn promise to dismiss Deborah the following day. The assurance given, Elizabeth at last fell uneasily asleep.

On the evening of the 12th he went first to sit with Elizabeth in her room and then summoned Deborah to a meeting in his chamber. There he dismissed her in front of his wife, advised her to be gone as soon as possible and warned her that he did not want to meet her again in the house. He spoke with tears in his eyes, bitterly resenting every word he used, and Deborah too broke out crying, partly, Pepys felt, because she knew him still to be her friend.[19] If love is a many splendoured thing, there persisted in Pepys an elementary aim which he did not deny. The following day he returned home to find that Deborah was moving out, which troubled him but left him with the same lascivious ambition.[20] He woke on 14 November determined to write Deborah a note and give her some money, but his wife would not let him out of her sight. He protested angrily, whereupon Elizabeth instantly flew into a rage, calling him a dog, a rogue and rotten at heart.[21]

At last Deborah left the house and Pepys made his way to the Office with a heavy heart. He could not expunge the girl from his mind. That night he made love to his wife – passionately, it seems – and reflected that he had lain with her more since their falling-out than in the twelve previous months – and, above all, with more pleasure than at any time before. Was he seeking redemption through love-making or was he thinking of Deborah all the while? Deborah at seventeen almost matched his wife when he married her at fifteen, and he must have had a sense of recovering those heady days. Deborah also reconstructed the power relations between Pepys and Elizabeth. Once dominating his wife's everyday habits, he now found his authority over her undermined. She was watching his every movement. As if to break out of her surveillance, no sooner had he sacked Deborah than he set about trying to trace where she had gone. Here, unwittingly, Elizabeth was his ally. She let drop the name Dr Allbon in connection with Deborah and Pepys discovered that he lived at Whetstone Park, a rather shady area near Holborn. There he repaired on the Monday following Deborah's weekend dismissal, but could find no trace of Allbon. Searching his memory he recalled Elizabeth saying that at one time Allbon lived in Eagle Court and while he himself returned to the Office, he sent a boy to reconnoitre. A chain of persistent enquiries eventually led to a new address in Fleet Street where Allbon now skulked to escape his creditors, reduced to 'a poor broken fellow' who 'dare not show his head'.[22] On 18 November Pepys lay long in bed with his wife because she still did not trust him and was afraid, whenever he left the house, that he would go in search of Deborah. Vehemently denying any such intention, no sooner had he escaped her surveillance than he went directly by coach to Somerset House 'and there enquired among the porters for Dr Allbon'.[23] One porter said that he had changed his address yet again to Lincoln's Inn Fields and he knew a second porter due to deliver a chest to that address. One clue led to another and Pepys spent the whole day going from one informer to the next and from the Strand to Whitehall, loitering along the way, looking up at windows, hoping he might see Deborah's face. Suddenly his luck changed and by accident he met the porter who had carried the chest to

Dr Allbon. At first, full of suspicion, the porter would not yield Allbon's address, but Pepys convinced him that his interest lay with Deborah not Dr Allbon, and he agreed to carry a message to her. In a sweat of anticipatory frustration, Pepys paced up and down until the porter returned to say that she had agreed to see him. 'So I could not be commanded by my reason but must go this very night.'[24] Post-haste he took a coach through the darkness, met Deborah and coaxed her into the coach.

And *yo* did *besar* her and *tocar* her thing but *ella* was against it and
laboured with much earnestness such as I behoved to be real; and yet
at last *yo* did make her *tener mi coso* in her *mano* while *mi mano* was
sobra her pectus and *yo* did *hazer* with grand delight. [And I did kiss
her and feel her thing but she was against it and laboured with much
earnestness such as I believed to be real; and yet at last I did make
her hold my thing in her hand while my hand was on her breast and
so did do with grand delight.][25]

Whether she shared his delight is unknown but like all lovers full of a fresh conquest, he wanted to preserve her as his exclusive property. He even warned her to take care of her honour which he had already violated. She must go in fear of God. Pepys then extracted a promise from her that she would not allow any other man to '*para haver* to ... *con* her – as *yo* have done'.[26] Coming dangerously close to converting her into a whore he gave her 20s – a relatively trivial sum – and instructed her to leave any change of address in a sealed envelope with Herringman, his bookseller. Back home he concocted a story of the day's events to Elizabeth, 'with which the poor wretch was satisfied, or at least seemed so'. At the Office the following morning his heart was full of joy to think how he had arranged the perfect balancing act between Deborah, his wife and himself.

    The self-congratulation was short-lived. At noon he went home to check on the work of some upholsterers and found Elizabeth sitting in silence in the dining room. Whether she was now sure of her intuitions or whether someone had betrayed him, she burst out in anger that he was the most 'false, rotten-hearted rogue' in the world. Thinking it impossible that she could so quickly have discovered his betrayal he continued to deny it for several minutes. Then, suddenly, he collapsed in abject confession. Dragging him away to the bedroom she cursed on him all afternoon, her invective mounting to the point where she swore she would slit the nose of the girl and leave him. In the midst of her fury the calculating side of her nature asserted itself and she demanded 400l in exchange for her silence or she would tell the whole world what a scoundrel the great Mr Pepys had become. On and on continued the tirade until a cowed Pepys, who thought that there would be no end, was finally driven to summon his clerk, Will Hewer, as if to redeem his sins by making them semi-public. By now Hewer was privy to much of their private life and in the midst of her wrath Elizabeth still trusted him far more than her husband. Hewer heard her account of what had happened and himself burst into tears like a child to find such hatred between his master and mistress. Patiently Pepys set to work and in due course Elizabeth, now calmer, accepted, with Hewer as witness, an undertaking that never again – but never – would Pepys see, speak with and certainly not caress Deborah Willett.

'But I have the confidence to deny it, to the perjuring of myself.'[27] Clearly, he was still not completely committed to the undertaking forced upon him. That night he made love to Elizabeth passionately, apparently to her great satisfaction. The pages of the Diary at this time are scattered with references to his and her chamber which might have meant that they were sleeping in separate rooms, and that night he describes how 'alone in [his] chamber' he actually fell on his knees to pray to God that He would give him the grace to remain true 'to my poor wife'. In the morning, the evening's peacemaking was shattered once more with 'mighty words between my poor wife and I'.[28] At last they came to the extraordinary arrangement that Pepys would not leave the house without a keeper who would guarantee his complete isolation from Deborah.

The keeper was to be Will Hewer or Elizabeth herself, and on that morning it fell to the lot of Hewer. Against all his protestations, and the fury he risked, Pepys now persuaded Hewer to carry a message to Deborah telling her not to deny anything if Elizabeth should interrogate her. Returning from his mission, Hewer fell into a full-scale discussion of Pepys's marriage with him in St James's Park. On his way home that night Pepys called on his coach-maker because part of his reconciliation with Elizabeth meant fulfilling her desire to have a coach of their own. A fresh outburst greeted him back home, and Elizabeth did 'fall to revile me in the bitterest manner in the world', rising to a climax when she struck him and pulled his hair. Taking it all in penitent silence, he was at last reduced to tears and prevailed upon her to grant an interval of peace. Within the hour it was broken again and she fell into a 'raging fit' worse than before, threatening once more to 'slit the girl's nose'.[29] Hewer, now established in the role of peacemaker, once more intervened. While Pepys flung himself in despair on the bed, Hewer reasoned with Elizabeth and together they concocted a plan. If Pepys would write to Deborah saying that he hated her and never wanted to see her again because she was a whore, this would convince Elizabeth that she could trust him. Pepys began to write the letter but his pen wavered on the word 'whore', which he omitted. Elizabeth read the letter and finding the word missing tore it into shreds in a new fury. Now Pepys produced a piece of circumlocution which avoided the brutality of the direct charge but conveyed a similar meaning: '... as that I did fear she might too probably have been prevailed upon to be a whore by her carriage to me and therefore as such I did resolve never to see her any more'.[30] As he wrote, Will Hewer winked at him, indicating that he had no intention of actually delivering the letter. From the moment the missive was handed over to Hewer, Pepys and Elizabeth kissed and were friends again. The next morning he hurried down to the Office where Hewer was waiting with that part of his letter which used the word 'whore' erased. Hewer had warned Deborah that Pepys must never see her again and 'did give her the best Christian counsel he could'.[31]

Throughout five weeks of this prolonged quarrel, Elizabeth had neglected her own person and the house, but on the day following their reconciliation Pepys came back to find his wife freshly washed and powdered and his home pristine. Still her suspicions simmered under the surface and when he was abroad in her company he dare not look at a pretty girl. Even lying beside him in bed he suspected that she had access to his very dreams. 'She ... will not be persuaded but I do dream of Deb and do tell me that I speak in my dreams, and that this night I did cry "huzzy" and it must be she.'[32] In all this Deborah's voice is never heard. Pepys found himself torn between two women whom he loved simultaneously but differently. His wife blazes to life in the Diary but Deborah remains a demure shadow who never speaks. It is unclear whether she returned his love and we do not know her ultimate fate, but the break certainly reduced her to a miserable way of life. Among the presents Pepys now showered upon his wife was the supreme one which she had coveted for years – a coach. He had earlier bought an unsatisfactory vehicle for £53 which turned out to be clumsily old-fashioned. Swiftly it was exchanged for a much more elegant affair and on 30 November he and his wife drove out with all the panoply of liveried coachman, painted panels and coloured reins 'to take the maidenhead of [my] coach'.

Chapter 14

The Diary ends

Professional matters which had simmered in the background at last rose to sweep aside domestic considerations. They took the form of an enquiry into the miscarriages of the war. Three times between October and November of 1667 Pepys stood bareheaded before committees of the House of Commons answering penetrating questions, preserving throughout a remarkable calm. Sir William Coventry, also in trouble as we shall see, gave Pepys a classic piece of advice for anyone dealing with parliamentary committees: 'to be as short as I can and obscure, saving in things fully plain ... to say little and let them get out what they can by force'.[1] Pepys offered such clear expositions, answered questions so frankly and was such a master of his subject that even surly old MP Colonel Birch admired his painstaking advocacy. Wholesale changes had overtaken the staffing of the Navy Office, with Penn in deep trouble over the Medway invasion, Carteret resigning as Navy Treasurer to become Deputy Treasurer of Ireland, and Coventry abandoning his secretaryship to the Duke of York. In October Batten died suddenly and unexpectedly, but Comptroller Sir John Mennes, who gave every appearance of being dead, suddenly recovered and outwitted opponents hell-bent to replace him.[2] On 10 December Pepys wrote a long, masterly letter to Sir Robert Brook, MP for Aldeburgh, in which he set out preliminary answers to a new set of questions.[3]

When the House reassembled in February 1668 it was overwhelmed by a rush of committees enquiring into accounts, prizes, bribery, payment by private ticket and, most delicate of all from Pepys's point of view, privateers. He hurried from one committee to the next having briefed himself on all issues, and displayed his remarkable expository powers, rebutting charges which should have been answered by his colleagues. The Committee for Miscarriages was no blundering aggregation of bureaucrats bent on destroying rivals. Pressing home questions about the Dutch invasion of the Medway, the Committee had already uncovered its own culprit in the person of Lord Henry Brouncker who was alleged to have given the fatal order to shorten sail off Lowestoft in 1665, allowing the Dutch fleet to escape destruction.[4] Knowing every documented source, Pepys did not draw this conclusion himself, but the Committee presented the evidence forcibly, revealing their interrogative power and putting Pepys on his mettle.

The night before, Pepys could not sleep and tossed restlessly until five in the morning. He then called Elizabeth, who managed to calm him but only after he had agreed to resign a post which gave him so much distress. On the morning of 5 March he drank 'a dram of brandy at Mrs Hewlett's ... with the warmth of this did find myself in better order as to courage truly'. He then spent the whole morning re-marshalling his evidence with such persistence that he missed dinner and had to hurry to the House of Commons. Travelling in Lord Brouncker's coach, he and his colleagues discussed the one main issue with which they were collectively involved – the discharge of seamen by ticket. All were aware that they could expect no royal help because the King had revealed a streak of disloyalty towards some of his former friends, including Brouncker. Once Pepys confronted his adversaries all his nerves disappeared and he began his exposition picking and choosing with precision between the papers placed beside him. In Grey's *Debates* Pepys is demoted to 'a clerk' and the resumé of his speech fragmented and inadequate. Hour after hour it continued, with Pepys's confidence mounting as his case cohered in all its detail until darkness fell over the chamber, candles were brought and at last he came to his triumphant conclusion. In this preliminary hearing Pepys rose above petty factions and jealousies to become the central figure in the Committee. In the midst of all his professional preoccupations he readily surrendered to the now obligatory infidelity. He slipped away from his wife on 31 December to Mrs Martin's where he did '*hazer con ella*' what he desired.[5]

He was again beset by a problem which had begun to haunt him as far back as 1663 – his deteriorating eyesight – and was certain that one day he would go blind.[6] The previous year he had written: 'I perceive my overworking of my eyes by candlelight do hurt them as it did last winter. Thus by day I am well and do get them right but then after candlelight they begin to be sore and run so that I intend to get some green spectacles.'[7] According to D'Arcy Power, in a thoroughgoing examination of Pepys's eye trouble in the *Lancet* (1911), Pepys was in fact suffering from hypermetropia with some degree of astigmatism, which was not unusual and certainly posed no threat of blindness.[8] The trouble grew worse in February 1668: 'My eyes mighty bad with the light of the candles last night which was so great as to make my eyes sore all this day ...'.[9] Pepys took some advice from a spectacle-maker called Turlington which Power regarded as superlatively bad because he recommended concave instead of convex glasses. Finally, Pepys resorted to an extraordinary contraption of paper cylinders, which gave him false hopes.

The timing of medical advances has sometimes changed the course of history. Pepys would have continued writing his Diary far beyond its eleven years given modern ophthalmic treatment. Early in May 1669 he records readjusting his tube glasses with high hopes but little success. 'At the Office all this morning and this day the first time did alter my side of the table after eight years sitting on that next the fire. But now I am not able to bear the light of the windows on my eyes.' A terrible decision pressed in on him. Should he abandon the Diary to relieve his eyes? First, he decided to appeal to the Duke of York for three or four months' leave away from papers and writing in the hope of recovery.[10] Then came the crucifying moment when he made the last entry after eleven years in which every other act was reproduced on the page and rendered doubly rich by a confidant closer even than his wife. 'And thus ends all that I doubt I shall be able to do with my own eyes in the keeping of my Journal.'[11] He resolved, as he wrote the last entry, to have his friends or clerks continue the Diary in long hand excluding references to his love life. Such episodes would, in future, become marginalia written in shorthand by himself. 'And so I betake myself to that course which [is] almost as much as to see myself go into my grave.'[12] He had indeed lost a life. He never kept his marginalia resolve. Journals later composed by his clerks under his direction recorded episodes like the Brooke House enquiry and what is sometimes called his Second Diary gives a short account of his voyage to Tangier. Both of these were completely without any personal references and excluded whatever love life continued after the death of the Diary.

Tremendous power struggles had now left political competitors redistributed in different patterns with two of Pepys's patrons, Sandwich and Coventry, no longer eminent as they had been. Rumours that powerful forces were working against Coventry dismayed Pepys, but Coventry was still a member of the Privy Council and a Commissioner of the Treasury. Pepys's respect, indeed affection, for Coventry remained unchanged. Continuous references in the Diary put his loyalty above the buffeting of ordinary politics. Pepys anticipated Coventry's downfall in his Diary late in October. 'The Duke of Buckingham is now all in all and will ruin Coventry if he can; and that ... Coventry doth now rest wholly upon the Duke of York for his standing.'[13] Pepys also found Sandwich in circumstances very different from the old days. First he was kept waiting – 'as his best friends are' – and then Sandwich talked about nothing but his own affairs. Together they proceeded to the meeting of the Committee on Tangier where Sandwich gave an account of his stewardship, '... yet he did it with a mind so low and mean, and delivered in so poor a manner that it appeared nothing at all'.[14] Dismayed that he had been torn out of the centre of affairs and sent away to Spain, Sandwich allowed his depression to show before the Committee.[15]

Meeting him again, two weeks later, Pepys found him so deeply lost in his own affairs that he gave the appearance of 'moping'. Above all, a new reserve characterised his manner with Pepys. This seemed explicable in terms of their relative fortunes; Pepys had skilfully negotiated his way through the first official enquiry with his reputation enhanced and suffered no setback equivalent to Sandwich's. A discussion ensued between the two men about the creation of a local paymaster at Tangier which almost reversed their roles in the hierarchy to their mutual embarrassment. Sandwich had nominated Sir Charles Harbord for the job, but the Duke of York referred the matter to Pepys for his opinion. Lord Sandwich then told Pepys that he took it very ill coming from the Duke of York and he bit his lip as he spoke. Later, he reacted very ambiguously, saying 'that he was glad ... the Duke of York might come to contend who shall be the kindest to me'.[16] With great daring, Pepys underlined the shift in power by inviting Sandwich to dinner at his house for the first time in their long acquaintance. Sandwich at once accepted, which indicated that he acknowledged the reversal of fortunes. The dinner itself reaffirmed Pepys's new status, consisting of six or eight dishes 'as noble as any man need to have I think ... and I have rarely seen in my life better anywhere else, even at court'. The wines too were carefully chosen with a newly sophisticated palate and a preference for 'the strong ... Greek, Italian, Spanish and Portuguese'. An undertow of hostility in public affairs remained which, despite his dazzling defence of the Navy Office, threatened to remove Pepys from office, if only there were sound reason. Pepys himself believed that 'they do think that I know too much'.

On Sunday 24 January 1669 Pepys was summoned to appear before

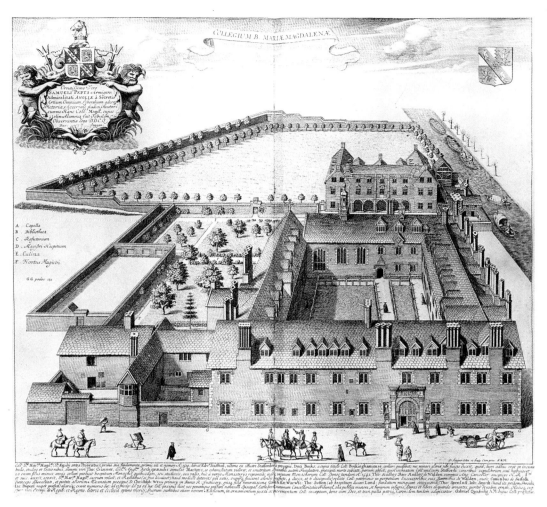

Magdalene College from Loggan's *Cantabrigia Illustrata* (1690). The quadrangle is as Pepys knew it from his undergraduate days.

Below
Elizabeth, wife of Samuel Pepys: engraving
by Thomson, 1828.

Opposite
Pepys had these spectacles specially made
to shield his eyes from candlelight. The
Diary records that they 'pleased him
mightily'.

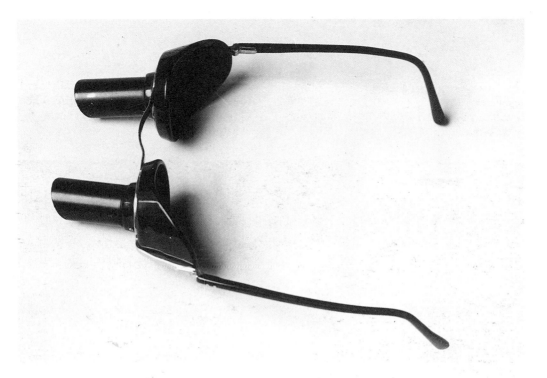

Below
Model of a new ship built for the Dutch in 1651 being shown to the Navy Board: painting by Seymour Lucas. Samuel Pepys is on the right of the model; Lord Sandwich on the extreme right taking snuff; and John Evelyn in the background, bending over the model.

Pepys aged about thirty-seven. From a portrait by Peter Lely at Magdalene College, Cambridge.

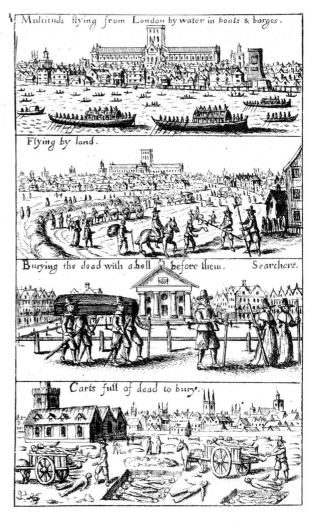

The Great Plague claimed its first victims in June 1665. People fled from the city en masse. The plague had hardly subsided before the Great Fire of 1666 engulfed the city of London.

The fire overwhelmed an area from the Tower to the Temple, a great stretch of the Thames. This engraving by Vischer after Schut shows London in flames.

Will Hewer, Pepys's clerk, who became his lifelong friend: painted by Sir Godfrey Kneller *c.* 1685.

Christmas merrymaking in Pepys's time.

The Popish Plot of 1678. A satire of 1681.

Commissioners of the Navy Board: Sir William Penn by Lely (*below*), and (*below right*) Sir William Coventry by John Riley.

PEPYS! see over →

Samuel Pepys in full panoply: painted by Riley.

Coventry

the King and Council at Essex House and learnt that the Government intended to 'set out' a new fleet for which he would have 'large responsibility'. He was asked how quickly the big ships could be repaired and contradicted the surveyor's estimate of two years. While Pepys was still balancing his interests between Sandwich and Coventry, a dramatic episode intervened to throw Coventry into the Tower. The Duke of Buckingham saw himself not only as a distinguished politician but a clever playwright. He let it be known that he intended writing a satire with Coventry sitting at a desk in the middle of a round hole, surrounded by his disordered papers. Coventry immediately threatened to slit the nose of any actor who dared to take the part. Uproar followed since the Duke was a royal favourite and Coventry's star already waning. By sending the challenge and not executing it Coventry incited arrest which duly followed with his incarceration in the Tower. Abandoned by most of his friends who feared guilt by association, Pepys was one of few who risked visiting him; he also won fresh respect from the Duke of York who hated every member of the Buckingham faction. The Duke visited Pepys at Deptford bringing a number of court ladies, among them the notorious Lady Castlemaine, the King's mistress, and they played absurd love games sitting on a carpet in the open air. Excited by this entertainment, Pepys took the opportunity to slink away intending to visit Mrs Bagwell, but there he found a former maid, Nell, who greeted him so joyously he desired nothing else than 'to stay with her'. For a time he hesitated, and then wisely he hurried back to his wife to have her, as ever, firing suspicious questions at him.

Several times over the next month he went to visit Coventry seeking advice and information, but his attitude was ambivalent. Coventry had not yet received the King's pardon and on the last occasion 'I did take the pretence of my attending the Tangier Committee to take my leave.'[17] It was still not circumspect to be seen in Coventry's company and he tried to excuse his expediency with the words: 'to serve him . . . I should stick at nothing.'[18]

Although Pepys was somewhat chastened and had put a bridle on his sexual appetites they were still clamouring for satisfaction. When in March 1669 he seized the chance to attend a court-martial at Chatham, no sooner was the business over than he took a trip to Maidstone and re-encountered an old love, Mrs Jowles. She proved more than willing, and but for lack of privacy he would have pressed home his advantage – this despite his assessment of her as a whore – '. . . but a very brave and comely one'.[19] They stayed together until almost midnight and then, with a lantern, he walked back over 'fields, as dark as pitch', covered with snow and bitterly cold. This was not by any means his last adventure. Early in April he went to Westminster Hall one day and 'took occasion to make a step to Mrs Martin's' but his advances were hindered by her period.[20]

He then deliberately engineered another meeting with Deborah. Still accompanied by his guardian Will Hewer, he managed to give him the slip and set off in what he thought to be 'Deb's direction'. Luck was with him. 'I away and through Jewen Street, my mind God knows running that way ... but going down Holborn Hill by the Conduit I did see Deb on foot going uphill.'[21] She saw him and he tried to speak to her but she hurried on and for a moment he abandoned the chase. The he stopped in his tracks, about-turned and went back after her. Overtaking her, he persuaded Deborah to follow him and 'led her into a little blind alehouse ... and there she and I fell to talk.' He at last was able to fondle her breasts with the inevitable consequences. She was, he later wrote, 'mighty coy', but 'with great force' he persuaded her to take his penis in her hand. Treachery to Elizabeth could go no further. He gave her 20s in a paper and arranged to meet again the following Monday. A further episode with Doll Lane in mid-April was followed by a last worried reference in the Diary to Deborah.[22] She then passed out of the Diary and out of his life. The deprivation must have distressed him but a much greater deprivation was shortly to change his whole way of living. Thoughts of a mute, inglorious Deborah pursuing her life in a semi-slum troubled Pepys, but in reality she was gone for ever.

Pepys had steadily widened his acquaintance among members of the Royal Society in 1668 and on 22 June went to a gathering especially to meet the great chemist Boyle, seeking his advice about his eyes. Boyle had referred him to 'one Turberville of Salisbury, lately come to town which I will go to'.[23] Paradoxically, it was reading and struggling to understand Boyle's books which had aggravated his eye trouble. Having so many diverse interests, overburdened with work, love affairs and professional anxieties, it is remarkable that Pepys found time to read Boyle's works. In April 1667 he had been 'mightily pleased with Boyle's book on colours and only regretted that lack of time prevented his full understanding of its theories'.[24] Early in June his eye trouble had become acute but 'weary and almost blind with so much reading' he boarded a boat and proceeded upriver studying Boyle's book ever more closely without grasping its full meaning.[25] Boyle, he concluded, was a most excellent man.

Within forty-eight hours, disregarding his eyes, he had plunged into yet another Boyle book, *Hydrostatistical Paradoxes*, to escape from a quarrel with his wife.[26] Remarkably it was not just the casual interest of a man anxious to keep up with the fashionable theories of his day. His reading had continued over many days in an effort to master Boyle's thinking. By the summer of 1669 Pepys's eyesight had become so troublesome that he found his professional paperwork was causing him constant pain. His letter to the Duke of York on 19 May petitioning for leave of absence to give relief to his eyes had led the Duke to invite him to his closet to discuss the matter.[27] Full of sympathy, the Duke agreed that he should take a trip to Holland to observe the Dutch Navy where, as the government's leading naval expert, he would be given Dutch facilities. There is very little documentary evidence of this trip, which began in late August and lasted two months. We know that Elizabeth accompanied him, that he carried letters of introduction from his friend John Evelyn, and that he was joined by Elizabeth's brother Balty.[28] He seems to have gained very little naval intelligence from Holland and quickly proceeded to Paris where his sparkling company made him a number of friends.[29]

It was when they reached Brussels that the first intimations of tragedy surfaced. Elizabeth became ill, whether from a bug or drinking polluted water is not known. Still able to travel, she arrived back safely with Pepys in London on 20 October 1669, but three weeks later, without any preliminary warning, on 10 November 1669 she died. It happened so suddenly it seemed incomprehensible. Fourteen years he had shared life at all levels with Elizabeth and despite his deviations she remained the centre to which he returned for comfort, security and an undercurrent of love. Now she was gone and without the Diary the record is thin. Just one carefully detached letter to Captain Elliot remains:

I beg you earnestly to believe that nothing but sorrow and distraction
I have been in by the death of my wife increased by the suddenness
with which it pleased God to surprise me therewith after a voyage so
full of health and content could have forced me to so long neglect of
my private concernments.[30]

At thirty-six years of age Pepys was left to face the future alone.

While Pepys was away in Holland, a group of politicians led by the Duke of Buckingham conspired to undermine the Duke of York's influence on the King. This was accomplished by an outright attack on the Navy Office associated in public opinion with the Medway defeat and misappropriation of funds. A commission had been established in 1667 which included Sir George Savile, whom the King had tried to buy with a peerage, Lord Brereton, an Irish peer believed to be a man of integrity, and George Thomson, described by Harris as a fanatic.[31] Pepys's grief at Elizabeth's death did not prevent him from pre-empting the enquiry by preparing the groundwork for his defence. One way of containing grief was to plunge into work and that he certainly did, without pausing to consult his colleagues. By January 1669, according to the Brooke House Journal, Pepys had persuaded the King to withdraw from a Council meeting into his closet, 'where I presented him a copy not only of my several answers but of another bound up copy ...' Pepys even took the liberty to read 'certain parts to the King'.[32] Elizabeth had died on 10 November yet by 25 November – despite his alleged neglect of his professional life – Pepys wrote to the Commissioner of Accounts saying that he had completed his answers to their charges. He would deliver these the following Saturday or Monday.[33]

The complaint launched against the Navy Office by the commissioner covered eighteen points, among them the long contested charges of corrupt purchase of supplies at extravagant prices, gross favouritism towards some contractors, and the failure of discipline among subordinate officers. Pepys's replies ran to fifty pages of cogent argument interlaced with sarcasm and occasional flashes of wit. They kept strictly to the facts but put those facts in new perspectives which occasionally ridiculed and frequently defeated the commissioners' charges. Pepys proceeded on the principle that if a charge had some validity it was better to acknowledge a degree of guilt while at the same time showing that it was inevitable. Of course there were discrepancies, he said, in storekeepers' provisions, but it was impossible for the Navy as a body to be present at every delivery of stores. As for the stores being bought extravagantly, that was simply the result of vendors not trusting Parliament to pay their debts which forced them to increase their prices to cover possible default. Insubordination – well, if this existed on any real scale it was the result not of lax authority but the inevitable limitations of a captain's ability to oversee every activity of lesser officers. There remained the major charge of corruption, and here his defence weakened, first because corruption was undoubtedly rife and, second, he could not altogether escape suspicion himself. The very awkward occasions when he sold flag material to the Board of which he was a member were noted in the charges and certainly improper. As for Navy Board corruption, Pepys did not hesitate to use the language of 'proud and unyielding scorn' in challenging anyone to provide a single example of the Board sanctioning payment for goods not certified as satisfactory by the local officer responsible. Thus any corruption, if it existed, derived not from the Navy Board itself but from the relevant port or dock official.

The ingenuity of his argument backed by a mass of documented evidence drawn from carefully organised papers came as a surprise to the commissioners, who were momentarily halted in their tracks. Page upon page of flowing evidence masterfully categorised and sometimes openly on the attack, revealed to them the formidable nature of their opponent. His evidence concluded – magisterially – 'I beg I may without offence confess my present inability to discern the cogency of the commission's conclusions.'[34] The very power of Pepys's analysis was bound not only to shake the case against the Board but to create enemies. Stealthily, behind-the-scenes evidence had accumulated about this self-important, bright-eyed little man who had taken office worth some paltry £200 and now commanded at least £10,000. Consider, the rumours said, the rapid rise in his standard of living, such that now he had a house in Seething Lane full of treasures and drove a brand new coach drawn by elegant horses.

Before the enquiry could take full effect the proceedings produced an eruption in Parliament. There was a premature demand for a report from the commission and a vote of censure was launched against Sir George Carteret, erstwhile Treasurer of the Navy. With alarming rapidity, one climax led to another as Sir George was suspended and the King driven to prorogue the House until February. The King then proclaimed that he would cut through all the confusions by himself hearing the joint charges against the Navy Board and Carteret in the presence of the commission. Preparing a written brief drawn from the honeycomb of Pepys's documents was one thing; presenting that evidence in person before a commission empowered to press home questions by the King's presence was another. The evidence for what followed is contained in the Brooke House Journal, a manuscript written by Pepys's clerks, comprising one hundred and twenty-five pages in the Pepys Library at Magdalene.[35] It reveals Pepys from the beginning of 1670 deeply involved behind the scenes with Sir George Downing and Carteret examining the now widely accepted charge that £600,000 voted by Parliament for the Dutch War had been dissipated to different ends. This was really a challenge to the financial conduct of the crown in the War and elevated Pepys from a Clerk of the Acts to advocate for His Majesty. It marked a new royal appreciation of his abilities and gave him fresh authority when, finally, he appeared before the commission.

On the night of 2 January Pepys spent many hours mastering his brief, but we have no details of his personal feelings. The Brooke House Journal is political not personal. The following morning he was escorted from the Treasury to confront a commission which included the King, the Duke of York, the Duke of Ormonde, the Lord Keeper (Lord Brereton) and two secretaries of state. It must have been an intimidating moment calculated to shake the confidence of the most practised advocate. As Pepys prepared to rise to the occasion an adjournment was called. The commission's chief adviser on naval matters, an old-fashioned naval administrator called Colonel Thomson, had been taken ill and Pepys, all geared up to confound this awe-inspiring company, retired home again. Now it was a home without Elizabeth, and this must have rendered the interruption more distressing, but at least Will Hewer was present to curse the absent Colonel. All the evidence for what follows was written by Pepys's eleven clerks and the whole drift of the argument is so partisan as to be suspect. Moreover, the evaluation of identical people in this and the earlier Diary frequently differs widely. So does some of the evidence.

The King opened the proceedings on 5 January with a short analysis of the disposal of £514,000 which had not, according to the commissioners, been spent on the war.[36] The members of the commission worked persistently, sitting all day, with little more than a bit of bread and a glass of wine for sustenance. Indirectly, the commissioners' report implied that Charles II had embezzled the £514,000 for private purposes and this view had spread throughout the country. The King immediately confounded his accusers by quoting from one of the commissioners' private papers where it was asserted that the money had in fact been spent on the Navy. He drove home the point by adding that he had dipped into his private purse to add another £300,000 for war expenditure.

It seemed extraordinary that a group of reasonably intelligent commissioners could have been so accepting of such immediate contradiction. Called upon to assess the reliability of the commissioners' report, Pepys, according to the Brooke House Journal, plunged in without any sign of nerves. He knew all too well that once a single apparently straightforward issue could be turned into a cloud of administrative detail he became the master of the situation with his intimate knowledge and readily available papers.[37] Immediately, he isolated one issue. The commissioners' assumption that finances should be reckoned from 1 September 1664 excluded previous expenditure in fitting-out the fleet for action and Pepys drove home the point. Lord Brereton immediately jumped up and objected forcefully to any offi-

cer of the Navy Office taking it upon himself to interpret an act
of Parliament in contradiction to the interpretation given by the
commissioners appointed by the act. Pepys equably replied that such
acts were not open to exclusive interpretation. Any member of the
public could give his own reading and he, Pepys, deserved 'that
[his] might be admitted on behalf of the King'.[38] When Pepys revealed
a second serious flaw in the report, Brereton again came to his feet
and exploded. Pepys would never dare to say in public what he
now said in a privileged place.[39] According to the Brooke House
Journal Pepys expected the King to reply to Brereton and when
he remained silent Pepys did not respond himself. There were no
laws of libel at this time but such public differences could lead to
duels and Pepys might have been silenced by a lack of confidence
in his inadequate swordplay as much as by prudence.

When he woke the next morning Pepys felt that he had gone
too far with Brereton and, dining with the King, craved his pardon
for such effrontery. At this point the King attacked Lord Brereton
and showered Pepys with praise for his performance. Emboldened,
Pepys then took it upon himself to advise the King to 'consider
by what ways ... to rectify the opinions of the world occasioned
by this report of these gentlemen, that His Majesty had employed
[for] his private uses of pleasure etc., not only the £514,000 here
mentioned but near £300,000 more ...'[40] Throughout the whole
of the Journal Pepys invariably gets the better of his opponents, and
it is thus suspect. Lord Brereton, seen as a simple-minded country
squire in the Journal, had in the last year of the Diary been a 'sober,
serious, affable man' who was very tough in discussion. Now he
and even Bryant regarded him as 'the bucolic chairman of quarter
sessions'.[41] Pepys's performance is even more remarkable when we
know that privately he regarded the King's record as not deserving
the respect of the country. He becomes in effect a leading counsel
defending a client in whom he does not entirely believe.

Throughout the early stages, the Journal has Brereton, Colonel
Thomson and Pepys circling one another, meeting thrust with counter-thrust, evading awkward evidence and flashing into attack through
any available gap. The odds, however, were weighted heavily in
Pepys's favour, with the King in the chair ever ready to respond
to an appeal from what he quickly came to regard as his little champion
from the Navy Office, who had a boldness out of proportion to
his size and position. The enquiry took place while Sandwich was
in Madrid and his friends wrote to him urging him to return immediately or false evidence would prevail against him. A network of

varying alliances saw Coventry changing sides and attacking Sandwich as well as Penn.[42]

Presently, however, Sandwich, and Coventry, faded into the background in the Brooke enquiry, while Pepys held direct allegiance to the King, the Duke and the Stuart colours. Beyond that lay the rivalry between Colonel Thomson's support of the government in the First Dutch War and Pepys's defence of the new Navy Office in the Second. Pepys found it hard to treat Thomson's rivalry with civility and as Ollard succinctly puts it 'a successful rival was not to be endured'.[43] Early in the enquiry the King decided to accept the advice of Lord Arlington that it should all be taken down as a matter for historical record and Pepys seemed to be the ideal historian. Hence the main record we have is an account which lacks the intimacy of the Diary, but remains highly charged. Pepys's asides about personalities could be more crushing than the factual evidence, as when his adversaries came to swear to their papers on oath. Of Sir John Mennes, Pepys said that he had not seen one word of such papers but 'did the like'.[44]

One of the commission's charges was that the efficiency of the fleet had been impaired by putting the men on a lighter diet more suited to Mediterranean than European waters. Pepys answered the charges with a specious plea based on the presence of a number of supernumeraries aboard the ships; these were the wounded seamen who – extraordinarily – multiplied to the point where it was necessary to 'fling overboard much provisions'. His explanation in the *Journal* developed the point: 'Fleets come in for want, men mutinying and ye contractors but for the friendship some of them found had probably been hanged for it.'[45] That seemed to defeat his own argument but it apparently passed unnoticed. The enquiry pressed on and hardly a single aspect of naval affairs escaped the commission's charges.

Victualling, masts, timber, anchors, sails, pay, all were examined in such detail that there was great danger of bringing the enquiry to a halt from boredom. The spectacle of Pepys and Thomson engaged in a technical argument about whether masts were commonly measured from the butt or the partners (where the mast and deck met), had many observers on both sides of the argument close to yawning. Pepys summed up: 'If there is a new way of doing it that is better than the old then I know nothing of it.'[46] Masts, none the less, were a tricky issue and Pepys only escaped severe censure by sheer skill. Commissioner Pett had sworn in his evidence that the Board accepted a more expensive offer for masts than that of a rival firm. Moreover, Sir William Warren, Pett claimed, had received large payments of 'imprests' at a time when money was said to be unavailable, and these imprests were greater than those required by contract. Pepys adroitly switched the argument to the general question of if and when imprests should be paid at all, elaborating a web of detail which seemed to obscure the original issue. He then gave an analysis of the mast market, accusing the King of Sweden of creating a shortage by forbidding tree-felling for seven years and automatically sending prices soaring.[47]

At a certain stage in the proceedings it became clear that the attack on Carteret and the crown was losing its force and the commissioners decided to turn their fire on Pepys's documentary evidence – or 'Answer To Their Observations' – which he had by now elaborated. At this stage he wrote: 'I was extremely sick ... being I confess after so elaborate and elegant a discourse ... unwilling to expose myself to its contradicting.'[48] His new material was much more personal and attempted to justify his 'performance and uprightness'. By the very nature of its subject the paper was charged with self-righteousness and rose to proclaim: 'My conscience in its strictest retrospection charges me not with any wilful declension of my duty.'[49] Analysis of his own 'emoluments', a term which should have included fees as well as salary, revealed a man so modestly paid it would have surprised no one if he had surrendered to corruption. But did he? Knowing as we already do the fees, the occasional presents and the rewards of his privateering, the answer seems a foregone conclusion, but not for Pepys. The commissioners pointed to private trading by officers of the Navy and drew special attention to an item for £757.17.5¾d accepted by the Clerk of the Acts in 1664 for supplies. Pepys sidestepped rather than admitted the charge. Paid far less than the commissioners, Pepys was legally within his rights to accept perquisites which brought salary discrepancies into balance, but he had never invited the payment of fees, gratuities or rewards from anyone. Moreover, Pepys claimed, from the day he entered the service ten years before – and these the most valuable in his life – his estate had not increased by even as much as £1,000 from salary or perquisites. By 1669 his wealth had, in fact, become substantial. Bryant calls this a daring lie. The word 'daring' loads the evidence very much in Pepys's favour. Is a lie any less a lie for being daring? Most chroniclers of Pepys are partisan and criticism easily converts into praise as when an accurate piece of self-examination about cowardice becomes courageous personal insight.

Throughout the whole of the commission's enquiry several very telling charges are levelled against Pepys which he never directly answers. His encyclopaedic knowledge, swift mind and debating skills enabled him to mask his answers most convincingly. That Pepys felt uneasy about his performance by 6 January can be deduced from a letter he wrote to the King claiming that it was the previous Commonwealth administration which had been guilty of spendthrift behaviour, not the current Naval Office.[50] In the defensive language of previous chroniclers, it was once again an audacious reversal by Pepys of the commissioners' case. On the following Monday morning, before the commission met, Pepys casually remarked to the Duke of York that it would be wise to have Sir William Coventry support the evidence of the Navy Office, to which the Duke replied that it was 'too much in all conscience to loose both of them at once on the unfortunate commissioners'.[51] Questions about supplying masts to the Navy were repeated and took several dramatic turns. When Lord Brereton rose to underpin his charge about improper mast contracts Pepys came to his feet and swept into a lengthy oration which drove Brereton into a towering rage expressed in such unconstitutional language that the Duke of York personally rebuked him.[52] There is no doubt that the enquiry was biased by the presence of the Duke and the chairmanship of the King. They were interested parties and Pepys was clearly their advocate. Seen in that perspective, Pepys's performance loses some of its brilliance. For instance, when the commissioners produced an affidavit from 'the learned' Peter Pett to draw attention to the accumulation of unnecessary masts clogging the stores, Pepys complained that Pett personally should have confronted him with the charge. It was every Englishman's right in any other court. He then produced Pett's signed certificate confirming the contract which seemed conclusive. Pett returned the charge at once, claiming that competitors had offered the same masts at lower prices. The King then intervened with a piece of information available only to him. Their price, he revealed, was conditional on the suppliers being allowed to trade – simultaneously – with the enemy, an impossible proviso. This revelation struck the commissioners dumb according to Pepys.[53] Perhaps the commissioners did not dare question the august word of Charles. The next day Pepys was missing from his seat for the remarkable reason that he wanted to see a highwayman executed at Tyburn. Such a distraction in the middle of his own attempted execution may have made psychological sense but seemed dangerously irresponsible.

Back before the commissioners the next day, the question of paying seamen by ticket brought up the corrupt practice of purchasing discharged seamen's tickets at cut rates and re-selling them at a profit.

James Carcasse, originally a clerk in the ticket office, stated that Pepys had been involved in this practice. Pepys must have felt shaken because he had committed a related offence. He admitted in March 1668 that he had diverted money intended for paying seamen in the King's ships, to the crew of his own *Flying Greyhound*, jointly leased to Penn, Batten and himself. Carcasse had that day come to him with evidence of the charge and Pepys wrote: 'The thing upon recollection I believe is true and do hope no great matter of it'[54] as the commission swung into its stride. Then a member of the commission suddenly recalled – to Pepys's relief – that Carcasse was none other than a clerk he had dismissed from the ticket office for improper conduct.[55] It prepared the way for Pepys's defence, which assumed the character of an attack. Pepys had always regarded ticket-buying as despicable, seeking ways to act against its practitioners and pressing for reforms. His denial was couched in such vehement terms that Lord Brereton challenged him: 'Do you defy the whole world in this matter?' 'Yes,' Pepys reiterated, 'I do defy the whole world and My Lord Brereton in particular if he would be thought one of it.'[56]

Before the next hearing Pepys was warned that fresh evidence might wreak havoc on this defence. Entries in the Journal and Admiralty letters make this clear.[57] Lord Brereton did indeed produce a bombshell in the form of a ticket entered in the name of a seaman serving on the *Lion*, with a written inscription stating that it had been paid to Mr Pepys. Pepys replied that there must be an explanation of such a ticket but he did not know one. Realising the weakness of the answer, the King once more swayed the evidence in Pepys's favour by enquiring ironically whether a man handling hundreds of thousands of pounds would bother to incriminate himself for a trivial £7.10s. Later, Pepys was to take the trouble to write a letter to Anthony Stephens (Sir George Carteret's secretary), demanding an explanation. 'I do desire . . . you do transmit to me an impartial account of the whole in writing . . . that upon which I am to proceed in obtaining the right to myself.'[58] No reply survives.

Slowly, there creeps into the Brooke House Journal a touch of the tedium which began to invade the committee's proceedings. The King, the Duke of York, Pepys, the commissioners and witnesses were becoming bored with one another. Pepys's final speech was vehement. Two years of witch-hunting had produced a plethora of inadequate evidence and he was surprised that such an undertaking had been launched by people calling themselves gentlemen. Nothing was more calculated to create enemies and some of the commissioners never forgave him. In the end an element of surprise entered his successful conclusion of the whole affair and he commented in his *Naval Minutes*: 'Remember to reflect fully upon ... the ridiculous success of that terrible commission to Brooke House.'[59]

Chapter 15

Secretary to the Admiralty and MP

Pepys returned day after day to his Seething Lane house with Elizabeth no longer there to greet him. He had become used to her talk and reassurance. He now had very different company in Will Hewer, the servants and the cat.[1] Hewer had become so deeply part of Pepys's life it was almost as if they were blood relations, but he could hardly replace the warm embrace of Elizabeth or reproduce those moments of self-revelation such as had frequently occurred with his wife. The bickering and quarrels were nothing beside her living presence, and she was irreplaceable. There remains the possibility that his marriage had reached a state of stalemate which diminished the impact of her death. Whether this highly sexed man revelled in his new freedom is unknown.

Now thirty-seven years old he was at the height of his powers, a man of authority with widespread influence which extended far beyond the Navy Office. He mixed at ease on equal terms with men and women of distinction, and if they occasionally detected his humble beginnings, they relished the company of a man who talked so well and had such a zest for living.

What lay beneath the sparkling surface of his everyday self? He frequently revealed motivations normally concealed by others. His guilt, his cowardice, his capacity for rationalising, his self-deception, one after another they rise to the surface in the Diary of a richly complex man. Towering above it all was the mind which he considered the real core of a man, a truism with special meaning in his case.[2] For years now he had been a member of the Royal Society and found its proceedings fascinating. Unlike the court, he took its work seriously and recorded with distaste how the King laughed heartily at 'Gresham College for spending so much time only in weighing air ...'[3] Not that the King was anti-science. He dabbled in biology and his interest in anatomy drove him to request a dissection for his exclusive observation. The Royal Society prided itself upon its famous collection of instruments and Pepys was familiar with air pumps, microscopes and lodestones. Mixing freely with scientists who were laying the foundation for the new and exciting thinking of the coming centuries, Pepys encountered that high priest Sir Isaac Newton. Unfortunately, he gives us no pen-portraits of Newton, Hooke and Boyle. His struggles with Boyle's books were transient, perhaps because his cast of mind was alien to abstract thinking. The very profundity of Newton's thought also made it inaccessible. Pepys does not himself reflect in the Diary on the nature of the Universe and he is not temperamentally introspective.

There remains the charge that he left no portrait of these great men and failed to report even their social talk. His dalliance with science was out-matched by his interest in the arts, and in particular, music. 'Musique', he wrote, 'is the thing of the world that I love most. Musique and women I cannot but give way to ...'[4] The Diary passionately celebrates being sick with love of a woman – Elizabeth – and swept away into the ecstasy of music. His own musical accomplishments were considerable. He took his part as a 'bass' [bass baritone] in the choir of the Chapel Royal, he could play the viol, the violin, the lute, the therobo (a close cousin), and the flageolet. *theorbo* He made consistent attempts at composition and believed that he could make a contribution to musical theory.[5] None of this, however, went very deep. In Chapter Two of Bryant's excellent biography there is a six-page encomium of Pepys which seems to escape into hagiography. According to Bryant he was – fastidious; confident; sensitive; generous; dedicated; gentle; aesthetic; prudent; shrewd; and recoiled from wickedness and debauchery. [6] Taken as a whole, Bryant's volumes do not burke Pepys's shortcomings, but the early pages of the second volume come close to fashionable idolatry.

Bryant remarks halfway through his encomium that 'to some perhaps he seemed rather too near the angels', and briefly develops that qualification. This went hand-in-glove with a confidence which could sail through the Brooke House committee almost unscathed and thank God for his mercy in blessing Pepys with 'taking pains and being punctual in [his] dealings'.[7] Bryant states that 'in the whole of his life there is no record that he ever betrayed a trust' which brazenly ignores his behaviour towards Elizabeth.

However, his loyalty and consideration for his down-at-heel relations continued until his middle age. He frequently 'carried the burdens' of old servants and even helped their children when there remained no direct connection with his own affairs. John Evelyn paid tribute to his instances of 'your friendship and what I shall ever value your counsel'.[8] Experience had tempered the arrogant streak in Pepys's make-up and he was capable now of tenderness towards friends which sometimes brought him close to tears when he was parted from those closest to him. His charity expressed itself with a necessary prudence since his reputation for having a free purse had in some quarters produced inordinate demands upon it.[9]

A man who had survived the plague and the Fire of London, come through the Brooke House ordeal, faced the threat of the Tower and lost his wife, was inevitably a changed man. He tried now to practise Epictetus' precept that we should learn to co-operate with the inevitable,[10] but found it difficult. He continued to practise his old skill of condemning corruption in others while rationalising his own. His church attendances remained regular but escaped the dogma of belief with a touch of the *boulevardier* which distinguished his everyday life. His divinity now practised an admixture of benevolence and austerity, and constantly sought for order in a chaotic world like the best naval administrator. He had written in 1666: 'But Lord what a conflict I had with myself, my heart tempting me a thousand times to go abroad about some pleasure or other ... However, I reproached myself with my weakness in yielding ... and prevailed with difficulty but did not budge but stayed within and to my great content had a great deal of business.'[11] This conflict troubled him again in 1670. The picture would be incomplete without including the constant efforts he made to help his brother-in-law Balty, his younger brother, John, and Elizabeth's impoverished parents. Having set Balty up as muster master in Deal, Pepys next, by intense lobbying with the Duke of York and Lord Sandwich, ensured John's appointment as clerk of Trinity House.

His activities on behalf of the Chatham Chest affected the lives of ordinary seamen for years to come. He wrote to the governors of the Chest: 'As there are few things wherein I do desire to be found useful so I have in nothing been more affected for my unusefulness than my relation to the Chest.'[12] Established by Hawkins and Drake after their spectacular defeat of the Armada, the Chest provided funds for sick and aged seamen with every employed sailor contributing 6d a month from his wages. Embroiled in the general corruption of naval finances the Fund frequently found its coffers dangerously depleted. In July 1671 there was a new crisis in the Fund's affairs and this saw Pepys searching for money from any available source. One such source was the ex-Navy Treasurer, the Earl of Anglesey, who had illegally withheld £3,000 due to the Fund. This

malpractice stopped the annual distribution of money and led to
elderly and disabled seamen making their way – painfully – to London
from all over the country to meet refusal when they arrived. Letters
from Pepys to Anglesey invoked the cunning piety of that gentleman.
He replied to Pepys late in 1672: 'I need not tell you how much
I was surprised ... to find him who was cash keeper acknowledge
a remain due and not have ready the money when the occasion
is so pressing.'[13] In short, his debtor's failure to pay him rendered
Lord Anglesey unable to refund the missing £3,000. On the same
day Pepys wrote to Anglesey: 'I perceive by Your Lordship's this
afternoon that which the Board found necessary to write to Your
Lordship since dinner was not come to your hand wherein you will
find that I have already been obliged to engage myself for £800
for the Chest ... More than this I am not in a condition at this
time to do.'[14] This was hardly borne out by his bank account, through
which in the previous year £43,000 had passed in no small part
due to Hewer's stewardship, but such quibbles are irrelevant. He
did noble service for ailing seamen and was genuinely concerned
for their welfare. His was one of the first voices to suggest pensioning
off 'maimed or decayed' seamen. In general, we return to a richly
complex person with now one, now another characteristic rising
to dominate, but never to destroy that underlying warmth and zest
for living which embraced pleasure, friends, companionship, music
and even those who sometimes made his life a burden. Pepys was,
at heart, a simple man – but grandly simple.

A new figure had appeared in his life by 1670 to give another
expression to his inner self. The merest outline of her life and personality are known. Mary Skinner was the daughter of a city merchant
whose business had suffered one setback after another until even
his respectability became threatened. Admiring Pepys and no doubt
pleased to have such a distinguished friend, he assumed that his
daughter's relationship with him was non-sexual. One of seven children baptised in St Olaf's parish between 1655 and 1668, she would
have been a girl in her late teens when he met her and as such
irresistible to him. Regarded by his neighbours as a rich widower
who received and sometimes entertained many distinguished people,
Pepys now epitomised respectability. His salary had risen from £350
to £500 but his wealth came mainly from the 25s payment which
he received for each pass granted to a ship trading in the Mediterranean. Since at least a thousand ships applied every year paying 25s
each, it was a lucrative source of income paid directly in hard cash.

Externally, his Seething Lane house preserved its courtyard garden, with the roof top on which he could walk of a summer evening, but inside the furniture had luxuriated and his library had developed in all directions. To the outside world the now middle-aged, somewhat dumpy figure of Pepys enshrined the virtues of a public man and it came as a shock to Mary Skinner's parents to suspect that he had become their daughter's lover. More dangerous from Pepys's point of view, at the same time he became friendly with her brother Daniel who had once been secretary to the radical poet Milton. Daniel was deeply in debt and suspected of writing mischievous pieces against the Church.[15] The evidence for Pepys's seduction of Mary is in a letter written in Latin by Mary's brother Daniel describing the breach in Pepys's relationship with the family. Daniel wrote that:

it was no small damage . . . in the course of relations which took place
between you [when] you violated my sister. But whether these
allegations fit in your case, or you can have deserved these reproaches
which parents are most ready to offer under such circumstances as these,
it is not my place to examine . . . Whatever the mischance was which
at all events caused me extreme pain, the consequences fell upon me
alone in as much as your friendship which I have regarded as among
my most valuable assets was broken and destroyed.[16]

The timing of the episode would perfectly fit the circumstances of his life. According to his will he had known Mrs Skinner for thirty-three years, taking us back to 1670, the year after his wife died leaving him griefstricken and lonely. Mary Skinner slowly became an important figure in his life and if she did not replace Elizabeth in Pepys's eyes, their relationship was close, possibly tender, certainly enduring.

Pepys's double standards had allowed him to womanise indiscriminately but he recoiled from the idea of living openly with Mary unblessed by the Church. Lord Brouncker had suffered in the Diary for just such indulgence and it quickly became evident that something prevented Pepys from marrying Mary. There were several possible explanations. His friendship with Mary's brother linked him in some eyes with the revolutionary ideology of Milton and that was highly undesirable; Mary revealed a lack of scholarship in letters which she later wrote for Pepys; Elizabeth was still too fresh in his mind for final commitment to anyone else; or Mary simply did not attract him enough. Suspected as their daughter's lover, Pepys found his relations with the Skinner family strained if not broken, but his affair deepened to the point where Mary became his resident housekeeper. Whether she was subjected to the same infidelities as Elizabeth we do not know, but the absence of the marriage tie must have encouraged Pepys in habitual indulgences. For many of his friends she quickly became his wife and Robert Hooke, the scientist, referred to her as such in his Diary.[17]

There emerged in Pepys's early relationship with Mary a mellowing man who was less combative, less embarrassed by his new consort's small peccadilloes. She was much younger and not accustomed to the distinguished company he kept. Whether she accompanied him to official dinners or celebrations is uncertain, but she certainly mingled freely with his friends who included Evelyn, Sir Christopher Wren, Hooke and Sir Robert Southwell. Ollard believed that Sandwich had launched Pepys, Coventry developed him and Evelyn added the cultural gloss which marked him out from ordinary naval administrators. Evelyn cherished ambitions to sit with him on the Navy Board, and when the honoraries expressed astonishment at such aspirations, he wrote to Pepys: 'I might yet perhaps have been subservient to such a *genius* as Mr Pepys and by his direction and converse not altogether an unprofitable member.'[18] Evelyn continues to move in and out of Pepys's life at many levels and in February 1671 he entertained him with Wren and Hooke.

Once again great events were reaching a climax which took over Pepys's preoccupation with his private life. An elaborate conspiracy involving Charles II's sister Minette had led to the Duke of Buckingham visiting Paris in 1670 empowered to sign a secret treaty with France. Simultaneously, Sir Thomas Clifford, First Lord of the Admiralty, collaborated with Sir George Downing, ambassador to the Dutch, to make impossible demands on the Dutch. The plan was for the French to attack the Dutch on land backed by the English at sea, a combined operation which nothing could stop. By the end of 1671 Europe was in a state of general alarm, aware of Louis XIV's one hundred and thirty thousand troops ready to carry out the grand design. English maritime activities had not passed unnoticed either.

Charles suddenly found himself confronted by a group of recalcitrant bankers demanding payment of their £2,500,000 debt, without which no more money would be advanced for any undertaking whatever. One party blackmailed the other until the King employed the audacious Sir Thomas Clifford to suspend payment of the bankers' assignments, prepare for any necessary liquidation and fix interest rates at six per cent. Panic ran through the city with the bankers refusing all payments and seizing the deposits of private merchants. National bankruptcy was imminent when the resourceful Charles sent for the bankers and managed to reassure them that their debts and interest would be paid in full whatever happened.[19] Within a few days £750,000 was made available, preparations for setting out the fleet were begun with great urgency, and Pepys was found in the middle of all these events.[20] Dutch attempts to negotiate a peace settlement were brushed aside and the government was committed to war. Ordinary seamen who hated everything Dutch actually volunteered to man the ships to Pepys's surprise.

While the snow lay thick outside his office window, Pepys drew up a balance sheet which showed – in his precise figures – a sum of £1,337,292.9s. required by the Navy to pay off its debts and maintain twenty-three thousand men. By the end of January, with the help of the bankers and the French King, all the first-, second- and third-rate ships were said to be ready for sea but that proved to be over-optimistic. Hatred of the Dutch was not enough to produce fully manned ships and ruthless pressing took into its net labourers and riggers from the yards. By 3 March 1672 a fleet of eleven ships put to sea. Theoretically, Holland was an easy prey for the combined navies of France and England, but the perfidy with which the English now broke all the rules and openly attacked the Dutch merchantmen reaped an unfortunate consequence.[21] What first appeared to be a lucrative haul of six prizes at little cost was revealed by the official report as an expensive exploit. The Dutch had put up a tremendous fight and the prizes taken by the English cost them many killed and wounded, with rigging and sometimes masts severely damaged. All this before any open declaration of war, which shocked Evelyn and was for him 'worthy of reproach'.[22] The pretext for the attack given in Pepys's Diary was the Dutch Admiral's omission to strike his flag when the English ship *Merlin* passed through his lines. 'Surely this was a quarrel slenderly grounded and not becoming Christian neighbours,' Evelyn wrote.[23]

Always a compassionate man, he went to visit the Dutch wounded and left a graphic description:

Having seen that morning my chirurgeon cut off a poor creature's leg
. . . first cutting the living and untainted flesh above the gangrene . . .
and then sawing off the bone in an instant; then with searing and stoopes
staunching the blood which issued abundantly; the stout and gallant
man enduring it with incredible patience and that without being bound
to his chair as usual . . . What confusion and mischief does the avarice,
anger and ambition of princes cause in the world who might be happier
with half they possess: this stout man was but a common sailor.[24]

The three nations were now close to full-scale war, but the English went about their business unmoved while the sound of guns echoed back from the Channel. Presently, the Declaration of Indulgence by the King astounded some and dismayed others. Given the French alliance, it seemed the most inappropriate moment to relax the laws against Roman Catholics and Dissenters. A new upsurge of anti-Catholic feeling broke out which reached such menacing proportions that the King was forced to withdraw the Declaration.

Religious intolerance has frequently undermined enlightened legislation and the King's aim to please all sects including the Catholics might have changed the course of British history. The passion it aroused can be judged by the reaction of Evelyn, the most tolerant of men, who gave a satirical account of the French ambassador's representation of Christ which he displayed to Londoners from the window of his residence at Somerset House.[25] Faced with such hostility the King not only withdrew the Declaration but passed the Test Act which debarred Roman Catholics from holding any office of profit under the crown.[26] The Duke of York did not hesitate to admit his Catholicism and immediately resigned from the office of Lord High Admiral. The powers of this office had steadily declined because the King, in his anxiety to keep the Navy under his control, had constantly intervened administratively. These events were to change the direction of Pepys's career, but for the moment he and Hewer were struggling to meet the demands of a Navy which was, once more, inadequately equipped despite protestations from merchants and suppliers to the contrary.

The fleet at last mustered at Spithead and the King carried out a royal inspection of one hundred ships and thirty-four thousand men – a spectacle witnessed by the ever observant Evelyn: 'The Duke of York with his and the French squadron in all one hundred and seventy ships of which above one hundred men-of-war sailed by ... Such a gallant and formidable Navy never I think spread sail upon the seas; it was [a] goodly yet terrible sight to behold them.'[27] Charles II launched into the Third Dutch War with the audacious idea of asserting Britain's sovereignty over the seas. It was an old-fashioned concept which Pepys regarded as a great risk, if not an actual abuse of naval power. Pepys recognised that this was in fact simply a war to develop Britain's trade routes, with the international power games taking second place. At the outset the Dutch attempted to prevent the English joining the French fleet and confronting De Ruyter with an overwhelming force. Daring as ever, De Ruyter sailed out of his sand dunes with no more than seventy ships and reached the mouth of the Thames, but he arrived too late.[28] The French and English ships had already merged and were waiting for him, only to lose contact when fog came down. Against the King's advice, the Anglo-French fleet then put into Southwold Bay.[29] While the rival fleets were trying to outwit one another to gain the advantage of surprise and position, Pepys dictated a stream of memos from his office in an attempt to acquit his colleagues of once more under-supplying the ships. Indeed, a quick and minor enquiry took place into their shortcomings under the Committee for Foreign Affairs from which Pepys again emerged unscathed. Fiercely engaged in this enquiry, Pepys sat in his office day after day unable to escape the stream of questions which included some from Prince Rupert, ever ready to exploit the slightest scrap of evidence against him.

The allied fleet was at last confronted by the formidable De Ruyter in Sole Bay on 28 May 1672. Numbers of English seamen were still enjoying carousals in Southwold, which meant that the fleet was undermanned. Seamen were ordered on pain of death to complete their crews, but 'several skulked away and hid about the town'.[30] These confusions were compounded when the Duke's squadron led by Sandwich sailed northward and the French – inexplicably – moved south. Questions later arose about such tactics but for the moment no fleet was in the desired position. The battle which followed put to the test the 'formal' and 'mêlée' principles which conditioned naval warfare at the time, both believing in an orderly approach to the enemy, subject to variation once contact was made. The forma-list school believed in massing at a decisive point a superior force capable of breaking the enemy's lines. The alternative school set one half of the fleet sailing round the enemy's flank preserving the other half for a frontal attack. This maintained a carefully calculated order without allowing the free play of individual initiative. Given 'preponderance' at a selected point, the mêlée school believed in abandoning concerted manœuvres with each ship independently aim-ing at a knock-out.[31] Sandwich found himself trapped between the two theories. When his leading ships overran the advancing Dutch, he used the third formalist tactic of going behind the Dutch fleet to take the strain off hard-pressed Prince Rupert. 'Jordan, the officer leading the "doublers"; seems to have mistimed this blow ... Sailing too far down the back of the enemy's line, he attacked the Dutch centre as it engaged the Duke in the English centre.'[32] Thus the formalist Duke, driven to abandon his cherished tactics, converted to mêlée practices which ended in temporary disaster. The flagship of the fleet, the *Royal James*, was sunk, and Lord Sandwich went down with it to his death. Forebodings of death had haunted Sand-wich for some time and the night before the battle, dining in Mr

Digby's ship, he 'showed a gloomy discontent so contrary to his usual cheerful humour'.[33] There are many versions of the last moments of the *Royal James* but none gives a clear account of Sandwich's death. Bryant draws a dramatic picture of a great fireship emerging out of the roar of fire and smoke 'disguised as a battleship with blue guns and dummy men' to crash into the *Royal James* which finally exploded and 'flew into the air', but this is not borne out by Montagu's biography of Sandwich. Montagu claims that Sandwich waited until the *James* was almost burnt out and threw himself into the sea.[34] All day from the cliffs above Southwold knots of people watched the flames flare and die until the *Royal James* was a silent hulk in a calm sea on a beautiful summer night.[35]

Despite this disaster the Dutch were eventually driven to retreat towards their own coast. But fog and lack of shot forced the English to give up the chase. Losses in the end were said to be evenly divided, but the English had set out with the idea of victory and now neither side could claim success. The Dutch had the reassurance that sufficient numbers of their fleet had survived adequately to protect the coasts of Holland and that in itself was a remarkable feat against such odds. Pepys continued working frantically throughout the engagement with news filtering through uncertainly. Not until 10 June was Sandwich's swollen body, still decorated with the Star of the Garter, found by a ketch and brought to lie in splendour by the King's order at Deptford.[36] There followed on 3 July the pomp and ceremony of the funeral procession up the Thames with a last salute from the Tower guns before the cortege arrived at Westminster.[37] Pepys was amongst the group of distinguished mourners who watched Sandwich's body pass through the double file of the King's Guard to be met by the Dean.

Pepys had another reason for sadness. The Duke of York's secretary, Matthew Wren, had been badly wounded at Sole Bay and his recovery remained in doubt, leaving his job vacant and vulnerable. It reawakened an old ambition in Pepys. He had for some time coveted the secretaryship and now he persuaded Sir William Coventry to write to the Duke of York on his behalf. Unfortunately, Coventry's nephew, Harry Savile, was already appointed as Wren's deputy and Coventry felt that he could not intervene. Those in the know assumed that Pepys would win the appointment and some wrote to congratulate him in the beginning of a chain of embarrassments.

In the background of his personal struggle the war had taken a new and decisive turn, and Pepys was overwhelmed with work to put a battered fleet back to sea once more. News from Holland created mixed feelings in England. The French assault on Dutch towns led to capitulation one by one, but the first delight in England was tempered by the spectacle of 'a nation of free Protestants' surrendering to Catholic authority. The smouldering dislike of the French, never entirely extinguished, was enflamed again and crusty Admiral Spragge immortally enshrined in it the words, 'the French who will never be as they ought to be'.

Bad weather dogged the English fleet as it cruised off the Dutch coast for two weeks without coming in sight of the enemy. By the third week the weather had torn sails and rigging, damaged cables and bowsprits and reduced the crews to a sorry state of sickness. It was decided to run for home, and on 23 August a depressed King went down to greet the Duke of York who told a tale of battered ships and men so weary that 'they had scarcely ... energy enough to weigh anchor'. A witness wrote: 'I never saw people so intolerably weary.'[38] One depressing fact crowded upon another to dampen any ardour for further expeditions. The victualling stores were empty, the victuallers clamouring for unpaid accounts, the seamen's wages bill at bursting point, with £340,000 due within a few months, and the press gangs reduced to gutter scrounging. Caring for the sick and wounded always proved difficult, but now the number of cases choked the southeastern ports. Evelyn drew a pitiful picture of their plight and Pepys's difficulties were only minimally reduced by the efforts of his brother-in-law, Balty. Work invaded his sleeping hours and he became accustomed to calls by night with fresh cases that had to be dealt with immediately. The fates seemed to combine to defeat the Anglo-French plans, bad weather driving the fleet home in disarray, while the Dutch forces stiffened their resolve and held back the French on land.

Meanwhile, Pepys's fortunes at home changed. Behind the international scene the small drama of Pepys's ambition to become secretary to the Duke of York reached a new stage when Harry Saville lived up to his reputation and proved unsatisfactory in the role. At first, a second candidate was selected in preference to Pepys – a young diplomat called John Werden – regarded by Pepys as a nincompoop in naval affairs. On 22 June Pepys wrote to his brother-in-law Balty complaining of some slight illness and warned him 'that diligence and integrity is [sic] not always defence enough against censure', referring obliquely to his loss of the secretaryship.[39] Luck, however, was with Pepys. Success in the struggle for the Duke's secretaryship would have denied him a much more influential post which now came within his grasp. The most distinguished casualty of Charles II's

Test Act was James, Duke of York, the Lord High Admiral, who could not easily disavow his Catholic beliefs. One Sunday morning after the Test Act had been passed, members of the Chapel Royal crowded to see whether the Duke of York would join his brother at communion. The Duke's seat remained vacant, and Charles was able to put out of commission the office of Lord High Admiral, creating the new Committee of the Navy. All the great officers of state sat on the Committee but Charles reserved for himself the powers he had filched from James over recent years and became not only First Lord of the Admiralty, but his own Lord High Admiral, retaining the perquisites of both offices.[40] There remained a major difficulty. Not one of the distinguished gentlemen attending Board meetings had anything more than a superficial grasp of naval affairs. The solution seemed to be with Samuel Pepys whose knowledge and skills were becoming legendary. Charles duly appointed him Secretary of the Board of the Admiralty, quite unaware that Pepys would not only reconstitute the Navy Board but create that all-powerful and majestic office which became known as the Admiralty. Once appointed, he began to plan the great reforms which were to convert naval posts into clearly defined ranks requiring specific qualifications. 'We can still watch the indefatigable little Secretary engaged upon this moulding of posts into the rough cast of "ranks" yet with no clear idea of what he was doing.'[41]

There was a clear distinction between the new-born Admiralty and the Navy Board. The Admiralty was essentially political, which explained why Charles, who believed in the absolute power of sovereignty, never relinquished any important part of its control voluntarily. The Navy Board was almost exclusively concerned with the supply and maintenance of naval material although occasional sallies into politics became essential to preserve its boundaries. Pepys, who kept meticulous records, believed in creating order out of chaos and exercised remarkable administrative skills, was not only the perfect candidate for the job but, in effect, the first civil servant. Within a short time, following the example of Charles, he had centralised control of the Navy Board and organised a weekly meeting with the Admiralty at eight o'clock on Saturday mornings.[42] The sacred English weekend had not yet been conceived and the Admiralty Board was accustomed to assemble – irregularly – three times a week. When Pepys took over, the Admiralty had no postal address but was enshrined in the person of the Lord High Admiral and his three secretaries. It seemed a natural consequence of Pepys's appointment that the Board should begin meeting at the Navy Board's offices in Seething Lane, but in January of 1673 a fire broke out in Lord Brouncker's lodgings which spread to the Navy Office.[43] Temporary accommodation was found in ancient Trinity House, but this was unsatisfactory and soon the Board moved to a Council Chamber at Derby House on the river between Whitehall Palace and West-minster.[44] Pepys arrived once a week to confront a vast green table surrounded by candelabra, silver standishes and ornate chairs, with heavy velvet curtains, portraits, rich hangings and a display of world power conveyed by spheres, maps and charts contributing to an impressive background.[45] When the King himself took the chair, it was one of the most distinguished gatherings in the kingdom. Somewhere – feigning a modesty he no longer felt – sat squat little Pepys, the man manipulating vital strings in the whole naval puppet show. Certainly, his power and prestige had increased to the point where the court, Parliament and Navy had to take cognisance of his views and people as eminent as Sir William Coventry now asked him for favours.[46]

Much of his work was far less grand and positively domestic in his early days. Ollard gives details of a typical day on 25 September 1673 which began with a letter releasing two commandeered fishing smacks, followed by a warning to a privateer owner anxious to have his vessel employed by the Board and a memo agreeing to honour a bill for stores. Pepys took more serious matters in his stride: allegations of cowardice, false excuses for delaying return to service and encouragement to depressed captains. No longer responsible for the details of shipping equipment he now superintended these operations, which were carried out by others. He still found time to expose malingerers, and demands for pressing men into service were balanced by warnings about too much zealotry. His principal responsibility once again came to the fore with the fleet now under the exuberant command of Prince Rupert waiting to be commissioned and sent to sea. This was achieved on 19 July, but the results were discouraging.

All buccaneering panache, Rupert set out for the Dutch coast but the wily De Ruyter carefully manœuvred his ships, choosing the right moment to launch his attack. The battle was short and sharp and gave little satisfaction to either side. Sir Edward Spragge behaved with the indomitable courage which was expected of his kind and died shifting his flag from ship to ship as each threatened to sink under him.[47] Yet again the French were accused of failing to play their part and the English exploded with predictable wrath. The King, accompanied by Pepys, travelled down to welcome home a fleet once more subdued but seething with rage. Peace negotiations began, for both nations by now were tired of the expense of running battles which resolved nothing. The Dutch took advantage of the lull to launch sporadic attacks on British merchantmen and drove the East India Company to propose a system of convoys quickly implemented by Pepys.

It became clear from the mass of Admiralty letters that Pepys's decisions in this matter would have been subject to the King's imprimatur. Pepys was in fact accused by a number of people of toadying to the King: there were stories, for example, about Pepys submitting the appointment of a mere cook for His Majesty's approval. Meticulous in some details, the King remained cavalier in others. He was quite capable of granting commissions on the spur of the moment, without reference to competence, and this infuriated Pepys. Yet Pepys seldom, if ever, expressed anger against the King and his criticism when it occurred was always balanced by praise, as in the naval minutes: 'He understood the business of the sea better than any prince the world ever had.' He 'sported himself with the ignorance of the commissioners and was pleased to declare to me his dependence ... upon my service to keep them right'.[48]

As we have seen, the year 1673 was not an easy year for Pepys. Over a million pounds in debt, the Navy Board struggled with a jungle of creditors, among them seamen, whose discharge tickets remained unhonoured. They threatened to burn down the Navy Office, Pepys and all his vainglorious array of papers. Balty, his brother-in-law, struggled to meet the clamour of unpaid householders who had sheltered the sick and wounded. Politically, Pepys ran into trouble when he decided to stand for Parliament because a distant suspicion of sympathy with Popery was now exaggerated out of all proportion by the rival candidate in Castle Rising, Otley. Why did a man like Pepys, unaccustomed to the rough and tumble of a sometimes brawling House of Commons, want to become an MP? Mainly, he wrote to Sir William Coventry, it was so that the House would have someone who could adequately defend the Navy.[49] No hint of a desire for power appeared in a letter surprisingly addressed to his former rival for the Duke of York's secretaryship. Status meant a great deal to him and MPs carried more weight in those days than they do now. Pepys worked diligently preparing the ground for his candidacy in letters which enshrined the orotund convolutions of his writing skills. Disentangling meaning from the interlocking phrases, complicated by elaborate ingratiation, demands concentration. One such letter to Lord Howard opened:

Having by His Royal Highness's appointment understood His Highness recommending me with success to Your Lordship for the Burgess-ship of Riseing upon the expected removal of Sir Robert Paston to the House of Lords I hold it my duty to make this my humble and thankful acknowledgement of it to Your Lordship. Not that I dare imagine Your Lordship's favour to me therein arises from any other consideration than that of my being an humble creature of His Royal Highness.[50]

Similar letters to the Earl of Norwich pleaded that only the Duke his master's desire could have justified the presumption of his ambition to become a member of the House, by which ambition he was duly embarrassed.[51] Mr Otley now summoned all his forces to destroy Pepys's reputation insisting that he 'was a bluddy Papist'. He organised public demonstrations against him with a rabble of soldiery led by a band.[52] Thus when Pepys first arrived at Castle Rising, the Mayor and burgesses interlaced their polite reception with religious interrogation. In the seventeenth century only certain classes of people had the right to vote and they were more impressed with the recommendation of the Earl of Norwich than by Otley's smear campaign.

When Parliament reassembled in January 1674 Pepys was among its Members representing Castle Rising. On the same day, 7 January, Otley laid a petition on the clerk's table of the House implicating the Catholic Duke of York in Pepys's election.[53] Simultaneously, Lord Shaftesbury was dismissed from office and his supporters rallied round the petition claiming that Shaftesbury had actually seen a crucifix and altar set up in Pepys's house. Anti-Catholic feeling steadily mounted and presently its organisers demanded a Committee of Enquiry on which, fortunately, one of the three members was Sir William Coventry. While the enquiry rumbled on, Pepys underwent his first baptism of Parliamentary fire when two MPs challenged him with supplying cables and anchors to the French in the middle of the war. Pepys had, in fact, strongly resented the cable transfer but was overridden by the King. Cross-questioned in the House he admitted that he had countersigned the warrants as Secretary of the Admiralty, but was not responsible for the actual decision.[54] The second attack involved the time-honoured process of pressing men for the fleet. Lord Cavendish presented a signed document from a group of officers belonging to the merchant navy who asserted that they were pressed into service illegally. Pepys seems to have summoned the full force of his personality to deny the charge and one MP came to his feet to call him 'cocksure'. Exchanges steadily became more heated until Pepys declared that if the time-honoured principle of pressing were abandoned, no British fleet would ever put to sea fully manned. The argument seemed incontestable but now outbursts were directed more at his personality than his argument. Members of Parliament had followed with fascination his defeat of the Brooke House commissioners and were anxious to avoid a similar humiliation at his hands in the House of Commons.[55]

Pepys now suffered a dramatic reversal of fortune. The Committee of Elections and Privileges made public its enquiry into his election and declared it null and void. This was engineered by one of Lord Shaftesbury's supporters who maliciously exaggerated the charge of guilt by association into full-blown Popery. He made his case unequivocally with blatant lies. All these years, he claimed, Pepys had remained a secret Papist with ceremonies performed behind closed doors in his house. These practices 'had nearly broken his wife's heart because she refused to turn Papist'.[56] The Diary revealed the opposite. It was Pepys who had suspected his wife of Catholic sympathies. Searching for corroborative evidence he wrote to Balty who replied with a long, reassuring letter. Elizabeth's father had once said to him that her marriage to Pepys had quite 'blown out her Popery'.[57] Balty's testimony went for nothing in the House, but an aroused Pepys demanded to face his accusers in person and Colonel Birch supported him. He pointed out, with great vehemence, that all the evidence was nothing but hearsay. Undaunted, Sir Robert Thomas, one of Shaftesbury's lieutenants, repeated the charge and Garroway, a Country Party MP, retold the story of Pepys breaking his wife's heart. Asked once again whether he had an altar and crucifix in his house, Pepys vehemently denied it. He was in fact lying because a crucifix in the seventeenth century was sometimes a mere representation and Pepys did have such a picture of a crucifix.[58] Sir William Coventry re-entered the argument and the Speaker was forced to ask him to name his witnesses. It came as a shock to the whole House to learn that evidence of the crucifix came from Lord Shaftesbury himself, which first shook Pepys and his supporters and then drove them to demand Lord Shaftesbury's appearance before the House.[59] As a member of the House of Lords it was within Shaftesbury's power to refuse this order and he did so. He then wrote explaining that dim memories of a long-forgotten visit to Pepys's house were not material to which he could swear on oath.[60] When the committee finally interrogated Shaftesbury he denied seeing an altar in Pepys's house and was so imprecise that any threat to Pepys from his evidence disappeared.

At this point Pepys gave such a forceful account of his life as a devoted civil servant and practising Protestant that it should have convinced everyone. As he recounted his attempts to communicate with Shaftesbury he was 'almost incoherent in … anger' and this seemed to turn the tide in his favour. The question of the veracity in his accusers was now overtaken by the much less serious one of how far gentlemen should go in abusing one another. At this point the debate was adjourned until late February and by that time the House prorogued itself with no vote taken on Pepys's case. It left Pepys somewhat precariously in possession of his seat, but his expenses defending it were out of all proportion to what he expected. He had still to survive another skirmish, minor in substance, but damaging to his integrity. Thomas Povey, the former Treasurer of Tangier, had an agreement with Pepys that when Pepys became Treasurer, Povey remained entitled to half any fees paid. Povey first wrote to Pepys asking whether any profit had accrued and Pepys gave him 'no other satisfaction than a sullen and uncomfortable return'. Pepys claimed that he had made 'no other profits but from the bare salary'. Povey then wrote again asking for further information.[61] Pepys had, in fact, received for the pay of the garrison £852,573.1s and had claimed – but not yet received – £28,007.2s 1d in fees. He wrote the kind of angrily defensive letter to Povey which characterises a guilty party and revealed once more his occasional skill at parading guilt as innocence.[62] Maybe, he said, he had taken some trifling profits, but not enough to make him Povey's debtor. Compounding his guilt the concluding paragraph of his letter delivered a schoolmaster's reprimand to Povey: 'Let us have no more of this sort of correspondence between us.' The final insult to Povey came with a payment of fifty guineas on account.[63]

These were uncomfortable days for Pepys. The Povey affair remained minor but the House of Commons exchanges left him with a sense of insecurity. Since there is no descriptive record of his behaviour as an MP we have to rely upon the truncated reports of his speeches in Grey's *Debates*, and these do not convey the same flair which he displayed before the Brooke House committee. A judicial enquiry carried out under relatively strict rules was very different from the hurly-burly of the House of Commons. An outraged sense of honour in the House could lead to a duel and even death, but wide licence was allowed before such extravagances really threatened. Pepys had shown that he could think swiftly on his feet, present a well argued case and strike hard when roused, but the constant interruptions of Parliamentary proceedings did not encourage his gift for exposition. This characterised a second enquiry into his professional life conducted under conditions where few holds were barred.

In the international scene negotiations were moving towards a peace treaty between the Dutch and English which was ratified by the Dutch on 20 February 1678. Intended as a preliminary to a more complicated agreement, it never reached ratification in England. The suave and disingenuous King Charles had no real desire for such an alliance and used the treaty as a means of playing for time.[64]

Chapter 16

Reorganising the Navy –
Colonel Scott appears

Pepys's reflections on the nature of the British Navy reveal an ambitious vision of the fleet keeping the peace on the international high seas, but the ships at his disposal were totally inadequate for such a purpose. His vision had arisen as the result of raids launched from the ports of North Africa which not only seized with impunity richly laden ships, but even invaded the Channel to kidnap innocent inhabitants off the Devon coastline and carry them off to slavery. In a burst of misplaced patriotism the Tangier Commission had built an artificial harbour at Tangier hoping to control the piracy. Pepys, as Treasurer of the Commission, took a special interest in its activities, but the situation steadily worsened. As he recorded in the naval minutes: 'Our policy [is] quite altered, our neighbours being so much stronger than before and there being a quite different use and service for men-of-war now than there was then ...'[1]

The development of the English Navy had widespread implications. Not only North Africa but Holland, France and Spain changed their policies when they realised that England could defend its trade routes from the Atlantic down to the African coasts. In the event, the establishment and supply of squadrons in foreign stations presented huge problems. One of these problems – discipline – proved highly intractable. Once a captain had left his home base and was no longer in communication with the Navy Board or Admiralty he became a law unto himself. The Navy was riddled with piratical abusers of privilege and captains were found loitering for months in port when they should have been at sea; others used their ships to carry contraband merchandise for which they were richly paid. Fraternising amongst officers, gross insubordination, abuse of power, dereliction of duty, every kind of deviation was, to the distress of Pepys, widely practised.

In the summer of 1674 under the influence of the new Treasurer,

Osborne, it was proposed that the expenditure granted to the Navy should be reduced to £200,000. This immediately inspired the ship-builder Sir Anthony Deane, a survivor of many past disputes, to urge the building of new ships in readiness for any fresh outbreak of war. Pepys replied that the King was more disposed to get out of past debts than to create new ones. He admitted that the Navy was not capable of tackling the Dutch without the aid of the French and this saddened him, but the immediate climate was not propitious for Deane's proposal.

J. S. Corbett has given a vivid account of the need for expanding the Navy when the North Africans, led by the Dey of Algiers, launched a number of attacks on shipping, and Pepys's friend in the East India Company complained to him of growing depredations.[2] Sir John Narborough was sent in the *Henrietta* to reinforce the few ships operating in the Straits and he opened negotiations with the Dey. The trouble began in the autumn of 1674, but by March of 1675 the Dey was still evasive and piracy continued. The latest dispatches arrived when the King and court were at Newmarket, whereupon Pepys promptly joined them and in the middle of horse-racing extracted a decision from His Majesty. Narborough was to cut short diplomatic niceties and deliver an ultimatum to the Dey: either the piracy ceased or the King would open hostilities. When it came to reinforcing Narborough's squadron Pepys was forced to fit out and victual frigates of the fourth and fifth rate which were not best suited to the purpose. The clamour of the merchants and the lack of first-rate ships reinforced Deane's claim for new ships. Pepys now changed his mind and supported Deane's proposal. 'On April 22nd Mr Pepys was ordered to bring to the House a true statement of the condition of the Navy and supplies.'[3] He went to work far into the night producing a re-examination of the fleet which revealed twenty ships in a sad state of repair and many others in need of modernisation. France and Holland were not only rapidly expanding their fleet, but modernising them with stronger sides and better fire power. They constituted another and quite different threat to peace. Deane offered Pepys the benefit of his brilliant technical knowledge and managerial skills, and together they reassessed the requirements of the Navy. Armed with a new prospectus Pepys then addressed Parliament with what he thought to be an irrefutable case. His first attempt to railroad the House into agreement failed dismally. One opponent argued that his figures showed nothing to be wrong with the Navy and another, Sir Thomas Meres, said that he was prepared to lay his hand on his purse in order to preserve what it contained.

The debate gave way to side issues and, before anything useful could be resolved, Parliament was prorogued.

A brief interlude at Portsmouth nearly led to the death of King Charles. He had travelled to Portsmouth intent on launching a new ship, the *Royal James*, and immediately after the ceremony he boarded the *Greyhound* homeward bound for London. A storm blew up and the ship was lost all night at sea to the alarm of his retinue which included Pepys. Not until the following morning did fires appear on the hills beyond the Solent announcing the King's safe return. Anthony Deane had specially designed the *Royal James* and when the King returned to Portsmouth he knighted him for his services. It remains a mystery why Pepys was never knighted since his services to the King were more important than many of his contemporaries, including Deane. Bryant's explanation that it was easier to maintain his disinterested stance undecorated, is unconvincing, and his belief that Pepys no longer coveted such honours, doubtful. It is difficult to imagine a man whose ambitions embraced a love of public distinction not hoping for a knighthood. At a time when commoners and aristocracy were ranked so decisively apart, for the son of a tailor to become a knight would have been a tremendous feat.

When the House of Commons met again on 13 October the battle for new ships broke out afresh.[4] The only reliable historical record for these proceedings is Grey's *Debates*, but Pepys gets a very poor showing in the crucial volume three.[5] Coventry, Sitwell, Sir Thomas Lee, Vaughan and Garroway are all quoted with some frequency but Pepys's appearances are minimal and out of proportion to his influence. The general tenor in the House was strongly against the building of new ships and summed up in the words of Sir Thomas Lee: 'We are told that there's always spent yearly on the Navy £400,000 and yet there is no Navy.'[5] The very succinctness of the phrase is telling. The opposition clamoured for a detailed account of why the new ships were necessary. Pepys rose to the occasion with what has since been regarded as one of his most impressive speeches. First he justified the King's use of money for the Navy and seemed to play into Sir Thomas Lee's hands.

Is the state of the fleet worse [he continued] than when the King came in? No. In quality, rate, burthens and force, men and guns, 'tis in better state then when the King came in. Let any man offer a contradiction that 'tis not the best fleet the kingdom every knew. There are eighty-three sail, great and small, more than in all his royal predecessor and he has built more ships in fourteen years.[6]

The same question repeated itself. Why did they need new ships? Simply because, Pepys answered, the French and the Dutch outnumbered and outgunned the English.[7] Pepys had already given the House similar information in April 1675 and even between then and now the disadvantages had grown.[8] His polemic steadily mounted until he declared that they had reached a crucial historical moment in which to take action against the 'envious Dutch' and 'imperious French'.[9] For the moment the House was carried along by Pepys's oratory and the opposition first wavered and then surrendered. Sir John Cotton thereupon moved to grant the King £500,000 for refurbishing the Navy. This proposition led to a resolution that work should begin at once on building twenty new ships of the line. No sooner was the resolution agreed than the opposition attempted to undermine it. The Ways and Means Committee proposed that the money should be paid not to the King but to the city of London. This caused a mild uproar since it expressed distrust of the King's financial dealings and seemed to imply a constitutional revolution.[10] Sir George Downing then warned the House: 'Some are hot enough that the Exchequer is not to be trusted, but when that trust is gone the government has gone.'[11] The whole long and tortured debate at last reached a conclusion on 6 November when, largely due to Pepys, the House agreed that twenty new ships of the line should be built. It never came to pass. The recalcitrant opposition went to work once more and quickly prevented the necessary £500,000 from reaching the King who – in despair – prorogued Parliament.

This was only the beginning. Within a short time the indomitable Pepys was hell-bent on building thirty not twenty ships, and no sooner had Parliament reassembled in the new year than he launched his new attack. Another virtuoso performance by Pepys followed during which he answered questions covering every aspect of shipbuilding. Inevitably, the key question was put to him in many guises – why were thirty ships now necessary where before he had settled for twenty? His answer came forcibly. The Dutch had taken advantage of the delay involved in these long, drawn-out debates to build continuously. The English Navy, both in numbers and design, was in a worse position – relatively – than before. Grey, in February 1676, suddenly relents and gives Pepys no less than three pages to make this and many other important points. There were now a series of minor attacks on Pepys, some openly sneering, others deliberately ambiguous, but he emerged undiminished. It was finally resolved that one first-rate, nine second-rates and twenty third-rates would be built at a cost of £600,000. It was a triumph for the Secretary.

As Pepys slowly came to grips with the gigantic task of reorganising – indeed transforming the Navy – two other naval issues demanded attention. Since the Middle Ages the Navy had conducted itself with the bohemian disregard for the few regulations thought suitable to such a free-roving and buccaneering organisation. Great leaders like Drake were able by sheer force of personality to impose a rough and ready discipline on their men, but respect for encoded laws implied, to many, a lack of virility. The trouble centred around the distinction between the tarpaulins and gentlemen. Sailing and navigating men-of-war was a skilled *trade*, but fighting and directing battles was the prerogative of the aristocracy. Saddled with captains whom he regarded as land-commanders having no real knowledge of the sea, Pepys complained constantly about their inadequacies in his naval minutes.[12] Some even tried to bring 'land luxuries' aboard their ships in the form of hen hoops which 'pestered and annoyed' everybody. Much more serious was their insolent attitude to orders and a cavalier disregard for the authority of the Navy Office.

The classic story which recurs in the records concerns Captain Priestman, who regarded his responsibilities as a serious interruption of his land-based pleasures.[13] Sauntering through Covent Garden on 9 July 1675 Pepys – in search of those self-same pleasures – suddenly sighted Captain Priestman idling his way through the crowds and at once recalled the instructions he had issued: 'Proceed to Portsmouth for ship repairs.' Confrontation would have produced a drama worthy of Pepys's pen but he decided to bide his time and later addressed a letter about Priestman to John Holmes.[14] A very well connected man whose most distinguished patron was the King, Captain Priestman regarded himself as relatively impervious to official instructions. Pepys's letter revealed once again that streak of courage which could outface rank, in order to tell the truth. Priestman's dereliction of duty was confirmed by the muster books and, coming straight to the point, he said: '... your forbearing to give your attendance on board to the dispatch of your ship seems to imply such a deportment towards His Majesty's service and the instructions of the Lord High Admiral as ... I shall not without manifest unfaithfulness be able to omit the making known both to His Majesty and My Lords and to His Royal Highness'. It was written in Pepys's characteristic manner. The elliptical style and circumlocution might have muffled its meaning but they made subtle what might have become crude. Whatever the style, the letter had no effect. Once the group of captains to which Priestman belonged became aware that this little busybody in the Admiralty was serious in his attempt to reinforce discipline, they conspired together to frustrate him. The King was simultaneously a useful but ambiguous ally for Pepys. Every well connected captain could proceed to Whitehall, await the right moment and get the personal ear of the King. Priestman first reacted by calling Pepys a scoundrel and then managed to dilute Pepys's accusations to the point where any threat to his career vanished.[15] Indeed, for the rest of his career he remained resilient. As fast as he lost one command he negotiated another.

More spectacular but less documented was the case of Captain Harris, accused by his first lieutenant of having 'accommodated his mistress' aboard his ship 'three nights in succession'. An adroit manipulator, Captain Harris claimed that the lady in question had fallen ill while visiting the ship and since her symptoms were serious he had thought it better not to have her moved. Asked where she was accommodated, he claimed it was 'in a separate cabin', which the lieutenant vigorously denied. Once ashore, the roistering habits of some captains certainly involved women and Captain Harris aroused such widespread sympathy that the lieutenant was ostracised and Harris, for lack of evidence, escaped with a reprimand.[16]

The easiest method of avoiding discipline was by 'loitering in port' and whenever ships put into Mediterranean stations delays and disruption became endemic. Penn was dead now but Pepys's dislike of the man lingered on and when he discovered the 'gross indiscipline' of Penn's relation Sir Richard Rooth it had a special savour for him. Rooth was away from England for nearly two years on board the *Adventure*. It was intended to act as a service ship, but 'he spent only four months on that duty, thirteen months in port and ... forty-three days in Cadiz when ordered not to spend above six'.[17]

Among the many ingenious alibis for loitering, captains sometimes conspired with their officers to invent sickness among the crews, which meant endangering life if they were forced to put to sea under-manned. Relations between the captains and the Naval Board reflected itself in insubordination between different ranks on board ship. Officers frequently split into factions, conspiring to undermine authority without quite provoking mutiny. Cowardice was by no means unknown and some ships when in danger from enemy attacks surrendered with alarming alacrity. Absentee officers were another cause of worry to Pepys. Having docked in a big port full of loose women, a lieutenant might easily slip away for a few days – and sometimes months – with or without his captain's permission. In the well-known case of Lieutenant Aylmer it was his highly eccentric Captain Roydon who caused a drunken scene and struck him with a cane. In another dramatic incident Captain Vittels broke a boat-hook over the head of the purser, John Trevor, who was going ashore without permission. Surprisingly, he was dismissed from service.[18] Many another captain behaved more outrageously and got away with it, but things were changing and at the very heart of the change, struggling against a tide of paperwork, sat the now ubiquitous Pepys.

Another major abuse had much more serious consequences since it began as a legitimate activity. Merchants had long used the Navy to transport their gold and silver because a warship was the best protection against the pirates swarming the high seas. It had unforeseen consequences. First, merchants began bribing commanders to carry special cargoes quite different from bullion. In order to justify the bribes, certain captains avoided going into action when danger threatened. The practice became steadily more sophisticated until captains not only offered bargain prices for certain commodities, but took the risk of advertising their services at ports of call. So lucrative were the returns that being cashiered by the Navy Office was no threat when a captain could retire in comfort on the proceeds. Bryant describes the case of Captain Poole who transported the new Governor to Barbados and remained anchored there enjoying the wonderful climate for six months without permission. Pepys informed him on his return that such gross dereliction of duty 'threatened to ruin His Majesty's honour, service and treasure'.[19] Pepys's attempts to bring him to heel were met with strong opposition. Poole, like many captains, could call upon the court and even the King to intervene before any sentence was passed. 'Our King, being a seaman, has appeared rather to have rendered our navigation worse by reason of our commanders (especially gentlemen) finding so easy access and talk to him.'[20] Pepys's original aim to have Poole court-martialled was met by the alternative proposition that he lose his pay for the voyage. Poole was asked to choose and – laughing, one supposes, all the way from the Navy Office – chose the latter.

Efforts to introduce discipline constantly came to nothing until Pepys at last decided that captains as well as subordinate officers must be subject to checks by the muster master. In future they were to verify their presence on station. This was the beginning of a sweeping set of new principles which quickly involved the recruitment of officers. Clearly, Pepys alone had no power to impose such changes on the Navy and the beginnings of his revolution can be traced to the Navy Board meeting of November 1674. There, an intricate discussion had arisen about those sixth-rate ships which, unlike larger vessels, did not carry a master. If the captains of such vessels were expected to play the double role of captain and master then they should face an examination in seamanship at Trinity House. Priestman, the delinquent captain, had overcome this problem by employing a master and persuading the Admiralty to pay his wages. Pepys used the master–captain problem to mask the beginnings of an entirely revolutionary method for selecting officers. Exercising all his cunning, Pepys drew from the Board the request that he should draft a list of skills required by lieutenants and methods by which they could be tested. Pepys completed the task in record time, but one among his recommendations – that service as a midshipman was a necessary prerequisite for elevation to higher rank – received short shrift from Prince Rupert in 1677. The Prince claimed that the commonplace duties of a midshipman were beneath the dignity of an officer and a gentleman.[21] The deep class divisions within the Navy which bedevilled its whole operation not only produced the clash between gentlemen and tarpaulins, but court versus country, the sophisticated Londoner and the country squires. Pepys found himself driven by forces moving in four directions but he rode the conflict skilfully and referred the question to a special committee. Present at its first meeting were representatives of the gentlemen and tarpaulins, the principal officers of the Navy Board and Pepys. The composition of the committee disturbed Pepys because it represented the very class distinction which it was his prime motive to remove. 'For no man living can be more inclined than myself to favour a gentleman that is a true seaman, so neither is there any man more sensible than ... I am of the ruinous consequences of an over hasty person admitting persons to office and charge of seamen upon the bare consideration of their being gentlemen.'[22]

It must have come as a surprise to Pepys to find that the committee repudiated the idea that gentlemen were demeaned by first serving as midshipmen. It also fitted his master plan which slowly emerged step by step. Lieutenants in future were required to show the following qualifications: three years' experience at sea, one year of which must be undertaken as a midshipman; familiarity with the duties of an able seaman and the ability to carry them out; an understanding of the principles of navigation vouched for by three senior officers, a flag officer and commander of a first- or second-rate ship. Against a history of go-as-you-please gentlemen given command of ships with a cavalier disregard for skills, this was strong stuff. The new regulations went even further. Naval training and skills were to be matched by character assessment, with an emphasis upon obedience, diligence, sobriety and the willingness to study. These principles were far removed from those Pepys accepted in his somewhat shady deals with men like Warren and Cooke in earlier years, and they mark the emergence of a new Pepys who practised what he preached. Assailed on all sides for favours, his replies varied from the courteous and tactful to the blunt and even, on one occasion, rude. Take the case of the pursership for the first-rate *Royal Sovereign* which had become vacant in the autumn of 1676. Despite Pepys's new rules, pursers remained privileged men who could expect rich rewards. Several friends of Pepys, including the wife of his old friend Pearse, and Sir William Coventry himself, wrote on behalf of their relations soliciting the post. Pepys replied to both with evasively polite letters and the following day, in consultation with the King, the position was granted to the purser of the *London*. A much blunter letter went to a man in the Chatham Yard who tried outright bribery for a similar post. What, Pepys demanded, made him think that any offer of money could obtain anything which 'bare virtue' could not.

Nepotism was commonplace in the seventeenth century and Pepys, in his early days, had of course introduced Balty to his job as muster master and John, Balty's brother, into the Navy Office, but now he subjected any such concessions to new austerities. The introduction of new principles coincided roughly with a revival of the troubles which had harassed English shipping off the coast of Tripoli. Admiral Narborough had blockaded Tripoli itself throughout 1675 and one of his lieutenants had broken into the harbour to destroy four of the Dey's warships. Narborough had then gone in pursuit of the remaining four which were still at sea and although outnumbered and outgunned he had 'cut them to pieces' and forced them to fly into Tripoli.[23] This drove the Dey to see reason and on 5 March 1676 a treaty was signed conceding maritime rights to England and the payment of $80,000 indemnity. The news had reached Pepys a week later and seemed a good omen for his new regime.

Meanwhile, applications for commissions, purserships, masterships and every kind of lesser job were pouring in. The power to make such appointments should have rested with the Admiralty commissioners, but the King had kept it within his purview. His reaction to the sometimes startling innovations that his busy little Secretary continued to propose varied but as he grew accustomed to change, his attitude settled into a good-humoured resignation. He had already come to trust Pepys as a man whose loyalty was unquestionable and now in practice he frequently relinquished his power of appointment. Aware of the dangers of such an anomaly, Pepys never made appointments without first indicating the constitutional limitations of his actions. Occasionally, he was overruled, to his embarrassment. Usually he pre-empted trouble by demanding the certificates which justified employment and gave what sometimes became an empty gesture of 'making them known to the King'. Did all this mean that a new Pepys, uninterested in fees or the returns on privateers, had emerged from the old opportunist?

Dictating his later Diary to his clerks, it is clear that the searing honesty of the personal Diary could not prevail. If he continued to take illegitimate rake-offs he would not place them on record with third parties as witnesses. Certainly, merchants were still protesting to him about the fees which he continued to accept for securing their protection from North African corsairs. Such fees he had in fact actually reduced after scrupulous examination from 30s, the then 'going rate', to 25s. There remained deviations. These, by their very nature, were open to public record. The real truth is that without the personal Diary we do not know whether Pepys was intrinsically a different man. We simply know that he successfully went into the Augean stable of the Navy and cleaned it up. He had certainly come a long way from the days when he wrote: 'A purser without professed cheating is a professed loser.' Yet he was not above minor transgressions. Sixteen lesser ships – small but very navigable – were held ready off the Palace Wall at Greenwich for ambassadors or important visitors who needed swift passage at a moment's notice between England and France. This traffic offered rich possibilities for Pepys to dispense special privileges to his friends. He was not above offering an enemy a quick trip across the Channel to soften his hostility, but it was friends like James Houblon or his old tutor Joseph Hill who usually benefited. Theatrical celebrities could always warm his heart and Nell Gwyn the actress distinguished the passenger list on occasion. Some compensation for the kiss she gave him in January 1667 was clearly required.[24]

That Pepys was no less concerned to improve the lot of the able seaman comes through clearly in letters and memoranda, but here a moral ambiguity once more appeared. A brief, discursive, but very informative document, *Memoirs of the Royal Navy*, included a classic passage about the commission which was set up to improve the system of paying seamen. Comparison between merchant and naval seamen revealed the former enjoying punctual payment but at a lower rate. The higher rate became meaningless, however, when payments were months in arrears and threatened starvation to disembarked seamen. Pepys seems in his memoirs to fudge the issue, saying there was 'not a penny left unpaid to any artificer or merchant for any service done or commodity delivered to the use of the Navy either at sea or on shore within the whole time of their commission where the party claiming the same was *in the way to receive it and had (if an accountant) done his part as such towards the entitling himself to payment*.[25] The italics are mine. Because of cumulative delays in payment seamen were frequently once more at sea when they should have been claiming back pay. A man in mid–Mediterranean could hardly fulfil the conditions of being 'in the way to receive it'. Not infrequently the abuse of pressing meant that men were forced to rejoin their ships without seeing their families or having time to pursue wage claims.

We have seen that Pepys had a mixed record on pressing. He was against pressing men on ships outward bound even in time of war, but he overrode the political fears of the Governor of Dover who had refused to execute his press warrant. 'The impressing of men for the supply of the King's ships', he wrote, 'must not be stopped notwithstanding the inquiries on foot in Parliament touching the matter.'[26] Beating warrant officers for relatively minor offences had become a common practice. This could take place in public or private. Pepys was against the practice in general. An Admiralty letter dated 4 July 1676 to Captain Dickenson had explained – elegantly – alternative methods for enforcing discipline. Conditions for ordinary seamen were frequently such that only the starving or destitute volunteered for service. Edward Barlow, a very ordinary seaman, who followed the sea from the age of thirteen to sixty, once wrote in a remarkable Diary he kept: 'I always think that beggars had a far better life of it and lived better than I did for they seldom missed their bellies full of better victuals than we could get and also at night lie quiet and out of danger . . . We seldom in a month got our bellyful of victuals and that of such salt that beggars would scorn to eat.'[27] Theoretically, seamen were liable to impressment only in wartime, but common practice had long undermined that principle. Surprisingly, surgeons had equal cause for complaint, being treated as seamen rather than officers. Pearse, Pepys's old surgeon and friend, on one occasion appealed to him to prevent a number of surgeons from being impressed.[28] Pepys first refused the warrant but later succumbed to the need for such men in a national crisis. There were other occasions when he did intervene to override impressment, as when two Charterhouse schoolboys were 'seduced from Southwark fair and shipped against their wills'. Pepys summed up the situation: 'Till this liberty of pressing men without consideration to the safety of the vessels they [are] pressed out of, be once severely corrected, the King's service can never be free from clamour.'[29]

A remarkable number of seafaring men kept journals which tell a sorry tale of hardship, bad food, indiscipline and quarters resembling prisons. 'Every writer relates stories about buttons made from cheese, as hard as horn, sour beer, stinking water, inedible meat, weevily biscuits full of large black-headed maggots.'[30] Pepys's famous minute still rings in the ears of those who supply the Navy: 'Englishmen and more especially seamen, love their bellies above everything else and therefore it must always be remembered in the management of the . . . Navy.' Yet all his efforts to feed the Navy fell far short of the ideals enshrined in his historic victualling contract of 1677. This included one pound of good, clean, sweet wheaten Bisquet, one gallon of high quality beer, two pounds of beef from 'a well fed Ox not weighting less than 5 cwt'. Translating this into reality was impossible given the victuallers' bad debts. The victuallers were middle-men and if they were not paid they in turn were refused supplies. In the clash between political protests for free citizenship upheld by Parliament and the demands of the Navy to allow 'pressing', the Navy usually won. Whether Pepys was more concerned with renovating the officer class without which the Navy could not function and gave less attention to the seaman is open to question. The seamen had no contact with, or influence on, the King and were forced back on direct democratic action. This usually proved ineffective unless the sailors withheld their labour long enough to threaten starvation. All in all, a seaman's lot was not a happy one. There remains no evidence that the King ever supported the seaman's cause – it was irreconcilable with his role – and even less evidence that Pepys pleaded their case through the King.

At the age of forty-three Pepys now lived and worked in Derby House, Canon Row, which overlooked the river and had one vast room on the first floor capable of accommodating the activities of his clerks. His own rooms were spacious and he looked down from the back windows on a small garden 'put in order' from the day of his arrival in 1674. Meticulously displayed were his rapidly growing library, his ship models, his flageolet and viol, and an accumulation of bric-à-brac. The household itself embraced a whole family of servants subject to a carefully imposed order which assumed that a servant must simply do as he was told. As we have seen, domestic and professional life were not so distinct as they are today, with Pepys's clerks following the example of Will Hewer and sharing some domestic duties. A coachman, footman, butler, a cook and a scattering of maids completed the below stairs staff with the charming Mary Skinner omnipresent in the background. It is reasonable to suppose that since she shared Pepys's love of order and beauty, she ran the household to his satisfaction, but she remains a blurred figure in the records. Inevitably, he would make comparison between Mary Skinner and Elizabeth. We know nothing of Pepys's and Mary's sexual relationship, but it is difficult to imagine so sensual a man as Pepys being satisfied with a platonic relationship. Since his importance brought him into contact with many fine ladies, it would be remarkable if he had ceased to indulge casual encounters. The rigours imposed by the marriage tie no longer troubled him and given such freedom the world should have been rich in adventure. Pepys at forty-three might, of course, have grown out of his *boulevardier* habits and found compensation in obsessional work. That he still rose at dawn and frequently worked fanatically is certain.

For the rest, we can visualise him being dressed in the morning by one of the maids in a blue camelot tunic with gold trimmings, silken hose, and buckled shoes, the picture finally completed with the ornate periwig which gave him – to the modern eye – the air of a presiding judge. From all the available records he appears overweight and must have cut an impressive figure as the footman told him the coach was ready at the door and he left the house. The decorations on his splendid coach included battle scenes, harbours and magnificent ships of the line – which led the less reverential to address him ironically as Admiral. We follow him downriver to talk to Phineas Pett, the master shipwright, who had already worked wonders with Pepys's boat, converting it into a barge.[31] Matching the ornate coach, the barge carried a freshly built superstructure and its cabin, enclosed by silken curtains, had windows which were being converted into sliding windows. It was all very impressive and marked him out now for what he was – a very distinguished person. Perhaps the barge journey took him to an appointment with Sir William Coventry, or a dinner with Pett, or, more likely - since all his finery had been assembled – to some gathering of ladies well connected with the Commissioners or the court.

In relaxed moments he visited still surviving relatives including Balty his brother-in-law and Roger Pepys, where young women found his company sympathetic, if not exciting. In the early days Pepys had followed such models as Evelyn, Sandwich or Coventry and dressed accordingly. In those days he had been preoccupied with 'my first fine cloth suit', 'my camelott cloak with gold buttons', 'my fine buckled shoes'.[32] Creed had warned him against too much ostentation and told him 'to avoid being noted for it',[33] which Pepys had taken to heart. Now confidence had replaced uncertainty and he sallied forth to one function after another employing all the resources which his relative wealth made possible. Accustomed as he had become to hobnobbing with the great, a hard morning at the Admiralty was sometimes followed by an elaborate dinner served from his best plate with fine wines. The guests might include the merchant Sir John Bankes, whose wisdom he appreciated, and James Houblon, his long respected friend. The old jollity, ballad-singing, heavy drinking and bawdry had given place to more refined gatherings. Pepys would protest that his rich food was too simple for his guests. At his best, he sometimes provided potage of duck, a whole salmon, roast turkey, Lombard pie, lobsters, prawns, creams and syllabubs and liberal quantities of champagne and claret. He knew all the gentry's tricks and made so casual his invitation to see his collection of silverware, glittering glass and beautifully intricate clocks that guests frequently believed that their own curiosity had inspired his conducted tours. Such a tour could become prolonged. There was so much to see. Central to this display were the growing number of fine books, from the *Life of the Renowned Sir Philip Sidney*, the *Workes of King Charles the Martyr*, the *Canterbury Tales*, *Brittain's Glory*, Bacon's *Natural and Experimental History of Winds*, to Gregory XIII and Defoe's *An Argument* showing that a standby army with consent of Parliament is not inconsistent with a free government.[34] His collection of maps, his world globes, microscopes, calligraphical specimens and mathematical curiosities, all were available to the willing and sometimes unwilling guest. There were other, lighter touches from the flowers in the garden to the canaries whose singing delighted him.

His growing fame as a public figure was matched by his developing reputation in cultured and scientific circles. Minor and major projects were hatched and discussed at his dinner parties, from his intention to write a history of the Navy to a misconceived attempt to penetrate the Northeast Passage. This led into a disastrous joint investment with the Duke of York, Lord Berkeley and Sir John Bankes in a frigate called *Prosperous* which should have opened up new trade routes, but foundered in icy water.[35]

There is some evidence that Pepys suffered from spells of hypochondria at this time. He would concentrate his mind on examining in detail every minute illness which had ever attacked him. Remembering the number of untreatable illnesses and health hazards during this period, hypochondria seemed a natural accompaniment.

On 7 November 1677 he brought this indulgence to a pitch of

perfection with a long rambling account which included such a glittering array of illnesses as would make him the perfect guinea pig for medical science. It began with shortness of breath, pain in the joints (particularly the wrist), 'spitting and sprawling in wet weather', 'falling down of the palate of my mouth, pains in the bowel and bladder, stoppage of urine, constant attacks of wind, frequent losing of my voice for days together', attacks of colic, an aptness to be dizzy in the head, and above all continued trouble with his eyes. He vividly recollected the days when he was writing the Diary: 'As long as I was able to work with my own eyes by daylight and candlelight [I would work] for a little less than eighteen or twenty hours a day … in a constant smoke of candles till I have wrought my eyes to such a weariness as at last [was] hardly able to see my way out of my office.'[36] Not until he relinquished the Diary and developed the new version written by his clerks did he control, but not entirely banish, the pain in his eyes. His growing eminence had brought with it demands for memos, letters and shorthand notes. During the Brooke House commission and the debate on building thirty new ships he had frequently had resort to note-taking and always suffered as a result with his eyes. His Admiralty Journal (1673–9) begins in a clear handwriting, becomes large and struggling in April 1675 and does not recover confidence until January 1676. He continued to experiment with aids but none overcame the pain of intense reading or the early-morning headaches. There are few references to Pepys consulting a doctor but he was 'bled' once or twice a year and had faith in a mixture of green hazelnuts and lapis cullminaris. In his forty-fifth year he made a remarkable statement: 'I have during my whole life been in constant heat of body little below a fever.'[37] It is unlikely that he had a permanent temperature. Pepys could, on occasion, become the professional hyperbolist, as when he claimed to work twenty hours by candlelight. For the previous ten years he claimed that the nature of his employment had meant irregular meals. Dinner was frequently taken 'at or after midnight', with the result that he suffered from a complicated form of dizziness which in straightforward language probably meant blood pressure. His current responsibilities allowed him regular meals and he had given up late eating with beneficial results. Once a great eater, he had graduated to moderation in food and in drink, with a preference 'for the most part … [for] the wines that are reckoned strong … Greek, Italian Spanish and Portuguese'.[38] Modern medicine would diagnose some of his symptoms as psychosomatic, such as a persistent pain in the wrist and loss of voice.

In 1677 his father's affairs became more confused than usual and he wrote several letters in an attempt to clear the air. While Parliament revived its interest in the fees paid to Pepys, his cousin Roger suddenly died and he hurried home from defending himself in the House to conduct a long correspondence intended to clear up worse confusions in his affairs. Meanwhile, Pepys's enemies conspired with dissatisfied merchants to renew the charges of extravagant abuse of the fee system. Merchants alleged that it cost them £80 apiece to get passes, whereas, as we have seen, according to Pepys he received a paltry 25s. It remained true that the system made men like Pepys rich. Scrupulously recording the key passages in one attack after another, Pepys rose to defend himself three times in Parliament. He denied every charge and then – with his unfailing faith in committees – demanded that the whole question be submitted to yet another one. Abstracting the facts from Grey's record it is clear that he set out to blame his predecessor for the high cost of fees which then prevailed. The full facts are not easily established, but the account given by the West Country magnate Seymour differed from Pepys's.[39]

Seymour also questioned Pepys's annual fee income of £1,000. Acknowledging the extravagance of some fees, Pepys still refused to reduce them. By now a very well set-up gentleman, he could have offered to meet his critics but he was still very money-conscious and insisted on his right to be paid properly. Pressing home his case, he pointed out that under the new rules his work would increase heavily as if unaware that he himself had instigated those rules. Familiar with every nuance of protocol, skilled in repudiating evidence, knowing just how far he could go in self-assertion before the Admiralty Board, Pepys presented his case effectively. He also humbled himself at the right moment when he made his submission to the King for maintaining his fees at the same level. Sympathetic to this remarkable little Clerk with whom the Lord had seen fit to endow him, the King granted the concession without a quibble.[40] Still bent on increasing his estate as well as wealth, Pepys did not hesitate to put in a claim for the estate of Francis Gurney whose suicide made it forfeit to the crown. Stating that Pepys never became a rich man on the grand scale, Bryant claims that he valued office for what he put into it and not for what he took out.[41] His motives were more complicated. Pepys had for two years been a warden of Trinity House and in May 1677 he achieved an ambition dear to his heart when he became its Master. Despite his dislike of too much display, Pepys enjoyed ceremony. As Master of Trinity he began the pilgrimage every Trinity Monday to the annual sermon and great feast given by the corporation at Deptford, returning by state barge to London for another and no less splendid feast.

In his forty-fifth year Pepys could reflect that he had set in motion three reforms in the English Navy which, taken together, amounted to a revolution. Major among them were his new regulations for the recruitment of lieutenants. As we have seen, the naval minutes reveal a picture of well-born amateurs invading the trade of the tarpaulins with a cavalier disregard for their skills. In future this would become much more difficult. By 3 November 1677 his second reorganisation meant that ships' companies would be in proportion to the guns carried and the retinues granted to flag officers carefully controlled against all the explosive objections of the aristocrats.[42] The third innovation involved widespread reading and study to determine who among the proliferation of solemn young chaplains eager to taste the life at sea was most suitable for the spiritual reassurance of men liable to face death and injury on every voyage. A new set of highly discriminatory regulations was presented to the Admiralty Board on 19 December 1677. Henceforth the Church would receive advance notice of sailings and have the right to appoint chaplains who carried a certificate from the Archbishop of Canterbury or the Bishop of London.

Medical treatment for sick and injured seamen remained another controversial issue.[43] As far back as January 1666, Pepys had given an account of his conversation with Evelyn when they discussed a project for an infirmary at Chatham.[44] Evelyn explained the project to the King on 8 February and Pepys laid it before the Navy Board and the Duke of York on 14 February.[45] The plan took the form of two hospitals, one for four hundred, the other five hundred seamen, and on 17 March Evelyn had gone to Chatham to select the site. After that the project dwindled away and nothing more was heard of it.

After all his extraordinary efforts Pepys seemed to have emerged triumphant in 1677. He was unaware that hidden forces were at work which would subject him to far greater pressures and possible disaster. Anti-Catholic feeling in the middle of the seventeenth century had steadily increased and by 1677 could generate hysterical outbursts which outraged Pepys's essentially rational thinking. The King's alliance with France had encouraged smouldering suspicion, the Declaration of Indulgence had reaffirmed it and popular thinking still regarded the Great Fire of London as the result of a Catholic conspiracy. Europe was dominated by the diplomatic and military power of Louis XIV, but by 1678 he still faced the coalition of

Holland, Spain and the Holy Roman Empire. French Protestants' immunity from persecution which had been guaranteed by the Edict of Nantes in 1598 was in danger of collapse. Louis shared the English view of Catholicism as an attempt to dominate the world under an absolute Catholic monarchy. An accumulation of Catholic minded people in high places in England began with the Catholic Queen Mother and Queen Consort, developed when James, Duke of York, declared his conversion to Catholicism and reached a peak with the King's interning of troops intended for a joint attack on the French. Fear of external aggression became fear of internal traitors. Writers and politicians made great play with suspicion. According to Grey, Lord Russell echoed the feelings of the country with the words, 'I despise such a ridiculous and nonsensical religion. A piece of wafer broken between priest's fingers to become our Saviour. And what becomes of it when eaten and taken down you know.'[46] The poet Marvell's attacks on Catholicism were more eloquent but none the less virulent.[47] Transubstantiation – the symbolic conversion of the wafer and wine into the body and blood of Christ – had become a crucial question under the Test Act of 1673. If you denied its validity you were safely Protestant.[48] History underpinned the fears of what we would call a fifth column with the 1571 conspiracy to depose Elizabeth, followed by assassination plots in 1580 and the spectacular never-to-be-forgotten episode of the Gunpowder Plot in 1605. Pepys had become steadily more aware of the growing agitation and his own vulnerability.

Central to this was the raffish, if not piratical figure of so-called Colonel Scott, a man whose melodramatic story is related by Pepys in his 'two volumes of Mornamont' which is elaborate enough to rate as another work of literature.[49] Bryant accepts the veracity of these two volumes without question. Certainly the narrative thrust of the account and the interlocking details come together convincingly. The title colonel is a music-hall disguise for many a first-class rogue and Scott distilled every characteristic of that classic figure. Like his forebears, tales of valour on the field fade before the actual facts into ignominious dismissal from a rank which probably never existed.[50] Born the son of a poor Kentish miller, he was taken as a child to New England and rose from helping to run a pig farm to heights of villainy. These reached a peak when he returned to England, lodged with Mr Gotherson, a Kentish Quaker, debauched his wife and persuaded her to surrender her whole fortune to his care. He then fled once more to Long Island, taking with him her son and several young people, seducing the girls and selling the boys to the highest bidder.[51] How much dislike of Scott led Pepys to exaggerate the details is difficult to estimate. Throughout his career Scott revealed all the panache and daring of a very gifted criminal and seemed able to talk people into unconvincing schemes apparently intended for their, not his, own benefit. Described as a tall, powerfully built man, his commanding presence and lustful eye meant that frequently he won his way with women. Above all, he was a master of bluff.

Posing as an expert on American foreign policy, he returned briefly to England and began a new career as an agent in Holland when the Third Dutch War broke out. Never at a loss for grandiose titles he elevated himself as Major General Scott of Scott's Hall, Shield Bearer and Geographer to the King of England. It is some measure of his powers that even the great commander De Witt believed his story and was alleged to have given him command of a regiment.[52] He cut a swaggering figure in his new role, happily followed a polygamous path which rewarded him with first one and then another wife, while his original wife still languished in Long Island struggling to support three children. Living in Bergen-op-Zoom he persuaded its influential politicians that his proliferating charts of the English coast could open the way for Dutch ships to penetrate deeply into the river Thames with the promise of untold plunder. Never able to miss a prize when he saw one, he made the fatal mistake of embezzling the regimental funds and fled to Flanders with the spoils, leaving behind a reputation so damned that his effigy was publicly burnt.[53] He also deceived Sir William Temple, the English ambassador to the Dutch, who believed in Scott's integrity and accepted a present from him. It was '... his map of England signed by himself as our King's Geographer ... which he had not only stolen from the Dutch but is in itself most notoriously fake'.[54] Mornamont gives the background to Scott's future behaviour towards the Duke of York under the subheading *Information of Morals about Scott.*[55]

The Duke of York, having a spleen against him, caused him to be put out of ... employment [in New York], after which he came to England to make a complaint about the King ... of the injustices of the Duke of York ... the King made him no satisfaction for the injuries he had received which was the reason he made his address to the Parliament but received likewise no satisfaction ... upon which he swore God's blood and wounds he had a thing in hand which would make the King and Duke of York repent.[56]

By the time he returned to England in 1678 his talents had become known to the erratic but witty Duke of Buckingham already conspiring with Lord Shaftesbury to undermine the state. Buckingham passed between England and France bent on 'who knew what mischief', and in the autumn vacation the first murmurs of a possible plot to assassinate Charles, destroy the Protestant hold on the country and appoint a Catholic ruler began to gather force. The main target of the early rumours centred around the Duke of York and he now made the mistake of challenging them with a public enquiry. Running the risk of giving substance to what had been denied, the King agreed to have the charges examined in Council.

Chapter 17

Titus Oates and the Popish Plot

Plotting in the middle to late seventeenth century was a widespread sparetime activity which bred a rich array of informers, secret societies and spies. People were preoccupied with rumour and hearsay which failed to apply truth-testing rigour and swallowed with avidity the flood of half truths and half lies which ran from tavern to club, club to court, and court to Parliament.[1] Scrupulous insistence on religious observance was matched by unscrupulous plotting and counter-plotting. There were countless activities in which false papers were planted on unsuspecting people, incriminating documents found behind wainscots, weapons hidden inside bran tubs, confessions as readily recanted as sworn and professional informers brought to perfection the art of Papist hunting. It was all to reach its climax with Titus Oates.

A crazy London clergyman called Israel Tonge became the first focus of a whole forest of such conspiracies. A mental casualty of the Civil War, Tonge had temporarily settled in comfort at St Mary Stayning when overnight the Fire of London destroyed his church and most of his parish. Thereafter his behaviour changed and presently reached psychopathic proportions.[2] The Society of Jesus became for him a satanic organisation responsible for the execution of Charles I, the Great Rebellion and the Fire. Called before the King's Council, he asked leave to introduce Titus Oates, whose chequered career had led to his expulsion from university and a naval chaplaincy for 'unnatural vice'. A highly skilled perjurer who escaped from one lie by inventing another, he now saw his chance to elaborate a whole tapestry of lies backed up, when required, by a little forgery. The tale he told reinforced the suspicions which coloured much Protestant talk.

Oates opened his assault with a threatened rebellion in Scotland, to be followed by the assassination of Charles II in London, the burning of the capital, the massacre of Protestants and the welcoming of the French Army at any convenient English port. The names of distinguished Catholics who would replace the current government were said to be known, among them Edward Coleman, secretary to the Duchess of York and a fanatical Catholic.[3] Coleman revealed all the excessive piety of the convert and was alleged to have solicited money from the Pope to back the proposed overthrow. In September Oates made depositions to this effect before a popular London magistrate, Sir Edmund Godfrey, who revealed them to Edward Coleman. There is no more colourful story in English history than the Popish Plot with its interminable twists and turns, threatened stabbings, lies exposed and reformulated, and recanted beliefs; but it all led inexorably to one conclusion. On 28 September Oates left the Council armed with a number of warrants for the arrest of suspected Catholic conspirators. The following morning, once more before the Council, Oates was cross-examined by a very sceptical Charles II, whose questions undermined Oates's evidence. By now, however, rumours were circulating in the city and within a few days the die was cast. At this crucial point, which threatened to wreck his whole regime, Charles II quietly took himself off to the races at Newmarket. By a supreme piece of luck which was to provide Pepys with an indispensable alibi, the King decided on the spur of the moment to ask Pepys to accompany him.[4]

A number of distinguished people now fell into Oates's net. Edward Coleman was shown to have conducted a long and treasonable correspondence with the Jesuit confessor to Louis XIV which gave further credence to Oates and led to Coleman's arrest. Suspicion next fell on Catherine, the Catholic Queen, and Oates, emboldened by success, accused her of treason before the bar of the House of Lords. Charles had long abandoned faithfulness to Catherine and sired numerous children by several mistresses, but he took the accusation coolly and defended her vigorously. This was followed by the startling murder of Sir Edmund Godfrey, the magistrate who had taken Oates's depositions.[5] As North records, Godfrey 'is the easiest man to be trapped of any man living ... His daily custom was to go about alone creeping at all hours in lanes and alleys ... and besides he was a man so remarkable in person and garb ... He was black, hard-favoured, tall-stooping and wore a broad hat.'[6] His death sent a shiver through the capital and the gossip of informed citizens encouraged unthinking uproar in several quarters. The rapid circulation of the story seems to have been engineered because normally news travelled slowly. The conspiracy theory was paramount.

The manner of Godfrey's death has been subjected to a most elaborate investigation by Kenyon without arriving at any firm solution.[7] His body, found in a ditch at the foot of Primrose Hill, had been run through by a sword with marks around his neck which indicated strangulation. Curiously, the sword was bloodless, indicating that the thrust had been made after he was dead and the evidence was still further complicated by severe bruising on the chest. Accusing fingers (including Oates's) pointed remorselessly at the Catholics who wished to have their revenge on the man who had taken Oates's deposition. No money or valuables had been stolen from Godfrey's person and the position of the sword indicated a classic suicide. As one detail after another came to light the suicide theory receded. The tracks around Primrose Hill were muddy and yet his shoes were newly polished: the sword had been run through his body after his death, a remarkable performance for a suicide; signs of a struggle were evident; and the post-mortem indicated that he had not eaten for forty-eight hours before his death.[8] One reconstruction suggested that he had been beaten up and killed in another place, brought by coach or cart − tracks were found − and then run through with a sword to make it look like suicide.[9] The murder came at the precise moment when Oates's spectacular statements were suffering a setback from the King's persistent interrogation. Doubts about the veracity or validity of the anti-Catholic case were reinforced by Sir Robert Southwell's statement that, despite the accumulating evidence, nothing seemed to corroborate the explanations for Godfrey's death.[10]

The populace thought otherwise. The funeral which followed was spectacular. 'The crowd was prodigious both at the procession and in and about the church and so heated that anything called Papist, were it cat or dog, had probably gone to pieces in a moment. The Catholics all kept close in their houses and lodgings.'[11] Godfrey was in the classic position of the man who knew too much and who was almost bound to be murdered. This overlooked the fact that all the depositions in Godfrey's hands had been presented to the Council before his death. Moreover, Godfrey had distinguished Catholic friends, among them Edward Coleman − already arrested − whom he had secretly warned of Oates's accusations.

John Scott now reappears in the story and the dates of his movements coincide suspiciously with the death of Godfrey. Scattered through the Rawlinson manuscripts in the Bodleian is a collection of depositions about Scott which, rather than explaining his erratic movements, simply show how much he was disliked. According to a Mr Bastinik, Scott had arrived at Folkestone under the name of

Johnson en route for London, but Bastinik gave no dates.[12] Godfrey left his house in Hartshorn Lane on 13 or 14 October, but it was not until 17 October that his body was discovered. Scott's movements in London are more precisely known. He left his lodgings at Mr Payne's the haberdasher in Connor Street on 15 October, two days before Godfrey's body was discovered. Any enquiries about his whereabouts, he said, must be met with the reply that he would be back in a matter of days. This message was especially directed at his republican associate Mr Wentworth, a young companion to whom he revealed that the Jesuits had threatened his life. Scott appeared in London the following day, but wrote a letter as if from Somerset. He then reappeared in Gravesend under the name of Godfrey. Apparently, he arrived in Gravesend on a horse 'all covered with lather'.[13] The Rawlinson manuscripts contain a number of descriptions of him at this time – one from a local dealer who took him for a highwayman. The dates of his movements make it perfectly possible for Scott to have been the murderer, a hypothesis which is not unreasonable given his unsavoury reputation, but what was his motive? Were any of the many people in Godfrey's entourage familiar with his litany of crimes, and was Godfrey liable, as a magistrate, to have him arrested? Both are possible but there is no real evidence. Certainly, Scott came under suspicion from one of the agents of the Clerk of Passage who set a man to shadow him. It had become customary since Oates's revelations to check all ships leaving Gravesend for absconding Jesuits. One such investigator discovered Scott in the King's Head making enquiries about a ship, the *Assistance*, outward bound for Lisbon. Once again he seemed set on escaping – from something. The investigator recorded that when Scott drank a toast to the Duke of Buckingham another was called for the damnation of all involved with the Popish Plot, and Scott showed great reluctance to raise his glass. Events moved swiftly from this point onwards. Scott managed to board the *Assistance*. Pepys was informed and gave orders to the commander in chief in the Downs to arrest him. Scott promptly left the *Assistance* at Margate, hurried to Folkestone and sailed for Dieppe. Scott was accustomed to bluff his way out of one embarrassing situation after another by producing easy alibis, but murder – if murder it was – called for more drastic action. He escaped but he left behind a trunk full of 'incriminating papers' such as Army and Navy estimates, details of the state of the fleet and republican pamphlets.

It is impossible to know whether Scott murdered Godfrey, but by that series of irrational connections which frequently bring the innocent into agonised complicity, attention next shifted to Pepys. Returning home from a sympathetic exchange of views with his old friend James Houblon on 1 November, Pepys discovered that Samuel Atkins, one of his clerks, was missing. Pepys, organising his office and household on strict lines, had imposed a curfew hour requiring clerks to be safely back home at nine o'clock. When Pepys heard the news he first fell to cursing Atkins who had twice before broken the curfew, and on one occasion returned drunk and disorderly. Pepys then gave orders to shut the doors and refuse him entry whenever he did return. He never did. The following morning a messenger called with the news that Atkins had been arrested on the evidence of a namesake Charles Atkins, once a captain in the Navy. This Captain Atkins had inexplicably made accusations which linked Atkins and, at one remove, Pepys, to Godfrey's murder. According to Captain Atkins a man called Child had approached him to commit a murder for a very distinguished gentleman who wished to be rid of an enemy. He elaborated the charge claiming that Atkins, the clerk, had asked him to confirm that Child was a reliable person who might conspire to dispose of Godfrey, a sworn enemy of his master Pepys. Captain Atkins then introduced Child to Pepys and was himself invited to join the conspiracy. Immediately on his arrest, Samuel Atkins was taken before the Popish Plot committee which included a fine array of Pepys's enemies: the Duke of Buckingham, Lord Shaftesbury, Lord Halifax and the fanatically Protestant Bishop of London. Atkins was then subjected to ruthless cross-examination pressed home by Shaftesbury in an attempt to implicate Pepys. 'The pinch of the question was if Mr Samuel Atkins had not told Captain Charles Atkins that there was a want of friendship between Mr Pepys and Sir Edmund Bury Godfrey ... Mr Samuel Atkins denied the whole matter ...'[14]

Pray Mr Samuel Atkins [continued Lord Shaftesbury] do you know one Mr or Captain Charles Atkins?
Samuel Atkins: Yes, My Lord.
Shaftesbury: How long have you known him?
Atkins: About two or three years, I think ...
Shaftesbury: Did you ever tell him upon discourse about the Plot that there was no kindness (or want of friendship I think it was) betwixt Mr Pepys and Edmund Godfrey?
Atkins: No, My Lord, I never mentioned Sir Godfrey's name to him in my whole life upon any occasion that I remember, nor ever talked with him about the Plot.

Lord Essex then took up the questioning.

Essex: Do you know one Child?
Atkins: No, My Lord: I have heard of such a man being concerned
in the victualling of the Navy . . .
Essex: No, no this is another sort of man, one whom you will be found
to know very well . . .
(Whereupon Child was called and appeared to be an ordinary seafaring
man.)
Essex: Now pray don't you know this man?
Atkins: No, sir. I never saw him in my life . . .
Essex: . . . What say you, Child, don't you know him?[15]

To the total confusion of the prosecution Child replied, 'No, My
Lord, I never saw him in my life.' Something had gone wrong with
the preparation of the case, to Pepys's delight. Shaftesbury decided
to try a different approach. Confronted by Captain Atkins, Samuel
Atkins was asked whether the captain had sent Child to Derby House
enquiring for his master, Pepys. 'No, My Lord, not in my life one
word like it.'[16] Captain Atkins challenged this vigorously: 'You
know', he said, 'this discourse was between us in the Lords' Room
at Derby House in the window.' A touch of comedy intervened.
Samuel Atkins said: 'Captain Atkins, God, your conscience and I
know 'tis notoriously untrue.' He then identified the purpose of
their last meeting. Atkins wished to borrow half a crown.[17] Shaftesbury next tried to shake Samuel Atkins's evidence by 'wheedling
him'. 'Captain Atkins', he said, 'has sworn this positively against you
to whom he . . . bears no prejudice . . . I do not think he has wit
enough to invent such a charge.' Quite unshaken, Samuel Atkins
replied, 'I assure Your Lordship upon my faith which I am ready
to bind with my oath . . . I never said one word in all my life like
it.'[18] Shaftesbury retorted angrily: 'Are we to take Captain Atkins
as a common rascal?' Samuel Atkins immediately reminded the court
that he had once been branded a coward for surrendering his ship.[19]
Step by step as Shaftesbury tried to trap Atkins, the aristocrat was
outwitted by the commoner. A simple man devoted to the belief
that lying would put him in danger of hellfire, his precepts held
firm against the pressures of his questioner. The cross-examination
once more changed its direction.

'Pray Samuel Atkins, what religion are you of?'
'My Lord, I am a Protestant and my whole family before me.'
'Yet you now frequent the Catholic Duke's Palace of St James.'

Atkins admitted this was true, but it in no way affected his Protestantism. His interrogators were getting nowhere and Shaftesbury at

last asked Atkins to withdraw while they considered his case. When he returned, Shaftesbury's manner became more threatening. He told him that he would have to consider committing him to Newgate if he did not tell the truth. Atkins remained obdurate, whereupon Sir Philip Howard, the justice of the peace, reinforced Shaftesbury's threats. If he did not confess, he said, his punishment would be severe. Atkins then confounded all their arguments: 'Sir, I very well know it and I know also that the laws of God will bring me into a worse guilt if I lie.'[20] 'So he was delivered with a warrant ... to the Keeper of Newgate and there he lay in a thinking condition without pen, ink, paper or liberty to write or speak with any person whatsoever.'

It is not difficult to imagine Pepys's consternation as the case concluded. One member of his houschold reinforced these anxieties – Morelli – the Italian musician whose company and playing was one of Pepys's special delights. A Catholic, Morelli made Pepys vulnerable to attack since he had lived so long in Pepys's household. Scared now and searching for every means to stop his enemies, Pepys did not hesitate to ask his friend James Houblon, a Huguenot, to 'go to work upon Morelli' in the hope that he might be persuaded to convert to Protestantism.[21] It was all in vain. Conversion to Catholicism was common, but conversion to Protestantism! It became clear that Morelli must be removed from Pepys's household and Houblon quickly arranged for him to be taken into a friend's house at Brentwood. Simultaneously, Pepys laid it down that everyone in his household must avow their Protestant beliefs by taking the sacrament on Sunday. There followed a mass exodus the following Sunday of all the clerks led by the secretary to St Margaret's, where it was afterwards agreed that all should be equipped with certificates of their faith. There was worse to come, from Oates himself, who claimed that he had uncovered a sub-plot within the master-plot – to take over the fleet by Catholic force. Pepys immediately ordered all his captains and commanders to scrutinise their religious beliefs and to check when they last took the sacrament.[22]

Meanwhile, matters had taken a turn for the worse for Samuel Atkins. A man called Bedloe, whose reputation as a rogue exceeded that of Captain Atkins, brought fresh witness against him.[23] Atkins had been held in irons and solitary confinement but reappeared before the House of Lords committee preserving the same dignified manner. 'Being entered [Bedloe] came up to [Samuel Atkins] and staring him in the face saluted him. Then came the question [to Atkins] Do you know that man? Answer: No. Then did Bedloe know him? Answer: He had seen him somewhere – a clerk? belonging to Derby

House.'[24] Bedloe then told the committee how the murder had been committed in the Queen's Palace, Somerset House, by a hired gang including Samuel Atkins, who was discovered two nights later standing over the corpse. Unless the compulsive necessity of returning to the scene of the crime had driven him there it seemed remarkable even to the prejudiced committee that Atkins should have exposed himself in such a way. Bedloe's evidence was duly noted without comment.

In the interval, Pepys had launched an enquiry – working day and night – into every aspect of Atkins's life, concentrating carefully on the three days between 12 October and the 14th when he was said to have been involved in Godfrey's death.[25] On 21 November Pepys's lawyer, Mr Hayes, and Atkins's sister were admitted to the prison, bringing with them the results of Pepys's research covering several pages. Still in irons and convinced that the death penalty awaiting him, their visit changed his mood. Here were clearcut alibis for the three nights. The prosecution now proceeded more cautiously and decided to allow Atkins pen and paper to give his own account of the vital days.[26] 'And so it was found that Atkins could clear the whole time in question particularly 14 October ten at night which was the precise time Bedloe charged him or his likeness to be at the murder. All which doings were so extraordinary as perhaps will not be believed ... After this the zeal of the prosecution began to languish ...'[27]

Towards the end of the year the Atkins investigation was temporarily swept aside by much bigger and more dangerous events. The English ambassador in Paris suddenly produced evidence of a clandestine correspondence between French and English naval officials which suggested an elaborate conspiracy to undermine the English government. This silenced all Pepys's attempts to press the financial needs of the Navy on the House. Shaftesbury met his appeals with a request that Pepys should first explain how Popery came to be so widespread in the fleet. Pepys realised that the cumulative evidence was now becoming dangerous. Atkins's trial, the accusation of naval Popery, the rumours of explosives discovered beneath Parliament and the threat of a French landing on the Isle of Purbeck, all boded ill for his future. Suspicion, by its nature, feeds upon itself and even the least likely person was in danger, but Pepys called for special attention. His chance visit to Newmarket with the King suddenly became a vital piece of evidence. On the night of the murder he could claim that he had been in the company of His Majesty and it was difficult to better a royal alibi. However, the King himself was hard-driven as much by domestic as foreign conspiracies against him. The notorious republican Green Ribbon club operating from a tavern in Fleet Street co-ordinated the spreading of libels and rumours to influence mob opinion and did not hesitate to contemplate the death of any inconvenient opponent, including even the King. Deeply embroiled in their machinations, John Scott had mysteriously resurfaced amongst appropriate company.[28]

This alone was disturbing enough for Pepys, but more serious enemies were gathering their forces. Frustrated in all his efforts at reconciliation, Charles II decided to cut his losses, challenge his enemies and dissolve Parliament. Pepys immediately looked to the safety of his own seat and finding Castle Rising unenthusiastic made applications simultaneously to Harwich and Portsmouth, both naval affairs constituencies. There followed a tide of electoral excitement which swept the country and involved every kind of conspiracy. Violence broke out in some constituencies but Shaftesbury and the Green Ribbon club used subtler methods. From their headquarters in Fleet Street they attacked their opponents with half truths and lies. The under-educated electorate was easily gulled and republicans began to defeat their opponents. Within a few days Pepys became their target. A letter to Captain Langley said: 'For what you write me touching ... ye election at Harwich [the discourse has] made ... Sir Anthony Deane and me as if he were an atheist and myself a Papist.' Such discourse was 'so foolish and malicious that I shall not give myself the trouble to ... answer thereto'.[29] A pamphlet entitled 'Samuel Pepys. Plot, Popery and Piracy' gave him special attention, but its effects were negligible. Two constituencies were prepared to have him as their candidate, and by March 1679 he was elected MP for Harwich.

Meanwhile, Atkins at last came to trial before the Court of the King's Bench in Westminster Hall and was charged with being an accessory to the fact of Sir Godfrey's murder. The evidence for the actual murder was now planted on three apparently innocent men – Green, Berry and Hill – who were sentenced to death on such flimsy evidence that Pepys felt a surge of sympathy. Those trials lasted till three in the afternoon when Mr Atkins came to the bar, but was told he must stay for trial till the sessions and he was asked if he had bail ready. He said he was better prepared for his trial than to give bail. And upon his insisting to be tried and 'shewing his witnesses were sea-faring men who could not stay so long' the Bench agreed and the trial began.[30] Big, burly Sir William Jones, the Attorney General, opened the case with a description of Bedloe discovering Atkins on Monday 14 October looking down at Godfrey's body in discussion with his fellow murderers. Captain Atkins was then called and Jones put the question to him 'What is the name of Mr Samuel Atkins's employer?' 'Mr Pepys.' 'What, Mr Pepys of the Navy?' 'Yes, My Lord.'

It is not difficult to imagine Pepys's feelings as his name began to dominate the exchanges. Then a new and totally unexpected witness was produced – a boy – who was prepared to swear that Samuel Atkins, the so-called Protestant, had frequently been seen by him at Mass in Somerset House. Before he gave evidence the boy stood hesitating in an outer ante-room where Samuel Atkins deliberately accosted him and asked: 'Do you know me?' Unaware that Atkins was the prisoner, the boy said no. Thus, at the outset, his evidence was invalidated. Bedloe, still a key witness for the prosecution, suffered a similar fate. Pepys's carefully documented account of Samuel Atkins's activities for the three days covering the murder so confused Bedloe that he modified his statement and said he was no longer certain of the identity of the man standing over the body – 'the light being so poor'.[31] Finally, the jury retired to return a verdict of not guilty. Samuel Atkins fell on his knees and cried 'God bless the King and this honourable bench.'[32]

Pepys might have repeated this cry with a different cast of characters. He had reason to thank Samuel Atkins for his unfailing courage in the face of brutal questioning and the threat of death. He had probably saved Pepys's life. No sooner had the threat receded than it renewed itself. On 14 April 1679 one of Shaftesbury's henchmen, Bennet, rose in the House of Commons and demanded an enquiry into the state of the Navy. Preliminary references to wild extravagances allowed under Pepys were followed by the renewed charge that Popery riddled the Navy. Overtaken by the rush of his own rhetoric Bennet shouted at the House, 'I will prove Popery in your fleet at the bar.'[33] Pepys replied with equal vehemence and declared that all his vigilance had been engaged to defeat Popery. There remained the inescapable fact that the Lord High Admiral was associated with Catholicism which tarnished every argument Pepys presented.

Once again the indefatigable Secretary set about collecting evidence and building a detailed case, this time in his own defence. Surrounded in documentation Pepys suddenly came to a cliff-edge. The rising tide of anti-Popery among the populace was reflected in a House of Commons which constantly clamoured for sacrificial victims. Now, unexpectedly, the King dismissed his privy councillors and ministers and replaced them with the shadow council from the Opposition. The Admiralty passed into alien hands. Shaftesbury became President of the Council and a new commission took over the office of Lord High Admiral. The majority of the seven members of the commission belonged to the Opposition and three were waiting to discredit, if not ruin, Pepys. Once again Pepys the survivor escaped the purge. It was strategically important for the King to assuage the rising tide of public opinion without destroying that symbol of steady continuity represented by Pepys. There remained a major difficulty. How could Pepys work with new commissioners already predisposed against him? Any doubts that remained in his mind must have disappeared when on Monday 28 April came the announcement of a parliamentary committee to enquire into miscarriages of the Navy. Once again the committee was alive with his enemies, including William Harbord, son of Sir Charles Harbord, Lord Sandwich's friend.

The committee met for the first time on the same afternoon in the Speaker's chamber and post-haste sent a letter to Pepys demanding a list of all officers in the Navy with the names of their sponsors.[34] Pepys's first answer was evasive. He himself had not recommended exclusively any officer nor had he taken fees which might have accrued – legally – to him. The commission found this answer very unsatisfactory and pressed home their enquiries among his clerks. The time had come for Pepys to decide whether he could tolerate yet another inquisition. He now wrote a detailed and very persuasive letter to the Duke of York in which, in effect, he offered his resignation. Whether he liked it or not, he said, his enemies were determined that he must be a Papist because he was favoured by His Royal Highness, which forced him to consider leaving his Secretaryship providing certain provisions were made for him. 'I should be in a very ill condition to bear its not being made up to me by His Majesty ... or at least making some other provision for me as one superannuated in the service.'[35] On 1 May a second letter went to William Harbord in response to the committee's enquiries, giving an answer in full to the committee's charges. These charges included money misapplied, gentlemen appointed as commanders, ships left to decay, new ships unfinished and stores empty.[36] The letter repeated his offer of resignation but still without making it final. Pepys struggled on for another month trying to accommodate the committee's requirements and only surrendered when it became clear that the new powers given to the Admiralty Board would override his.

John Scott then reappeared once more. Following orders from Shaftesbury he had landed in England only to be arrested under an outstanding warrant and thrown into Dover gaol. Quite undismayed, he immediately wrote a letter to Shaftesbury who was now in effect the Prime Minister. Investigation of his movements revealed a man arriving secretly by fishing boat, carrying maps of English coasts and harbours which showed England's innermost defences. Before his arrest he was known to have drunk toasts to the downfall of the House of Stuart and, in particular, that of a man called Samuel Pepys. On 20 May the committee declared that the Secretary of the Admiralty Office was guilty of piracy, Popery and treachery. Each charge carried severe penalties and, taken together, made death certain. It is not difficult to imagine Pepys's reactions. Shortly afterwards the House of Commons, packed with republicans, arraigned Pepys in an atmosphere clearly hostile. The lobby too was crowded with Green Ribbon members and a riff-raff of paid informers set to create disturbance. Among them, resplendent in lace and silver, strode the 'tall form and dark leering countenance of Colonel Scott'. Shortly afterwards he 'swaggered up to the bar of the House of Commons' to reveal that his friend John Browne had seen Sir Anthony Deane giving M. Pellissary, Treasurer General of the French Navy, a packet of highly confidential naval charts. Deane and Will Hewer had both been received at the French court and moved in circles which included French naval ministers. Pepys not only suffered guilt by association but was said by Scott to be the inspiration behind a Popish invasion of England from France. Scott summed up his attack: Pepys was a great betrayer of his country and one of the arch-traitors of the kingdom. There were reasons, as we have seen, why Scott should seek to revenge himself on Pepys, but he was politically implicated with Shaftesbury, Buckingham and Harbord. Did they provide the liberal finances required to pay for his continuous travelling and relaxed way of life? Pepys accepted all the circumstantial evidence which implicated Shaftesbury. Harbord was equally suspect. Chairman of the Miscarriages committee, he coveted the perquisites of Pepys's office.

Whoever held the purse-strings, Harbord himself introduced the next witness, John James, an ex-butler of Pepys's. Morelli, Pepys's musical friend – banished from his household – had one day discovered James in bed with, apparently, Pepys's housekeeper. It might have been Mary Skinner, which sets off intriguing speculation about Pepys's reactions. Pepys had sacked him. In any event, James's evidence was very damaging.[37] According to him, Pepys kept the Jesuitical Morelli in his household for religious as well as musical reasons. Morelli composed masses which they indulged on Sunday mornings accompanied by specially selected psalms. Pepys's accusers specialised in colourful detail and now James decorated his evidence with a secret door in Morelli's chamber, giving on to a closet full of weapons, beads and crucifixes. According to James, Pepys himself had frequently admitted in his presence that only those given preference by the Duke of York stood any chance of employment in the Navy.[38] Several minor witnesses now rose to drive home the attack. Replying, Pepys first examined the case against the Duke of York.[39] If the Duke of York had named some officers, Pepys said, that was no reason why a general reproach should be cast upon the Navy. 'The Duke is unfortunate and with my life I will rescue him . . . From the moment I have been in employment I never knew that the Duke gave countenance to anyone Catholic.'[40] Pepys's loyalty to the Duke was admirable since the mood of the country was against him. Pepys turned to the evidence of his butler. 'Mr James was recommended to me by Sir R. Mason . . . it was his [James's] ill luck to fall into an amour with my housekeeper and, as fortune was, Morelli overheard their intrigue and catched them together. . . . It was Sunday at three o'clock in the morning . . . I turned him away and he was never in my house again . . .' As for psalm-singing with Morelli: 'I entertained myself harmlessly with him . . .'[41] Detail by detail Pepys undermined James's evidence and presented the true picture: a sacked butler had decided to have his revenge on his employer. There exists a retraction of all the evidence James gave, dictated the following year in March 1680 which named those who hired him, including Harbord.[42] It also revealed links with Scott.

The conspirators against Pepys had laid their plans carefully. If the charge of Popery lacked sufficient conviction they were to divert their attack to his piratical use of the sloop *Hunter*. During the Third Dutch War, Sir Anthony Deane and Pepys's ubiquitous brother-in-law Balty formed a partnership to borrow the sloop *Hunter* from the King and equipped her to operate as a privateer. Pepys belonged to the exclusive school which learnt by experience but his previous venture with Penn and Batten did not warn him that where he himself had failed Balty was hardly likely to succeed. Thomas Swaine, the *Hunter*'s captain, had deliberately misinterpreted his instructions, widened his predatory range and harassed and plundered English ships.[43] Now, four years later, a charge of piracy was laid by the committee. It put new life into the case against Pepys which was showing signs of flagging. In the summer of 1679 Colonel Scott again reinforced the charges before the committee by saying that Monsieur Pellissary, Treasurer General to the French Navy, had shown him many incriminating papers signed by Pepys. On the same day Pepys began his reply ironically, 'It is a mighty misfortune that I am charged with so many cumulative ills at once ... As to what related to the *Hunter* ... I answer I never was at the Admiralty nor was I directly or indirectly interested in anything of it. I know neither ship nor share in her.'[44] Given the known facts, this was a remarkable statement. He then turned to his alleged complicity with Monsieur Pellissary. 'That papers in France were signed by me, 'tis Scott's "Yes, by report" – 'tis my "No, before Almighty God." I have ever industriously avoided being within the smell of the French ambassador.'[45]

Behind the scenes Pepys continued preparing evidence to defeat his by now hell-bent opponents. His clerks drew up a list of the names, salaries and wages of all naval officers beginning with Prince Rupert, Vice Admiral of England and Lieutenant Admiral of the Narrow Seas, earning £469.5.9d. Next came Pepys, Secretary, deliberately left blank by the clerk. Pepys entered the word 'nothing', which was a deliberate lie.[46] Matters came to a head on Thursday 22 May. A bill was passed excluding the Duke of York from succession to the crown and Pepys and Deane were brought once more before the House in the face of renewed charges.

Overwhelming hostility confronted them and, within a few hours under the Speaker's warrant (which did not contain a reason), they were committed to the Tower. It was left to Harbord to present the evidence to the Attorney General with a view to prosecution. There followed a series of delaying tactics which infuriated Pepys but did not stop him concentrating on the exposure of the true nature of Scott. His papers in the Pepys Library include a document headed 'A brief of the Case of Sir Anthony Deane and Mr Pepys' which gives a day-by-day account of what followed. There is no evidence in these documents that Pepys felt any fear the trial might prove fatal. Clearly, he remained so confident of his innocence that, given the judicial atmosphere of the courtroom, he was sure that truth must prevail. Nine days after his arrest a number of incidents took place. 'They were brought by Habeas Corpus to the King's Bench and upon occasion of the Attorney General being ill ... were remitted back to the Tower till Monday following.'[47] On Monday 2 June they were brought again to the King's Bench and, denied bail, they moved for a speedy trial.[48] On this occasion the Attorney General acknowledged that he had sufficient evidence for the charge of piracy but not for that of treason. However, until he could gather additional evidence he must renew their commitment to the Tower.

Most accounts of life in the Tower reveal that it was relatively relaxed, for gentlemen of private means could import outside 'luxuries'. The rules, according to the diary of General Williamson, Deputy Lieutenant of the Tower, theoretically made this impossible. The Orders for Close Prisoners read:

1. That no message be carried to the prisoners but by the gentleman gaoler.
2. That the sentinel posted on a prisoner suffer none to come within their posts or to go into the prisoner's house ...
3. The warder appointed to keep a close prisoner shall not presume to leave him for a moment either by day or night ...[49]

None of this seems to have troubled Pepys. Heating in the Tower was erratic but summer had begun and neither imprisonment nor regulations could quite quell his spirits. On one occasion Evelyn sent a ready roasted fowl ahead to the Tower and they dined together convivially. At the outset Pepys had the support of the Duke of York, who wrote to the King asking him to do everything in his power to help someone who had spent 'so many years in your service and to your satisfaction'.[50] A tide of letters poured from Pepys to everyone capable of exposing Scott's true character or willing to bear witness on Pepys's behalf. One went to Henry Savile, now English ambassador in Paris, saying that no less than Pepys's life was at stake.[51]

Much of the evidence against him emanated from Paris and Savile had all the powers required to check on Scott. Saturated in Parisian life, a streak of the *boulevardier* enabled him to disregard diplomatic niceties and make indiscreet enquiries. Another stream of letters went to friends and lawyers, putting Pepys's affairs in order in case of his death and – surprisingly – borrowing £100 for legal fees. His correspondence indicated his range of friends and contacts, one written to Evelyn who represented the world of learning, another to Houblon representing commerce, a third to Sir Robert Southwell in political life.[52] Still dissatisfied, Pepys sought for a personal envoy in Paris and his brother-in-law Balty presented himself as a devoted relation with 'a knowledge of the place and the language'. Whether influenced by Pepys or not, the King released Balty from his new appointment as muster master to Tangier and granted him leave to visit France. Hopelessly unstable in personal relations and reckless with money, Balty had yet shown himself an efficient muster master and he leapt at the chance to visit his beloved Paris and serve his brother-in-law. Originally intended to operate under the surveillance

of Brisbane, secretary of the Paris embassy, Balty found himself free
and at large to indulge himself when Brisbane was suddenly recalled,
and the self-dramatising egoist was slowly converted into the shrewd
secret agent. Accustomed to mix with dubious characters in naval
dockyards, Balty must have found communications with the crooks
and conmen, who were Scott's cronies, relatively easy. Pepys's letters
explore what followed between them, but most of Balty's reports
have not been preserved.[53] Some depositions remain in volume six
of Rawlinson's manuscripts and Balty seems their obvious source.
One such manuscript was headed 'To Prove John Scott a Scandalous
Person not to be believed – A particular account of what passed
between me, William Rooper and Colonel Scott . . .'[54]

Most significant among the motley crew Balty encountered was
John Joyne, a man thought to be a watchmaker who had sheltered
Scott while on the run in Paris. Scott had absconded in the middle
of the night owing Joyne forty pistoles and he was hot-foot for
revenge. Pepys wrote to Balty: 'I do . . . repeat my desire of his
[Joyne's] coming over with all speed. And as to what you wrote
that his intention of coming . . . should not be published . . . I will
keep it as little spoken of as may be.'[55] When he arrived, the story
Joyne unfolded became steadily more complex, involving a whole
network of people. One among them, named Sherwin, swore that
on the very day Deane was said to have been seen by Scott handing
over charts to Monsieur Pellissary in Paris, Scott was in fact at Nevers
in France practising his old craft of gun-casting.[56] Sherwin also recalled
remarks that Scott made about the King: 'All his family came from
nothing but whoredom and witchcraft . . .' A third witness unearthed
by Balty was a member of a distinguished English family named
Foster, then living a debauched life in exile. He had, he said, seen
Scott preparing his confidential maps and heard him say that he was
going to have his revenge on a man called Pepys who had long
hounded him.[57]

Pepys hastened to point out to Balty that hearsay evidence was
insufficient when dealing with his powerful adversaries. Every detail
must be substantiated by corroborative evidence capable of standing
searching cross-examination. He wrote to Balty: 'And therefore by
the way, pray learn of me this one lesson . . . to be most slow to
believe what we most wish to be true.'[58] Pepys himself momentarily
believed that written depositions would be sufficient if witnesses
refused to appear in person, but his counsel reminded him that English
law required live witnesses capable of being cross-examined. By

20 June the law term had opened but still the prosecution was not ready to proceed.

The brief Diary in the Rawlinson papers records Pepys's renewed attempts to get bail, instead of which he was removed from the Tower to the Marshalsea prison. And then at last on 9 July he was granted bail for the huge sum of £30,000. A long procession of witnesses arriving in England from France now began, some of them uninvited, but as late as October Joyne was still missing.[59] On the day before the next term began, 23 October 1679, Deane and Pepys had once more appeared before Sir William Jones the Attorney General and requested an acceleration of the long delayed trial, only to find that the King had decided to rid himself of Sir William without nominating a successor. Surrendering to bail, they were told to reappear once more on the last day of the term. A series of incidents was to lead eventually to Pepys's concealing himself behind a curtain listening to the actual voice of Scott.

The arrival of Joyne in London on 27 October set the whole drama in motion. On the 30th Pepys found himself entertaining, at the Crown tavern near the Royal Exchange, a set of highly dubious characters amongst whom Joyne was relatively innocent. For the first time Pepys was in touch with a demi-world of roguery, and the stories they unfolded left him more alarmed than optimistic.[60] The prospect of an early trial also diminished despite the King's intervention to pressurise the appointment of a new Attorney General.

By 13 November it was clear that no trial would take place until another new term and on the same day there was a dramatic demonstration of one hundred thousand Protestants parading through the streets to burn publicly, at Smithfield, an effigy of the Pope. One central figure was still missing from the scene – Scott – but Joyne discovered that he had returned to London and immediately set about tracing him. Accident intervened on 24 November when Joyne, leaving his lodgings in Long Acre, observed a familiar figure entering Drury Lane. It was Scott and their mutual embrace – recorded as warm – must have been a remarkable exercise in hypocrisy. That evening, Joyne spent a few hours with Scott at the Dog and Dripping Pan which yielded nothing more than a description of Scott's political manipulations. Joyne sought out Pepys to announce his first success. Uneasy with anything but concrete evidence, Pepys instructed Joyne to keep a journal of everything that transpired between himself and Scott.[61] Incapable of the discipline required for such an undertaking he had to be supervised by Paul Lorrain, Pepys's copy clerk.

The delay in coming to trial meant that Balty was confronted by a number of French witnesses kicking their heels in bad lodgings and clamouring to get back to France. Pepys proceeded to Westminster Hall on 28 November to press vigorously for immediate trial or discharge from bail. The Lord Chief Justice remained evasive. Nothing could be done without a new Attorney General. John Joyne next reported disturbing news from Scott. He had eleven new witnesses arriving from France and had procured incriminating papers alleged to have been delivered by Deane to the French Naval Secretary. When Parliament met he would 'deluge the Members' with this damning evidence. The King then upset Scott's plans and – out of countenance with the government – prorogued Parliament.[62] This gave Pepys and Joyne the opportunity to pursue their enquiries. By now Pepys was beginning to be sceptical about the stream of villainy pouring so conveniently from Scott's lips. Joyne thereupon arranged a theatrical climax. The Colonel would be invited to a meal at a tavern where Pepys could listen to his conversation, concealed behind a curtain.[63] Joyne arranged for his sister, the owner of St Clement's tavern in the Strand, to provide a meal for Scott while Pepys sat in an adjoining closet. The scene belonged to melodrama. The great gentleman from high places in his fine clothes crouched in a dark 'hole of a room' listening to the conman's confidences. Unfortunately, these secrets did not amount to much. They consisted of a series of boasts about Scott's love life, a maudlin lament at the death of his mistress Lady Vane, the threat to kidnap and marry her daughter, and an occasional burst into bawdy singing.[64] Pepys left reassured, if a little alarmed, at the obvious camaraderie between Joyne and Scott. Joyne put the evidence on paper and since Pepys had heard much of it, there was some corroboration.

It was flimsy, but Scott had incriminated himself in two ways. He had taken a vigorous part in pressing the petition from the city intended to force the hand of the King to reopen Parliament. He also said that one of the Duke of York's few friends was that rogue Pepys.[65] Almost simultaneously a new pamphlet attacking Pepys appeared called 'A Hue and Cry After Pepys' which renewed the charges of illicit fees paid to him for permissions and protection. Its authorship was uncertain. Pepys suspected Scott but his ex-butler James and a clerk Donlius came under suspicion.

Throughout his bail period Pepys had taken refuge with Will Hewer and his mother in their house in York Buildings where his room looked out on the river. Still well to do, with his financial resources shrewdly preserved, Pepys could afford to set up a minor menage of his own including Katharine the maid, Paul Lorrain his copy clerk, and his coachman. No mention appears of Mary Skinner.[66]

Pepys's campaign to collect evidence now reached its climax and great names – the Duke of Buckingham and Lord Shaftesbury – recurred with increasing frequency. Time, however, was running short. If the petition from the city and other pressures forced the King to recall Parliament before Pepys's case was tried he would be subject to the rough justice of Parliament instead of the rule of common law. It must have been a testing time for Pepys. Having exhausted himself collecting evidence, he now faced the possibility of all his work becoming useless. Dining one evening with Anthony Deane they determined to force the issue with the new Attorney General fourteen days before term began. Together they met the Attorney General in his chambers and explained their predicament with witnesses from France needing support so long as the trial was delayed.[67] He retaliated with the news that more evidence had been found against them but was not yet confirmed. It began to appear as if these artificially created frustrations would multiply indefinitely. Once again the persecuted pair gathered their resources and forced an appearance before the Court of King's Bench. Represented by no less than four counsels led by 'the fat, jovial' Mr Saunders and flanked by all their French witnesses, they applied for immediate release under Habeas Corpus or a trial within ten days. Judge Pemberton bore out his reputation by wrapping the application in a cloud of legal technicalities. Irritated by the battle between his counsel, Saunders, and Pemberton, Pepys intervened personally to say that he simply wanted a trial not a discharge. The Court then agreed that the Attorney General must answer the question one way or another by the following Tuesday.[68] The Attorney General himself faced the complication that Harbord's witnesses refused to testify unless Parliament was in session.

Matters became even more complicated when the butler James was accused of receiving money from Harbord by one of Pepys's former clerks Phelix Lewis. He gave a statement to Will Hewer and Paul Lorrain enlivened by slang redolent of the street language of the day.[69] According to Lewis, James expected employment in return for bearing false witness against Pepys, but when no job materialised he remarked: 'The devil take me if I believe any one of them any more for they are my arse all over.' Once again the end of term made legal proceedings impossible. Whether spontaneously or at Pepys's request, the King again intervened asking the Attorney General to resolve the issue – punctiliously. The Court reconvened on 12 February when the Attorney General spoke again of incriminating letters delivered to him via an intermediary of Scott's. The Court then called for Scott's appearance in person only to be told that he refused to attend. He had picked up rumours of Pepys's activities and was averse to meeting him personally in a court of law. Under pressure, the Court at last agreed that Pepys and Deane could be discharged from bail with certain provisos. Pepys was disinclined to accept these but Deane, sitting anxiously beside him, whispered urgently 'Take it! Take it!', knowing how suspicious it would seem should Pepys insist on a permanent discharge.[70] No longer able to board and lodge his crowd of witnesses, Pepys spent the next fortnight taking depositions and packing them off to France. It left him in a relatively weak position when suddenly another witness, James the butler, fell dangerously ill. Considering James's evidence crucial, Pepys began keeping a new Diary around his last days. Harbord and his friends paid several visits to the dying man trying to get him to sign a document which accused Pepys of persuading him to bear false witness. They did not hesitate – according to his mother – to disturb the sick room with their argument, persuasions and even quarrels. It was all in vain. Instead, before he died James signed a document admitting that his accusations against Pepys as a Papist and Morelli as a Jesuit were lies. This became an important part of Pepys's defence. Scott was now fully aware of the dossier of damning evidence built up by Pepys which, unfortunately for Pepys, defeated the whole exercise: Scott refused to go to court or to the House to face such detailed revelations about himself. On 11 June Deane and Pepys returned to face a court ruling and were dismayed to be told that they must wait until the last day of term. On 28 June the Attorney General was again asked what remained to be said against discharging the prisoners. He found himself driven into a corner. He had to admit that there was – 'nothing'. So, at last, a painful and prolonged episode, testing Pepys's nerve to breaking point, was over.[71]

Chapter 18

Temporary retirement – the Tangier expedition

By the winter of 1680 the Popish Plot was beginning to falter.[1] Shaftesbury, trying to create the threat of an Irish Plot, let it be known that he was in danger of assassination, but the public did not react with any great alarm. The King's attempt to relieve Parliamentary pressure and take the heat out of the plot was beginning to work, but international affairs were reacting against the new stability. The English alliance with Spain and negotiations with the Dutch made the French highly suspicious of English policy. Louis had spent a great deal of money buying English neutrality but now he was called upon to bribe Parliament, and the Duke of York let it be known that any surplus money available should rightly be his. Clearly, Louis had complicated motives, at the heart of which were economic interests. He sought a balance of power across Europe which was centred on the restoration of Catholicism in England. When Charles's fourth Parliament opened on 21 October 1680 the main business of the House of Commons was the second Exclusion Bill which rendered James guilty of high treason if he returned to England after 5 November 1680 and hence would debar him from succession.[2]

In the Lords, Shaftesbury and Essex were passionate advocates of the Exclusion Bill and the debate ran far into the night with MPs and even the King in attendance as spectators. A long and damaging exchange between Shaftesbury and Halifax saw Halifax steadily wearing down his opponent and rallying waverers against the Bill. In the intense atmosphere swords were drawn, threats made and the Speaker (Orator) had to be protected. The Lords finally rejected the Bill by sixty-three votes to thirty.[3]

Pepys saw these events from a different perspective. He was now a man free from persecution, breathing the sweet air of acquittal, but as yet unaccustomed to his new leisure. Throughout his fifteen months' persecution there is no evidence of Mary Skinner in his life, but one of the first people he wrote to was her mother. His letter to Frances Skinner said:

I would not omit giving you the knowledge of my having at last
obtained what with as much reason I might have expected a year ago.
I mean my full discharge from the bondage I have from one villain's
practice so lain under. However . . . justice ought to be welcome at
any time, and so I receive it with thanks to God Almighty. . .[4]

Several similar letters went to people like Houblon and Evelyn celebrating his newfound freedom.[5] Temperamentally, Pepys was a man most at ease when most engaged and as the pressures fell away sought something to fill the relative vacuum. Almost immediately he set to work with his clerk Paul Lorrain to begin the compilation of the two volumes of Mornamont to enshrine for posterity the story of Scott and his persecution.[6] When drunk Scott was liable to lay claim to a magnificent castle which he called Mornamont and Pepys appropriated the name for his title. Meanwhile, Pepys's social life expanded and he spent many a pleasant afternoon in the hot June sunshine with his cousin, Lady Mordaunt, who found his conversation irresistible. Indeed, long ago, in the time of Salisbury Court, she was said to have been desperately in love with him.[7]

It is doubtful whether Lady Mordaunt slept with him, even though it would have been remarkable for Pepys to have been completely free of his former urges. Evelyn also kept him company for many an evening where 'everything under the sun' was tirelessly discussed. Their friendship had steadily deepened and Bryant records Evelyn's staying up all night to write a sixteen-page letter in reply to Pepys's persistent historical probings. It was Evelyn, too, who urged him to resume his attendances at the Royal Society which had 'fallen into disrepair'. Pepys the amateur scientist had widened his interests to include experiments with the elasticity of glass, transfusion and infusion. 'By invitation' he had also been 'to see an experiment of killing a dogg by . . . opium'. With cold scientific detachment he recorded: 'the dog did presently fall asleep and so lay until we cut him up.'[8]

With his zest for living, Pepys's newfound liberty sharpened his appetite for every minor and major pleasure. As one sunny day followed another in congenial company, one cloud remained to trouble him. There were large sums owed to him by the government which needed the King's authorisation before they could be paid. Cleared of all charges, Pepys was respectable company for the King who still valued his advice and as the summer drew to a close he accompanied His Majesty to Newmarket. Bucolic life quickly called on Pepys and once again he refused to remain idle. There, in the midst of company which enjoyed hunting and shooting, enlivened by court ladies and some of easier virtue, he settled down to record, at the King's request, the story of his long drawn out escape from Worcester in 1651.[9] The King never ceased to marvel at Pepys's shorthand feats which enabled him to lie back at leisure and pour out the story. From the pace of the condensed narrative it is clear that Pepys greatly edited Charles's ramblings. His opening sentence was nicely calculated to arrest the reader's attention. 'After that the battle was so absolutely lost as to be beyond recovery I began to think of the best way of saving myself . . .' The two men must have worked intensively since they completed the narrative in three days. The social historian was in his element.

Personal tragedy then intervened. News arrived – a day late – that Pepys's father had died at Brampton of a mysterious ague which also afflicted his sister Pall. Before he could reach Brampton his father was buried but Pepys hurried over to attend his sister. There he found his father's affairs in the expected muddle but his sister on the road to recovery. Hurrying back to London he acquired a power of attorney for his father, cleared up his own delayed affairs and returned to risk the infection. For nearly a month he ignored the political news from London and tried to accommodate the dull routine of country life, with winter coming, his sister still bedridden and his father's papers a poor substitute for the grandiose affairs of the Navy. Pepys was also coping with a row of letters from Balty which excelled in his special combination of complexity and self-pity. Muster master at Tangier, Balty set out in September 1680 and addressed his benefactor: 'Most ever honoured Sir . . . After my having given your dear honour millions of thanks . . . for the present employment . . . I have in so much confusion, pain, disquiets and discouragements . . . I am sacrificed and torn from the bowels of my sweet little family and from my fine small babes who cried after their own father . . .'[10]

Meanwhile, away in London, the possibility of civil war seemed dangerously real. The Popish Plot persisted but Charles had revealed unexpected skills in parrying, sidestepping and even risking occasional confrontation. The threat of violence crept closer to his person when his royal physician Sir George Wakeman was charged with plotting to poison him. Coincidentally, the King did in fact fall ill, but from natural causes. Now the King's defence against the republicans showed signs of crumbling until it seemed that every friend of the

Duke of York was in danger. By December 1680 the two camps were heading for direct collision, one led by Lord Shaftesbury, and the other by the King. A small fish in these waters, Colonel Scott had become a member of the Green Ribbon club and was busy arranging to arm the mobs which had already burnt an effigy of the Duke of York in public. The threat of civil war was further heightened when rumours circulated that Shaftesbury intended to draw a line round Whitehall and arrest everybody within its circumference, including the King. Unknown to Shaftesbury, Pepys or anyone except those directly involved, the King was in contact around the clock with agents who kept him informed of plans for armed revolution, which steadily dominated Shaftesbury's thinking. Still living at Brampton, Pepys had turned his attention to writing an account of his late defence. Houblon and Hewer continued to feed him the latest political news from London.[11] They reported that members of the Green Ribbon club were circulating rumours of a frightened Pepys who had 'fled to join the Duke of York in exile in Edinburgh' and Hewer advised him to return to London to confound the lie.[12] Excluded from the political arena, Pepys fretted, impatient for action, and when Hewer revealed that the King had referred a dispute before the Council to 'our Mr Pepys', he resolved to return immediately.

According to Houblon, Pepys's managerial mind was very much missed at the Admiralty Board where political intervention had undermined much of his reconstruction. The distribution of the Navy for the defence of England was in disarray and England's Mediterranean interests were unprotected by a single warship. The ever faithful Hewer offered his house as a London home for Pepys and prepared an elaborate welcome for him. Two days later on 17 November 1680 Pepys set out for London only to encounter six highwaymen who systematically robbed him. After fourteen months' persecution and three months living in the sticks, it was to him no great matter. On the very day Pepys returned to London, Halifax, Sir William Coventry's nephew, led the debate in the House of Lords which dramatically threw out the Exclusion Bill. In furious reaction the House of Commons impeached and ruthlessly condemned to death the ageing Lord Stafford for what seemed no other reason than his Catholic faith. Parliament then refused to continue supplies to Tangier unless the Bill was reinstated. Tempers mounted, positions hardened, the debate slipped back to the Fire of London and forward to refusing supplies in any form for Tangier. A harassed and gloomy King Charles, his patience exhausted, first prorogued Parliament and then considered dissolving it. Fear ran through London. An address was made to the Lord Mayor of London, '. . . humbly recommend[ing] . . . as highly necessary the doubling of night watches . . . and . . . the city gates be locked'.[13]

Bills and pamphlets were published from the republican presses openly challenging the gathering forces of the crown. Throughout the country rusty pikes and breastplates were refurbished in the growing belief that they would soon be needed once more. Meanwhile, the Admiralty Commission and the Council were rapidly changing their complexion. Several members resigned from the Commission and the rebels on the Council suddenly found it expedient to withdraw, a move which the King welcomed. The Army trained its guns on the city, soldiers patrolled the gates and the main roads to Oxford, a favourite retreat in time of trouble, came under surveillance. In the Treasury chambers, debates about sending troops to protect the Tower if the city opposed them became heated.[14] The King decided to remove Parliament to Oxford away from the influence of the London mobs who could so often be manipulated to desired ends. Arriving in Oxford the crowds cheered him as he drove in full panoply through the streets, and one bystander shouted, 'Remember your royal father and keep the staff in your hands.'[15] Nobody knew that the King had signed a new agreement with Louis of France providing Charles with funds independent of Parliament which would enable him to pay the Army and Navy without surrendering to political demands. He agreed to make some concessions. In private negotiations he surrendered to the demands that the Duke of York be banished in perpetuity. He also agreed to vest the crown on his death in the regency of Mary of Orange. These propositions were rejected without debate in the Commons. Driven to act, on 28 March Charles simply dissolved Parliament. The republicans had cut their own throats.

Pepys played no part in all this, but he kept his ear to the ground and resisted any temptation to visit his old haunts or make contact with ex-colleagues. The weather remained atrocious with persistent snow which did not encourage the recovery of his sister Pall, now brought to London for consultation with leading physicians. Late in March Pepys himself fell seriously ill with the mysterious ague – which might have been the forerunner of flu.[16] For the whole month of April the illness dragged on and put to the test the sturdy resistance of his basically healthy body. Never inactive for long, he continued to work perfecting his account of the King's escape from Worcester with the thoroughness of the born historian. By May he had fully recovered, and was busy procuring a loyal address to the throne from Trinity House as part of the royal celebrations at Oxford. These celebrations were somewhat premature because the King could not dislodge Shaftesbury from his city stronghold. He continued to control the sheriffs who appointed London juries, which made it impossible for any loyalist to get a fair hearing.

Pepys meanwhile completed his history of the Worcester escape and tried to occupy his days with trivia about his small properties. After prolonged hesitation he decided not to sell Brampton in case he should eventually retire there. Certain repairs were necessary to the house and on a hot summer's day he set out to look over the property himself. Walking in the beautiful countryside with his cousin Joseph Maryon he remarked how marvellous it was to relax 'next to nature' and spoke for the first time of retirement to such a place. No sooner had he expressed this thought than he returned to London and learnt that Sir Thomas Page, the Provost of King's College, had died. His politically sophisticated cousin Joseph wrote to tell him that he was the ideal man to replace Page if the King would mandate his preferment.[17] It was a very tempting proposition. Academia offered in those days an even more relaxed way of life than it does now, with the pleasure of scholarly company and his own home almost within walking distance. Contemplating the disorder of the papers he had collected for his great history of the Navy, he reflected on how pleasant it would be to catalogue them and have sufficient leisure to begin writing. The whole proposition was suddenly undermined when he approached Colonel Legge, the Duke of York's London agent, and learnt that he had already committed himself to support a different candidate as Provost of King's – Doctor Copplestone. Once again chance had influenced his destiny. If Colonel Legge's decision had not pre-empted Pepys, it is possible that Pepys would have settled back in the groves of academia preoccupied with academic politics.

A close circle of friends and relations still surrounded Pepys, some already supported by him, others clamouring for aid of one kind or another. Morelli continued to receive an annual retainer from Pepys although no longer living in his house or providing musical entertainment. His maid, coachman, and the clerk Lorrain, had to be paid and, with Balty away in Tangier, Esther St Michel, his wife, complained that she lived under conditions worse than those of the poorest servant. Pall was still not well enough to look after her sons, Samuel and John, which forced Pepys to board the two boys with a schoolmaster in Huntingdon, and provide them with an allowance, although it was minimal. Mary Skinner's lazy brother Daniel was packed off to Barbados with letters of introduction to Sandwich's one-time steward. In semi-retirement Pepys fulfilled more activities than the average professional man. On 25 March 1681 he was 'on the rampage' about the mathematical master at Christ's Hospital and sent Dr Wood an ultimatum. Wood was a learned man trapped in the 'lowliness and drudgery' of teaching ordinary mathematics and Pepys insisted to the governors that they must find someone without over-reaching ambition who was ready to be a 'bare land navigator'. He wrote to Sir John Frederick:

you will in nowise content yourselves ... with a person knowing only
... the theory of mathematics without practice; it seeming to me not
only in itself absurd that a foundation expressly instituted for the
improvement of navigation should be under the conduct of one wholly
unconversant with ship or sea and therefore unable to properly even
discourse of the trade he is to teach.[18]

He would relax with his lively young cousin Lady Mordaunt, Thomas Hill his long-time merchant friend, and Morelli, who sent him new transcriptions from the opera. There is no evidence of Mary Skinner's whereabouts at the time but it would be impetuous to conclude that she still played a part in his life since every avenue of possible attack on his reputation had to be sealed against the revival of persecution. Was he living in sin with her, and did her republican association remain dangerous? Was he by now too grand a person casually to indulge an evening in the taverns, and had he lost interest in the theatre? The ladies of the town at this juncture of threatened civil war were doing a roaring trade. He wined and dined with several members of the Royal Society, including Sir Robert Southwell, Sir William Petty and Sir Christopher Wren. Correspondence flowed between them when they were out of London. In December 1681 Evelyn wrote a long, effusive letter which warned Pepys of the labyrinth of 'papers, treaties, declarations, letters and other pieces' into which the would-be historian of the Navy must be sucked, which caused 'fatigue unendurable'. It concluded with an even more intimidating list of letters, petitions, bonds and obligations: '... perfidious men betraying divers loyal persons, copies of letters from His Majesty and other letters and transactions there are yet by me many thousands'.[19] Pepys remained undismayed.

By April of 1682 the Duke of York's expectations had changed for the better. Once at the mercy of his enemies, his fortunes were again in the ascendant, but it was necessary for the heir presumptive to clear up any confusion of his Scottish affairs before reoccupying his place at the court of his brother Charles. Pepys was delighted to receive an invitation to accompany the Duke on his journey to Edinburgh. The Duke pressed Pepys to join him on board the *Gloucester* due to sail from the Margate Roads on 4 May but the ship was overcrowded and Pepys chose to transfer to the *Catherine*, one of the accompanying yachts. He did not foresee the dramatic consequences. They set sail with a friendly southerly wind, but by the evening the wind had shifted to the north and the weather steadily worsened. Fog came down in the night to be cleared by a gale the following day. On the second night they turned away from the shore to avoid running on Yarmouth sands and an argument followed between Captain Ayres, the pilot and the navigator. Encouraged by the Duke, the pilot was anxious to complete the voyage as quickly as possible and given his wide experience in these matters, he refused to take the longer tack to the south against the combined advice of the captain, his master and mates. While the ship battled through huge seas the argument continued fiercely, but the pilot would not give way. 'His Royal Highness was still of the opinion to stand off longer' and once more asked the pilot's opinion. The pilot said 'he would engage his life that if we tacked presently we should without hazard weather all sands'.[20]

Disaster struck at five-thirty the following morning. Grinding on treacherous sands, the *Gloucester* first reeled over and lay exposed to terrible seas. Then a huge wave simply tore away her rudder and split open the ship. Someone shook Pepys awake at six o'clock and he hurried on deck to witness a scene which must have astonished him. There before his eyes the ship he had abandoned was rapidly sinking and with it the Duke of York, Pepys's one hope of returning to high places in public life. Pepys wrote graphically to Will Hewer the following day: 'Our fortune was and the rest of the yachts to be near the *Gloucester* when she struck; between which and her final sinking there passed not, I believe, a full hour; the Duke and all about him being in bed and, to show security, the pilot himself, till waking by her knocks.'[21] The captain of the *Happy Return* had been following fast in the wake of the *Gloucester* and only the swift order from her captain to drop anchor saved her from suffering the same fate.[22] The seamen aboard the *Gloucester* made way for the Duke, Colonel Legge, Sir Charles Scarborough and others of the Duke's retinue to clamber into a boat and pull away towards the *Happy Return*. Even the Duke's footman and dog took precedence over the seamen. Later the pilot was arrested and brought to trial.[23]

Two days later a somewhat chastened Pepys had settled into his duties at Edinburgh and decided to take the opportunity to explore further north than Castle Rising, his old constituency. He visited Berwick, faced sea hazards once more to land on Holy Island, was ceremoniously received in Newcastle and emerged from these experiences disgusted with the personal hygiene of the Scots. Back in Newcastle, on the return journey, Pepys received good news by letter from Will Hewer. A warrant was out for Scott's arrest and in his absence a coroner's jury arrived at a verdict of guilty on a charge of wilful murder. Hewer also wrote to Pepys: 'You can't imagine what consternation all your friends in general were upon the report of you being cast away, but more especially [the ladies] at Cratched Friars, Winchester Street and Portugal Row.'[24] Houblon and Lady Mordaunt wrote similar letters revealing their despair that he might have sunk with the *Gloucester*.[25]

At last he was back in London again and quickly immersed in his historical research. The selection of a new master for the mathematical school led to conflict with Sir Isaac Newton backing a candidate in opposition to Pepys.[26] The original list of candidates was limited and Pepys expressed surprise in his naval minutes that many months of searching had produced so few.[27] Only two candidates on the shortlist had any experience of the sea, but against all Pepys's advice one of them, Edward Paget a Fellow of Trinity Cambridge, was on the verge of appointment when Pepys broke into indignant protest. It was of no avail. This lack of concern in naval literacy reflected itself in the activities of the new Commissioners at Derby House where Pepys's revolution in naval ratings was flouted at every turn. Pepys's evidence cannot be taken as objective and the picture he drew must be seen in the light of his resignation from the service. Not a single admiral, according to his findings, had any 'education of the sea'. Pepys complained of £100,000 lost on an Irish project; of merchantmen captured for lack of protection; and of the Chatham Chest three years in arrears of payment. Much larger sums than £100,000 frequently disappeared in naval projects, merchantmen were picked off from time to time, and the Chatham Chest was always in arrears. The administration had fallen into some disarray but Pepys's criticism was sweeping. None the less, in April 1683, Pepys took coach with Deane and Hewer to witness the launching of the ship *Neptune* and saw for himself the sad state of the yards. The *Neptune* was the last but one of the thirty new ships Pepys had pressed on the Navy and enormous industry had gone into their building.

By the autumn of 1682 the whole political background had undergone another dramatic change. The election of a loyal Lord Mayor and sherriffs had helped to challenge a last despairing attempt to overthrow King Charles, whereupon Shaftesbury had fled abroad to be followed by the notorious Scott. King Charles had begun to age and found his regular ten-mile walks exhausting. He led a less active social life and tried to get to bed by nine. His visits to Newmarket were still frequent and there, on the evening of 22 March 1683, a groom smoking a pipe knocked out the burning ashes and tried to smother the small fire which they caused.[28] It quickly ran out of control and by dawn the King's residence had turned to rubble. Paradoxically, the accident saved the King's life. A plot to murder him planned to put a haycart across the road on his return journey to London and riddle his coach with bullets from a ditch below the causeway. Delayed by the fire the coach was a day late and the conspirators had given up waiting in vain.[29]

Meanwhile, in London, events were becoming more propitious for Pepys every month, but it was a relative distraction which concentrated his attention. When the fourth Parliament of King Charles had opened on 21 October 1680, Charles had announced with some pride that during the prorogation he had negotiated an alliance with Spain, which made the defence of Tangier against the Moors an unnecessary proposition.[30] Immediately, the charge had arisen that the Tangier garrison consisted of a nest of Papists which might embezzle any money voted for its defence. These threats had receded but Tangier continued to swallow large sums of money and was a ceaseless drain on the King's finances. Early in the summer of 1683 the King decided that enough was enough. Beneath his easy-going nature Charles occasionally revealed that he was purposeful and could relentlessly pursue specific issues when the mood overtook him. The King planned in great secrecy to send a small fleet commanded by Lord Dartmouth with instructions to destroy the city walls, the forts and the greatly admired Mole.

In this the problem of compensating the inhabitants had to be considered. Searching for the right man to make such a complicated assessment, the name Pepys arose spontaneously.[31] When the proposal was put to Pepys his precise role was not immediately revealed to him. Fearing an outbreak of popular indignation from Tangier province, the King decided to keep his precise plan highly confidential. None the less Pepys received with pleasure the royal command to join the expedition. Whatever his precise duties, it meant that he was back in business as a top naval civil servant.[32] Pepys had collected no small part of his wealth from his Treasureship of Tangier in the past, and he was now about to become a major figure in its obsequies.

The party selected for the undertaking included George Legge, Lord Dartmouth, Will Hewer, the current Treasurer, Dr Thomas Kerr the Canon of Winchester, and Dr William Trumbull a Fellow of All Souls, steeped in legal learning. Henry Sheeres, an internationally known engineer who had been responsible for the Mole's construction, was also a key figure. His name stirred a small tremor in Pepys's mind as a one-time would-be seducer of Elizabeth.

Pepys left London for Tangier at two days' notice but in those two days performed an elaborate preparatory exercise. His naval minutes give a breakdown of the items he considered necessary for the expedition. First, letters of recommendation were carefully garnered from those naval persons in touch with Tangier. Then outstanding debts were meticulously listed and struck through as he paid them.[33] Books rated high in his priorities and were listed under different headings – marine, musical, fortifications. Small details of clothing were immaculately recorded, from four pairs of Linsey drawers; three pairs of shoes; one pair of galoshes; three pairs of worsted stockings; eight cravats and cuffs; thirteen handkerchiefs; two stomachers; flannel which might contain the colic; and a new sea gown.[34] The list continued over two pages. He also read up on local Spanish customs, some of which shocked him. Spaniards, he read, 'won't piss in streets' but in doorways and 'shit in pots' or even in household utensils. Mastering a smattering of Spanish phrases he learnt to use 'tu' only among the highest persons. Letters of farewell went to all his friends including Evelyn, Deane and Lady Mordaunt. On Monday 30 July he set out to meet Dr William Trumbull at Lambeth and together they travelled by coach towards Godalming. Trumbull's role in the expedition was at this stage even more mysterious than Pepys's who still had no inkling of why the King had torn him out of his retirement to send him to a place all too familiar in his correspondence with Balty. Trumbull, a lawyer, subsequently left an account of their expedition claiming that Lord Dartmouth waited until they were off Cape St Vincent before divulging its nature to Pepys. This was contradicted by Pepys's Tangier Journal. A letter from Evelyn said, 'You leave us naked at home that till you return from Barbary we are in danger of becoming Barbarians.' He expressed delight that Pepys had one more returned 'into the publique . . .'[35]

They set sail on Sunday 19 August from Plymouth and the rough weather quickly brought Pepys to bed with seasickness. It did not last long.[36] Pepys, contradicting Trumbull, in his Journal describes the nature of the mission thus:

14 August: Tuesday . . . into My Lord's cabin, where he took me into
his closet within his bedchamber and gave me his commission under
the Great Seal and his instructions referred to therein . . . At noon to
dinner and then into his cabin where I slept and after sleep he asked
me whether I had read those papers. So answering that I had not I
took a time . . . to leave him and went upon the poop quite abaft and
there alone not overlooked by anybody I read them over and over . . .[37]

According to Trumbull, Pepys was indignant at this delay in unveiling
the true nature of their work. No hint of discomfiture appears in
the Journal.[38]

At least three gladiatorial battles had taught Pepys the importance
of documented evidence and it was no surprise that he kept yet
another Journal in shorthand. The King's intentions were still
unknown to the public because highly charged questions would inevitably arise in the House of Commons. Englishmen had first looked
eagerly on Morocco as opening the way to untold wealth, fame
and empire. Now, at a single stroke, it was to be destroyed without
explanation. Pepys as the King's emissary might again become fair
game.

Saturday 25 August: So at night to bed a little sickish the weather being
bad and very bad indeed it was all night we being then about Land's
End.[39] Sunday 26 August: Very much out of order with last night's
weather and the noise at my head from the steersman.[40]

Early Diary entries made no reference to the faithful Will Hewer
who was aboard ship playing an ambiguous role in the service of
Pepys and the King. Whether class divisions excluded Will from
higher conclaves or whether his seasickness rendered him immobile
is uncertain. On Friday the 31st Pepys recorded: 'The wind came
fair in the night and continued so and the weather very fine all
day so as I was pretty well but poor Hewer still much out of order.'[41]
On Sunday, Hewer had recovered sufficiently to talk to Pepys about
the nature of their work, but only 'by implication and not in clear
words'.[42]

A whole month the voyage dragged on, testing Pepys's patience
to the utmost, but his reactions were muted and he showed no sign
of boredom. He had the advantage of his books and many a concentrated hour was spent reading Fuller's *Crusades* and studying – at
last in detail – Butler's *Hudibras*. And then on 13 September they
entered the Straits and anchored in the Bay of Tangier the following
day. Pepys took one look at the fortifications 'overseen' everywhere
by Moors and came to the conclusion that they were no defence

at all – 'so as to be amazed to think the King had laid out all this money upon it'.[43] Colonel Percy Kirke, the Governor, had picked up news of their arrival and before they entered the Bay all the guns of the town fired salvoes of welcome. Kirke then came aboard and when the news of the King's intention to blow up the Mole was broken to him he proved unexpectedly co-operative. On their first encounter Pepys found Kirke a 'very forward' man, which in the event he recognised as a serious understatement. After dinner the quarterdeck was alive with officers walking and talking, and there coming to greet Pepys effusively was his brother-in-law Balty, '. . . who is mightily altered in his looks with hard usage as he tells me'.[44] Dartmouth commented privately to Pepys that it was well they had come because Kirke and the Alcaïd were already on bad terms, provoked not so much by the Alcaïd's intransigence as Kirke's hot temper. On Monday the 17th more firing of guns greeted Dartmouth and his entourage as they were conducted in state to the castle for dinner. Throughout Monday Pepys was badly bitten by chinches which did not stop him riding out after dinner with Dartmouth and Kirke 'to see the town . . .' He did so 'with no pleasure but great danger'. Moving through the narrow, dirty streets Pepys was very aware of the clear blue sky, the warm scented air and the vines 'mightily laden with excellent grapes of divers sorts'. It did not impress him. He was too conscious that wandering into the country involved the risk of kidnap and conversion to slavery, and the lightning speed of the Moorish cavalry moving along the shore seemed particularly threatening. Already he was beginning to share the King's desire to be rid of Tangier and all its works.

This mood was reinforced as he unravelled Governor Kirke's character and found him to be a coarse, heavy drinking man, who encouraged dirty stories and frequently behaved with brutality. Never a prude, Pepys tolerated the stories but he recoiled from the brutality. According to rumour, soldiers had been beaten to death in ruthless punishments, women raped, citizens bullied and refugees surrendered to the Spanish Inquisition. Under the luxurious surface, vice was rampant. Whoring, drinking, cursing: these were the stuff of everyday life, and many women were as libertine as the men. The climax came at dinner one evening when Kirke boasted to Dartmouth that one sixteen-year-old girl of his acquaintance had given syphilis to at least four hundred soldiers. Laughing uproariously, he recalled that his own secretary was 'one that got it most pockly'.[45] According to the Rawlinson manuscript Kirke had built himself a bath-house and filled it with whores, each with her own speciality. Not to be outdone, his wife promptly summoned her own lovers and fully indulged her lusts. Kirke had even made his wife's sister pregnant.

Work had now begun apace assessing compensation but Pepys failed to take into account the congenital laziness and indifference of the Tangerines. First he drew up a list of questions to be put to any claimant: where was the evidence of their tenure? by what right did he or she hold the property? what covenants with the crown were involved? what rents were fixed and, if fixed, paid? could the appropriate papers be produced when required? A proclamation issued on 19 September required 'proprietors' to appear before the commissioners the following day with answers to all the questions. The next morning the Mayor of Tangier, resplendent in scarlet robes, sat next to Pepys in the Town House and Pepys opened the proceedings to an almost empty chamber. The church, ever aware of its property rights, was represented by two black robed fathers, and one or two other claimants arrived with totally inadequate answers to Pepys's questionnaire. The farce repeated itself the following morning when some claims were made but in Spanish, which had to be sent back for translation. In the afternoon Pepys fared no better.[46] A handful of claimants appeared with illiterate answers to his questions and were carefully instructed on how to give acceptable alternatives. By now Pepys's hopes of returning to London in time to eat Christmas dinner with his friends were fast fading.[47] One more unsuccessful day drove Pepys on 27 September to issue a final proclamation making it clear that no claims would be met which were not delivered that same evening. A flood of paperwork descended on him and kept him busy far into the evening, but the results remained dismal. Complete confusion characterised so much of the evidence recorded that Pepys decided some other method must be found. In the event this took the form of a survey carried out by Pepys and his clerks during which he made his own assessments. These were open to objections by the proprietors at a specially convened meeting when Pepys forestalled much of the criticism by putting the prices demanded in historical perspective. In an extraordinary piece of double-thinking he claimed that rents were artificially inflated because reinforcements had poured into Tangier since 1680. Thus the King could not be asked to repay rents at rates which he himself had inflated. Once a reduction of the garrison began, rents would fall and such rents were the genuine market value. Pepys finally drew up a list of repayments which the King could increase if he chose. The estimated net total payable by the crown was £11,234.17.4d, £4,000 of which went to leaseholders and £7,000 to freeholders.[47]

Much more serious difficulties threatened the whole expedition. Sheeres revealed to Pepys and Dartmouth that blowing up the Mole was a major operation which could not be carried out in less that three months. A depressed Dartmouth protested that supplies were running very low. He came to Pepys's cabin one night to discuss the situation, where Pepys revealed his recent conversation with Admiral William Booth, 'he telling me his dreadful prospect of the condition of the fleet in a few days when the seamen shall know what provisions they have and no more ... He told me too that he had now stated the victuals of the fleet ... clearly which is three months ... and nothing as he hears in the garrison or very little to spare for the fleet.'[49] Dartmouth's depression deepened because he could not make up his mind whether the time had come to tell the Alcaïd that he intended blowing up the Mole. Pepys seems to have persuaded him out of this, cogently arguing that it might release the Moorish hordes against them at the very moment when engineers were handling very powerful explosives, 'all of which put together made him very melancholy so he left me and I to bed where I was worse troubled than any night since my coming'.[50] In fact Pepys's worries were unnecessary because the Alcaïd's spies had already discovered the truth and even knew about the 'deliberations of the council at home'.[51]

By October Sheeres had begun his attack on the first layer of the Mole which was to be destroyed in sections. In spite of a cold Pepys went to watch. 'I ... to the water gate and saw it blow up and it was ... wonderful ... [the] stones did fly to the endangering of the small vessels in the harbour. Going down to the Mole I saw the effects of the blow which was very great.' Sir Hugh Cholmley and Sheeres, the joint creators of the Mole, had done their job well, and destroying a construction 1,500 feet long, weighing 167,000 tons, was virtually impossible in the seventeenth century. Meanwhile, the threat of violence from the Moors drove Dartmouth to arrange an imposing review of troops on 28 September intended to impress the enemy. A thousand seamen under the command of Sir John Berry reinforced the garrison, decked out in new red coats brought over from a Scots regiment. Others were 'clothed with white and blue striped linen fitted with muskets, pikes and pole-axes ...'[52]

Pepys's role as consultant to Dartmouth continued but, with his main tasks finished, he turned his attention to naval observations. He must have been aware that his Tangier days would deepen his experience and prepare him for a new and predestined role far removed from the Mole, explosives and Moors. Dartmouth's instructions from the King specifically required that he attempt to recover some discipline in that part of the Navy under his control, but Pepys found him lacking the moral courage required. They talked incessantly about the Navy's problems and agreed that the King too easily made free with commanders, undermining the authority of the tarpaulins. Fear of making enemies at home prevented Dartmouth from carrying his views into action. Pepys himself remained in an ambivalent position. Freed from the tangle of political and naval loyalties, he could survey the scene serenely with a new independence and honesty. Whether this derived from his battle-scarred past or whether persecution had taught him not to meddle unnecessarily in political affairs is speculation. He was not content to see his conclusion of the Tangier expedition as a self-contained success without wider implications. The discussions with Dartmouth clearly indicated that Pepys had undoubtedly changed with age but that he was still preoccupied with the Navy. As for Dartmouth, he was never a man to take risks – as became clear when Kirke secured a grant for government stores which he turned entirely to his own profit. Pepys remonstrated with Dartmouth, who replied: 'What would you have me do? I come not here to stay and for me to oppose and cross him, for so little a time, is to little purpose to the King or his subjects, but a great deal to me to the drawing of enemies about my ears at home ...'[53] Dartmouth was in an embarrassing position. He knew that Pepys had once had great influence and that in his present role he might recover that power. What if his report to London of Dartmouth's work in Tangier was negative? He needed Pepys's goodwill and went out of his way to establish a camaraderie with him which became quite intimate, based upon personal frankness and their common view of the Navy's problems.

Pepys's observations of Dartmouth's squadron revealed that the new regulations which he had so painfully established were frivolously flouted. Dining one afternoon off Tangier, on board Captain Priestman's ship *English Tiger*, they discussed the question of seniority when a flag officer was incapacitated for one reason or another. The choice might lie between a third-rate ship with a captain steeped in thirty years' experience, or a second-rate ship commanded by an elegant gentleman with no seamanship. Which should be given priority – the 'eldest captain' or 'greater ship'? Pepys answered unequivocally – the eldest captain, eldest meaning the most experienced. Priestman expostulated and the exchanges became fierce. Priestman, of course, had been found guilty of lying ashore without authority and Pepys gently reminded him of his delinquency which merely intensified the atmosphere. Pepys invoked the French Navy as an example of how the rule of seniority applied and worked well, which drove Priestman to pour scorn on everything French. What a fool the man was, Pepys reflected. The question of granting commission then arose and Pepys remarked that here all his regulations were equally disregarded. He concluded his argument with the case of Captain Dering. Dartmouth told the story of Dering coming aboard his ship for the first time and, observing the 'great bits of timber' which encumbered the decks, said that they would clearly 'hinder the ship's sailing' and must at once be taken away.[54] Dering had failed the examination established by Pepys and was considered unfit to serve as a lieutenant, but 'he was soon after made [one] and presently ... a captain which he is now.'

Pepys's last days in Tangier were beset by his persistent cold and the appalling weather. His departure for Spain, where he planned to take a holiday, was delayed from one day to the next. He packed away all his paraphernalia from books and flute to razors and spectacles, meticulously noting each item. At last, on 30 November, he set sail with the ever faithful Will Hewer on board the *Montagu* bound for Spain. Pepys did not remain to see the end of the Tangier station. The Mole was demolished, the ports were dismantled, and the Peterborough Tower was brought down in a roar of masonry. When the Moors saw the Englishmen abandoning Tangier out of what they assumed to be 'sheer fright' they were delighted.[55]

When Pepys arrived at Cadiz, James Houblon's agent in southern Spain, Mr Hodges, took him into his house. Great excitement broke out as war with France was proclaimed and parades and demonstrations burst on the streets. The news set Pepys thinking about King Charles's reactions and the readiness of the British Navy to meet possible developments. However, there was no hint of nostalgia for home or the high places of power in his letters. The weather remained a major preoccupation. It was terrible. In a letter to Lord Dartmouth headed Cadiz, seven days after Christmas began, he wrote: 'Notwithstanding what I told you by my journey with the *Lark*, I am still here, the height of the floods by the late rains continuing such.'[56] And then the next day, against all expectations, the weather changed. The sky turned blue, everything was brilliant with sunshine, and at last he set out with Hewer and a man called Fowler, who knew the country well, to cross the bay to Puerto de Santa Maria. They travelled by mule and it is tempting to picture the ex-grandee of the Navy, accustomed to travelling splendidly by coach, suddenly transformed into a roughshod itinerant astride a mule led by pack-loads of his belongings. The roads were flooded and dangerous, the rain returned to plague them and their discomfort must have been great, but the ever adaptable Pepys pressed on, determined to see Spain and, in particular, Seville.[57]

When at last he came to 'the most beautiful city on earth' with flowers overflowing on balconies, interiors mysterious behind shutters and beautiful women on every street, it was all under the persistent, relentless drenching rain. Pepys's curiosity remained insatiable. Wearing heavy boots and cape he pressed home his enquiries with the relentlessness of one of His Majesty's inspectors. Nothing was too big or too small to come under his scrutiny and, in some cases, cross-examination. Confronted by the claims of the Saludadors that they could sit without burning in red hot ovens, he brought a priest and an oven together and invited one to enter the other.[58] Every detail of life was scrutinised, right down to cloths used for sanitary purposes.

Still matters of the sea remained his constant preoccupation and in his Journal he gave a detached description of the life and training of Spanish pilots. The methods seemed to him slipshod but the Spanish Navy had brought the wealth of the New World pouring into Spain. Pepys found hypocrisy no less widespread in Spain than in England. False pretensions to noble birth were frequent, men who could not read wore spectacles, and citizens contributed funds to a fleet for protection against the Moors when no such fleet existed. This humbug repeated itself on a vital issue of great interest to Pepys: the question of whether the King's ships were permitted to carry merchant goods as they so flagrantly did in England. At first sight he was pleased to find the practice forbidden, only to discover, that since the King accepted fees for granting captains places, they expected his secret indulgence to carry goods.[59]

Meanwhile, the rain continued ceaselessly. Elaborate pageants were arranged calling on God to stem the torrent, but either the faithful had sinned grievously or the elements were out of divine control. Early in February Pepys wrote to Dartmouth: '

Here the weather hath been such, that after having finished . . . all my curiosity aimed at and could perform . . . I have been by the height of the floods kept out of any capacity of quitting it. The ways by land have become wholly impassable; and the river so overflowed that notwithstanding all endeavours used for preventing it . . . above one third of the place within the walls hath been drowned.[60]

Pepys was forced to remain in Seville for six weeks. Restless and uneasy about his commitments to Dartmouth, there were so many unexplored distractions in Spain that he never fell into depression or became bored. An urgent letter came from Dartmouth who badly needed his help in his attempt to recover English slaves from the Moors. 'Do not hesitate', he told Pepys 'to board any convenient man-of-war in order to get back to Tangier quickly.' At last he set sail and arrived at Cadiz on 23 February. Immediately, he asked Sir John Berry, who had a man-of-war under his command, to send his barge across from the *Henrietta* to pick him up. Sir John received the request jocularly, explaining that previous orders given by the Admiral made it necessary from him to remain at anchor in Cadiz until the main body of the fleet arrived. Knowing the wily ways of naval captains Pepys at once exposed this evasion. For Berry this was sanction to launch quite openly into a narrative about whole new forms of corruption. Admirals now shared their captain's profits and even allowed clerks representing the merchants on board to keep accurate accounts. The intricacies of the conspiracy were unravelled before Pepys's highly critical eyes. In exchange for fifty per cent of the profits admirals would order captains to warmer climates or convenient stations. As a result, the Mediterranean fleet had degenerated into a kind of private trading corporation presided over by a master racketeer flying the King's flag.[61]

Dartmouth himself did not escape criticism. Turning a blind eye to disciplinary detail, Dartmouth made no attempt to stop the barbarous practice of flogging seamen in the round. Justice was different for officers and seamen. Officers made money out of malpractice and escaped without even a reprimand; seamen suffered brutal punishment for relatively minor offences. Pepys himself witnessed the flogging of two deserters, first on their own ship the *Lark*, before being circulated in a boat to be whipped before each ship in turn. 'And as they were brought round ... the whole company cried out upon the deck they would be glad all of them to be whipped as they were [if they] might be cleared of serving under that commander.'[62] Pepys recorded sadly that the lack of a court-martial allowed 'more powerful sinners to escape punishment and continue swaggering round the decks'.

Rumour circulated early in February that Dartmouth had finished his work and was heading for Tangier. Pepys swiftly set about packing his belongings, accrued trophies and presents. There followed yet another example of supreme skill in protesting about corruption only to endorse it. 'It was worth observing what care and shift Mr Reresby and Hodges did use upon the coming in of the fleet ... to make up a little sum for a compliment ... on board My Lord's ship. And upon their asking I could not advise them against sending it ... to him though I knew it not to be very fit to go to My Lord's own ship.'[63]

Dartmouth sometimes appeared to be more principled than Pepys. He protested to Pepys that he would have preferred not to have the bullion on his ship in case it was thought to be for his profit.[64] The fleet lay at anchor three days taking in provisions and Pepys bade many farewells, especially to Houblon's friends. At seven o'clock in the evening of 26 February nineteen men-of-war and twelve merchantmen put out to sea and Pepys, on board the *Grafton*, took a last look at Spain.

Within a few hours the weather began to worsen. The captain's log recorded: '27 February: At noon this day it began to blow very hard; at two in the afternoon our main topsail blew from the yard.' By eight in the evening, 'it began to blow ... a storm of wind that we could hardly maintain a pair of low sails'.[65] By the following day at three o'clock in the morning the mizzen split and at four-thirty the mainsail itself gave way. We have no record of Pepys's reaction. Pepys's Tangier Journal ends on 1 December 1683 and there remain only scattered references in his general notes: 'Consider the mighty care of an admiral [in this case, Herbert] for a whole fleet ... that came ... about thirty-five ships ... and in one night all parted by foul weather ... many missing, some drove into the Straits and ourselves and the rest all with loss of masts or such or rudder ...'[66] The fleet took twenty-four hours to re-assemble and in the afternoon cast anchor in the Road of Tangier where they began a refit. From the Road, Pepys caught an occasional glimpse through cloud and rain of the blackened ruins of Tangier, now overrun by Moors, a stark symbol of failing empire. The captain's log recorded on 3 March: 'This day a fair gale and fair weather. Between one and two in the afternoon got our yards and topmasts and between four and six we unmoored in order to go to sea.'[67] What followed revealed to Pepys not only the necessity of properly trained seamen but a new and healthy respect for God who had the power to conjure such majestic destruction out of 'the deep'. Above all, he gained an experience of life at sea he had never had before.

Trouble really began on 9 March when a great gale blew up with clouds coming down almost to sea level and rain driving horizontally across the deck, reducing visibility to a few yards. 'We endeavoured all we could to go to windward', the log recorded, but it was of no avail.[68] As morning broke on 11 March the main yard of the *Grafton* cracked and a heavy swell developed which made it difficult to man the rigging for examination and repairs. For eight hours while daylight lasted, the crew and carpenters struggled to put a 'brace' upon the main yard and tentatively re-raised the mainsail. Pepys must have watched this operation with apprehension as the ship wallowed in the great seas and he, for all his new sea legs and freedom from seasickness, felt the incompetence and unease of the landlubber. He was not, and never would be, a man of physical action. No heroic struggle with a broken main yard or dexterous feat among the rigging would ever distinguish his career, but there is no hint in his general notes of any great fear. Torn from his desk and civil service security, Pepys appeared to match up to the great storm and the fates remarkably well. But this was not the end. What followed comes through vividly in the captain's log for 13 March: 'At twelve noon we were still under our low sails being squally weather . . . but at half an hour past eight at night we . . . did not think it hazardous to set our main topsail, which proved very unhappy.'[69] Scarcely half an hour passed before, with a resounding crack, the main yard broke again to be followed at once by a 'sprung' foreyard. It is not difficult to imagine the confusion which ensued, but the cool entries in the log gave a wonderful distance to the event. The ship must have floundered for nearly three days battered by gigantic seas and gale-force winds, while the crew struggled to keep her under way with a handful of sails. The fleet had long lost its formation and ships were driven to the south and west of their proper courses. They were in fact farther from England than when they first set sail from Cadiz three weeks before. For Pepys it crystallised the unpredictability of the seaman's life and led him to reflect: 'I know nothing that can give a better notion of infinite eternity than the being upon the sea in a little vessel without anything in sight but yourself within the whole hemisphere.'[70]

Remarkably, in the midst of great danger, the threat of capture by the Moors, and death by drowning, Pepys philosophised about the Universe and the seaman's role in it. It was a rare moment of introspection. All class discriminations were of little moment when the *Grafton*, dwarfed by the immensity of the ocean, relied for its survival on the skills of ordinary seamen as much as lords and captains.

As Secretary to the Admiralty, Pepys had insisted on daily logs being kept by sea captains but he now discovered that Admiral Herbert openly boasted of blank pages in his own record. 'What is it good for to remember where the wind was after it was over?'[71] Herbert did not even possess a rudimentary knowledge of the rigging of his ships, and all too frequently he commanded his men to 'haul up that which am there'.[72] By 23 March another gale was at its height and the following morning the *Grafton*'s mainsail once more broke away. Men were sent aloft to cling to the mast like bobbins and suddenly a great sea gathered its force, advanced upon the ship and smothered it, reaching high into the rigging. Six men were torn away and dashed to sea, three of them drowning while the remaining three, 'with great difficulty', were saved.[73] It reminded Pepys again of the great difference between seamen and gentlemen. Seamen were forced into the trade to earn a living and came to respect its unwritten codes; gentlemen were determined to make a quick two or three thousand pounds – and the devil take the hindmost. Many of his reflections in the midst of storms and hazards were in favour of the common seaman.

Conversations with Dartmouth on the quarterdeck ranged over every aspect of naval life, but they always came back to two subjects: the threat of France making herself the master of the Mediterranean by an alliance with the Moors, and the menacing figure of the one-eyed Admiral Herbert whose reputation as an audacious leader made him popular with the King and Duke of York. Dartmouth was fascinated by Pepys's accumulated evidence which stripped Herbert of his glamour to reveal an immoral man with a sneering contempt for discipline. Discipline: the word continued to recur on board the storm-tossed *Grafton*. Together Dartmouth and Pepys agreed that if they were to save the Navy, discipline must be given high priority. Next, trafficking in goods must be stopped and replaced by a system of pay which did not fall into arrears. The removal of the distinction between tarpaulins and gentlemen remained a necessity, as did an insistence on the inspection of logs. Central to this revolution was the removal of admirals ignorant of seafaring such as Admiral Herbert. Pepys's dossier on Herbert was damning. 'Of all the worst men living, Herbert is the only man that I do not know to have any one virtue to compound for all his vices.'[74] Faced with evidence, Dartmouth had to agree with this assessment. As Pepys wrote: 'It would not be for the King's service for them both to continue together in it.'[75] Above all, Herbert was a cruel man who starved hundreds of prisoners to death simply in order to enrich himself with their victuals allowance. In the meantime, in his more intimate conversation with Dartmouth, Pepys discovered that he had become obsessed with the fear that the King would forget him in his absence and might even disown him on his return. Anxious to re-establish himself as quickly as possible, Dartmouth deliberately abandoned the supply ships to press ahead at high speed, but the bad weather continued with a persistence which Dartmouth read as ominous. At one point Dartmouth and Pepys agreed that they must collaborate when they returned home to confront the King and the Duke with their joint plan for saving the Navy.

Throughout March 1684 the *Grafton* was torn and traversed by storms but on the 28th they glimpsed the beginnings of the English Channel and ran before a fresh wind. Yet again on the 29th the weather worsened, 'it blowing very hard and thick weather. At six in the morning we sounded and had seventy-five fathoms of water, small white sand. At two in the afternoon we sounded again and had sixty-five fathoms water, peppery sand and small white shells.'[76] The point of greatest danger for ships in the seventeenth century was the approach to inadequately charted coastlines. The nature of the seabed indicated how close ships were to shore and might contribute to establishing their position, but disputes frequently arose and, as we have seen, could prove fatal. On the 30th the navigators and crew of the *Grafton* could not agree their readings until suddenly the sun came out and there, reaching into the sea, was the Lizard of Cornwall. Some had said they were likely to run aground on the Scillies, others that they were in danger of the French coast, but now 'everybody endeavours to make himself be thought to have been in the right.'[77]

Despite the burst of sunshine, spring seemed remote, but there was the coastline of beloved England, with the possibility of sound sleep, fresh food and the liveliness of an English tavern. Such a prospect quickly overtook what remained of naval discipline. Men went ashore carousing far into the night and every captain in the fleet found new excuses for delaying his departure on the last leg of their journey to Spithead. Indeed, when the *Grafton* set sail once more from Plymouth Sound on the afternoon of the 31st, Dartmouth was humiliated to discover that not a single ship followed him. Every explanation except the real one – another night ashore – was given and Dartmouth grew angry as he hove to with the wind likely to drop at any moment. For the last time Pepys fell into argument with Dartmouth about his failure to impose discipline and Dartmouth rationalised his weakness, claiming that the very chiefs of the Admiralty became his enemies when he pressed his authority too far. In his anger Dartmouth had ordered shots to be fired at the delayed ships *Dragon* and *Tiger* – 'shot and all' as Pepys's Tangier Journal recorded.[78] Twenty-four hours later the fleet at last sailed for Spithead.

Fast on the heels of landing, Pepys took the first coach he could find to drive with Henry Sheeres up the Portsmouth Road to London, urged on by Dartmouth who desperately wished to pre-empt any trouble with the King.

Chapter 19

James becomes King – Monmouth invades England

An exhausted, but relatively happy, Pepys returned to London considerably richer than he left it. His expenses had been minimal and with an income of £4 a day for nearly two hundred and fifty days he amassed the considerable sum of £1,000. Even more satisfying, within a short time he was received by the King 'bare headed in his bedchamber'. Their discussion was conciliatory and all Dartmouth's fears of the King's displeasure were confounded. The Duke interrupted their conference and shared the King's appreciation of the work accomplished in Tangier. Lord Sunderland, the Secretary of State, joined the company and Pepys continued his enquiries about the King's expected criticism of Dartmouth. Once more Sunderland's report was favourable. Then, late at night and tired, Pepys sat down and wrote to reassure Dartmouth. 'Abating what some fanatics out of jealousy of the court can but forbear wishing ... I do not find any charging the least crime on Your Lordship on the whole matter.'[1] As he finished the letter, news reached Pepys which aroused once more his ambition to return to public life. Lord Brouncker had died suddenly. This left a vacancy on the Admiralty Board and no one was better suited to fill it than Pepys. Dartmouth seized the opportunity to recommend his appointment to the Duke of York in a letter which complained bitterly about the tricks played on him by the Admiralty. Their lordships of Derby House, he wrote, had ignored him to send instructions direct to captains of the Tangier fleet, 'endeavouring to lessen my command'.[2] As if to pre-empt and flaunt his and Pepys's plan to rid the Navy Board of land admirals, the unprincipled Lord Herbert was appointed to replace Brouncker. Pepys was furious but bided his time.

Social life renewed itself in London as Evelyn welcomed him home and invited him to join a party intent on witnessing the eclipse of the sun.[3] Shortly afterwards Pepys gave Evelyn a copy of Thomas

Burnet's massively detailed *A Sacred Theory of the Earth* which combined an innocent belief in the beginnings of life with a healthy
scepticism about the Flood. Foreshadowing modern thinking, Burnet
concluded that 'the antediluvian earth was of a different form and
construction from the present.' Evelyn responded enthusiastically,
but also stressed his scepticism: 'I am infinitely pleased with his
thoughts concerning the Universe (intellectual and material) in relation to this despicable molehill on which we mortals crawl and keep
such a stir about as if . . . this all were created for us little vermin.'[4]
On a brief excursion to Hampton Court Pepys carried a petition
for the Clockworkers' Company which led to his presentation to
the King by the Duke of York. Back once more among elegant
company, Pepys heard rumours which led him to believe that something big was in the air. No sooner had he returned to London
than he received a message via Dartmouth to repair once more to
Windsor where the King desired to see him urgently. The big news
followed. The King had decided to dissolve the hopelessly incompetent Admiralty Board and was pleased to appoint Pepys as the
new Secretary at the generous salary of £2,000 a year.[5] The wheel
had turned full circle, placing him back in high places. Pepys had
reached the advanced age of fifty-one and there were signs of his
old illness – stone in the bladder – troubling him. A medallion carved
in ivory about this time – said to be a vivid likeness – reveals a
plump face with a double chin, a bold nose and large eyes, the sculp-
tured mass of the head heavily bewigged, epitomising a successful
professional man of his time. It is the face of a fully mature, thoughtful
and still sensual man showing few marks of the experiences which
had affected him deeply. His bladder trouble soon became complicated by symptoms indicating an ulcer, and his sleeping habits
changed. He no longer fell asleep easily. Never a man to convert
mental stress into physical symptoms, ulcers notoriously had psychological components and the stress of returning to confront naval disorder
must have been intense. It did not diminish his private activities.
He developed his library, pursued his naval studies, followed psychical
research, befriended scholars and considered dumping rubbish into
the Thames to create a causeway.

Previous biographers have either reflected a touch of adulation
for a cult figure or given him the benefit of the doubt in circumstances
where he hardly deserved it. At the very heart of Pepys's naval criticism
lay a personal contradiction. Admiral William Booth told him that
he knew at least five captains who reckoned themselves among gentleman captains of the fleet, yet they were nothing more than upstart

footmen with false pretences. In his desire to further damn Admiral Herbert, Pepys put the promotion of 'these mean rogues out of the street' down to Herbert's homosexuality.[6] Pepys himself came from a class which supplied many a footman and his own early relationship with Sandwich was not far removed from that position. It was common for members of the lower classes to attach themselves to distinguished persons and rise under their patronage. There was also exaggeration in his description of the corruption of the Mediterranean fleet because the mantle he assumed of the objective observer concealed his predisposition to find what he wanted.

That Pepys was no paragon is clear in his condemnation of black people to life-long slavery for relatively mild offences. Pepys sold off his black servant in 1679 and has been defended on the grounds that his standard of living had to be cut when he ceased to be Clerk of the Navy. A worse example followed. In the winter of 1684–5 he '*kindly* interested himself in the recapture of a negro slave ... who had been *so ungrateful as to run away to sea*' (my emphasis).[7] Later in 1688 he disapproved when prisoners were transported to Virginia 'there to be treated according to their deserts' but qualified his disapproval. Transportation for blacks meant being 'sold entirely ... to slavery for their whole lives or how long the King may choose'.[8] 'The lives and happiness of a rabble of unknown west country peasants who shared the political principles of Shaftesbury and John Scott weighed nothing with him set in the scales against the claims of a deserving naval officer.'[9]

Pepys, of course, was a man of his time. Both Ollard and Bryant appreciated that Pepys's values were socially acceptable in his day, but Ollard rejected this justification. 'Such mercilessness towards the poor illiterate dupes of political gamblers is repellent.'[10] He could be considerate to strangers, he identified with the sufferings of common seamen and cherished his relatives and friends, but slavery left him untouched. If we are to accept the image of Pepys as a sensitive, socially caring man, Ollard was right. Even close employees sometimes suffered similar fates. Josiah Burchett had served him faithfully for seven years and was an intimate of his household, but when his accounts were not ordered enough for Pepys's new regime, he was first sacked summarily and then had all his appeals ignored. Early in August of 1687 Burchett wrote a heart-searching letter pleading with Pepys to reconsider his verdict.

I find it equally difficult to persuade myself that there is not those in your family who have made so poor use of their time in my absence

as to insinuate to you that this fault of mine is accompanied with many
more . . . I know well enough that whatever you do you do by the
rules of justice and therefore will not despair but that this letter will
be a little favourable . . . I should have been more cautious of troubling
you did not my present condition force me.[11]

This was met with silence. Repeated apologies and appeals were
of no avail. James Southerne would shortly suffer a similar fate. He
was ruthlessly thrown out of his house to make way for a newcomer
appointed by Pepys. There were also the sailors and their wives besieg-
ing the Navy Office clamouring for long overdue wages, exciting
sympathy in Pepys who simultaneously pocketed moneys which
should have been theirs. None of this disturbed his friends. They
were accustomed to such reactions as part of everyday seventeenth-
century life.

He was welcomed back from Tangier by many of those friends
– James Houblon, Evelyn, Mary Skinner, the Duke of York – and
made a round of visits. He returned to his old haunts including the
bookshops around St Paul's and was reunited with the glitter of
expensive shops where he spent money freely, but there is scant
reference to the theatre, which had once been so irresistible. In an
unwelcome visit John Joyne appeared hat in hand at the door of
Derby House having abandoned Paris for London. Inevitably it was
money he needed, and a loan of £20 quickly changed hands.[12]

It was to Derby House, the administrative headquarters of the
Navy, that Pepys now made his way daily through the scorching
summer heat of 1684, gliding almost gondola-fashion via the Thames
past Northumberland House to Westminster Stairs. There, next door
to his private office, his clerks sat in a great room at high desks
writing innumerable letters to commanders, captains and muster masters. Meanwhile, Pepys grappled with the gigantic task of reassessing
the state of the Navy. Rumours had reached his ears that the thirty
new ships built at the cost of so much effort had been allowed to
warp and rot at their moorings. The overall picture which emerged
was even worse. Ignoring members of the Navy Board, Pepys took
the risk of writing over their heads to the dockyard managers request-
ing the number and state of ships and the estimated cost of repairs.
Dismayed by their replies, early in August he decided to visit the
dockyards to see for himself. There he found harbour masters reluctant
to conduct him on surveys which quickly revealed an unbelievable
state of affairs. Ship after ship was literally rotting at its moorings
with toadstools between decks 'as big as my fists', bowsprits crumbling
and timbers warped. Efforts to disguise the decay with shotboard

and canvas merely made it more evident. Pepys was reminded of the condition of a defeated fleet returning from battle, and at last faced the fact that the splendid Navy he had conjured to life was no longer capable of commanding the seas or even coping with an enemy of any consequence. His vision of England as the greatest naval power in the world dissolved as he moved from one ship to another. When politics had driven him from his job as Secretary of the Admiralty, he left behind a fleet of seventy-six ships at sea with 12,640 fully paid-up men equipped for any emergency.[13] When he returned in April 1684 there remained twenty-four ships at sea manned by three thousand and seventy men and the value of reserves was down to one hundred and fifty thousand.[14] There must have been a point, as the evidence unfolded, when he despaired of rectifying such wholesale neglect. It did not last long.

At first cautiously and then emboldened by results, Pepys began to investigate and expose the men whose neglect had brought the Navy so low. A Captain Russell, for instance, having acquired enough money by illicit trading, had decided that 'he would never more go to sea but upon conditions of his own liking.'[15] Pepys reminded him that if he did not report for duty the source of his wealth might be subject to investigation, 'on which its reality might fade'. The purser of the *Mordaunt* had steadfastly refused £10 to a creditor and Pepys informed him that, unless he appeared at Derby House to explain his conduct on the following Monday, he would face immediate arrest.[16] The purser of the *Mermaid* received a similar warning: if he continued to neglect his duties in refitting his ship for sea, he would be replaced by another, more efficient purser.[17]

Pepys infiltrated the dilatory habits, if not gross negligence, of the officers and commissioners of the Navy Board itself. Ignoring their responsibilities, they had left naval affairs largely to their clerks. Life suddenly became uncomfortable for them with the return of this alert, probing, inescapable little man who informed them that the Duke of York required their attendance on him, and suddenly appeared himself at the Duke's side. Much more embarrassing, he brought with him the lords of the Treasury, who pressed home questions about the fate of the large sums of money granted by their lordships to the commissioners. Pressure steadily increased. Every audience with the King meant another flurry of letters repeating the King's desire that the report on the state of the Navy should 'be brought to quick fruition'. The commissioners used this pressure to produce an alibi for their neglect of the Navy. It was all due to buying the wrong kind of timber known in the trade as Eastland timber, and who behind the curtain of high office was responsible for this gross error of judgement – the revered but justly sacked Pepys. Timber could explain decaying ships but not corruption so widespread that the Navy was being run as 'a gigantic swindle' for the benefit of captains and commanders who quarrelled among themselves for the best pickings of the spoils.

There was a special satisfaction in the peremptory letter Pepys despatched to Admiral Herbert demanding an explanation for his capture and starvation of slaves earlier in the year. Herbert received it with disdain. Still a court favourite to be found swaggering in the Duke of York's company, he felt secure against any attack. Temporarily that was true, but not for long. In May 1684 Pepys completed yet another of those splendid reports he liked to deliver to the King on some recognised anniversary: *The State of the Royal Navy of England at the Dissolution of the late Commission of the Admiralty*. Bound in black morocco, the volume still has pride of place in his library.[18]

Behind all this Pepys's private life was not running as smoothly as he desired. First there had been a serious fire at the house in Buckingham Street which he shared with Will Hewer and his mother. Sparks flying from a nearby chimney set several houses on fire, including Number Twelve.[19] At midnight it looked as if the house would be consumed and in the general panic Pepys collected his precious belongings into one room ready to hurry them away. Then the guards arrived and decided to blow up Number Thirteen next door, as it stood, without troubling to remove the furniture. They were just in time.

Balty had once more become a problem after the closure of Tangier. Pepys searched for some new opening for him while Balty's relentless correspondence continued without any modification of its high-flown intensity. At the same time, Pepys was writing letters to the captain of the frigate *Phoenix* asking him to accept on board as a cabin boy his nephew Samuel Jackson, 'the nearest of kin to me I have of any relation next to his mother'. Pepys did not hesitate to submit his nephew of fifteen to a fate he knew to be very rough. The boy was slow to learn, he said, but must quicken the process in order to earn a living despite his expectations of some inheritance. Commuting to work was a problem which rarely troubled seventeenth-century employees, but Pepys found his daily river journey to Derby House tiring and in the middle of September he decided to move the office to his own home at Number Twelve Buckingham Street. The King gave his permission and for three days vans and horses were busy transferring priceless documents from one place to the other. The move enabled Pepys to live at the King's expense and sleep at his workplace, a convenience which became pressing as his rehabilitation of the Navy gathered pace.[20]

In the wider perspective the course of his private and professional life was to be quite transformed. Moving with the ease of a seasoned diplomat among royal company, Pepys became aware that the King's health was deteriorating. Pepys no more approved the court circles which he occasionally entered than did Evelyn, who vividly evoked the relaxed way of life of King Charles:

I can never forget the inexpressible luxury and profaneness, gaming and all dissoluteness and as it were total forgetfulness of God . . . which I was witness of, the King sitting and toying with his concubines . . . a French boy singing love songs in that glorious gallery whilst about twenty of the great courtiers and other dissolute persons were at basset round a large table, a bank of at least two thousand in gold before them.[21]

On the evening of 1 February 1685 Lord Bruce, son of Charles's old friend Lord Ailesbury, had seen the King disappear into the apartments of the Duchess of Portsmouth where he 'regaled himself' with her company. Bruce called at an agreed hour to collect him and escort him to his bedchamber. 'As he passed the candle to the page at the door the flame went out though there was no gust of wind in all that dark long gallery.'[22] The King donned his nightgown and in company with Bruce went to 'the place of easements' where he sat talking and laughing with him for some time. Both went to bed but the King tossed and turned in his sleep which the groom of the bedchamber remarked was an 'ill mark and contrary to custom'.[23] In the morning the King's whole countenance had changed. His surgeons came to dress a wounded heel and were alarmed to find him looking as pale as a ghost. Instead of his usual cheerful greetings he spoke over their heads in French to someone not present in the chamber. Next, he went to the barber but was no sooner settled in his chair than he dropped back foaming at the mouth, his eyes rolling upwards 'revealing their full whiteness'.[24] Every medical device of the day from bleeding to applying blisters, purgatives and pans of coal to his body was used throughout the day.[25] A momentary recovery was overtaken by a further collapse and by Wednesday evening the doctors said he would not survive the night. Then, at night, the Duke of York hurried to the Queen's room and told Barrillon, the French ambassador, that the King had consented to see a priest. The King then struggled to rise from his bed as he made full confession to the priest and expressed a desire to die in communion with the Catholic Church.[26] About six o'clock on Friday morning he asked for the curtains to be drawn that he might 'once more see day'. His breathing became difficult and they tried to raise him on his pillows. By twelve o'clock he slipped into unconsciousness and died.

It was 6 February 1685 and the King was in his fifty-fifth year. For three days Pepys hovered near the royal bedchamber hoping the King would recover enough to give the Navy Board an audience. He was one of the select few moving in and out of the chamber and saw the desperate struggles of the physicians to keep the King alive. Despite his failings, or perhaps because of them, the King had aroused a response in his subjects which revealed the authority of the throne in public life. As a man he had wit and charm which enabled him to absorb and ride out criticisms which too easily discomfited his enemies. His dissolute sexual life had a secret appeal among many courtiers and despite his devious manipulations he remained loyal to those who won his love. Resenting the powers of Parliament to interfere with his desires, he had exercised a new kind of personal rule which drew its strength from the Church of England in whose dogma he did not believe.[27] The cost of such a reign was high, relegating his country to 'a dissolute annexe of Versailles', but the people were prepared – uneasily – to accommodate him. His last years were sustained in relative tranquillity by the devotion of his brother James and two loyal mistresses.

The country held its breath as a Catholic King prepared to accede to the throne. The ports were closed and troops summoned to arms, but the expected uprising failed to materialise and even the disturbances were minimal.[28] The inconceivable had come to pass as James ascended the throne of England without bloodshed. It must have stirred tremendous expectations in Pepys who had remained loyal to James in exile and under threat of death for twenty-five years. James was crowned in an Anglican ritual which kept ceremony to a minimum and avoided the sacrament. Pepys played a minor role as one of the King's canopy bearers.

The omens at the coronation were not good. Momentary confusion arose when the King's canopy split and almost simultaneously the crown slipped precariously on his head. A tremendous gust of wind split the standard above the White Tower as the guns fired a welcome to the new monarch. Later in life Pepys was to recall these incidents with amusement, but at the time they caused unease. The usual pomp and pageantry continued for some hours but was kept within strict limits. Nothing was done to evoke comparison with the rich ceremonials of the Catholic Church. Pepys was an honoured guest at the banquet in Westminster Hall, occupying a seat among the barons, judges and bishops at one of the top tables. It was all very different from the coronation of Charles II when he sought out an observation eyrie and scavenged for what food he could get. The sumptuous feast of dishes of hot-larded leverets, Battalio pie, soused carp and beef-à-la-royale[29] continued hour after hour to the music of Purcell, the singing of ballads and elaborate toasts drunk to His Highness. There was a display of fireworks which 'so frightened some that they felt the joy of the Lord had turned to anger'. Pepys, watching from his window, was delighted with the 'stupendous torrent of fire'. Throughout the night there was singing and dancing, 'and not the first streaks of dawn could quite quell their spirits'.

The new King was a man above middle height with a long face, fair hair and a quick nervous manner. Hesitant in speech, he relied – to Pepys's relief – on reason in preference to fine phrases and was a great enemy of drinking and gaming.[30] Bishop Burnet said of him: 'If it had not been for his Popery he would have been if not a great ... a good [King].'[31] As for Pepys, his devotion to James tended to blind him to any possible shortcomings. The contrast between Charles's fickleness and debauchery and James's morality and industry pleased Pepys. There was a different atmosphere at court where the *boulevardiers* and buffoons were banished and a high serious-ness was introduced. By now, Pepys had completed the second of his great reports on the Navy and within a few days entered the royal presence to begin reading the results to the King. Unknown to Pepys, James had already entered into diplomatic negotiations with Barrillon, King Louis' ambassador, to explain why he intended sum-moning Parliament into session rapidly. On the wave of the imme-diate enthusiasm for his accession it was necessary to act quickly, and summoning Parliament would encourage it to grant him revenue for life.[32] The following day Rochester called on Barrillon to elaborate the explanation which was intended both to pre-empt Halifax's mal-contents and make it easier for the King to favour Catholicism. If Pepys had known of these secret negotiations he would have found reason to worry. Indelicately, the King was already beginning to practise his religious rites with some ostentation, which caused a certain amount of unease. Pepys's supremacy in the Navy was now unchallenged. No new Lord High Admiral or Commission had been appointed and the King alone took precedence over him in naval matters. Bryant believed that if Pepys had been driven by personal ambition alone he could have pressed for a title carrying great wealth – such as Secretary of State.

His devotion to the crown at this stage was certainly not 'founded upon private advantage'. Pepys, who had a large sum of money owing to him[33] from the crown, did not press his claim despite supporting evidence. Unexpected characteristics of James II slowly unravelled their contradictions to Pepys as he struggled to carry through his rehabilitation programmes. Pepys had regarded James almost as a saint in exile, whose warmth and generosity was vouched for by so many, but he now allowed his own nephew 'to grovel for mercy before him and then refused it'.[34] When the Earl of Argyle was tortured he expressed a wish to be present to witness it. His first speech to his Council reaffirmed his support and defence of 'the Church of England' but his negotiations with France were seen to be disingenuous. At first enthusiastic for the new monarch, Pepys was to witness a slow erosion of his popularity, but since he was not consulted beyond naval commitments, for a time Pepys himself escaped any association. His responsibilities involved accepting the political line followed by the government and did later implicate him in policies which ill suited his temperament. Carried along by his unbreakable loyalty to James, he was to find himself giving evidence in an assault on the rights and liberties of Protestant Englishmen. For the moment, however, resurrecting the great structures of the Navy and examining complaints, injustices and derelictions of duty kept him working far into the night in the tall book-lined rooms with their glimpse of the river at Number Twelve Buckingham Street.

There he conceived policies which were to become embedded for years in what he regarded as 'the spirit of a great service'. Henceforth all in the service were to subscribe to the new commandments of naval integrity. First, the acquisition of the necessary knowledge for responsible seamanship; second, the readiness to fulfil one's duty without complaint even if it meant facing death on low wages; third, the willingness to obey orders immediately; fourth, the practice of a scrupulous honesty incapable of corrupt private profit. In the tumult of seventeenth-century individualism these were romantic principles and Pepys encountered widespread resistance. There was also respect and admiration.

Evelyn had long been aware that hidden behind the bustling civil servant was a person who might conceivably have a touch of greatness. This was reflected in a quite different and, for some, much more discriminating world when the Royal Society elected him as its President. In a letter to James Houblon, Pepys described himself as a

Tory, but he was a born cross-bencher whose cast of mind might have flourished as well in science as in the civil service.[35] He believed in the rational analysis of problems, he was expert at collating evidence, and there remained a streak of scepticism which left a trace of doubt about the most established truths. Deeper still, his respect for authority made him an enemy of revolution, and opposition – except when it was his own – did not appeal to him. Ollard remarks that 'there is no thing in Pepys's life or writings to suggest that he would not have served the dynasty of Oliver Cromwell ... with the same loyalty that he gave to the Stuarts.'[36] Perhaps that marked him out as the perfect civil servant, and indeed, sifting through all classifications, nothing fits him better, with one reservation. His versatility of mind and range of interests put him in a class of his own. Moreover, there was another, quite different, side to Pepys's personality. *Force majeure*, politics periodically entered his life and as a spokesman for the Navy Pepys could not ignore the streak of the politician in his own make-up.

In the general election which followed hard on the heels of James's accession, after the fashion of the time Pepys was returned simultaneously for two constituencies, Harwich and Sandwich. Complications among disenfranchised voters at Sandwich made him accept his old seat, Harwich. It must have given zest to his parliamentary return that the day after his first appearance Titus Oates was whipped by the common hangman from Aldgate to Newgate.[37] On 22 May Oates was dragged from prison on a sledge, unable to stand after his scourging, and whipped once more all the way to Tyburn, which, as Evelyn put it, 'some thought to be very severe and extraordinary'.[38]

At precisely the point when the King needed a period of quiet to reinforce his position, the dramatic news that the exiled Whig Earl of Argyle had landed in Scotland and rallied his supporters to invade England broke the peace.[39] The King entered the Lords and Commons on 22 May 1685 and made a long speech swearing to support the Church of England, and 'preserve its government as by law now established'.[40] Evelyn reported that 'at every period [of his speech] the house gave loud shouts.' The King was pleased to find both houses prepared to support him against Argyle, some adding that they would do so 'with their lives and fortunes'. In the emergency Pepys was once more frustrated by the state of the Navy. Very few frigates or ships were available to protect home waters and Pepys had been forced to rely upon a mere yacht, the *Kitchen*, to 'trail the Dutch coast'. The principal business of the House of Commons after the declaration of an emergency was to provide the King with funds to put the Navy to sea once more in full force. Against all expectations Parliament proceeded to vote James a larger revenue for life than it ever granted Charles II. Unfortunately, this was adequate for peace but not war, and did not take account of Charles's considerable debts. The new King repeated his appeal for money on 30 May assuring the two houses that for all his shortcomings 'he had a true English heart'.

The Commons again responded by authorising the imposition of extra taxes on tobacco, wine, sugar and vinegar over a period of eight years. A third appeal for money two days later might have strained the goodwill of his most enthusiastic supporters, but once again duties on a new range of goods was granted for five years.[41] The hereditary revenue averaged about £1,500,000 and the new taxes £400,000, which meant that the King launched his reign with twice the revenue of Charles II. This was music to Pepys's ears. It now became possible to fund and implement his great naval rehabilitation.

Another event reaffirmed the need for a large and completely overhauled Navy. The 'Protestant Duke' of Monmouth had been busy for months gathering support from exiled republicans in Holland, news of which trickled through to England and Pepys. He immediately sent an urgent message to the captain of the *Oxford* to trail and survey as much of the Dutch coast as possible. Another dispatch went to Captain Skelton of the *Portsmouth* with more explicit instructions from the latest intelligence. The Duke of Monmouth had bought, equipped and manned a thirty-two-gun ship for the apparent purpose of making a landing somewhere on the English south coast in support of Argyle in the north. The plan was to draw off English troops to repel the Scottish landing while Monmouth faced less resistance in the south. Simultaneous risings would take place in London and Cheshire, making any co-ordinated attempt to contain the revolution difficult. Pepys's dispatch to Captain Skelton stated: 'It is His Majesty's pleasure that you endeavour by all acts of hostility to reduce, sink or otherwise destroy' Monmouth's ships.[42] The plan failed completely. On 11 June Monmouth landed unscathed at Lyme Regis where he was given a tumultuous reception.[43] Pepys at once ordered every ship available in the vicinity to go into the attack and within ten days the Navy had boarded and captured Monmouth's ships. Bottled up in Lyme Regis it looked as if Monmouth's fate was sealed but he showed no signs of surrender. Instead he issued a vigorous proclamation declaring that he was the true heir to the throne, that James had poisoned his brother Charles and was even responsible for the Fire of London.[44] Braggadocio of this kind did not impress James who believed from intelligence reports that Monmouth remained trapped in his Lyme Regis base. News filtered through to Pepys in the following ten days of Monmouth's men spreading through the countryside gathering new recruits until he reached Taunton with an army of seven thousand. They were an ill-trained rabble of peasants and he was forced to mount his cavalry on cart-horses which reared and bolted once the guns went into action. None the less, Pepys was disturbed to learn that when Monmouth came face to face with the militia, despite their lack of discipline, his motley army came out best. Momentarily, this seemingly ill-timed conspiracy without sufficient resources began to be taken seriously. In a letter he wrote that Monmouth reaches Taunton and begins to threaten Exeter. Extraordinarily, it was the villainous Admiral Herbert whom Pepys hastily ordered to reinforce the Duke of Albemarle in defending that city. On the night of 5 July 1685 Monmouth gathered his bedraggled forces together and made a reckless attack on royal troops encamped on Sedgemoor. Feversham, the royalist leader, whose dilatory ways should long ago have dismissed him from the service, was sound asleep, but the fates were against Monmouth. Lord Grey misunderstood a vital command from Monmouth and led the cavalry in a direction which hopelessly entangled the horses with Monmouth's infantry. The fight continued through the night but in the early morning the royalists overwhelmed Monmouth's guns and the battle was more or less over.[45]

While the infantry were subjected to devastating fire, Monmouth and Grey simply fled leaving them to their fate. Pepys wrote to Captain Faseby early in July describing 'the total defeat and rout given to the Duke ... who fought very stoutly at the head of the foot [and] escaped ... [it] does not yet appear whether live or dead'.[46] They had, Pepys added, 'nothing left ... to save them ... but the King's mercy'. It was a hollow hope as Pepys well knew. Clemency was not a Stuart virtue. James required vengeance dressed, if possible, in the finery of the law and Monmouth was executed. As for his followers, they were handed over to two notorious judges, George Jeffreys and Pepys's old enemy, Colonel Kirke. The Bloody Assizes were responsible for the deaths of over three hundred men, but death was sometimes preferable to transportation to the West Indies. Some pardons were sold at high prices, while humbler prisoners were bought and sold for £10 or £15. Edward Prideaux, a rich landowner, escaped scot-free for £15,000. Even the Queen and her maids of honour were not above acquiring consignments of transportees and selling them for large profits.[47] Pepys regarded the sentences of the Bloody Assizes as inevitable, did not raise a voice against the sale of pardons and approved the application of one sea captain for a thousand rebels to be transported to Virginia, knowing full well what that meant.

During this period a certain Thomas Phelps escaped from slavery under the Moors and wrote a book which he dedicated to Samuel Pepys in flattering terms. Pepys reciprocated by introducing him to the King but for what purpose and whether anything came of it is unknown.[48] When the nation had at last closed ranks behind the King and the dust had settled, Pepys received, for the second time, an honour quite unconnected with the uprising. On 14 July 1685 he was appointed Master of Trinity House, but the official ceremony had to be postponed until the 20th because the compilation of the enormous charter – mostly Pepys's work – could not be completed in time for Trinity Monday.[49] Among the large and distinguished company which gathered to acclaim him was his old colleague Lord Dartmouth who with eighty others enjoyed what Evelyn described as 'a most . . . magnificent . . . feast'.[50]

The role of the Navy in defeating the rebellion had reaffirmed Pepys's case for urgent rehabilitation and in the autumn of 1685 he persuaded the King to make a tour of ships and dockyards at Portsmouth. After dinner, on 16 September, as became Pepys in his new grandeur, a coach with six horses was hired – at the cost of the crown – to carry him, accompanied by Evelyn, to Winchester. There they met the King in the deanery where he was deeply lost in argument with Bishop Ken about the miracles alleged to have been performed by the Saludadors. The King was predisposed to believe their stories but Pepys recalled too vividly the occasion in Spain when his scientific scepticism required one of them to test his powers in a red hot oven. At a certain point, when dealing with royalty, Pepys always found it wise to go along with gullibility. He suppressed the Saludador's failure to stand up to his test. The following day they all left for Portsmouth and the King duly inspected the yards and fortifications which drove Evelyn to the usual fulsome admiration for his 'royal concern'. The constant toadying to royalty often involved a complete surrender of integrity, but in the climate of opinion of the late seventeenth century any criticism of this attitude would have seemed offensive. Royalty still had aspects of divinity shrouding its somewhat undermined image. It remains difficult to understand how a populace once clamouring for the head of every Catholic had accepted a new monarch who openly practised that religion. One man at least remained troubled – Evelyn. 'Such a prince never had this nation since it was one,' he wrote, and added, 'There could nothing be more desired to accomplish our prosperity but that he were of the national religion.'[51]

Shortly after their survey Pepys went to Windsor and encountered the King in a relaxed mood. Conversation moved away from naval and public affairs to religion. They discussed Lord Arlington who had sworn his allegiance to the Protestant Church to enable him to join the House of Lords, only to reveal his Catholicism on his death bed. The King said that he had long known him to be a waverer but for 'fear of losing his place [he] did not think it convenient to declare himself'. Encouraged by the King's frankness, Pepys was emboldened to ask – without offence he hoped – whether 'His late Majesty had been reconciled to the Church of Rome'. Before the King could answer Pepys took alarm at his audacity and asked his pardon if he had unwittingly 'touched upon a thing it did not befit him to look into'. 'On the contrary,' the King said, fully aware that no one could be more loyal than Pepys. He then beckoned him to follow him into a closet, opened a cabinet and produced some papers written in the late King's hand. From these it was clear that he had opposed the doctrine of the Church of England and even accused Church leaders of heresy. What thoughts must have raced through his mind as Pepys read these papers. The whole reign of Charles II had been based on imposture, the revelation of which would have brought it crashing in ruins and changed the course of British history. The shock must have been considerable, but for one fact. Unwittingly, Pepys had connived at the deception, and he must have remembered the doubts which had arisen in his own mind only to be smothered, perhaps because of his conscience. Was it possible that somewhere at the back of his Puritanism there flickered a sympathy for aspects of the creed he decried?

No sooner had he left the King than – his heart still racing with excitement – he went straight home and rushed off a letter to Evelyn: 'I have reasons to desire you will give me your company tomorrow noon, first because we will be alone and next I have something to show you that I may not have another time.'[52] A similar letter went to James Houblon and the following day all three men met for dinner. Afterwards, Pepys took them into a private room where he showed them the vital documents loaned him by the King. Pepys and Evelyn were familiar with the King's handwriting but Evelyn could not agree its authenticity. He remarked that the arguments advanced were old familiar ones used so often by priests proselytising against the Church of England. Pepys persisted that the documents were genuine but Evelyn felt some hand other than the King's had copied them from a priest's dossier.[53] It remained clear that the King was boldly reaffirming his Catholicism, which drove Evelyn – with remarkable tolerance – to praise his courage. Certainly, the majority of Englishmen did not share Evelyn's view as Pepys knew all too well.

In the wider world the Catholic–Protestant feud was becoming rapidly more entrenched. Suspicion of the French King Louis' motives was growing as he harassed French Protestants. In the autumn of 1685 these suspicions were reinforced at home when Judge Jeffreys, who had wreaked such vengeance on the Protestant rebels, was elevated to Lord Chancellor and against all expectations, the usual Guy Fawkes celebrations were forbidden. Carried along by his own success, Pepys did not read the signs as threatening. He was the right hand man of a King much more reliable that his brother, and had shared Pepys's downfall and recovery. If anything, the King trusted Pepys more than Pepys trusted the King, but Pepys moved with the times and was prepared to suppress suspicion in the King's favour. He was now simultaneously royal adviser, Secretary of the Navy, Master of Trinity House, and President of the Royal Society. Histories of the Royal Society are very unsatisfactory and Pepys receives scant mention, but his standing in scientific eyes must have been high indeed because he gave his imprimatur to one of the most original and influential scientific books ever published – Isaac Newton's *Principia*.

Pepys's paramount interest remained the salvation of the Navy. He made time to visit Hewer's ageing mother at Clapham and entertained a fourteen-year-old boy of no importance – Sir Robert Southwell's son – but these indulgences were rare. Nerves, mind and body were geared as never before to one purpose. In October 1685 Pepys issued a general instruction to the Shipwrights' Hall urging collaboration with shipbuilders in reporting the precise conditions of the King's ships lying at Deptford, Chatham and Woolwich. Consulting with Dartmouth, Pepys revealed a self-defeating circle which had to be broken if the ships were to be saved. Anxious to conceal the results of their neglect, the shipwrights deliberately underestimated the state of disrepair. Simultaneously, the Navy Office 'industriously demanded below the truth and then ... when the ships come under their hands [said] that the work upon further survey appears worse than expected'.[54] Pepys proposed to the King a Special Commission to take over the work from the Navy Board and immediately set about selecting its members. He turned first for advice to Sir Anthony Deane who had been removed from public life in company with Pepys. Deane had applied his brilliant talents as a naval architect for private fees far beyond those once paid by the state. In collaboration with Pepys he quickly prepared an analysis of the current state of the Navy which revealed that one hundred and forty-two of its one hundred and seventy-nine ships were completely unseaworthy. The credit for what followed has largely gone to Pepys, but one crucial element in the whole subsequent undertaking was Deane's.

Pepys, a superb administrator, had a vision, but it was Deane the practical architect who made its realisation possible. Given the £400,000 available, Pepys proposed to 'repair the entire Fleet in three years' and to have it fully equipped with six thousand men in the summer and four thousand in the winter. Nothing must stand in the way of his operations, and powers were required to 'put vigorously in execution the standing instructions and orders'.

Now an active MP in the Commons, Pepys found his energies diverted in defence of the Navy Board – ironically – since he no longer had any faith in its abilities. The main attack on the Board resurrected the charges of religious discrimination which he contemptuously dismissed with the categorical statement that every officer in the service had taken the King's required test. Another charge asked for an explanation of why, if the Navy Board was so efficient, Monmouth had managed to land with such ease on the English coast. 'It was always possible', Pepys replied, 'for a lucky invader to make a chance landing', only, he added with a suitable pause, 'to be thrown back again.'[55] He escaped cross-examination with nothing more than some rough handling. For the King it was altogether different. His sympathetic references to Catholics in his opening speech made it clear that the approval of his confessors mattered to him no less than the approval of the Tories.[56] When he then asked for 'indemnity and dispensations for Polish officers from the test', Parliament appealed to the law against any such concessions.[57] The Commons 'returned no thanks to the King' for his speech. When the question of the test came up again two days later, it was in fact carried by only one vote.[58] Meanwhile, the House of Lords demanded that the test laws be brought – unequivocally – into operation against Catholic office holders. The King's retaliation was simple. He prorogued both houses.

State papers provide extensive evidence of the King's constant manipulation to retain one Roman Catholic after another in office.

Given a free rein he would undoubtedly have permeated the Army, Navy, universities and Church with Catholics but the tolerance of the English had its limits. Extraordinarily, the deep attachment to the monarchy and resistance to change enabled the King and Pepys to survive unscathed until James made the fatal mistake of invoking force.[59]

The prorogation of Parliament left Pepys free to give his full attention to Sir Anthony Deane and the Special Commission. Immediately, the problem of Sir Anthony's salary arose. A deeply committed family man, he had fifteen children and their education and upbringing strained even his considerable resources. He needed a minimum of £1,000 a year to cope with all his responsibilities, he said, and the Lord Treasurer, backed by the King, found this extravagant. Were there not alternative candidates equally suitable at a lower figure? Pepys first replied no, and then named and defamed one alternative after another with that expedient invective which he could so readily command to undermine rivals. The Lord Treasurer thereupon offered Deane a compromise. He would be free to continue his lucrative private practice and be paid a salary of £500. They were asking Deane to undertake the Herculean task of cleaning out the Navy's stables and expecting him to make it a part-time job. For Deane such ignorance of the essentials of the situation was not unexpected in the Treasury but surprising in the King.

Pepys next brought together Deane, Lord Rochester and the Treasurer and a debate ensued which ended with Rochester losing his temper in an outburst of oaths.[60] On 11 March 1686 Pepys presented the King with his devastating analysis of the alternative candidates. It included phrases like 'illiterate and not of countenance'; 'a great drinker'; 'low spirited of little appearance or authority'.[61] Perhaps in fear that the sharp eye of the Lord Treasurer might see something suspicious in the very consistency of his attacks, Pepys did not warn him of his appointment with the King until the morning of the evening on which it was set. Such manipulation did not escape Rochester and he retaliated by simply failing to turn up. Kicking his heels in an antechamber, a very irritable Pepys decided that tougher methods were necessary. The next morning he simply invaded the royal closet when he knew that Rochester would be 'in audience'. The spectacle of Pepys reading – maybe with relish – his defamatory account of Deane's rivals appeals to the romantic imagination but may not be true. The conclusion was foregone. The King appointed Deane at the £1,000 salary he demanded. Other members of the Commission were drawn from the resident commissioners of Dept-

ford, Chatham and Portsmouth, supported by distinguished sea officers like Sir John Narborough. The ever faithful Hewer reaped part
of his reward when he found himself in a new and powerful position
as Pepys's right hand man on the Commission. There was one last
and perhaps surprising appointment – the wordy, emotional, somewhat feckless brother-in-law Balty – who had, none the less, shown
his mettle in the Tangier office. Pepys protected himself against
charges of incompetence by keeping the Comptroller and Surveyor
of the old Navy Board who would remain responsible for the accounts
of the previous five years. On 17 April the new Commission began
the work of repairing and equipping ships and yards, recruiting seamen, preparing estimates and contracts.

Chapter 20

The Special Commission –
the trial of the bishops

Now at the pinnacle of his career Pepys was rich, powerful and widely respected, a man whose gravitas required that he dressed soberly and travelled in his ornate coach. His favours were endlessly sought by some of the most distinguished men in the land and he lived elegantly both at home and in his office. Comfort and culture marked the first and efficiency and order the second. Portraits at this time indicate a man grown much plumper with jowls beginning to overwhelm his chin, a man considering the outside word with calm confidence. He had bitten the dust, risen and was now in full flower again, looking positively magisterial in an expensive wig – one of many – and a silk shirt in the latest fashion. On his desk the day collection book was beautifully bound in dark green morocco and set out in perfect order a complete account of the fleet with the ratings of ships, and regulations governing pay, pensions, flags and salutes. Each day he carried with him a set of notes registering each item due for attention, from audiences with the King or meetings with the victualling officer, to the manifold commitments in a life once again busy from morning to night. There continued to fall away – either by dictation or from his own pen – such a flood of letters, documents and memos as filled to overflowing his complex filing system.

Old friends were dying and he was no longer so facile in making new ones. Mary Skinner receives scant mention in the documents, though we know that Pepys arranged to send her brother Peter on a trip to the Mediterranean. Among his relations, Balty continued to flourish in his correspondence and wrote shortly after his appointment to the commission: 'I have to say ... I shall perform my duty with care, diligence, faithfulness and industry; to the uttermost of power for the King's service as well as my benefactor's honour ... after which if malicious fortune unjustly be my ruin I must rest content.'[1] Sir William Coventry remained close in Pepys's affections but while taking the waters at Tunbridge Wells in June 1686 he died suddenly. His death reminded Pepys of his own advanced years and for several days he was depressed. There were other reasons why death crept a little closer in the autumn of 1686. Balty's wife died in childbirth in September which threw Balty into despair. Mrs Evelyn wrote Pepys a letter of condolence.[2] For once his grief rendered him unable to put pen to paper but he may have dictated a letter addressed to his assistant. Given Balty's incompetence as a family man, it meant more nephews and nieces needing the watchful eye of Uncle Samuel. His own health began to trouble Pepys again and by early December he wrote to Balty: 'It was not without very much ground that in one of my later letters ... I cautioned you against depending on my support much longer ... I now cannot hide ... that pain which I at this day labour under (night and day) from a new stone lodged in my kidneys and an ulcer attending it with a general decay of my stomach and strength that cannot be played with long nor am I solicitous that it should.'[3]

His professional life had achieved a new harmony. Deane, Hewer, Narborough, Berry and Godwin were to concentrate on repairing ships and recovering the lost Navy discipline. Drunkenness and debauchery would be dealt with by immediate suspension, although what qualified as debauchery lacked definition. In the interests of efficiency the new commissioners were asked to reside at their workplace, which meant summarily removing the old members of the Navy Board from their houses. Compensation on a relatively mean scale was granted. Pepys's new Commission was admired and his public reputation soared, but nobody in an age of institutionalised corruption could believe that he personally was not making 'a good thing out of it'. The new dispensation also made life difficult for those influential people with connections at court who expected to slip into easy sinecures. Ehrman has analysed and evaluated the work of the commission in his definitive work *The Navy in the War of William III*. He summarises Pepys's aim:

1. To maintain the ordinancing of the Navy ashore and in harbour and to repair the offices, storehouses and dockyard equipment where necessary;
2. To repair fully by the end of 1688 'the extraordinary decay under which the body of [the] fleet now in harbour labours';
3. To supply the whole fleet with stores for six months' use;
4. To put to sea in 1686 'instead of the three small ships assigned ...

a squadron of no less than ten ships' involving 1,310 men instead of the 275 contemplated';

5. To supply two 'nimble' frigates each year to rectify the shortage of such craft.[4]

It has always been assumed that in the event, the Commission carried out this work successfully in all areas, but there were qualifications. Maintenance, the first item, came under the supervision of Balty at Woolwich and Deptford, and he erected no less than fifty-four new dockyard buildings. The creation of reserve stores to supply the new storehouses did not come up to expectations and '... even the basic magazines turned out not to be sufficient in all respects to answer the demands of the first two – let alone the first eight months of the ensuing mobilisation'.[5] Ehrman comments: 'It is possible that Pepys displayed the same optimism about its state as did those later officials whose ignorance he was so quick to remark.'[6] The fifth item quickly surrendered to economies of space and labour and the frigates were never built. The real success of the Commission lay in the repairs programme. Repairs were fully and efficiently carried out, their cost did not exceed the original estimates and they were completed within the estimated time.[7] These facts were later challenged by a parliamentary enquiry in 1691–2, but proved to be correct.[8] 'Altogether the Special Commission repaired sixty-nine ships and rebuilt twenty. By the time it came to a close only four ships remained with their repairs not completed and four more with ... repairs not begun ...'[9]

Other aspects of the Commission's work were more successful in their delineation than their execution. The rules governing the carriage of freight and bullion now meant instant dismissal for any proven infringement, with any profits immediately turned over to the coffers of the Chatham Chest. The new rules for admission to the Navy or appointment as lieutenant were rigorously outlined. Rates of pay, table allowances and prize money were all carefully codified. King James gave every appearance of backing the indefatigable Pepys on all these points, but that was no guarantee of their enforcement. While Pepys's devotion to his high naval principles remained complete, the same integrity did not characterise his personal conduct. He could take the risk of severely criticising the King's favourite officer, Sir Roger Strickland, when he left his command and drove to London without permission. He did not hesitate to tell the survey clerk at Portsmouth when he presented an unsatisfactory collection of tables that they were useless. He also dismissed the Duke of Grafton's candidate for a lieutenancy as unqualified to be the boatswain of a fourth-rate ship. Yet when Thomas Povey wrote yet another appeal to pay the fifty per cent of profits from his Tangier treasure ship, upon which they had agreed many years before, he ignored the letter. Rightly incensed, Povey turned to their mutual friend Sir Anthony Deane:

Common civility [he wrote] returns an answer in matters of lesser
moment and common justice expects a ... reply ... Contempt, neglect
or superficial evasions, or obstinate and affected silence were never
excusably admitted to be a decent way of proceeding, especially with
one not much inferior to them though not in so thriving and swelling
a condition as themselves.[10]

Bryant comments: 'The poor man never received any satisfaction.' It was an understatement.

Mrs Bagwell now resurfaced after many years when he conspired to sleep with her under dubious circumstances. Driven by her out-of-work husband, she began to haunt the entrance to York Buildings, pressing his claim for any suitable appointment that became vacant. It must have embarrassed Pepys in all his new grandeur, surrounded by an ever growing staff. When her pressure became intense Pepys did take the trouble to write a letter to her husband.

I am your friend and always have and will be so, your service to the
King well deserving it. But I cannot pretend to be able to do everything
that is desired of me even by those that do deserve it well, there being
a much greater number desiring and waiting for employment than the
Navy can find opportunity of satisfying ... And hence it is that I advised
Mrs Bagwell as I do everybody else not to lose their time attending
... upon me, because that occasions them but an increase of expense
in staying in town ...

Pepys explained that under the new rules, appointments were made without personal contacts, the candidates knowing nothing until 'word is sent them of its being done'. His letter, he hoped, would remove the misunderstanding of his apparent 'backwardness to do you the kindness on occasion of the late vacancies'.[11] Clearly, past sexual favours cannot justify present privileges, but Bagwell had a proven record as a master shipwright and jobs were available. No practical reason was given why he should not get one, unless renewed proximity meant renewed guilt.

In the wider world the King's steady infiltration of Protestant life with Catholic thinking disturbed Pepys's close friends Houblon and Evelyn. Until the summer of 1686 Evelyn remained convinced that the King was a tolerant man prepared to embrace all religions in proper proportion, but now he wrote of 'all enquiries being ... at work to bring in Popery again which God in mercy prevent'.[12] There was no doubt about it, the innermost chambers of James's life – the closet, the chapel and even the bedchamber – were seen to be full of priests and confessors who did not conceal their presence. James had successfully propounded the argument that as an openly avowed Catholic – accepted as such on the throne of England by the populace – he must defend the interests of his Church. He had, in the past, convinced Evelyn, Houblon and Pepys himself that his tolerance was intended fundamentally to protect the Protestant faith. By the summer of 1686 that belief was in disarray as he proceeded to infiltrate one area of public life after another until he reached the universities, which at last impinged on Pepys. His old friend, the heavy drinking Dr Peachell, Master of Magdalene College, Cambridge, was appointed Vice-Chancellor at the same time as the King was attempting to open university fellowships to selected Catholics.

Early in the new year Peachell wrote to Pepys:

His Majesty was pleased to send a letter directed to me ... to admit one Alban Francis, a Benedictine Monk of Arts without administering any ... oaths to him. None of the oaths of allegiance and supremacy being required ... I could not tell what to do: decline His Majesty's letter or his lawes: I could but pray God to direct, sanctify and govern me in the ways of his laws that so through His most mighty protection both here and ever I may be presented in body and soul ...[13]

If Pepys's reply exists, I could not trace it. Perhaps he did not reply because he too was caught between divided loyalties. Oxford and Cambridge were the centres of influence in the Anglican hierarchy and the example they set was liable to be followed by receding ranks of churchmen. If Pepys advised Peachell to refuse the King's request it would bode ill for him in court and add a small firebrand to the conflagration which was waiting to engulf him. Peachell had never emerged in the documents as a strong man prepared to sacrifice himself for his principles but he stood out against the King in great trepidation and was suspended as Master and Vice-Chancellor.

Much larger figures were presently involved in an issue which threatened to tear the country apart. It began when the Chaplain of the Ordinary at Chatham, Mr Loton, found himself unable to carry out the King's request to read the second Declaration of Indulgence from his pulpit. He lived by the precept 'first give to God the things that are God's and then to Caesar the things that are

Caesar's'. The Sundays of 20 and 27 May were the days selected by the King for the Declaration to be read and no less than seven bishops jointly refused to obey. They then compiled a petition to the King asking him to reconsider his Declaration, which must put him in the position of overriding the law. The King received the petition angrily, believing that it was tantamount to treason, but he could not prevent its wide circulation in taverns and coffee-houses. Convinced that his authority was at risk if he did not immediately prosecute the seven signatories, the King summoned them to appear before the Council where Pepys himself sat cheek by jowl with the forbidding Lord Chancellor, Jeffreys. Judicial calm was quickly broken by a heated interrogation during which the bishops not only admitted signing the appeal but refused to enter into recognizances even when repeatedly pressed. Anxious to avoid adding fresh fuel to the hostility growing around him, the King hesitated before committing them to the Tower.[14] In the end it was an unwise but, as he saw it, necessary move. The news of their arrest spread like wildfire and crowds gathered in boats and on rooftops to watch in sympathetic silence as the barges carrying the bishops moved down the Thames. Once in the Tower they were 'most mightily visited and courted by the multitude at Whitehall ...'[15] On 29 June they were duly brought to trial in Westminster Hall. A great crowd gathered outside full of noisy and frequently bawdy protests while inside the remarkable paradox of the aristocracy opposing the King packed the benches with a hardly more restrained audience.[16] For the prosecution the Solicitor General, Sir William Williams, was an unpopular man whose love of wrangling and short temper matched his moral courage. For the defence Pemberton had in the time of Charles II been Chief Justice of the King's Bench and was known for his humanity and tolerance.

The bishops were first charged with having written or published in the county of Middlesex 'a false, malicious and a seditious libel'. Several witnesses were called to prove the actual writing but produced evasive replies which pleased the spectators whose ribald reactions threatened to interrupt the proceedings.[17] Pemberton immediately contended that there was no evidence to go to the jury and, in effect, no case to answer. The crown then changed the charge from one of writing a libel to publishing a libel. This required proof of the delivery of the document to the King. Although several witnesses were interrogated the required answer was not extracted. Williams then began to put leading questions to which the defence immediately raised objections. Macaulay described what followed vividly: 'As witness after witness answered in the negative, roars of laughter and shouts of triumph which the judges did not even attempt to silence shook the hall.'[18] The Attorney General at last lost his temper and shouted back: 'Here's a wonderful great rejoicing that the truth cannot prevail.' Pepys then became directly involved in the proceedings. The ubiquitous, the reliable, the distinguished Mr Pepys, a close friend of the King and present at the first Council meeting, would surely have witnessed delivery and provide the necessary evidence. So crucial had Pepys's evidence become that the Lord Chief Justice took over his examination.

Lord Chief Justice: Were you at the Council Board when My Lords the bishops were committed?
Pepys: Yes, I was.
Lord Chief Justice: What were the questions that were asked either by the King or by My Lord Chancellor?
Pepys: My Lord, I would remember as well as I could the very words and the very words of the question were I think 'My Lords do you own this paper?' I do not think anything was spoken about the delivering but I believe it was understood by everybody at the table that that was the paper ... they had delivered.[19]

By the crucial phrase 'it was understood by everybody' Pepys had committed himself in favour of the King which meant weakening the bishops' case. The Lord Chief Justice then turned to the Attorney General and questioned him tartly: 'Well, have you done now?' Before the Attorney General could reply he continued: 'To satisfy you I'll ask [Mr Pepys] this question: Was this the paper you delivered to the King?' He flourished a paper. Pepys replied, 'No, My Lord.' This reply introduced further complications. The Attorney General took up the questioning:

Attorney General: Pray sir, do you remember whether the King himself asked the question?
Pepys: You mean I suppose, Mr Attorney ... [about] their delivering it to the King.
Attorney General: Yes, sir.
Pepys: Truly, I remember nothing of that.
[The Solicitor General pressed home the question:]
Did you observe any discourse concerning their delivery of it to the King?
Pepys: Indeed, Mr Solicitor, I did not.[20]

Pepys's evidence had become very ambiguous.

The case for the crown seemed on the verge of collapse when news arrived that the Lord President was prepared to give indisputable evidence of publication. As he was carried into the hall in a sedan chair several voices called out 'Popish dog' and his face paled. With his eyes fixed on the ground he gave evidence in a faltering voice. Publication was proved and the bishops' defence undermined. The question remained – could it be said to be malicious or seditious? Pepys followed the trial in close detail and found himself in difficulties. He did not want the King humiliated but he could not condemn the bishops.

On the last day of the trial it was dark before the jury retired to consider their verdict. They 'stayed together all night without fire or candle'.[21] The bishops' solicitor also sat throughout the night to prevent any interference with them. As for Pepys, he must have shared what Macaulay referred to as 'the intense anxiety of half the nation'. At ten the next morning the court met again with the public benches overwhelmed and everyone fell silent as the jury entered their box. When the words 'not guilty' were uttered the crowds on the benches and in the galleries 'raised a shout and ten thousand persons who crowded the great hall replied with a still louder shout'. The behaviour of the judges throughout the trial had been extraordinary and most remarkable of all was the direction of the court to the jury. It was reasonable for them to allow the jury to decide on the fact of publication but not to decide the issue of libel. It set the precedent for future libel interpretation for years to come.

The trial of the bishops rightly takes its place as seminal in English history because it produced a verdict opposing a whole system of government.[22] On the following day, celebrations echoed through the streets with church bells ringing, shots fired and the bishops having to be protected from their own excited supporters. Violence broke out near Derby House and Pepys witnessed the burning of an effigy of the Pope. Almost simultaneously the secret negotiations between the Dutch and the aristocracy came to a head with a formal invitation to William of Orange 'to invade England at the head of the Dutch Army'. The whole episode was surrounded by a cloak-and-dagger secrecy with the vital invitation conveyed by Sir Arthur Herbert (later Earl Torrington) disguised as an ordinary seaman. There were many precipitant factors but principal among them was the birth on 10 June of a son to Queen Mary of Modena who would be heir to the throne of England and educated in the Catholic faith. This did not dismay Pepys. Loyalty to the King overrode all religious and political considerations.

He wrote to Sir Roger Strickland wishing the child a long and happy life. This was remarkable; the strong possibility of a Catholic

King was so repulsive to a large part of the nation that it threatened civil war.[23] A new subtlety characterised the King's approach to a situation where the lines were being drawn for a gigantic struggle.[24] James's sympathetic relations with Louis XIV of France remained relatively cool but William of Orange was implacably opposed to Louis and everything for which he stood. Louis was about to challenge the whole might of Europe and this inevitably aroused the Pope's hostility. In the maze of complicated diplomatic relations James received conflicting reports from his advisers, but the news from Holland continued to be of ships gathering in unusual numbers. Rumour, lies and scare-mongering were rampant in London while Papists continued to circulate in the royal chambers, some managing to invade the natal chamber itself. The Dutch movements became more worrying and even the King's facile optimism began to crack. Early in April he made a weak gesture to the Navy Office allowing them to prepare victuals for an extra thousand men against an emergency.

By 27 April Pepys was writing to the commander in chief of the Downs a letter which stipulated 'that this command be not exposed to anybody's knowledge but such as are concerned in seeing it executed'.[25] Written in his own hand, the letter enclosed a duplicate order signed by the King for the fleet to be in readiness. The King had one purpose in sending the order and Pepys another. The Dutch had once before magically appeared in the Medway and a repetition of such daring might threaten the many ships in the Cinque Ports which Pepys had so painfully brought to a state of readiness. By June, Admiral Strickland was in command of twenty frigates with accompanying fireships which were ordered to cruise off the Goodwins and check the movements of any foreign ships. There remained a great weakness with which Pepys was all too familiar. The seventy-five ships of the main battle fleet were all in harbour and as yet unmanned. Verney in his memoirs remarked that 'drums are beating up about Wapping for seamen but few come in'.[26] Here was Pepys, after two years of unrelenting struggle, with a growing array of ships and rigorous new codes of conduct, but the men required were either abroad in merchant ships or belonged to a multitude of unemployed drifting around the sea ports. Short of press-ganging or mobilisation, the situation was alarming.

Pepys and Deane went to work with a will and Deane recorded total exhaustion one night from 'so many vexations, from ignorance, negligence and sloth'. It seemed remarkable that he could use these words when the Navy was in an advanced stage of rehabilitation.

A gap in fact appeared in Pepys's grand design. The ships, stores and discipline were beginning to shimmer in their new shape, but no less than fifty-nine of the line of battle were idle at their moorings as if for exhibition and not action. It can be argued that at this stage the threat of invasion was not sufficiently great, but that threat had been rumoured and counter-rumoured for months. In the final event mobilisation was the only answer, reinforced by the worst forms of press-ganging.

On 24 August the King ordered the Chancellor to issue writs for the meeting of a new Parliament on 27 November. Instructions were drawn up for the regulators of corporations which encouraged them to approve persons opposed to the King in the hope that such approval would guarantee their rejection as MPs. Lord Sunderland gave sweeping recommendations to the Lords Lieutenant for desired candidates to be promoted. The idea that Parliament would become a willing tool of the King was encouraged by those familiar with his carefully concealed inner machinations. And then on 21 September the King issued a proclamation undertaking to exclude Catholics from any new Parliament. Under pressure from a number of bishops he announced the dissolution of the Ecclesiastical Commission and restored the Charter of the City of London. Another proclamation followed, reactivating the franchise of business corporations, but these conciliatory gestures went for nothing.

In Holland persistent rumours of an imminent alliance between King Louis and James reinforced Dutch anxieties and underpinned the necessity of William's invasion plans. Late in September Holland openly declared that it was the intention of James and Louis to sweep away the Protestant Church and replace it with a Catholic equivalent.[27] In England confusion became confounded. The choice was between two unpleasant alternatives. Sharing the same religion with the Dutch did not diminish the distaste for invasion by a foreign army, but something stronger than patriotism recoiled from accepting French Catholic dominance. On the eve of events which should have led to bloodshed, this choice between two evils diminished the intensity of the clash. If there are such things as immutable historic forces they were certainly at work, with Europe arousing itself to resist Louis' expansionist policies and William of Orange aware that time was running short for any invasion of England. The great administrative reforms of the Navy were almost complete and the Commission about to be wound up, but Pepys realised that, if anything, events required an intensification of his work. The nation held its breath in the midst of an approaching climax, with the people,

clergy and nobles in unaccustomed alliance and the King hoping
that the imminent general election would give him an anti-Protestant
Parliament. Englishmen who believed that William could offer deliverance from the Catholic threat were matched by others who could
no longer follow the bewildering complications of the international
scene. The King himself was still not completely convinced of the
inevitability of invasion. Indeed, the domestic concessions he had
made at home were matched by a new twist in foreign affairs, the
result of the French King's announcement that any attack on England
would be an attack on France. The weather reinforced his doubts.
His advisers pointed to the lunacy of launching an invasion as late
as October, with ships not built to survive seasonal gales. One went
further and suggested that the gathering of Dutch ships was nothing
more than an elaborate bluff to reinforce diplomatic negotiations.
These views were reaffirmed by the stream of untruthful reassurances
received every other day from the Dutch ambassador.

Late in August there was inescapable confirmation of the Dutch
intentions. The English agent at The Hague spoke of an armada
of no less than ninety ships, all fully manned and in fighting shape,
about to sail for England.[28] Alarm resounded throughout the country.

Chapter 21

Prince William invades England

Dwarfed by these events Pepys's private life throughout the years 1687–8 underwent considerable changes. Will Hewer's role as Pepys's ever faithful collaborator and companion tended to conceal the fact that he was relatively rich in his own right. He possessed one of the finest houses in York Buildings – Number Fourteen – and it was to this house that Pepys, in the midst of whirlwind work, managed to move early in 1688. It was ideally situated, standing above the beautiful stone watergate past which the Thames flowed untrammelled by artificial embankments. The walkway beside the river, lined with trees, became a retreat on summer evenings where Pepys sometimes dawdled trying to escape the pressure of the impending crisis. As if to enhance his new grandeur, at the cost of the crown, he had a large gilded shield affixed to the house which enshrined the Lord High Admiral's anchor and royal arms. Those on foot, or travelling by boat, could not pass without being aware that a person of some distinction lived at this address. He furnished his new house elaborately with the help of Houblon who occupied a more and more important place in his life. It was Houblon who managed to purchase – 'at great sweat' – a beautiful tapestry to cover the inner walls of Number Fourteen at the bargain price of £80. Pepys's library had grown beyond the dimensions regarded as necessary for a gentleman and what little leisure remained was sometimes given to browsing in his old booksellers' haunts.

Whether Mary Skinner still presided over his household is unclear, but if she did it was not as housekeeper. Certainly, she remained in his life. The morality of the seventeenth century accommodated something equivalent to modern couples living together. 'Keeping', as it was called, had no defined limits and varied according to class, but unless some dramatic change had overtaken Pepys it is difficult to believe that he lived with Mary Skinner platonically. The role of housekeeper had been taken over in the autumn of 1685 by a Mrs Fane who was not a complete success. Houblon had given Mrs Fane a good character reference. 'I have known her from her bib upwards; and visible qualities and esteem for my wife and children made me her friend.'[1] Pepys quickly found flaws in this description. She had a 'bitterness and noise of tongue that of all womankind I have hitherto had to deal, do render her conversation and comportment as a servant most insupportable'.[2] Mrs Fane settled in as housekeeper but bickering and quarrels continued to be provoked by her shrewish tongue. Within eighteen months there was nothing for it but to sack her. He then employed a lady called Judy Robbins, but this was a failure too, because she had contracted a secret marriage to a man whose house she 'kept' at Chatham.[3] Mrs Fane in the meantime put her case to Houblon, anxious to return to Pepys's household. Houblon wrote to Pepys: 'As I protest solemnly that I have never before heard of this ill quality in her so I have had no other intention in endeavouring to make peace between you than what may justly have contributed to your satisfaction as well as hers in her earnest application to me to be her advocate.'[4] In the end it was as much Mary Skinner as Houblon who persuaded Pepys to take Mrs Fane back.

There were now at least nine people in the household and it was embellished by many valuable pieces which Pepys had only recently been able to acquire. Money flowed freely since his £2,000 salary was topped up with a whole variety of fees for new appointments, ranging from 10s for chaplains and midshipmen to £5 for master shipwrights and storekeepers. Despite external pressures on his new luxurious surroundings Pepys continued to find time to entertain guests at musical evenings, and he would go to great lengths to secure the best performers. Ignoring religious distinctions the devout Catholic Lady Tuke became his emissary in persuading the exclusive singer and eunuch Cifacca to perform for him. 'I showed your answer to Mr Dies who is so well satisfied ... and he [is] willing another day next week to give you an hour or two to hear him sing.'[5] Houblon and Evelyn were guests at the concert and Evelyn described Cifacca as 'a mere wanton effeminate child' who could none the less sing with 'incomparable softness and sweetness'.[6] Houblon attested Pepys's tolerance since Pepys was a Tory and Houblon a Whig, Houblon a Huguenot and Pepys an Englishman. That tolerance did not extend to Morelli, his old singing master, when he tried to return to the Pepys household. He had dared, it seems, to marry without consultation and Pepys expected his authority to be respected even by those who had left his family circle.[7] Pepys showed greater intolerance with the 'negro' servant he had recently acquired. The servant's capacity for 'lying, pilfering and drinking' reached a point where Pepys decided that he could no longer belong to a respectable household – a view vigorously endorsed by Mrs Fane. Without consulting Pepys she arranged for a local waterman to spirit him aboard a freighter then making ready to sail for the West Indies. This led to angry exchanges between the *Foresight*'s Captain Stanley and Pepys, who then came to an arrangement for the boy's disposal. He was to be kept on hard tack while on board and sold immediately the ship arrived in the Indies, the cost of his keep being deducted from the sale price. While at sea, Pepys insisted that the boy be subject to the strictest discipline.[8] These reactions did not surprise Bryant 'in that strained and cloudy time when Pepys's temper grew a little acrid'.[9] They were indeed strained and cloudy times. When public pressures disturbed his peace of mind, Pepys still took refuge in his study to read, research and write on 'private matters', such as his planned life of Lord Sandwich. Such projects were swept aside once more by the manœuvres, lies and deceptions which characterised international relations. On 28 September 1688 the King publicly revealed what everybody already knew: that an invasion of England was imminent. Pepys accelerated his efforts to man the Navy, supported by his well tried aides Deane and Hewer. Working far into the night they moved between London and Windsor, frequently leaving the London office in charge of Samuel Atkins, the survivor of the Popish Plot. It was to be expected that Pepys's divided loyalties were resolved when a foreign country threatened his country – but the invader was bent on reaffirming Protestantism and this confused the issue.

Not until 19 October did the Dutch fleet actually set sail, only to be driven back by bad weather. It confirmed the worst fears of naval advisers that Prince William was mad to put his ships at risk in autumn weather. Speculation ran wild in England selecting one possible landing point after another. The coast of Scotland, Sole Bay – that old familiar battle ground – and even Bridlington Bay were favoured. Even at this late stage, the English Navy was not yet fully equipped and ready to face the enemy. Bad weather was a godsend to Pepys, still working relentlessly in York Buildings far into the night. Literally, the fate of England was at this stage in his hands and the gods were kind to him. The bad weather continued. On 28 September the entire English fleet was ordered to assemble at the Buoy of the Nore. A quarrel between Pepys and Strickland – Commander-in-Chief – had placed the fleet in the hands of Pepys's old friend from his Tangier days, Lord Dartmouth. Strickland had endangered good relations by attempting to have Mass celebrated on his flagship which caused a minor mutiny among his crew. The much less serious question of his rate of pay during operations in Portuguese waters caused an angry exchange, and a final breach with Pepys. Late in September Strickland was replaced by Dartmouth whose capacities Pepys could calculate with some accuracy. They were very mixed according to Macaulay, who did not share Pepys's evaluation. Consideration was given to sending frigates to the Zeeland Shoals in a pre-emptive strike but Dartmouth lacked the dash and daring of Drake. He believed in building up his resources to their highest pitch, meeting the enemy in English seas and attempting an element of surprise. English pilots who professed to know every shoal and sandbank could make this possible. It was a strategy which ignored the renegade English pilots in the Dutch fleet, no less familiar with English waters. In London the atmosphere produced in the King an uncharacteristic moodiness which seemed to weaken his resolution.

The politicians, divided in their views, were no help to him at all, and Dartmouth's early initiative had subsided into humdrum caution. It was left to the unbelligerent professional civil servant Pepys to rush by coach from London to Windsor trying to stiffen the resolve of all concerned while overseeing dockyard activity, holding a watching brief on the Navy Board and stirring the Chief of Ordnance to greater effort. Facing such challenges, Pepys seemed able to draw on reserves of energy which kept him active far into the night and made it possible for him to carry out jobs normally divided between three men. Royal diplomacy, naval direction and now political campaigning brought his activities to a pitch which seemed frenzied. Instead his letters and memos revealed a brain working with a calm rationality which expressed itself in long, uncoiling sentences intricately reaching their conclusion, driven home by the gravitas required of great decisions. There were those who regarded his professional letters as pompous but such language was a form of courtesy to professional people. Some were tart with the annoyance of an important bureaucrat.

The King had called a general election for the autumn. Ever watchful for his future, Pepys knew that his re-election to his old seat in Harwich was very uncertain and he intensified his political campaign. James now requested Pepys to issue fighting instructions urging Dartmouth to sink, destroy and disable, by any means, enemy ships wherever he could find them. Instead, Dartmouth's strategy kept him safely settled in the Thames estuary building up his resources.

Discussing possible manœuvres involved laboriously written letters dispatched on horseback and several days could pass before a reply was received. 'This morning by pack horse are despatched flags for the flagship and proper pendants for the whole fleet.'[10] The almost daily correspondence between Dartmouth and Pepys reveals that as late as October the fleet was still not completely equipped, with captains missing from their ships. On 19 October, the very day the Dutch fleet first sailed, Dartmouth wrote to Pepys: 'I cannot but very much esteem and applaud the great zeal and hearty care you testify in pressing so earnestly to strengthen the fleet by all means ... particularly by moving His Majesty to order to their commands ... the captains of those ships appointed for his service who ... are still paying their court at Whitehall.'[11] In the same letter he was rationalising his failure to go out in search of the enemy as a result of a prolonged consultation between flag officers and pilots.[12] At the most he intended to 'fall down to the Gunfleet that being I judge the properest post'. The fleet now consisted of fifty-two, third-, fourth- and fifth-rates, with seventeen fireships, mounting a total of 1,876 guns, very slightly inferior to the Dutch armament of fifty-four ships and 2,040 guns.[13] Pepys from his vantage point at the centre of intelligence wrote to Dartmouth at midnight on 10 November confirming this estimate. 'Contrary to the impression universally received touching the inequality of the two fleets, greatly to the advantage of the Dutch both in number and force to yours, the odds in number is very inconsiderable and in quality ... appears to incline to His Majesty's side.'[14] Quality meant design of guns and seamanship and Dartmouth found Pepys's letter reassuring. It is fascinating to reflect on these two men (or their clerks) laboriously writing in pen and ink missives of several pages on which the fate of England turned, one cut off in the state room of his flagship, the other in his – frequently – candlelit office. More than a touch of acrimony crept in from time to time because despite Pepys's efforts there were serious delays in victualling the ships. Dartmouth's impatience and occasional anger is understandable, but he had a gift for adding a cutting edge to a letter when roused: 'Sir, though I am very well assured you have assiduously performed your part as Secretary, yet other officers have not as I have often repeated to you and I do once more most earnestly desire that all excuses may be laid aside and everything eventually be done for His Majesty's service. The ... necessities thereof oblige me to give you my opinion that a further delay may be fatal.'[15]

As a result of these pressures, the Special Commissioners suffered from overwork extending far into the night and both Deane and Hewer fell ill while the indomitable Pepys ploughed on sometimes alone. In the eulogies penned about Pepys's rehabilitation of the Navy one sceptical note was struck by Ogg in his impressive *England in the Reign of James II and William III*. 'Whatever success may have been achieved ... *contemporary opinion was divided* (my emphasis).'[16] John Ehrman concluded that most criticisms were misplaced.[17] However, Pepys himself was clearly anxious in a letter to Dartmouth late in October: 'There is not one ship behind you from whose commander I do not daily hear of the want of guns, carriage ... or something relating thereto.' Dartmouth shared this view. He feared fighting battles, he wrote, 'with few ships and those not in the condition they ought to be'.[18] Equally disturbing were the subversive pamphlets circulating among men and officers. Gangs of pressed seamen suddenly revolted on board their transports, overcame their guards, swam ashore and disappeared. A number of gentleman officers had also slipped through Pepys's new regulations to put at risk the efficiency of their ships.

In all this doubt and confusion, it was surprising that Dartmouth at last managed to set sail from Gunfleet on 30 October while the wind was still in the southeast. His voyage was cut short when the wind turned easterly and drove him to anchor once more off the Longsands' Head. Winds could make a laughing stock of the finest pieces of strategical planning. Moreover, Dartmouth's policy to preserve the English fleet intact for the final defence of England was flawed, especially because it met an entirely different spirit from the invading Dutch. Under their banner they had 'half the adventurers of Europe' imbued with a daring which matched the recklessness of some of their leaders. Early in November they sailed once more from Helvoetsluys with the wind for which the Prince of Orange had prayed in their favour. Dartmouth was left still struggling to clear the Galloper sands. At the outset the Dutch set a deceptive northwesterly course, but suddenly changed direction to the southwest. Watchers on the English southeast coast could plainly see scores of ships hurried along by the easterly gale which sent great seas over their decks and threatened to drive them ashore. By 3 November, Dartmouth was at last on the high seas and entered the English Channel to reach Beachy Head on 5 November.[19] There, to everyone's surprise, he reported to the King the unanimous decision of all his captains not to launch an attack. Pepys was one of few who kept his counsel and made no complaint although Dartmouth's reputation was fast declining. Two equally attractive alternatives were available

to him and led to long hours of tortured debate. He could wait
until the Dutch had landed their troops somewhere on the English
coast and then proceed to disable their supply fleet, leaving the
invaders cut off. Or he could risk a running battle with the Dutch
at sea which might leave the English fleet in disarray and underpin
the success of any subsequent landing. On 5 November Dartmouth
indicated to the King that he could no longer pre-empt a landing
and the King told him to employ whatever strategies he felt fit.
By 12 November the King had changed his mind and Dartmouth
received new orders: 'Attack the Dutch wherever [you] find them.'[20]
This he singularly failed to do. Sea battles in the seventeenth century
– as we have seen – were frequently won not by ships, men and
bravery, but by the weather and now Dartmouth blamed the weather
for his failure to attack. With remarkable restraint for a man who
could be very frank in moments of adversity, Pepys reassured Dartmouth that he had done everything possible against a wind blowing
in favour of the Dutch fleet, a manipulation of the facts since the
wind had for a long period favoured the English.

Prince William's transports had landed at Torbay without much
trouble and on 5 November his soldiers quickly fanned out. The narrow lanes and hilly countryside around Torbay were soon full of
marching invaders. By 8 November a besieged Exeter had fallen and
was overwhelmed by a colourful throng of foreign troops which
arrived in bohemian disorder and marched through streets already
crowded by visitors to the annual fair. Still, Dartmouth claimed, bad
weather forced him to continue sheltering in the Downs. Not until
16 November did he set sail – forlornly – for Torbay.[21] Once more
the weather would brook no interference and drove him off course
as far southwest as Alderney. By this time the organisation of the fleet
had collapsed and many ships were leaking badly. Dartmouth wrote
to Pepys: 'I find my loss in the *Montagu*, *Centurion* and *Assurance* greater
than any recruit I am likely to have; so that nine and twenty men-of-
war are all I am likely to depend on.'[22] Back at his office at York
Buildings Pepys continued to work intensively writing letters to Dartmouth which spoke of more merchantmen and more fireships put
into his service. Still hard at work at two o'clock on the morning
of 11 November he wrote a letter whose delayed delivery must have
rendered it ironical to Dartmouth. The letter condensed the latest
intelligence received by Pepys about the relative strength of the two
navies and said that the odds still '. . . inclined to His Majesty's side'.[23]

Dartmouth finally arrived off Torbay on 19 November, by which
time the invading troops had established themselves and were living

off the land. The Dutch fleet lay snugly intact in Torbay and once again Dartmouth had to decide whether to attack or not. Reduced by the weather to a remnant of his former strength with many ships leaking badly, he decided yet again not to challenge the protected and undamaged Dutch fleet of fifty-four men-of-war. While Dartmouth sat wavering what to do, letters passed to and from Pepys which apparently accepted Dartmouth's inaction but urged him to close with the Dutch as soon as possible. A Council meeting on 12 November at which the King was present further compounded a confused situation. Aware as he was of Pepys's instructions to Dartmouth, the King sent a dispatch which seemed to contradict them. 'You best know your own strength and whether to make use of this easterly wind to attempt anything on them ... I must leave all to your judgement ... who can judge best what is to be done. ...'Tis late and I have not time to say any more ...' He then wrote 'It will be the end of this week before I think to leave this town.'[24] The words had a sinister note. Did they mean that the King was about to abandon his capital and run for it or was he preparing to join his troops in the West Country hoping that a bold confrontation at Sedgemoor would push them back towards their entrapped fleet? The second interpretation was never really in doubt. When William first assembled his forces at Exeter he was disappointed by the response from the ordinary people and the gentry. Those secretly enthusiastic lords and magnates who had encouraged his invasion remained discreetly in the background while the King's red-coats were still in their areas, but once they were seen heading southwestwards they began to speak openly.

By Sunday 11 November Pepys was called away from his pew in St Martin's in the Fields to return to his office where urgent news awaited him. Reinforcements were gathering in Rotterdam to join William's forces on such a scale as to upset the optimism of the English commanders. Pepys immediately sought audience with the King, only to receive the same vacillating answer as ever – that naval strategy must remain in Dartmouth's hands. The state of alarm into which the invasion threw the whole country was illustrated by a letter from Evelyn to Pepys. 'We are here as yet (I thank God) unmolested; but this shaking menaces every corner and the most philosophic breast cannot but be sensible of the motion.'[25] In the southwest military events fully justified Evelyn's anxieties. At the outset James had under his command twice as many men as William but in the course of the second week of the invasion, defections began to multiply. Before the King left the capital to join his troops Clarendon's son had deserted to William, and Lord Lovelace, hellbent to follow him, was only stopped in a bloody confrontation with the militia. On 16 November an express messenger brought a missive which, as he read it, stopped the King in the middle of his dinner. Leaving the meal uneaten he retired to his closet. It soon became known that Lord Cornbury, a commander of three regiments of cavalry, had taken them into William's lines only to have the ordinary rankers rebel and refuse to join the enemy. Lord Cornbury and his officers persisted in their desertion and were royally welcomed by William.[26] His quarters at Exeter began to take on the appearance of a court with 'more than sixty men of rank and fortune lodged there'.[27] Still Pepys did not see King James's position as hopeless. In his propaganda William had always presented himself as a liberator who would ensure that the Protestant religion prevailed, with James ruling a freely elected Parliament. Pepys also realised that William was considered by some as a possible lever to extract concessions from James should he win the battle.

Pessimism now overcame the King. He summoned his officers to conferences begging them not to desert him in the field and made a will to which Pepys was a signatory. Pepys then joined the King's cavalcade moving southwest until it reached Windsor where a remarkably astute manœuvre revealed Pepys in the middle of perhaps the greatest crisis of his life, still with an eye to the main chance. It is difficult to imagine the reaction of a King besieged on all sides by disaster, confronted by his Secretary of the Admiralty asking him to sign a letter guaranteeing that a sum of £28,000 due to him for past services should duly be granted him by the Lords Commissioners of the Treasury – whatever happened. Impassively, the King duly signed. 'It should be remembered he had refrained from doing so [demanding payment] during the four-and-a-half years of his second tenure of the Admiralty secretaryship.'[28] Perhaps it is a further tribute to Pepys the businessman, preserving some cool centre of his brain to calculate the commercial odds of his commitment to King and country.

He was no fighting man. He left the royal entourage on Sunday the 18th and returned to London to confront more disturbing news. Partly thanks to Pepys, Dartmouth had at last decided to commit his fleet in an attack on the enemy, but the fates were pitiless. Once more the weather broke and Dartmouth wrote that there was 'such a variety of winds and storms as frustrated all my hopes'. Bad weather continued for four days during which the English fleet was now battered and incapacitated while the Dutch were snugly protected by an English harbour. It is not difficult to imagine Pepys's anxiety as he dictated missive after missive trying to discover what had happened to his beautiful, newly equipped, but so ill fated Navy.

Reducing details of what followed to their bare outline, the battle on land found William, joined by many West Country gentry, leaving Exeter on 21 November to begin a march on London which met little serious opposition. In the capital, mobs had broken loose and no Catholic was safe from at best molestation, at worst death. Once again, an effigy of the Pope was dragged by cart down Whitehall, and as one representation fell in roaring fire, another quickly rose to suffer a similar fate. Groups of youths armed with pikes began combing Jesuit households, and cellar hideouts were broken into and set on fire. No priest dared to set foot in the streets and most went into hiding. Troop reinforcements from Ireland marching westwards through London came under ribald derision and occasional brickbats. Macaulay wrote: 'The very sentinels who guarded the palace hummed as they paced around the grounds:

The English confusion to Popery, drink,
Lillibularo bullen a la.'[29]

Everywhere passions suppressed for three years mounted and broke loose as news of William's rapid advance on London reached Whitehall.[30]

The King had long realised that there was nothing for it but to retreat and on 26 November he was again seen re-entering a disturbed London where his own security depended upon heavy military protection. A group of fifty peers and bishops had sought desperately to discover William's precise intentions, but he maintained a strict silence knowing full well that it would encourage division among his enemies. The same group demanded urgent audience with the King on the day following his return. Led by Clarendon they did not mince their words and made it clear that this was a time for drastic action. News of their meeting quickly reached Pepys and he found himself in some confusion when he learnt the terms which they had almost dictated. The King must summon Parliament, give full amnesty to his enemies, dismiss all Roman Catholic officers, separate himself from France, and arrange for emissaries to confer with William.[31] Once the most sycophantic of his ministers, the King's brother-in-law Clarendon presented his petition with an arrogance completely at odds with his former humility. Many courtiers reflected this changed attitude and the King's humiliation deepened.[32]

The royal commissioners were duly received at the Bear Inn in Hungerford by Prince William on 8 December. The delay allowed

William's troops to make further progress and increased James's anxiety. Revised terms were agreed with William, and the commissioners set out for London with high hopes and unaware that the King intended merely to gain time, not to commit himself to real concessions. In that time he successfully arranged for the Queen and her newborn son to cross the storm-tossed Thames in an open boat to meet Lord Powis waiting on board a yacht which would carry them to France. Dartmouth had already refused to be an accomplice to this act. On 10 December the King revealed his secret mission to the Lords and reassured them that he would remain to face the consequences whatever happened. He then wrote a letter to Dartmouth describing the *fait accompli* and sent it via Pepys in an open envelope allowing him to read its contents. He also revealed his plan in a letter to Barrillon.[33] Macaulay evokes the scene vividly: 'All those evil passions which it is the office of government to restrain … were on a sudden emancipated from control.' It happened to be the longest night of the year which brought out 'in their thousands the house breakers, highwaymen, cut pursers and ring droppers'. Roman Catholic churches were demolished and set on fire, and books and furniture were burned where a Catholic convent had once stood. Pepys saw the night sky ablaze with the lurid glow as one house after another went up in flames.

The mob then turned on the diplomats, ransacked and set the Spanish embassy on fire, howling round Barrillon's house in St James's Square until they were held back by a detachment of horseguards. Buckingham Street lay protected behind the Strand, but Pepys was afraid for his windows in York Buildings as they shook with the fury of the mob. A sudden fear that he might lose all his possessions drove him behind closed doors. A shaken man, he pulled himself together and issued orders from a newly created Council of Peers that no one should pass down the Thames without a passport and all ships bound abroad must be searched.[34] 'The morning of 12 December', Macaulay wrote, 'rose on a ghastly sight. The capital in many places presented the aspect of a city taken by storm.' During this period Judge Jeffreys shaved off his eyebrows and disguised himself in ordinary clothes hoping to pass as a seaman, but he was recognised, pelted with stones and dragged away – bleeding – to confront the Lord Mayor. It was all too much for the Lord Mayor and he literally collapsed. Only the intervention of armed militiamen safely escorted Jeffreys – blubbering with terror – to the Tower.

On the night of the 10th – the very same day he reassured the Lords that he would remain in London – James retired to his closet,

burned the writs for summoning Parliament and confiscated the Great
Seal of England, a symbol of government. At three in the morning
of Tuesday the 11th he rose, took the Great Seal in his hand, ordered
Northumberland not to open the door of the bedchamber till the
usual hour and disappeared through a secret passage. He then crossed
the Thames from Millbank in a small wherry and, as he passed Lambeth, flung the Great Seal into the river.[35] Unaware of his volte
face, Pepys was still happily writing to Dartmouth about the salaries
of muster masters and the victualling of ships, coming at last in his
letter to the very bad military news. A battalion of the Scots Guards
had deserted, the mob had taken over Dover, the Dragoons were
retreating and anyone with close Catholic connections was in flight
from the capital.[36] At four the next morning a special messenger
from the King awakened Pepys from uneasy sleep to reveal the shattering news that the King had flown the capital. He brought two letters,
one of which Pepys was to forward to Dartmouth. Dartmouth wrote
back immediately to Pepys. 'Since my last, yours of the 10th is come
to my hands ... with an order subscribed by several lords spiritual
and temporal ... requiring that all acts of hostility between His Majesty's fleet and the Prince of Orange should cease.'[37] By remaining
a link between the King and Dartmouth, Pepys, when he passed
on the royal message, opened himself to the charge of Catholic complicity in the eyes of the avenging mob who smelt Popery at every
street corner. Later that morning he was full of misgivings but events
now swept him up powerfully beyond the concern of any finer anxieties. James secretly boarded a small vessel anchored off Faversham
on the night of the 11th. Some mysterious bush telegraph had released
a rumour that he was flying the country and at the very moment
when his accomplices were about to weigh anchor, a handful of
ordinary seamen decided to investigate this vessel stealing away without any warning in the middle of the night.[38] Suddenly, they came
face to face with Sir Edward Hales with a pistol in each hand, who
threatened to shoot anyone approaching the King. Wisely, James
parleyed with the seamen and offered a bribe of £50 to give passage
to his ship. At first they refused, broke in on the King, robbed him
and returned on deck to light a fire in an open brazier. There was
nothing Hales could do but accept the situation and complain about
the smoke. Taken ashore the following day, James was accommodated
in the Queen's Arms where Sir Edward Dering called on him and
recorded: 'I observed a smile on his face of an extraordinary size
and sort, so forced, awkward and unpleasant to look upon that I
can truly say I never saw anything like it.'[39]

Dartmouth and Pepys found their loyalties divided. Co-operating with the council of war which met at the Guildhall on 12 December, Dartmouth had offered the services of the fleet to William of Orange, but when he learnt of His Majesty's sudden return to London he tried to rationalise his surrender. He dictated a letter to the King explaining that Pepys's advice of the King's return dated the 11th had been sent by common post and hence arrived after the council of war at Guildhall. This contradicted Pepys's statement that he sent the letter by express post. When life and death were at stake, it would have been uncharacteristic of Pepys not to express the letter. In the confusion which followed, Lord Feversham, General of the King's Forces, suddenly took charge and set out with a cavalry troop to escort the King to Rochester. The King then sent a letter to William suggesting a meeting and was disturbed when he heard that his envoy had been made a prisoner. Later the Prince accepted the King's invitation, providing they met at 'some distant place [where] his own guards [could] be quartered'.[40]

The King finally returned to London on Sunday 16 December and was met by a complete – but temporary – reversal of public opinion. People pressing around his small cavalcade greeted him 'with loud huzzas' and that evening bells were rung and bonfires lit. Momentarily, a reconciliation between Church and sovereign brought the Tory vision of a happily united England to life again, and even Pepys was swept along, half hoping that some new resolution was possible. Bryant – evocative as always – allowed his pen to carry him away. As Pepys hurried to the palace with the Admiralty correspondence, 'One suspects', he wrote, 'there were tears in his eyes.'[41] It was all in vain. Emboldened, partly by his welcome from the people of London, a mood of intransigence overtook the King and drove him to behave as if a conquering invader were not hammering on the doors of his capital. He severely reprimanded those ministers who had collaborated with rebellious peers and openly attacked Mass. This was followed by a resurgence of fear when he asked for protection from the Prince's advancing armies. None was forthcoming. Instead, the Lords assembled at Westminster and suggested that the King should take up residence at Ham near Richmond, where he could begin negotiations with William. It was clear that these were delaying tactics, but they proved useless. While James remained in England, Prince William could not be declared sovereign.

The Dutch were on the outskirts of the city and pressing into Chelsea and Kensington hot-foot for confrontation with the King. On the night of 17 December the King was deep in the sleep of despair when a messenger awakened him with the news that troops were flooding the Mall, and William's emissaries were waiting to see him. The atmosphere was funereal in the heavy rain, and in that steady downpour the victorious Prince of Orange drove along Piccadilly resplendent with his entourage. The mercurial mood of the populace changed once again, to provide a show of enthusiasm which none the less remained muted. The regulation bell-ringing took place and bonfires were duly lit, but something was missing at the heart of the celebrations, perhaps because the liberation involved an alien army.[42] Macaulay, however, saw things differently: 'In defiance of the weather a great multitude assembled between Albemarle House and St James's Palace to greet the Prince. Every hat, every cane was adorned with an orange band ... William who had no taste for crowds ... took the road through the Park ...'[43] A badly shaken, sick man, the King finally left England on the morning of 23 December. He reached France on Christmas Day, and was carried ashore in humiliating circumstances on the backs of seamen at the village of Ambléteuse. Waiting for him at St Germain were his wife and child in a refuge provided by Louis.

Pepys could not escape the King's disaster. He had served and collaborated with James for over twenty years, but the flower of his contribution to the nation, a strong and rehabilitated Navy, had proved impotent to save his master. Moreover, he realised at once that men who were old enemies – Edward Russell and Admiral Herbert – would be taken into the Prince's service, making his own role uncertain, if not impossible. Pepys quickly sought and was granted an audience with the Prince on a very cold Wednesday, which remained in his mind as a turning point in his life.[44] At the outset the omens were reasonable. It came as a pleasant surprise to find that the Prince required him to remain as Secretary of the Admiralty even if it meant nothing more than maintaining a temporary continuity. On the same day, his devoted Will Hewer wrote to him a warm letter. 'You may rest assured that I am wholly yours and that you shall never want the utmost of my constant, faithful and personal service ...'[45]

Prince William's first encounters with the temporal and spiritual leaders of England were reassuring to both. He would not accept the throne in place of the late King, nor would he interfere with a freely elected Parliament. Military and naval affairs were another matter. Military leadership would remain in his hands and naval affairs in Pepys's with the proviso that his new advisers Edward Russell and Admiral Herbert held an overseeing brief. Herbert's reputation as an irresponsible roué and bohemian captain could not possibly accommodate Pepys's new naval Puritanism and Russell had taken an active part in the earlier plot to destroy Pepys's reputation. It was one thing for Pepys to recognise the necessary naval continuity and rise above his partisan interests to serve whichever master was in power as became the perfect civil servant. It was quite another to co-operate with an invading foreigner and his hostile nominees.

The Prince was a very different man from James, preserving an aloofness from all but his Dutch advisers, and secretly hoping that all contact with James had been lost. Indeed, the news of James's flight came through on 23 December and almost immediately William sent the French ambassador packing, and summoned a meeting of parliamentary members, aldermen of the city and the Lord Mayor. The parliamentarians had been elected under the exclusionist influence of the Popish terror and the whole gathering was hostile to any reconciliation with the exiled King, which suited William's purpose perfectly. Pepys applied himself at once to his normal duties which cut short his Christmas festivities. On Boxing Day he settled down to write a very difficult letter to Dartmouth. Anxious to ingratiate himself with the Prince, Dartmouth had gone over Pepys's head to apply for instructions direct from William in consultation with Russell.[46] Sensing the indignity to Pepys, the Prince passed Dartmouth's letter on to him and he promptly sent off a chilly letter to Dartmouth. Another even more frigid missive went to Dartmouth's private secretary, Phineas Bowles, who had been his intermediary with the Prince. Their differences continued to rankle but late in December Dartmouth attempted to rationalise his deviousness. 'The only reason I sent up Mr Bowles proceeded wholly from my not hearing from you, and no disrespect or design of mine ...'[47] It was unconvincing but Pepys welcomed any explanation.

I thank you with all my heart for your last of 28 December under your own hand; for I must own, I thought your usage of me in the particular you mention somewhat unnatural, especially at a juncture so little needing it from one's friends. But My Lord, you have done yourself and me right in the trouble given yourself for my satisfaction. And I assure you nothing on't shall longer stick with me ...[48]

Throughout the country, the court, Parliament and the Church, a whole nexus of manipulators were busy trying to win appointments or favour from the Prince without much scruple other than personal gain. Evelyn, often the wise commentator on social upheavals, wrote: 'I look for no mighty improvement of mankind in this declining age.'[49] Pepys was not slow to seek reassurance of his own position. On New Year's Day he was busy cultivating his friends in Harwich hoping for re-election. It did not surprise him when he found them less than enthusiastic. He was no longer the grand naval deputy of the King and some like Mr Langley, the Mayor, were plotting against him behind his back. Two Whig candidates appeared in the field opposing Pepys and Deane, and the town clerk sourly indicated that perhaps some personal visit would not be out of place against such competition. On 3 January Deane decided to withdraw in order to concentrate his votes on Pepys, but he told Pepys it would be a tough fight with the voters favouring the Whig candidates. Further complications followed. The two Whig candidates, Middleton and Eldred, employed a certain Captain Ridley to spread the rumour that Pepys was still an unrepentant Papist. On this occasion Pepys became embroiled in the subtler coils of seventeenth-century election corruption. Certain factions disqualified from voting by law – dissenters and others – vociferously proclaimed their 'natural' right to vote, and when the Mayor ruled them out of order such an uproar arose that their votes were recorded. The town clerk, who had persistently campaigned in secret against Pepys, then announced that Pepys was bottom of the poll. One of his supporters, the vicar of Dovercourt Harwich, wrote him a letter of condolence overblown with the customary flattery.[50] Pepys took his defeat stoically, knowing full well that someone so committed to the old regime would be foolish to cherish high expectations from the new.

Great constitutional questions were now raised by the revolution and the arrival of William of Orange. A special committee led by John Somers, once Lord Chancellor, drafted the first Declaration of Rights, which included the old Whig doctrine of the social contract, proposals for uniting Protestants, the prohibition of buying and selling offices, and new procedures for trial of treason. In the event, these proposals underwent drastic change before the bill was finally passed in December. The social contract clause disappeared but the abdication of James II was considered a *fait accompli* and Church of England Tories were divided about the future of royalty. Some were for recalling the King, subject to austere conditions, while others thought of making Princess Mary Queen. These proposals ignored the undying enmity of the Whig Peers towards James, or the opinions of the all-conquering Prince William. Pepys continued to throw his energies into naval affairs, his vigilance and devotion undiminished. Continuity of service was first a prerequisite of naval efficiency, and inborn in his character. He sent off letters to the Prince which frequently matched in asperity those he was accustomed to render to the King. Officers seen without leave in town were duly reported, and captains who abandoned their commands threatened with courts martial. Even Dartmouth came in for somewhat summary treatment when he was ordered to relinquish control of the fleet to his second in command and prepare for audience with the Prince.

Pepys's powers, however, quickly revealed limitations which must have irritated, if not humiliated him. He was himself summoned to audience with the Prince on 12 January in company with his old enemy Herbert, only to be told that ten thousand men had to be maintained at sea in pay throughout the winter. Pepys tactfully pointed out the financial straits into which the revolution had thrown the victualling commissioners and was not encouraged when the Prince said he would put his case before the Treasury.[51] Pepys had understated the naval situation. Mobs of unpaid seamen were so rebellious that mutiny broke out on two of Dartmouth's ships. Pepys immediately circulated a proclamation which – somewhat recklessly – guaranteed that arrears would be paid.[52] There were other more pleasant tasks. On 17 January he selected a small yacht, the *Fubbs*, to sail for Holland where Herbert was to pick up the Princess of Orange and return escorted by Sir John Berry's squadron.

On Monday 28 January a cross-party committee was formed in the Commons to take stock of the confused constitutional situation. Expectations that the Prince and Princess of Orange would automatically ascend the throne were at once shown to be premature, since James remained – constitutionally – King. When Sir Christopher Musgrave, an old travelling companion of Pepys, asked whether they had the power to overthrow the King, Sir Robert Howard answered that the Divine Right of Kings was matched by a divine right of the people. The King had broken the social contract with the people and they therefore had the right to act. The Tory lawyers then questioned whether the social contract had any legal validity. Once again Pepys found himself torn between his loyalty to James and the necessity of facing the presence of Prince William waiting in the wings. On 29 January the Lords went into committee to consider the detailed resolutions submitted by the Commons. The assertion that James had broken the social contract and abdicated the throne was put before the judges who sidestepped the issue, claiming that they were unqualified to speak on matters which concerned the law of Parliament.[53] Rejecting by fifty-five to forty-one the proposition that the King had left the throne vacant, they accepted the social contract as still valid by a dangerously small majority. The two houses went into further consultation with long and tortured protestations on both sides. The Lords maintained that whatever role divine right played in the matter, the throne remained hereditary. The Whigs believed that the invitations issued to Prince William presupposed an unoccupied throne which remained, anyway, elective. Pepys was fully aware that behind this straightforward conflict lay many subtleties.[54] Sir Robert Sawyer, known to Pepys from his Cambridge days, claimed that the Commons had no power to exercise authority over the crown. The bishops, encouraged by Clarendon and Rochester, wanted to see William as Prince Regent with Mary, his wife, on the throne. Private consultation with William made it clear that he would not accept such a compromise. He now desired the full power and panoply of kingship and without it he would simply abandon all his successes and return to Holland.

This view became overwhelming when Mary wrote to Thomas Osborne, the Earl of Danby, stating categorically that she would have nothing to do with the throne unless her husband was King.[55] A week of wrangling followed, with the populace growing steadily more impatient, and Pepys more anxious as the mob once again invaded Palace Yard. The two houses then arrived at a compromise, accepting that James had abdicated and rendering the social contract invalid. It was also agreed that the laws of the realm must be cleared of ambiguity and the false notion that the royal prerogative was 'something more sublime and holy than those laws' abandoned. On 12 February Mary arrived safely from Holland and the two houses agreed on a joint Declaration of Rights.

Pepys did not abandon his long drawn out and sorely tested loyalty to James but he had tried to retain his seat at Harwich, which did not indicate any willingness to relinquish office. Bryant goes to some lengths to show that in the final analysis Pepys abandoned his secretaryship voluntarily, and Pepys certainly took equal trouble to justify the claim. His documentation carried the tremendous title: 'A Copy of the Entries of all the Acts of His Royal Highness the Prince of Orange prepared by Mr Pepys relating to the Admiralty and Navy from the Time of his coming to Whitehall and Entrance upon the Government to that of Mr Pepys voluntarily ceasing to act further therein'.[56] There remains some evidence that he was forced to retire.

By now, the shift in world power had put France in conflict with England and William needed the services of a man steeped in naval affairs like Pepys. Between 19 December when the Prince granted Pepys his first audience and his accession to the throne on 13 February

1689, Pepys suffered the full scrutiny of men like Russell who had invited William to England, and Admiral Herbert who escorted him to London. As we have seen, both men were hostile to what they still regarded as this upstart bureaucrat wielding power beyond his means. Once able to administer the Navy as he chose, it must have irked, if not infuriated, Pepys that these ill-trained aristocrats had swept aside all his attempts to limit their powers and literally had him at their mercy. These facts alone were enough to force his hand into premature resignation. There remained a few days during which, faithful servant to the last, he continued to write letters, one making 'points of official detail' to the commander-in-chief in Portsmouth and another to Lord Dartmouth about the disposal of equipment. On 20 February King William then issued a general order suspending all offices until fresh authorisation was granted from the palace. This was obviously a turning point for Pepys. The few letters he dictated in the following two days concerned generalities. One, for instance, encouraged the Navy Board to hold in readiness all ships for the King's need which, with the threat from France, was likely to be sudden and urgent.

Then, at last, it was all over. On 5 March the King approved the appointment of Herbert to control the new Admiralty Commission which was staffed by a number of Pepys's old adversaries, if not his enemies. Herbert wasted no time in appointing a new Secretary which confirmed his nepotistic methods. Phineas Bowles, once a storekeeper at Tangier and recently secretary to Dartmouth, found himself elevated to this relatively high office, but he did not replace Pepys. Pepys's office as Secretary to the Admiralty ceased to exist on the day he was asked to turn over all his official books and papers to Phineas. Pepys's last letter from the Admiralty Office in York Buildings was no more than three formal and detached lines to Herbert enclosing a handful of letters from foreign stations.[57]

Anyone forced to retire from office and asked to relinquish his papers, experiences uneasiness, but for Pepys this was a very special break – the final one – in his long and distinguished career. At almost sixty Pepys was still in full possession of his faculties, steeped in experience, and capable of directing the Navy for years to come. Stepping down to make room for a lightweight like Phineas must have produced a combination of gall and regret, matched by the fear that haunted public servants after a revolution. Seventeenth-century politics tended to make victims of those deposed from office with the ruthless aim of ensuring that one-time rivals could not rise again. Pepys's past record and avowed loyalty to James made him particularly vulnerable. A remarkable set of circumstances had produced a bloodless revolution, but the theory that English balance and commonsense were dominating influences was undermined by the power of natural forces. If the weather had allowed Dartmouth to attack the Dutch fleet at the outset, the revolution would have been anything but bloodless. Moreover, it was the Navy which he himself had created that failed to save Pepys.

The first skirmishes over his continued possession of premises at York Buildings were a prelude to more serious troubles. The machinations of a group of unknown adversaries – reminiscent of Scott – brought charges of 'dangerous and treasonable practices' against Pepys, Deane and Hewer. Notoriously, the three men were known to be close associates, once intimately in touch with James, and on 4 May 1689 they were arrested. Pepys was now a seasoned campaigner entirely familiar with the power of documents to meet such charges, but he had also seen injustice prevail in circumstances where the innocent were victimised. Memories of the Popish Plot, Scott's persecution, the Tower and the shadow of the gallows falling across his path were still very fresh.

Anticipating hostile reactions he had already prepared new and special justifications of his years as Secretary for his memoirs. The manuscript opened with a characteristically convoluted sentence from which can be torn the simple statement that in April 1679 Charles II put the control of the Navy into the hands of a Commission where before it had been 'managed under his own inspection'. The memoir was a densely written description of Pepys's administrative masterpiece, the rehabilitation of the Navy, which covered all the new regulations. The training and promotion of officers; discipline; fee-taking; dockyards; contracts for food and equipment – all were considered, but Pepys's preoccupation with detail did not prevent his speculating about policy. Whether Pepys presented this document as part of his defence against the charge of treason is unclear, but at the beginning of July he, with Deane and Hewer, was released. A new arrest in June 1690 had a dramatic sequel.

The effects of Pepys's first lithotomy years earlier returned suddenly to trouble him when the scar tissue became inflamed and necessitated new surgery. An 'Order for Mr Pepys's Liberation from the Gatehouse' was signed by Russell for the Commission and Richard Lowther, the most distinguished physician of the day. 'Whereas Dr Lower [sic] had this day certified by oath before us that Mr Samuel Pepys who was lately committed by this Board to the Gatehouse is so very ill with an ulcer in his kidnies that unless he be speedily enlarged from his present confinement he is in danger of death.'[58] Pepys had three new operations which must have tested his stoicism and courage to the utmost. A letter to his nephew John Jackson revealed the details: 'The cicatrice of a wound occasioned upon my cutting for stone ... all on a sudden ... breaks out again so as to make another issue for my urine to sally at besides that of its natural channel'.[59] He was fifty-seven and the operation was performed without anaesthetic. This was only the beginning. Not only the first operation proved unsuccessful but a second also. Pepys's survival under such treatment is remarkable. As for the third operation, which followed with reckless haste, that would normally have meant certain death. There is no evidence of the techniques used on these occasions, but the pain caused by the first operation must have made anticipation of a second and third a nightmare at which the mind boggles. Pepys had hardly had time to recover from the ordeal, yet his letter to his nephew showed extraordinary detachment and optimism. 'I am in no doubt of recovering my first state very soon ...'[60] During his convalescence Pepys spent long hours completing his naval memoirs. They gave an account of such devotion to duty carried out with an unrelenting energy that they lifted him above the noise of charge and counter-charge, and provided almost incontrovertible defence against any suspicion of treason.

The proceedings against him were in fact dropped in October and Pepys began to believe that perhaps he could escape the inevitable witch-hunt which follows even bloodless revolution. Celebrating the occasion he gave a splendid six-course dinner to his friends and bailors, Hewer, Houblon, Blackborne and Martin. The drinking went on late into the night.[61] Behind the scenes Pepys had, with considerable cunning, persistently evaded the Navy Office demands that he should surrender all the papers from his years in office. 'There were some gaps in the lists of the records transferred by Pepys ...'[62] He withheld some of the papers from James II's reign, the most important of which were his own letter books from 1684 to 1688.[63] Pepys's ex-clerk, Burchett, discharged by him in 1687, had become, to Pepys's dismay, Secretary of the Admiralty, and a sharp correspondence followed between them.

Burchett wrote demanding the return of the missing books early in 1689.[64] Pepys found one excuse after another for delay and made sure that he kept transcripts of those documents which he did return. As late as the summer of 1700 Burchett was still demanding the missing letter books.[65] Pepys held out against the pressure and surrendered only part of the material demanded and that in transcript form.[66] There remained one other threat to his peace of mind. A long-forgotten trouble suddenly resurfaced and led to a new indictment, launched with considerable publicity, before a committee of the House of Commons. The charge was that he had connived to seize ships and goods belonging to the King with the *Phoenix*, a man-of-war, which was the property of His Majesty. The situation arose because a piratically minded officer had taken matters into his own hands and broken the rules of the East India Company. Pepys had ordered the *Phoenix* to the East Indies to suppress what amounted to a minor uprising, but en route the *Phoenix* encountered another ship, the *Bristol*, then trading illicitly in Mozambique waters. Boarding the *Bristol*, the *Phoenix*'s captain found that her master had been killed and he took the ship in convoy as a prize ship. Within a few days it became apparent that the *Bristol* was unseaworthy and on the tenth day, with the *Bristol* foundering, the captain of the *Phoenix* ordered twenty bales of chintz to be snatched as a prize. All would have been well had not Pepys signed the original document ordering the *Phoenix* to proceed in search of the *Bristol*. In 1689 the owners of the *Bristol* took proceedings in Parliament for redress against Pepys for the Admiralty, Sir Josiah Child for the East India Company, and the captain of the *Phoenix*.

In the ordinary course of events this was nothing more than a storm in a teacup, but Pepys, in his apprehensive state, realised that it could become a political issue. The enforcement of the East India Company's rights might be read as political interference with the liberty of the subject under Stuart inspiration. Pepys, 'the lackey' of Stuart imperialism, was a highly suitable person to charge with complicity. Alerted to the dangers, James Houblon recommended consulting his distinguished lawyer friend Pollexfen and pre-empted Pepys by seeing him himself. The charge when formulated said that Pepys was guilty of 'high misdemeanour' by signing the instructions given to the captain of the *Phoenix*. Pollexfen quickly found a legal loophole. Pepys had, in fact, *countersigned* the document which made responsibility ambivalent.[67] Once more a gathering cloud was dispersed and now at last Pepys began to feel free from threat and harassment. One last aspect of the Admiralty's interest in his fate he treated with cavalier indifference: their attempts to eject him from his house in York Buildings. A complex machinery of bureaucratic persuasion was set turning against him without result, and at last the Admiralty gave up in despair. Sir John Lowther, on behalf of the Admiralty, wrote in the spring of 1689: 'The committee, finding their affairs could not bear the want of a house for so long time as you required to remove, have agreed for a house elsewhere.'[68]

Chapter 22

Correspondence with Sir Isaac Newton

That Pepys's finances were not crippled by his fall from grace is clear from the eight servants he still employed in 1690. They included a porter (£12), a footman (£10), a coachman and a housekeeper (£8 each), a junior footman, cook, laundrymaid and housemaid (£6 each). Finding himself crowded by these dependents, he also rented what he called a 'little house' in York Buildings at £25 a year for a man called Jones who seems to have been a kind of personal attendant.[1] Mrs Fane still fulfilled the role of housekeeper and Mary Skinner's relationship with Pepys remained close. Writing to Evelyn in the summer of 1700 Pepys said: 'I cannot give myself the scope I otherwise should of talking now to you at this distance from some care extraordinary I am at present under from poor Mary Skinner being fallen very ill here.'[2] Pepys was also extraordinarily tolerant of Mary's brothers who ceaselessly sought his assistance. As far back as the summer of 1676 he was busy extolling brother Daniel's virtues to Sir Leoline Jenkins, the Judge of the Court of Admiralty: 'I have not in all my conversation known any person set out better prepared for an admission to public business.'[3] As a result Daniel was briefly given employment, only to fall foul of a man called Williamson and immediately re-apply for help from Pepys. Pepys once more wrote an explanatory letter on his behalf and actually went to plead his case in person.[4] A similar patience characterised Pepys's relations with Daniel's two brothers, Peter and Corbett Skinner. In the spring of 1683 Mary Skinner's mother Frances was writing to Pepys in an attempt to save her son Peter from becoming a common seaman.[5] It seems likely that Pepys did intervene on his behalf because three years later a report was delivered to Pepys about his conduct as a junior officer during a voyage from the Mediterranean. Pepys himself then employed him in some unnamed capacity. Unfortunately, he behaved so badly that Pepys threatened him with dismissal. In fear

Mary Skinner wrote a humble, pleading letter which began: 'I am in the heaviest affliction ever I was since I was born about this graceless son of mine that he should abuse and slight so good a master as you have been.'[6] The letter ended: 'Sir, I beseech you for Christ his sake do not let him be ruined for if he goeth away from you he will be ruined body and soule.' Once again Pepys took considerable trouble to re-establish Peter in a naval appointment. The third brother, Corbett, not to be outdone, also applied to Pepys for help to rise above his dreary work in the Excise Office, and was promptly promoted to supervisor of collections in Bedford.[7] It can be argued that in his retirement Pepys wrote many letters on behalf of his friends, relatives and sometimes mere acquaintances, but his attention to the Skinner family was particular. One question remains which Ollard sought to answer. Why did not Pepys marry Mary Skinner? Mary's brother Daniel had as we have seen at one time been Milton's secretary and after his death planned to arrange the publication in Holland of a political tract entrusted to him by the poet. Moreover, a sonnet published in 1673 by Milton was addressed to Mary's uncle, Cyriack Skinner. Thus the Skinner family was already associated with the dangerously radical and republican Milton when Mary joined Pepys's household. Despite pressure from her parents, Pepys knew too well the dangers for anyone loyal to King James marrying a woman with such connections.

By 1673 the affair had sunk into the background and he settled into a warm and probably platonic relationship which suited his purpose. Although Mary's literacy was not comparable to Pepys's, she could hold her own in conversation among his friends. She also acted as his secretary from time to time, taking down letters from his dictation.[8] Her name recurs in his letters as his constant companion, and as a final tribute to her, he commissioned Sir Godfrey Kneller to paint her portrait.

When Pepys, still recovering from one of his operations, decided to accept Will Hewer's invitation to stay at his Clapham house, he took Mary Skinner with him. According to a letter written from that address early in May, some agency was still interfering with his incoming mail, opening and resealing a letter he had just received from John Jackson in Rome.[9] Years before in the Diary he had written with appreciation of Hewer's house in Clapham which belonged to his old merchant friend Gauden: 'I find the house very regular and finely contrived and the gardens and offices about it as convenient and as full of good variety as ever I saw in my life.'[10] Evelyn reinforced this view.[11] The house was within easy reach of the West End of London and Evelyn's country house at Deptford. Several previous visits had made its geography and daily routine familiar to Pepys and it was large enough to accommodate all his servants.

That Mary Skinner made Pepys's later life less lonely is evident, but she also created stormy incidents as a letter from Balty made clear.[12]

Honoured Sir,
After my late having groaned under some troubles . . . which at this unfortunate juncture of time have proved extremely heavy and grievous to me ; I understand that by the malicious inventive ill offices of a female beast which you keep, I am like also to lie under your anger and disgrace . . . but I hope and humbly pray (though she told me impudently and arrogantly you scorned to see me) that with your generous usual goodness, wisdom, manhood and former kindness you will not damn him unheard who should joy to hazard (as in duty bound) his dearest bludd for your service . . .[13]

Balty's affairs were in total disarray and this attack upon Mary Skinner did not improve his relations with Pepys who was struggling to find employment for Balty, a man about to be discharged from his job. In April of 1689 Pepys wrote to the naval administrator Sir Richard Haddock, anticipating Balty's dismissal. 'I cannot but with great earnestness bespeak your advice, furtherance and friendship . . . that he may not at this time of day be (with such a family as God Almighty has given him) exposed to the wide world.'[14] Pepys appears to have provided for Balty in some way, and he wrote to thank him in his characteristically overripe style: 'This late generous act of yours has . . . outdone all the former for that at this pinch, in this my later age and groaning under such circumstance of afflictions, and miseries of body and mind which none but the great divinity and myself knows and indeed such as I am sure hath no parallel: you were pleased to releave me . . .'[15]

For the last few years that Pepys occupied York Buildings it became a hive of intellectual life, where every Saturday his friends gathered to discuss new books, plays and science. Inevitably, the guests were introduced to his now extensive library which covered an enormous range, each volume bearing his bookplate and gold-stamped cypher. In a person said to combine good taste with learning, it was remarkable that he chose to order the books according to size and shape, not subject matter. Clearly, the civil servant's obsession with tidiness took precedence. Literary reputations surrendered to symmetrical order but some books refused to conform in height to their neighbours and were fitted with wooden 'hoofs' covered in leather. Instructions for renewing the library insisted that, where necessary, precise readjustments of size were made for greater harmony. Certainly, the results for the casual browser could be full of surprises. The range of the library was catholic, embracing literature, science, philosophy, poetry, theology, collections of rare pamphlets and the occasional erotic book. Rochester's erotic poems were delicately re-titled *Rochester's Life*, and, writing to Will Hewer in the winter of 1680, Pepys said: 'There is also ... a collection of my Lord Rochester's poems written before his penitence in a style I thought unfit to mix with my other books. However, pray let it remain ... for as he is past writing any more so bad in one sense so I despair of any man surviving him to write so good in another.'[16]

Collectively, the library consisted of some three hundred volumes now preserved in Magdalene College, Cambridge. There is an indiscriminate comprehensiveness in the collection, but Pepys's instructions to his old College indicate a desire to preserve intact the special Pepysian sensibility which it enshrines. Literature, art, history, survive alongside books like *The Counter Ratt*, and philosophy alongside *The Life and Death of the English Rogue*. Covering such a wide range it would be unexpected to find him studying any one subject in depth. This especially applies to philosophy. Locke, Hobbes, Newton are present in his library but there are no supporting writers and nowhere in Pepys's writings is there any attempt to evaluate their work.

Locke and Hobbes had suffered politically like Pepys, both becoming exiles and eventually returning to England. Hobbes had tutored Charles II in mathematics, was frequently seen at court and published his *Leviathan* in 1651. Locke, once under Shaftesbury's wing, fled to Holland in 1683 and when Shaftesbury died Locke returned on the yacht organised by Pepys to carry the Princess of Orange back to England. Newton lived through many of the historical events Pepys had experienced and he produced his *Principia* in 1687, the year before the revolution. These men were at the heart of the great seventeenth-century intellectual revolution, but Pepys moved on its fringes. There is only one exchange with Newton, not about the universality of gravity or infinitesimal calculus, but the mathematical probabilities of dicing.[17] This arose from a practical question.

Someone had discussed the possibility of raising funds by a national lottery and Pepys put the following proposition to Newton.[18]

A has six dice in a box with which he is to fling a six.

B has in another box eighteen dice with which he is to fling two sixes.

C has in another box eighteen dice with which he is to fling three sixes.

Question: Whether B and C have not as easy a task as A at even luck.[19]

Newton wrote a long analytical reply reformulating and sharpening the question. He then commented: 'If the question be thus stated it appears by an easy computation that the expectation of A is greater than that of B or C: that is, the task of A is the easier.' Newton's reputation in 1693 was already awe-inspiring but it did not intimidate Pepys who readily admitted his shortcomings in mathematics, but said that if it were not troubling Mr Newton too much he would like a sight of the computations proving the given answer.[20] Thus challenged, Newton got down to business. His next letter amplified his analysis and justified his conclusion with a growing complexity which might have brought the correspondence to a halt. It was some indication of the sharpness of Pepys's mind and the respect in which Newton held him that it did not. Pepys remained unconvinced, persisted in his questioning and humbly admitted that 'this is but fumbling and ... it ariseth only from my not knowing how to make the full use of your table of progressions'.[21]

Pepys's incisive interrogations disturbed the great man sufficiently to invoke an arbitrator. George Tollett was called in and delivered himself of an analysis five pages long which involved pyramids of figures incapable of any simple condensation. Pepys's last letter to Tollett revealed him halfway to understanding and still struggling valiantly:

I have taken all this time [to reply] and can scarce yet tell in what terms to thank you for your late admirable present ... namely that A has an easier task than B and yet more easy one than C such (I take it) being the doctrine of [your] paper ... full glad I am of my so seasonably meeting with it, as being upon the very brink of a wager (£10 deep) upon my former belief.[22]

Displaying a remarkable catholicity, Pepys broke out of his continuing preoccupation with the affairs of Cambridge University to become absorbed in a distinguished group of scholars at Oxford University.[23] His friendship with Dr Hickes, the great historical scholar, drew him into a circle which included Wanley the palaeographer, Charlett, Master of University College, and Gale the classicist. This brought together men from the Royal Society, philosophy and scholarship to pursue enquiries admirably overriding the boundaries of each group. A friend and patron of Godfrey Kneller, Pepys persuaded him to paint the portrait of Dr John Wallis, Savilian Professor of Geometry at Oxford, while corresponding with him about the mathematical relationship of notes in music. Nothing was excluded from their roving conversations which, at one point, returned to the question of extra-sensory perception. It had occupied Pepys's attention sporadically over the years. Lord Reay wrote him several letters exploring at length examples of second sight but Pepys was unimpressed. By November 1699 he appeared to retreat from his scepticism. 'This only I shall not now spare to say; that is to the business of second sight I little expected to have been ever brought so near to a conviction of the reality of it as by your Lordship's and the Lord Tarbutt's authoritys I must already own myself to be.'[24] Conviction was shortlived. Within a few months a letter from Roger Gale, son of Dr Gale, who died suddenly in his deanery early in 1702, reactivated scepticism.[25] The letter referred to Pepys as a man who would rather 'hear the truth than a strange story'. Roger Gale then related how a certain Mr Hally read the lesson and coming down from the lectern suddenly saw the dead Dr Gale seated in his usual place. Automatically, Hally bowed and receiving no response hurried into the coffee house to spread the story abroad. It then transpired that when a certain Dr Stainforth found his pew in the church filled he slipped into the dead dean's. 'Mr Hally's mistake then became an easy one, Dr [Stainforth] being very much of my father's size and . . . not very unlike in the face.'

That Pepys was still not entirely free from harassment as late as September 1692 became evident when he rented a house in Epping Forest which he did not occupy. Instead he shut himself up incognito in York Buildings where – apparently unaided – he set about sorting any papers which might be used as evidence against him. Every year, for the past four years, he had been subject to 'surprises and disquietings from the powers above me' and he decided to pre-empt any further 'interference' by disappearing from the social scene and destroying evidence.[26] His letter to Dr Gale, High Master of St Paul's, was not completely explicit, but the camouflage of an unoccupied house and the hint of isolation did indicate some very confidential activity. The intensity of his incarceration had made him ill, and, apparently, a Mrs Steward tended to him. 'My constant poring and sitting so long still in one posture without any divertings or exercise having for about a month past brought a humour down into one of my legs, not only to the swelling of it to almost the size of both but with the giving me mighty pains and disabling me to this day to put on a shoe on that foot.'

Pepys was able to move only between his study and his chamber which were on the same floor. He clearly needed the ministrations of Mrs Steward. He must have quarrelled with her at one point because he expects her to wish his right leg to become as bad as his left. However, he slowly returned to his old socially minded self, craving company. Taken at its face value Pepys had gone into hiding, and his fears of further persecution seem to have exceeded their expression in his letters. Writing to Evelyn he made light of the whole excursion as 'a small piece of work that lay upon my hands which I had no mind longer to trust futurity with'.[27]

Back in his old haunts he was wining, dining, meeting old friends and engaged in such a network of activities it made mockery of the word retirement. He retained some relatively tentative connections with public life – as when he was invited to become a member of the grand committee for Greenwich Hospital. Even royalty did not completely ignore him. An impersonal printed invitation to join the King and Queen on New Year's Day in Christ's Hospital arrived to his surprise, one morning. His acquaintance with Christopher Wren also blossomed when the great architect invited him to join him while viewing the site for the Greenwich Hospital. Ever interested in natural phenomena, Pepys drew from Dr Wallis a description of an eclipse witnessed by his daughter, and expressed his puzzlement by the forces which controlled it.[28] He remained in touch with the Archbishop of Canterbury and wrote to him on behalf of 'the wife and necessitus family of Mr De Galenere, one of the poor ministers of the ... Church'.[29] Pepys was also still busy helping his nephew John Jackson and financed a grand European tour for him.

By October he wrote complaining that Jackson was still in England when he should have been on the high seas. 'I shall be in dayly payne for your loss of time till I hear you are gone.'[30]

By the summer of 1700 his health was troubling him again and he went off to spend a short holiday with Will Hewer. Once more he wrote to his nephew John Jackson: 'I have been here four days and by Mr Hewer's kindness am with Mrs S. and a good part of my family likely to have the benefit of its whole summer's airing.'[31] The following spring there was tremendous upheaval when he moved permanently into Hewer's house where he was to spend the rest of his life. Correspondence continued to flow from his pen on science, art, music and mathematics, interspersed with advice to the young. He must have spent long hours dictating or writing hundreds of letters, frequently several pages long, which pushed speculative enquiry into fields closely familiar to modern thinking. His last circle of friends, Evelyn, James Houblon, Dr Gale and Sir William Petty, were all educated men capable of informed disputation.

Dr Gale, Fellow of Trinity College, Cambridge, Regius Professor of Greek, High Master of St Paul's and a Fellow of the Royal Society, was particularly adept at criticising university administration. Pepys's dinner parties showed no diminution in his zest for living and huge feasts were lavishly laced with drink, but there remained behind their talk a high seriousness. Men like Newton and Boyle were mentioned but whether they shared Merton's view that religion inspired their work is uncertain.[32] Pepys was aware that men of the calibre of Robert Crosse saw the Royal Society as a pseudo-Aristotelian-Jesuitical conspiracy against society. Several churchmen considered it axiomatic that scientific investigation undermined theological doctrines. Literary satires – Butler's *Elephant and Moon* – made mock of all scientific thinking.[33] Newton categorically stated: 'Plato is my friend, Aristotle is my friend, but my best friend is truth.'[34] Since the religious climate of the day found certain truths unpalatable, they were irreconcilable.

Before Descartes and Newton, Platonic archetypes formed a universe of ideal constructions of which earthly objects were shadowy representations, participating in varying degrees of permanence. God had so arranged this harmonious universe that Christianity offered a number of signs and correspondences which revealed the nature of the relationship between primary and secondary reality. The task of science was to catalogue and interpret these correspondences. After Descartes and Newton, perspectives changed. Mechanical interpretation became the scientific paradigm derived from Newton's methodology in his three laws of motion.

In the 1690s Newton sent Locke a copy of a manuscript attempting to prove that the Trinitarian passages in the Bible were a latterday conception, but when Locke proposed publishing it Newton retreated in fear. The threat of religious disapproval was too much for him.

Newton underwent a breakdown, the origins of which are mysterious, but Locke and Pepys were privy to the experience. In mid-September 1693 Newton wrote to Pepys: 'I am extremely troubled at the embroilment I am in and have neither ate or slept well this twelvemonth ... I never designed to get anything by your interest nor by King James's favour but am now sensible that I must withdraw from your acquaintance.'[35] Newton also wrote to Locke, strongly objecting to Locke's opinion that certain ideas were innate and claiming that such views struck at the root of all morality. Then came this remarkable comment: 'Being of the opinion that you endeavoured to embroil me with women . . . I was so much affected with it as that [when] one told me you were sickly and would not live I answered 'twere better if you were dead.'[36] It took Newton three years to escape from this incursion into near-insanity. Pepys was a level-headed realistic man still under the influence of his early Aristotelian indoctrination. Led by Descartes, philosophy had rejected Aristotle's geocentric universe, replacing it with an intricate impersonal machine constructed of particles interacting around the sun. Newton absorbed and brilliantly developed this concept but Pepys made no reference to this theory. Perhaps it was too alien for him. Certainly, his interest in science – that of a dilettante – was not inspired by his rather plodding down-to-earth Puritan religion; nor did it enlighten him about Newton's breakdown.

His views on the church were far less clear in the Diary than his views on society and they fluctuated according to the pressure of events. He could pinch the bottoms of pretty girls in church and escape from the boredom of immensely long sermons into the arms of his latest mistress. During the plague he had been given to asking God's protection and after his lithotomy he had thanked God for its success, but relapses into scepticism were not infrequent.[37] Clearly, religion in his view was something different from the church which he described in the Diary as nothing more than a human institution.[38] Moreover, that institution was heavily political. 'Religion . . . is made by a Parliament and not by any ecclesiastical authority . . . in the time of the late rebellion the Parliament would never suffer King Charles . . . to be at rest until they had got him to submit to our settled religion.'[39] His notes on religion may be said to foreshadow the thinking of Darwin and even Wittgenstein. 'How far', he asked, 'may mankind . . . be said to be made up of different species and where ye brute ends and man begins with the consequences thereof.'[40] That last phrase – 'the consequences thereof' – may well indicate Pepys's awareness of the explosion which must follow any proven connection between men and earlier species. Certainly, the consequences for Isaac la Peyrère (1596–1674) had been unfortunate. He was, according to Richard Popkin, regarded as the greatest heretic of his age, 'even worse than Spinoza who took over some of his most challenging ideas'.[41] It was his work which inspired Pepys's reflections. His contention that there were men before Adam involved a serious reinterpretation of the Bible. According to la Peyrère the holy book merely retold the history of the Jews and not the whole human story. Once again Pepys was interested in thinking which is directly connected with modern theories.

The Wittgensteinian link really came from Sir William Petty not Pepys. 'Much ye greatest part of all humane understanding is lost by our discoursing and writing ... in words subject to more senses than one, to ye rendering disputations infinite upon every proposition that can be made in any science whether divinity, law, etc.'[42] Wittgenstein had himself read some Pepys and adapted a code for confession about his sex life, like Pepys.[43] Throughout his life reason was dominant in Pepys's approach to all problems. Even faith itself must surrender to examination by reason and there he differed from Wittgenstein. Death, too, was rationalised as he approached his own death and encountered new strains.

Chapter 23

Retirement and death

Evelyn wrote to Pepys in the summer of 1700:

The scantiness . . . and little satisfactions of the things of this world, after all our researches in quest of something we feel worth the pains, but are indeed the images only of what we pursue . . . warn me that . . . there is another and better state of things which concern us and for which I pray Almighty God prepare us both.[1]

Explicit references to life after death are rare in Pepys's papers. Writing to Evelyn in the winter of 1701 he did express a hope of their meeting in another place which was 'a better and more lasting [one] for which God fit us'.[2] It was a throwaway remark later subjected to his usual scepticism. Evelyn's religion was more orthodox than Pepys's, whose motto beneath his portrait in the memoirs spoke of the mind not the soul as the core of any individual. His friends, Sir William Petty, Dr Gale and James Houblon shared his religious sentiments in different degrees and during their Saturday evenings together at York Buildings they had indulged many a critical onslaught on theological dogma. Now, settled at Clapham, those evenings were no more and Evelyn wrote full of nostalgia: 'In good earnest, sir, I pass not by York Buildings without serious regret. Saturday which was want to be a jubilee and the most advantageous and gainful as well as the most diverting to me of the weekly circles is from a real Sabbath and day of repose now become wholly saturnine, lugubrious and solitary.'[3] Throughout his life Evelyn had been a refining influence on Pepys. He consistently embodied a public spirit, a taste for learning and the arts, with a sensitivity and compassion unusual in the landed gentry. Pepys had developed from a man crudely concerned with his career into a complex, deep-thinking person giving compassion its appropriate place. In the dissolute days of the Restoration, Evelyn had displayed a humanity which Pepys acquired, and both men shared a cultural life which produced men of the calibre of Newton, Boyle, Hobbes and Spinoza.

Pepys did not lack visitors in his Clapham retirement. Mr Wanley wrote to him in the spring of 1701: 'I will therefore gladly wait on you, sir, on Easter Day when beside the feasting of my body I know ... that you will feed my mind and understanding.' His encomium was matched among a number of tributes to Pepys's stimulating company: ''Tis never any drudgery to wait on Mr Pepys, whose conversation I think is more nearly akin to what we are taught to hope for in heaven than that of anybody else I know.'[4] The correspondence with Evelyn continued in the last years and was full of references to coping with old age, health, and shared concerns. Pepys still put considerable faith in folk medicine: 'I am at this day ... under more care in all things relating to the passing and passages of my urine than I can remember myself to have been ... and owe it only to the leaving off of malt drink and betaking myself wholly to barley water.'[5] Evelyn had also been ill and wrote thanking Pepys for his barley water tip.[6] Pepys had now reached the very ripe age of sixty-seven and Evelyn a phenomenal eighty-one. Pepys's letters never show a hint of depression. He seems to have faced his ill health with an astonishing stoicism. By 29 October 1700 Pepys was writing to Dr Charlett, the Master of University College, 'impatient as I am to be among my old friends again ... my books, my friends on this side of the water are obstinately bent to prevent it'.[7] Pepys could never be at ease in idleness. Thinking, as he knew, could be hard work, and for a man with such a rich past to draw upon there was an infinite range of recollections. Among many last acts of generosity, his planning with James Houblon of his nephew John Jackson's grand tour had been inspired by the belief that a European dimension transformed the education of anyone, as witness his own far too brief sojourn in Holland.[8] It produced 'a degree of satisfaction and solid usefulness that has stuck by me through the whole course of my life'.[9] Jackson's tour had included France, Italy, Spain and Portugal and lasted two years. It had embraced such supreme moments as the opening of the Holy Door in Rome on Christmas Eve 1699, the cardinals' last supper at the Vatican and the 'ravishing' midnight devotions at St Lorenzo. Jackson's letters to Pepys must have sent a whiff of incense across his nostrils and reminded him of the threats that came over the barricades in the years of the Popish Plot. As his health deteriorated he continued to help refugees, to advise the Chatham Chest, to prepare Mary Skinner for life after his death and – above all – take an interest in naval affairs.

'I have too long outlived my relation to the Navy,' he wrote to Sir George Rooke, commander-in-chief of the fleet.[10] 'I return nevertheless (as I always shall) the same degree of concernment for its prosperity and respectful regard to the persons of its present directors.' The letter was written in John Jackson's hand with corrections by Pepys, which may have meant that he no longer wrote letters himself.

In April Pepys knew that the end was approaching and bluntly asked the doctors to tell him the truth about his condition.[11] On 19 April they admitted that he was mortally ill. Reporting this to Hewer, John Jackson wrote a letter which protested that he had no interest whatever in any inheritance, but 'would labour by all laudable methods to improve ... whatever he shall please to entrust me with'.[12] Jackson's reputation hardly bore out these lofty sentiments. On 14 May Evelyn recorded: 'I called in ... at Clapham to visit Mr Pepys now languishing with small hope of recovery which much affected me.'[13] The summer of 1703 began with prolonged sunshine and Pepys could witness its encroachment from the windows of the house. Dr George Hickes, now Bishop of Thetford, came to call on him one Monday afternoon and prayed beside if not with Pepys. It was a nice distinction which may have kept alive a small sceptical flame. The doctor then took his pulse and finding it very low told him that he had nothing to do but say, 'Come Lord Jesus. Come quickly.'[14]

That evening at about seven o'clock Pepys trembled all over and fell into a fit of convulsions. John Jackson sent for Will Hewer and prepared to stay with him all night. At four on the Tuesday morning Pepys was once again overtaken with convulsions. Jackson attempted to force some burnt claret between his lips but failed, and sent for Dr Hickes and Mary Skinner. Taking Jackson and Mary Skinner by the hand, Pepys said: 'Be good friends. I do desire it of you.' Jackson tried to kiss Pepys on the cheek but he 'turned his mouth and pressed my lips with an extraordinary affection'.[15] Hewer then reassured him, saying that Dr Hickes was coming, whereupon 'he ordered himself to be raised up in his bed'. When Hickes arrived he quickly performed the office for the sick and laying his hand on his head gave him absolution. Pepys murmured 'God be gracious to me' and prayed to God to reward them all. Mary Skinner then entered the room and he said: 'And thee in particular my dear child.' They all kissed Pepys and retired, leaving him alone. Hickes accompanied Jackson to his chamber to be in readiness for the final moments. Pepys called once more from his bed to Jackson who returned only to find him with little or nothing to say. Mary Skinner and Will Hewer then re-entered the bedroom and when he had once more blessed them he requested that they leave because 'he should be obliged to say a great deal to us which he could not with any ease do'. As they left, Arthur, one of his servants, entered. To Arthur Pepys said: 'I love you and thank you and so goodbye.' Three ordinary members of his household, all of them deeply distressed, came to pay their respects, including Betty Hamly 'who wept the least'.[16]

Pepys was, for some reason, carried from his bed to his couch and as night came down Mary Skinner and Jackson 'stole up to his bed to see him and shook him by the hand, he not discerning who it was'. Dr Shadwell, the physician, was called and felt his pulse. He said it was gone. Pepys died early in the morning of 26 May and his nephew recorded the event with Pepysian exactitude. 'It was forty-seven minutes past three ... by his gold watch.' Evelyn wrote a tribute to him in his diary: '... a very worthy, industrious and curious person, none in England exceeding him in the knowledge of the Navy ... universally beloved. Hospitable, generous, learned in many things, very great cherisher of learned men of whom he had the conversation ...'[17] Evelyn had been his friend for forty years and Pepys left a request that he should be 'one to hold up the pall at his ... obsequies'. Unfortunately, 'Indisposition hindered me from doing him this last office.' The funeral took place at nine o'clock in the evening of 4 June, the sunset coinciding symbolically with death. Pepys was laid beside his wife Elizabeth in front of the altar at St Olave's, Hart Street, in the parish of Crutched Friars. Over a hundred people gathered at the funeral, some identified in the pages of the Diary, many distinguished in law, politics and science, but scattered through their ranks were the ordinary domestics from his household like Mrs Fane. His lawyer, banker, doctors and book binder, the President and many Fellows of the Royal Society, the Archbishop of Canterbury and the Bishop of London, Dr Charlett Master of University College, Sir Anthony Deane and two members of the aristocracy, the Earls of Clarendon and Faversham – all were present. Persistent to the last, the ailing Balty appeared, supported by his daughter. The whole Board of the Admiralty arrived somewhat late, including Mr Burchett, the new Secretary. Jackson wrote: 'The magnificent character of the ceremony is suggested by the appearance among the mourners of a class described as retainers general.'[18] Dr George Hickes, Bishop of Thetford, conducted the service. There was no mention of Mary Skinner.

Dr Hickes wrote an account of Pepys's reaction to his coming death which some read as a reaffirmation of his complete belief in the Christian faith. The absence in either Hickes's or Jackson's account of any direct request made by Pepys to summon Dr Hickes to his bedside does somewhat alter the perspective. In Dr Hickes's encomium there is only one phrase which relates directly to a desire expressed by Pepys: 'I gave him the Absolution of the Church which he desired and received with all reverence and comfort.'[19] He concluded: 'The greatness of his behaviour in his long and sharp trial before his death was in every respect answerable to his great life; and I believe no man ever went out of this life with greater contempt of it or a more lively faith in every thing that was revealed of this world to come.'

Appendix

On the same day as Pepys's death Dr Shadwell left a gruesome document entitled *An Account of what was remarkable upon opening the body of the Honourable Samuel Pepys Esq.*[1]

The body was very much emaciated . . . The right kidney was of a larger size than ordinary, very sound and well coloured . . . the left . . . had scarce the form of a kidney . . . Upon opening it great quantity of a most foetid purulent matter gushed out, a large stone weighing an ounce and a half was found in the pelvis and several others viz VI weighing about three ounces were so firmly fastened to the kidney that most of the glandulous substance seemed to be petrified. The stones were all of very irregular figures with long sharp pointed angles one of which had almost pierced the parenchyma.[2]

According to modern medicine Pepys must have been in acute pain for weeks during his last illness but no hint of it appears in the documentation.

Notes

Abbreviations and Cue-Titles

Bryant I	Sir A.Bryant, *Pepys in the Making*
Bryant II	Sir A.Bryant, *Pepys: Years of Peril*
Bryant III	Sir A.Bryant, *Pepys: Saviour of the Navy*
Carte	Carte papers in the Bodleian Library
Chappell, *Letters*	*Shorthand Letters of Samuel Pepys*, transcribed and edited E. Chappell
Correspondence	*Private Correspondence and Miscellaneous Papers of Samuel Pepys 1679–1703 in the possession of J. Pepys Cockerell*, 2 vols, ed. J.R.Tanner
CPMSS	*A Descriptive Catalogue of the Naval Manuscripts in the Pepys Library at Magdalene College, Cambridge*, ed. J.R.Tanner
CSPD	*Calendar of State Papers, Domestic*
D.	Pepys's Diary, 10 vols, ed. R.Latham
DNB	*Dictionary of National Biography*
Evelyn	*The Diary of John Evelyn*, 6 vols, ed. E.S.de Beer
Further Correspondence	*Further Correspondence of Samuel Pepys 1662–1679*, ed. J.R. Tanner
Grey	A.Grey, *Debates in the House of Commons 1667–94*, 10 vols
Harris	F.R.Harris, *Life of Edward Mountagu, First Earl of Sandwich*, 2 vols
HMC	Historical Mss Commission Reports
Howarth	R. G. Howarth, *Letters and Second Diary of Samuel Pepys*
LBK	Letter Books, National Maritime Museum
Naval Minutes	*Samuel Pepys's Naval Minutes*, ed. J.R.Tanner
More Pepysiana	*More Pepysiana*, ed. W.H.Whitear
Ogg	D. Ogg, *England in the Reign of Charles II and William II*
Ollard	R.Ollard, *Pepys: A Biography*
Penn, *Memorials*	G.Penn, *Memorials of Sir William Penn*, 2 vols
Pepysiana	*Pepysiana*, ed. H.B.Wheatley
PRO	Public Record Office
Rawl.	Rawlinson Mss in the Bodleian Library
Sandwich, *Journal*	*Journal of the First Earl of Sandwich*, ed. R.C.Anderson

The Other Pepys

Smith	J.D.Smith, *The Life, Journals and Correspondence of Pepys*, 2 vols
Tangier Papers	*The Tangier Papers of Samuel Pepys*, ed. E.Chappell
Tedder	A.W.Tedder, *The Navy of the Restoration*

Prologue

1 *More Pepysiana*, 108. D. 30 Nov 1668.
2 D. 18 Aug 1668.
3 Sir D'Arcy Power: BM 011853 aa 2(8).
4 D. 19 Dec 1664.
5 D. 15 Nov 1664.
6 D. 3 Feb 1668.
7 D. 8 Apr 1662.
8 D. 23 Oct 1660.
9 D. 20 Dec 1666.
10 D. 1 Mar 1668.
11 *Pepysiana*, 14–15.
12 Admiralty Letters XIV, 407–9
13 Rawl. A 181 f 197.
14 D. 20 December 1664.
15 D. 23 Oct 1660.
16 *Old Bailey Session Papers*, 6–9 Dec 1693.
17 Cobbett and Howell, *State Trials* XII, 350.
18 R.L.Stevenson, *Cambridge History of Literature.*
19 D. 14 Jun 1662.
20 D. 31 Mar 1669.
21 Ollard, 286.
22 D. 6 Sep 1664.
23 Thomas Burnett, *The Theory of the Earth.*
24 Rawl. A 173 f 69.
25 D. 13 May 1665.

Chapter 1: The small years

1 E.Burton and F.Kelly, *At Home*, 47.
2 V.Brome, *We Have Come a Long Way*, 138.
3 H.B.Wheatley. The first edition of Pepys discusses the Pepys pedigree in detail. *Pepysiana*, 4–8. W.C.Pepys, *Genealogy of the Pepys Family.*
4 *Pepysiana*, 9.
5 Ibid.
6 *Genealogy of the Pepys Family*. A new genealogy traces descendants of the Pepys family down to the present day. This genealogy is the work of J.S.Gordon Clark.
7 F.M.Page, *Estates of Crowland Abbey*, 72.
8 *Genealogy of the Pepys Family.*
9 H.T.Heath (ed.), *The Letters of Samuel Pepys and his Circle.*
10 D. 30 May 1663.
11 *Pepysiana*, 12.
12 D. 30 May 1668.
13 D. 25 Apr 1664.
14 D. 25 Dec 1663.
15 Rawl. A 185 ff 206–13.
16 V.Wedgwood, *Thomas Wentworth*, 387.
17 Ibid., 389.
18 *More Pepysiana*, 14.
19 Bryant I, 15.
20 *DNB*, Carlyle, *Cromwell's Letters* XII–XIV.
21 D. 17 Dec 1662.
22 D. 9 Mar 1665.
23 McDonnell, *St Paul's School.*
24 Bryant I, 1–18.
25 Ibid.
26 Ibid.

Chapter 2: School days and early marriage

1 *More Pepysiana*, 108.
2 *Athenaeum*, 6 Jun 1914. See also *St Paul's School.*
3 *Academy* 1893, I, 372.
4 *DNB* Vol. 44, 360.
5 University of Cambridge, Mullinger III, 549–50.
6 W.T.Costello, S.J., *The Scholastic Curriculum at Early Seventeenth-Century Cambridge*, 142.
7 J.Hall, *A Humble Motion to the Parliament of England Concerning the Advancement of Learning and Reformation of the Universities* III, 372.
8 D. 26 Nov 1666.
9 D. 19 May 1660.

10 D. 21 Sep 1664.
11 *DNB* Vol 44, 360.
12 Ibid.
13 Bryant I, 23.
14 Rawl. A 185 ff 260–3.
15 D. 25 Nov 1661.
16 D. 11 Nov 1660.
17 D. 26 Jul 1663.
18 M.C.Whiting, 'The Wife of Mr Secretary Pepys', *Atlantic Monthly* Dec 1890.
19 Smith, *Pepys's Life, Journals and Correspondence* I, 147–8.
20 D. 3 Sep 1660.
21 D. 25 Feb 1667.
22 Harris I, 100.
23 Ibid.
24 Carte 15, 49, 27 Nov 1656.
25 'A Narrative of the Late Parliament', *Harleian Miscellany* III, 463.
26 M.C.Whiting, 'Profile of Mr Secretary Pepys', *Atlantic Monthly* Dec 1890.
27 Ibid.
28 D. 2 May 1663.
29 D. 21 Oct 1660. Known today as dysmenorrhoea.
30 D. 2 Aug 1660.
31 D. 15 Aug 1663.
32 D. 13 Aug 1661.
33 D. 17 Feb 1663.
34 D. 6 Dec 1665.
35 Rawl. A 182 f 329.
36 Evelyn, 3 May 1650.
37 Sir D'Arcy Power, *The British Journal of Surgery* XVIII, No. 72 (April 1931). Dr T.Hollier, 'Account of being cut for stone', Mar 1650, BM Add. 1536 ff 63. Sir H.Sloane, 'Account of his voiding stones', BM n.d. 4078 f 49.

Chapter 3: The Diary begins

1 D. 20 Mar 1660.
2 D. 12 Mar 1660.
3 D. 21 Jul 1664.

4 D. 8 Feb 1660.
5 D. 8 Mar 1660.
6 D. 9 Nov 1662.
7 Hall, *Antiquities of the Exchequer*, 107–9.
8 D. 16 Jan 1660.
9 Bryant I, 47.
10 Harris I, 176.
11 D.Underdown, *Royalist Conspiracy in England 1649–1700*, 310–14.
12 Ibid.
13 Pepys to Sandwich, 6 Dec 1659.
14 Latham I, Introduction cxvi–cxvii.
15 D. 29 Sep 1662.
16 D. 19 Jun 1661.
17 Bryant I, 69.
18 D. 1 Jan 1660.
19 Sir L.Jenkins, 'Key to [Pepys] cypher', BM Add. 40677.
20 D. 9 Feb 1660.
21 Westminster Hall.
22 D. 11 Feb 1660.
23 D. 24 Feb 1660.
24 Ibid.
25 D. 26 Feb 1660.
26 Ibid.
27 D. 6 Mar 1669.
28 Ibid.
29 D. 8 Mar 1668.
30 D. 9 Mar 1660.
31 Latham points out that it was usual for Exchequer officials to enter into bonds.
32 Harris I, 176.
33 *Clarendon Rebellion Book* XVI, 227.
34 D. 10 Mar 1660.
35 D. 12 Mar 1660.
36 D. 18 Mar 1660.
37 D. 19 Mar 1660.
38 D. 18 Mar 1660.
39 D. 17 Mar 1660.

Chapter 4: A voyage to King Charles

1 D. 17 Mar 1660.
2 D. 2 Mar 1660.
3 D. 23 Mar 1660.

4   Ibid.
5   D. 23 Mar 1660.
6   Ollard, 61.
7   D. 27 Mar 1660.
8   D. 8 Apr 1660.
9   Ibid.
10   D. 7 Apr 1660.
11   Ibid.
12   D. 8 Apr 1660.
13   Ibid.
14   D. 9 Apr 1660.
15   D. 10 Apr 1660.
16   D. 11 Apr 1660.
17   Ibid.
18   Macray, *Calendar of Clarendon*, Ms Bodleian.
19   Harris I, 176.
20   D. 2 May 1660.
21   Harris I, 183.
22   D. 14 May 1660.
23   Ibid.
24   D. 19 May 1660.
25   Ibid.
26   D. 20 May 1660.
27   Harris I, 185.
28   Ibid., 186.
29   D. 23 May 1660.
30   'An Account of the Preservation of King Charles', *Papers on the Escape of Charles II from Worcester*, BM Add. 31955.
31   Harris I, 187.
32   D. 23 Jun 1660.
33   D. 25 May 1660.
34   D. 28 May 1660.
35   D. 31 May 1660.
36   Ibid.
37   D. 18 Jun 1660.
38   D. 23 Jun 1660.
39   D. 24 Jun 1660.
40   D. 25 Jun 1660. Rawl. A 192 ff 179–81.
41   D. 29 Jun 1660.
42   D. 12 Jul 1660.
43   Ibid.
44   D. 13 Jul 1660.
45   Ibid.
46   Rawl. A 174 f 327.
47   A Commonwealth Admiralty official.
48   D. 17 Jul 1660.
49   H.B.Wheatley, *Samuel Pepys and the World He Lived In*, 135.
50   D. 2 Sep 1660.
51   D. 4 Sep 1660.

Chapter 5: Clerk of the Acts

1   Wheatley, *Samuel Pepys and the World He Lived In*, 189.
2   D. 9 Aug 1660.
3   D. 14 Sept 1660.
4   D. 20 Aug 1660.
5   Ollard, 82.
6   D. 8 Sep 1660.
7   *DNB* Vol. 44, 310.
8   Bryant I, 126.
9   D. 27 Dec 1660.
10   D. 18 Nov 1660.
11   D. 26 Nov 1660.
12   D. 6 Feb 1661.
13   D. 9 Jan 1661.
14   Ibid.
15   D. 27 May 1661.
16   Navy Records Society, Vol. 7. J.Holland, *Two Discourses of the Navy*, 1.
17   Ibid., 100–1
18   D. 8 Mar 1660.
19   M.Oppenheim, *The Royal Navy* VIII, 476.
20   Holland, *Two Discourses of the Navy*, 76, 'grasping'
21   Holland, *Two Discourses of the Navy*, 100–1.
22   LBK, quoted Ollard.
23   D. 29 Oct 1660.
24   At the Cockpit, Drury Lane.
25   D. 30 Oct 1660.
26   D. 31 Oct 1660.
27   Ibid.
28   Ibid.
29   D. 25 Dec 1660.
30   D. 23 Apr 1661.
31   Ibid.

32 Ibid.
33 Ibid.
34 D. 19 May 1661.
35 D. 2 Oct 1660.
36 D. 1 Apr 1661.
37 D. 31 May 1661.
38 *More Pepysiana*, 145–6
39 D. 24 Jul 1661.
40 *More Pepysiana*, 146.
41 D. Companion Volume 10, 439.
42 D. 26 Jul 1661.
43 D. 31 Apr 1661.
44 D. 31 Aug 1661.
45 D. 13 Jun 1661.

Chapter 6: Battles within the Navy Board

1 D. 1 Aug and 25 Aug 1661.
2 D. 6 Dec 1661.
3 D. 21 Dec 1661.
4 D. 29 Nov 1661.
5 A study of the dominion and ownership of the sea.
6 D. 3 Dec 1661.
7 Penn, *Memorials* II, 265.
8 Ibid.
9 PRO Adm. 7/633.
10 D. 5 Feb 1662.
11 D. 8 Mar 1662.
12 D. 5 Jun 1662.
13 D. 12 Apr 1662.
14 D. 29 Jun 1662.
15 D. 14 Jun 1662.
16 D. 26 Dec 1662.
17 D. 14 Jun 1661.
18 D. 14 Jun 1662.
19 Ollard, 20.
20 *DNB* Vol. 44 361. *Pepysiana*, 171–3.
21 D. 14 Sep 1662.
22 Holland, 61.
23 D. 13 Jun 1666.
24 D. 5 Sep 1664.
25 D. 23 Aug. 1662.
26 D. 10 Dec 1663.
27 D. 13 Mar 1664.
28 D. 15 Mar 1664.

29 D. 18 Mar 1664.
30 D. 2 Nov 1662.
31 D. 17 Nov 1662.
32 D. 12 Mar 1663.
33 D. 18 Mar 1663.
34 D. 15 May 1663.
35 D. 14 May 1663.
36 D. 16 May 1663.
37 D. 7 Sep 1662.
38 D. 26 May 1663.
39 D. 29 Jan 1663.

Chapter 7: Sexual adventures

1 D. 1 Jul 1663.
2 Ibid.
3 D. 5 Aug 1663.
4 Ibid.
5 D. 7 Aug 1663.
6 D. 3 Oct 1664.
7 D. 20 Oct 1664.
8 D. 3 Nov 1664.
9 D. 15 Nov 1664.
10 D. 20 Dec 1664.
11 D. 23 Jan 1665.
12 Ibid.
13 D. 12 Sep 1666.
14 D. 10 Aug 1663.
15 D. 9 Sep 1663.
16 D. 27 Dec 1663.
17 Harris I, 246.
18 Pepys to Sandwich, 18 Nov 1663.
19 Harris I, 246.
20 Ibid., 247.
21 D. 22 Nov 1663.
22 D. 13 Oct 1663.
23 Ibid.
24 D. 17 Nov 1663.
25 D. 20 Oct 1663.
26 D. 21 Feb 1663.
27 D. 23 Feb 1662.
28 D. 20 Feb 1663.
29 Ibid.
30 D. 29 Apr 1663.
31 D. 7 Aug 1664.
32 D. 12 Jul 1667.
33 D. 26 Oct 1663.

Chapter 8: First Dutch War and the plague

1 *Further Correspondence*, Pepys to Petty, 16 Feb 1663, Ms 96; Pepys to Coventry, 23 Feb 1663–4, Ms 97.
2 LBK, 89, 14 Nov 1663.
3 D. 21 Nov. 1663.
4 31 Dec 1664.
5 *Further Correspondence*, 143.
6 Quoted Ollard, 129.
7 LBK ff 45–6, 7 Mar 1663.
8 D. 21 Mar 1663.
9 Rawl. A 195, f 53.
10 D. 20 May 1665.
11 D. 15 Jan 1665.
12 Latham is unsure whether this lady was Betty Lane or a girl at the Rose tavern.
13 Dryden, *Essay on Dramatic Poetry*, quoted Bryant.
14 D. 3 Jun 1665.
15 D. 7 Jun 1665.
16 D. 8 Jun 1665.
17 Sandwich, *Journal* I, 296.
18 Harris I, 302.
19 Fighting Instructions 1665, article 7.
20 Lediard, *Naval History*, 578.
21 D. 8 Jun 1665.
22 Ibid.
23 Coventry to Albermarle, 4 Jun 1665.
24 Sir Henry Ellis, *Correspondence* (Ser. 1) III, 328.
25 Captain Roger Cuttance, Carte 75, 307.
26 Harris I, Appendix C: Clowes, *Royal Navy* II, 260.
27 D. 8 Jun 1665.
28 D. 22 Jul 1665.
29 *CSPD* 1664–5.
30 Pepys to Carteret, 24 Aug 1665.
31 Bryant I, 258.
32 D. 11 Jul 1665.
33 D. 10 Aug 1665.
34 D. 30 Aug 1665.
35 D. 3 Sep 1665.
36 D. 7 Oct 1665.
37 D. 22 Aug 1665.
38 Howarth, 4 Sep 1665.
39 Howarth, Pepys to Sandwich, 7 Aug 1665.
40 Smith, 7 Aug 1665.
41 Harris I, 314.
42 D. 7 Oct 1665.
43 *Further Correspondence*, Pepys to Coventry, 4 Nov 1665, 73.
44 D. 30 Sep 1665.
45 Sandwich, *Journal* I, 309.
46 Ibid., 248.
47 Harris I, 318–29.
48 Ibid.
49 Ibid., 329.
50 Carte 75, 337–8, quoted Harris.
51 Harris I, 339.
52 Johan de Witt I, 360–2.
53 Ibid., 341.
54 Tedder, 140–1.
55 Sandwich, *Journal* I, 351, quoted Harris.
56 D. 7 Sep 1665.
57 D. 9 Sep 1665.
58 S.B.Baxter, *The Development of the Treasury*, 9–11.
59 D. 10 Sep 1665.
60 Such was the avaricious chaos on this occasion that the Prize Court seriously thought of abolishing the system and substituting a part of the profits. Carte 34, 440.
61 Harris II, 4.
62 D. 12 Oct 1665.
63 Harris, II, 5.
64 Carte 75, 361, quoted Harris.
65 D. 22 Jan 1666.
66 Sandwich, Letters, 28 Sep 1666.
67 Sandwich, Letters I, 53.
68 Harris II, 10–12.
69 D. 24 Sep 1666.
70 'A Journal of my Proceedings in

the Business of the Prizes'. Pepys deciphered by Smith, 104–8, 17 Sep–13 Nov 1665.

71 D. 18 Sep 1665.
72 Rawl. A 174 f 93.
73 Harris II, 8.
74 Chappell, *Letters*, Pepys to Sandwich, 10 Oct 1665.
75 Ibid.
76 D. 7 Oct 1665.
77 Ibid.
78 Pepys to Sandwich, 12 Oct 1665, Chappell, *Letters*, ff 252–3.
79 D. 11 Oct 1665.

Chapter 9: First Naval Report

1 Chappell, *Letters*, 24 Aug 1665.
2 Chappell, *Letters*, 24 Aug 1665.
3 Tedder, 141–2.
4 Rawl. A 174, f 301.
5 D. 30 Dec 1665.
6 M. H. Nicolson, *Pepys's Diary and the New Science*, 19.
7 D. 16 Jan 1664.
8 D. 17 Oct 1666.
9 Ollard, 147–8.
10 LBK, 383, Jun 1666.
11 Pepys to Coventry, 14 Oct 1665, *Further Correspondence*, 59–61.
12 Tedder, 113.
13 Pepys to Coventry, 19 Feb 1666, *Further Correspondence*, 120–2.
14 *CSPD*, 15 Apr.
15 Pepys to Coventry, 28 Oct 1665, *Further Correspondence*.
16 Pepys to Coventry, 15 Nov 1665, Ibid.
17 Rawl. C 302 ff 46–63.
18 Pepys to Coventry, 1 Jan 1666, *Further Correspondence*.
19 D. 1 Jan 1666.
20 D. 3 Jan 1666.
21 D. 28 Feb 1666.
22 D. 16 Mar 1666.

Chapter 10: Second Dutch War and the Fire of London

1 D. 19 Dec 1664.
2 D. 1 Jul 1666.
3 Tanner, *Mr Pepys*, 191.
4 D. 29 Jun 1663.
5 Ogg, 736.
6 D. 13 May 1665.
7 D. 3 Jun 1666.
8 Sandwich, *Journal* I, 248.
9 D. 2 Jun 1666.
10 Ibid.
11 D. 2 Jun 1666.
12 Admiralty Letters VIII, 373, 375.
13 Samuel Daniel had risen from the ranks to become a lieutenant and was known to Pepys.
14 *CSPD* 666–7, 71. J. R. Powell (ed.), Rupert and Moncke Letter book, f 87.
15 Ollard, 151.
16 D. 7 Jun 1666.
17 D. 24 Feb 1667.
18 Ollard, 153.
19 Rupert and Moncke Letter book, 7 Jun 1666.
20 D. 1 Jul 1666.
21 Ibid.
22 Ibid.
23 Ibid.
24 Rawl. A 195 f 202.
25 Carte 72, 56–7.
26 R. Ollard, *Man of War*, 165.
27 D. 31 Jul 1666.
28 Ibid.
29 W. G. Bell, *The Great Fire of London*, 22.
30 D. 2 Sep 1666.
31 D. 2 Sep 1666.
32 Ibid.
33 Ibid.
34 Evelyn, 3 Sep 1666.
35 D. 2 Sep 1666.
36 Evelyn, 7–27 Sep 1666.
37 D. 2 Sep 1666.
38 D. 3 Sep 1666.

39 Bell, *The Great Fire of London*, 173.
40 Greenwich Ms, 406.
41 D. 4 Sep 1666.
42 S. de Pennefort, *Relation du premier voyage de la compagnie des Indes Orientales*, 1668, 336–8.
43 D. 5 Sep 1666.
44 Ibid.
45 Evelyn, 3 Sep 1666.
46 D. 15 Sep 1666.
47 D. 17 Sep 1666.

Chapter 11: Professional corruption and more affairs

1 Tedder, 179.
2 D. 2 Oct 1666.
3 Ibid.
4 Ibid.
5 D. 19 Oct 1666.
6 Pepys to Penn, 19 Oct 1666, *Further Correspondence*.
7 D. 19 Oct 1666.
8 D. 21 Jan 1667.
9 Pepys to the Commissioners, 20 Apr 1668, *Further Correspondence*.
10 Rawl. A 191, 182–93.
11 Penn, *Memorials* II, 459. 1 Feb 1668.
12 D. 24 Jan 1669.
13 D. 2 Aug 1666.
14 Ibid.
15 D. 1 Feb 1666.
16 D. 9 Jun 1667.
17 D. 5 Feb 1667.
18 D. 2 Dec 1666.
19 D. 18 Jul 1663.
20 D. 27 Jan 1667.
21 D. 11 Feb 1667.
22 Ibid.
23 LBK, 404, 25 Aug 1666.
24 D. 25 Mar 1667.
25 Ibid.

Chapter 12: The Dutch attack London

1 *SP* 84 (182), f 153.
2 C.P.Rogers, *The Dutch in the Medway*, 71.
3 Ibid., 75.

4 Admiralty Letters III.
5 D. 3 Jun 1667.
6 Ibid.
7 D. 5 Jun 1667.
8 D. 16 Dec 1666.
9 Tedder, 181–2.
10 D. 9 Jun 1667.
11 Rogers, *The Dutch in the Medway*, 73–4.
12 D. 10 Jun 1667.
13 LBK, 11 Jun 1667.
14 Ibid.
15 Summaries of Pett's two letters to the Navy Board. *CSPD* 1660–5, 189.
16 D. 11 Jun 1667.
17 Pepys to Coventry, 11 Jun 1667, *Further Correspondence*.
18 Journals, House of Commons, Vol. IX 1667–87.
19 PRO PC 259 f 227.
20 LBK, 491.
21 D. 12 Jun 1667. Rawl. A 195 f 128.
22 J.Millward, Diary, 2 Oct 1667.
23 Pepys to Brouncker, 1 Jul 1667, *Further Correspondence*.
24 D. 12 Jun 1669.
25 Tedder, 183.
26 Evelyn, 11 Jun 1667.
27 D. 13 Jun 1667.
28 Ibid.
29 Ibid.
30 D. 19 Jun 1667.
31 Tedder, 188–9.
32 D. 27 Jun 1667.
33 D. 18 Jun 1667.
34 D. 19 Jun 1667.
35 Ibid.
36 Rogers, *The Dutch in the Medway*, 192.
37 Tedder, 189.
38 Rogers, *The Dutch in the Medway*, 123.
39 PRO Adm. 2/1745.
40 D. 29 Jul 1667.

Chapter 13: The affair with Deborah

1   D. 9 Nov 1667.
2   D. 24 Sep 1667.
3   D. 25 Sep 1667.
4   D. 27 Sep 1667.
5   *Pepysiana*, 31.
6   D. 18 Aug 1668.
7   D. 10 Oct 1667.
8   D. 30 Dec 1667.
9   Ibid.
10 D. 25 Oct 1668.
11 D. 20 Oct 1668.
12 Ibid.
13 D. 27 Oct 1668.
14 Bryant I, 370.
15 D. 3 Nov 1668.
16 D. 10 Nov 1668.
17 Ibid.
18 D. 11 Nov 1668.
19 D. 12 Nov 1668.
20 D. 13 Nov 1668.
21 D. 14 Nov 1668.
22 D. 16 Nov 1668.
23 D. 18 Nov 1668.
24 Ibid.
25 Ibid.
26 Ibid.
27 D. 19 Nov 1668.
28 D. 20 Nov 1668.
29 Ibid.
30 Ibid.
31 D. 21 Nov 1688.
32 D. 5 Dec 1668.

Chapter 14: The Diary ends

1   D. 3 Dec 1667.
2   Bryant I, 345–6.
3   Pepys to Sir Robert Brooke, 16 Dec 1667.
4   D. 20 Oct 1667.
5   D. 31 Dec 1667.
6   D. 19 Jan 1664.
7   D. 13 Dec 1666.
8   *Lancet*, 24 Jun 1911.
9   D. 16 Feb 1669.

10 Pepys to the Duke of York, 17 Jun 1669.
11 D. 31 May 1669.
12 Ibid.
13 D. 27 Nov 1668.
14 D. 9 Nov 1668.
15 Ibid.
16 D. 18 Jan 1669.
17 D. 31 Mar 1669.
18 Ibid.
19 D. 24 Mar 1669.
20 D. 9 Apr 1669.
21 D. 15 Apr 1669.
22 D. 19 Apr 1669.
23 D. 22 Jun 1668. R.E.W. Maddison, *Notes and Records*, Vol. 9, No. 1, Royal Society.
24 D. 28 Apr 1667.
25 Nicolson, *Pepys's Diary and the New Science*, 32.
26 Ibid., 33.
27 *Further Correspondence*, 237.
28 Evelyn to Pepys, 21 Aug 1669, Howarth.
29 Bryant I, 390.
30 Pepys to Captain Elliot, 3 Mar 1699–70, Howarth.
31 Harris II, 190–1.
32 Pepys Ms 2874, Vol. VI, Brooke House Journal, 394.
33 Pepys to the Commissioners of Accounts, 26 Nov 1669, *Further Correspondence*.
34 Pepys Ms 2554.
35 Pepys Ms 2874, Vol. VI, 386 *et seq.*
36 Pepys Ms 2874, 390/2. Harris II, 191.
37 *Naval Minutes*, 37–8.
38 Pepys Library Miscellanies VI, 390–1.
39 Brooke House Journal, 392–3.
40 D. 5 Jan 1668.
41 Sandwich, Letters II, 81.
42 Ibid.
43 Ollard, 198.
44 Pepys Ms 2874, 481–6.
45 Ibid., 404.

46   Ibid.
47   Ibid., 343.
48   Pepys Ms 2874.
49   Pepys Ms 2554.
50   Bryant II, 26–7. Pepys to the King, 8 Jan 1670.
51   Pepys Ms 2874, 384–504. 'Journal of What Passed Between the Commissioners of Accounts and Myself'.
52   Pepys Library Miscellanies VI, 399–406, quoted Bryant.
53   D. 1 Mar 1668.
54   *Naval Minutes*, 197–8.
55   Brooke House Journal, 471.
56   Ibid. 473, quoted Ollard.
57   Pepys Ms 2874, 483. Admiralty Letters VI, 393.
58   Pepys to Stephens, 8 Mar 1668.
59   *Naval Minutes*, 152.

Chapter 15: Secretary to the Admiralty

1   It is alleged that the last descendant of Pepys's cat, Brutus, belonged to the National Gallery and died in 1933, Bryant.
2   Pepys's motto was 'Mens cujusque is est quisque' – 'What man's mind is, that is what he is.'
3   Nicolson, *Pepys's Diary and the New Science*, 103.
4   D. 9 Mar 1666.
5   D. Companion Volume, 258.
6   Bryant II, 47.
7   D. 16 Dec 1662.
8   Evelyn to Pepys, 9 Aug 1700.
9   Mary Evelyn to Pepys, 183–4, Howarth.
10   D. 9 Sep 1662: 'Some things are in our power, others are not.'
11   D. 17 Apr 1666.
12   LBK, 305, 25 Oct 1665.
13   Anglesey to Pepys, 4 Aug 1672. Smith I, 133.
14   Pepys to Anglesey, 4 Aug 1672.

Smith I, 136–7. Miscellanies VI, 399–406.
15   Pepys to Daniel Skinner, 17 Nov 1676, *Further Correspondence*.
16   *The Review of English Studies* VII (Jul 1931), 263.
17   15 Dec 1676, and Pepys to dinner.
18   Evelyn to Pepys, 6 Dec 1681, *Further Correspondence*.
19   Clarke, *James II* I, 455.
20   Family of Hatton, *Correspondence* I, 78–84.
21   *CSPD*, 14 Mar 1672.
22   Evelyn, 12 Mar 1672.
23   Ibid.
24   Ibid., 23 Mar 1672.
25   Ibid., 2 Apr 1672.
26   M. Lewis, *The Navy of Britain*, 361.
27   Evelyn, 5 May 1672.
28   CSPD 1671–2, 592.
29   Ibid., 541.
30   Harris II, 267.
31   Lewis, 456.
32   Ibid., 464
33   Duke of Buckingham, *Memoirs*.
34   Harris II, 284–5.
35   Ibid.
36   Ibid.
37   *London Gazette*, Jul 1672, 691.
38   *CSPD*, 1672, 370–1.
39   Pepys to Balthazar St Michel (Balty), 22 Jun 1672.
40   See Lewis, 362–6.
41   Lewis, 250.
42   *Further Correspondence*, Introduction.
43   Hooke, Diary, 29 Jan 1673.
44   Ibid.
45   Evelyn, 26 May 1671.
46   Coventry to Pepys, 25 Jun 1673.
47   Hatton, *Correspondence*, 113–14.
48   *Naval Minutes*, 71–2.
49   Pepys to Henry Savile, Sir William Coventry's nephew, 20 Aug 1672. Tanner wrongly identifies the addressee as Sir William Coventry. B. N. Ranft,

Journal of Modern History XXIV, No. 4, 368–75, quoted by Ollard.
50 Pepys to Lord Howard, 20 Aug 1672.
51 *Further Correspondence*, 274–5.
52 Rawl. A 172, 141.
53 Commons Journal IX, 304.
54 Grey II, 304. Chandler, *Debates*, House of Commons, 1673–4.
55 Ibid.
56 Commons Journal IX, 306. Grey 1673–4, 10 and 16 Feb.
57 Balty to Pepys, 8 Feb 1673–4.
58 D. 3 Nov 1666.
59 Commons Journal IX, 306.
60 Ibid.
61 Thomas Povey to Pepys, 16 Feb 1674. Rawl. A 172 ff 100–102.
62 Pepys to Povey, 15 Mar 1674. Rawl. A 172 f 107.
63 Rawl. A 191.
64 Ogg II, 549.

Chapter 16: Reorganising the Navy – Colonel Scott appears

1 *Naval Minutes*, 176–7.
2 J.S.Corbett, *England in the Mediterranean* II, 100–101.
3 *Miscellanies* V, 185.
4 W.Cobbett, *Parliamentary History* IV, 774.
5 Grey III, 319.
6 Ibid., 365.
7 Ibid., 377.
8 'Notes for my Discourse in Parliament introductory to the Debate of the Business of the Navy', *Pepysiana* 2266, paper 119.
9 Grey III, 323.
10 Ibid.
11 Ibid., 360.
12 *Naval Minutes*, 26.
13 Ibid., 322.
14 LBK, 891. Pepys to John Holmes, 15 Apr 1679; 10 Apr 1679.
15 CPMSS I, 195–6; III, 85, 92–3.
16 CPMSS II, 127–8.
17 Rawl. A 185 f 110, quoted Ollard.
18 Rawl. A 181 f 195. Evidence of Thomas Harman, 25 Oct 1685.
19 CPMSS II, 342, 383, 386, etc. See also Admiralty Letters XIII, Ms 2348.
20 *Naval Minutes*, 194.
21 *Tangier Papers*, 158–9. CPMSS II, 207–8.
22 CPMSS, Vol. 14, 1 Dec 1677, 232.
23 Corbett, *England in the Mediterranean*.
24 D. 23 Jan 1667.
25 Memoirs of the Royal Navy, 80.
26 Admiralty Letters VIII, 104.
27 Barlow, *Journals*, 2 vols, ed. Basil Lubbock, 60, 128.
28 Admiralty Letters XV, 226.
29 Admiralty Letters VIII, 104.
30 Christopher Lloyd, 232.
31 Pepys to Pett, 22 Jun 1677, *Further Correspondence*.
32 D. 1 Jul 1660.
33 D. 10 May 1669.
34 Catalogue of Library.
35 Evelyn, 26 Aug 1676.
36 Rawl. A 185 ff 206–13.
37 Ibid.
38 Ibid.
39 Grey IV, 204–17, CJ IX.
40 CJ IX, 405.
41 Bryant II, 172.
42 CPMSS I, 231–41.
43 Bryant II, 183.
44 D. 29 Jan 1666. LBK, 471, 17 Feb 1665.
45 *Further Correspondence*, 116–18.
46 Grey VII, 148.
47 J.Kenyon, *The Popish Plot*. Kenyon is the best source.
48 Ibid.
49 My Two Volumes of Mornamont, Mss 2881–2, Pepys Library.
50 G.D.Scull, *Dorothea Scott*.
51 Rawl. A 173 ff 138–59; A 175 ff 1–16, 16–40, 60–9.

52 Rawl. A 173 ff 139–60.
53 Ibid.
54 There are some interesting sidelights on Scott in J. Pollock, *The Popish Plot*, 61–3.
55 Mornamont I, 605 ff.
56 Ibid.

Chapter 17: Titus Oates and the Popish Plot – committed to the Tower

1   Ogg, 597–8.
2   Kenyon, *The Popish Plot*.
3   H.M.C.Ormonde IV, 482–3.
4   Admiralty Letters VIII, 231–3.
5   J.G.Muddiman, *The Mystery of Sir E.B.Godfrey*. Admiralty Letters VIII, 231–3.
6   R.North, *Examen*, 199.
7   Kenyon, *The Popish Plot*, Appendix A.
8   North, *Examen*, 203.
9   Ibid.
10 Yet another version was given by Williamson, *CSPD* 494, 30 Oct 1678.
11 North, *Examen*, 204.
12 Rawl. A 173 ff 189, 195–201.
13 Rawl. A 188 ff 114–19.
14 North, *Examen*, 244.
15 Rawl. A 173 ff 113 *et seq.* Samuel Atkins's account of 'His Examination Before the Committee of Lords appointed to examine the murder of Sir Edmundbury Godfrey', Cobbett, *State Trials* VI, 1474–1491.
16 North, *Examen*, 244.
17 Cobbett, *State Trials* VI, 1473.
18 Ibid., 1475.
19 Ibid.
20 North, *Examen*, 245.
21 LBK, Pepys to Houblon, 2 Nov 1670. See K.H.D.Haley, *The First Earl of Shaftesbury*.
22 Admiralty Letters VIII, 296, 319.
23 Rawl. A 181 ff 10–23.
24 North, *Examen*, 247.
25 Rawl. A 181 f 1. Admiralty Letters VIII, 313.
26 Samuel Atkins narrative. Rawl. A 173 f 113–32.
27 North, *Examen*, 249–50. *Further Correspondence*, 328–9.
28 Pepys's copy of the *Journal of the Green Ribbon Club*. Pepysiana, 2875. Miscellanies VII, 265–91.
29 LBK, 878–80, 6 Mar 1670.
30 North, *Examen*, 250.
31 F.Hargrave, *State Trials* I, 789–93.
32 Rawl. A 181. Samuel Atkins's account of the case, 25 Nov 1678.
33 Grey VII, 111–13.
34 *Naval Minutes*, 181.
35 Pepys to the Duke of York, 6 May 1679.
36 *Naval Minutes*, 181.
37 Rawl. A 173 ff 178–9.
38 Ibid.
39 Monday 14 Apr 1679. Grey VII, 111–12.
40 Ibid.
41 Grey VII, 111–12.
42 Mornamont II, 1245–9.
43 H.T.Heath (ed.), *The Letters of Samuel Pepys and His Family Circle*.
44 Grey VII, 111–12, 20 May 1679.
45 Ibid.
46 Rawl. A 181 f 197.
47 Rawl. A 173 f 87, 31 May 1679.
48 Ibid.
49 General Williamson, *Diary*, 27–8.
50 Evelyn, 4 Jun 1679. Duke of York to King Charles, 22 May 1679.
51 Pepys to Savile, 26 May 1679.
52 Rawl. A 173 f 69.
53 Heath (ed.), *The Letters of Samuel Pepys and His Family Circle*.
54 Rawl. A 188.
55 Pepys to Balty, 13 Oct 1679, Heath.
56 Rawl. A 194 ff 370–480.
57 Mornamont I, 229. 'Information of Captain John Browne touching

Colonel Scott's … maps pretended to be of his own design'.

58 Rawl. A 194 ff 80–81.
59 Mornamont I, 177. Joyne to Pepys, 30 Sep 1679.
60 Rawl. A 194 ff 94–100.
61 *Pepysiana*, 2881. Mornamont I, 283–330.
62 *CSPD* 1677–80, 307, 11 Dec 1679.
63 *Pepysiana*, 2881. Mornamont I, 310–30.
64 Joyne, Journal, Wednesday 17 December 1679, *Pepysiana*, 2881.
65 Ibid.
66 Mornamont II, 1226–70.
67 Rawl. 173 ff 69, 85.
68 Mornamont I, 61–6.
69 Mornamont II, 1237–44, quoted Bryant.
70 Mornamont I, 72–81.
71 Rawl. A 173 ff 66–9, 87–8.

Chapter 18: Temporary retirement – the Tangier expedition

1 Ogg, 598–9. The assumption that Shaftesbury exclusively inspired the plot against Pepys is denied by Haley, *Shaftesbury*, 521.
2 HMC Report, XI app. pt. II, 195–7. Grey VII, 418–20. See K.D. Haley's magisterial biography of the First Earl of Shaftesbury.
3 Cobbett, *Parliamentary History* IV, 215.
4 Pepys to Skinner, 1 Jul 1680, Howarth, 96.
5 Rawl. A 194 f 168.
6 *Pepysiana*, 2881.
7 Hill to Pepys, 14 Apr 1673.
8 Nicolson, *Pepys Diary and the New Science*, 67.
9 'An Account of the Preservation of King Charles after the Battle of Worcester in 1651'. Pepys Library 2141 recovery.
10 Balty to Pepys, 24 Sep 1680.

11 Houblon to Pepys, 30 Oct 1680, Howarth, 103.
12 Hewer to Pepys, 15 Nov 1680, Howarth, 107–8. Rawl. A 183 f 140.
13 *CSPD*, 11 Jan 1681.
14 *CSPD*, 166, 14 Feb 1681.
15 *CSPD*, 227–8, SP. Dom. Car. II 415 No. 100.
16 Pepys to Roger Pepys, 16 Mar 1681.
17 Joseph Maryon to Pepys, 8 Aug 1681, Howarth, 115.
18 Smith, 287.
19 Evelyn to Pepys, 6 Dec 1681.
20 Henry Ryde, Earl of Clarendon, *Correspondence*, ed. Singer, Vol. I, 72.
21 Pepys to Will Hewer, 8 May 1682, Howarth.
22 Houblon to Pepys, 13 May 1682, Howarth, 138–9.
23 Earl of Clarendon, *Correspondence*, 73.
24 Hewer to Pepys, 13 May 1682, Howarth, 136–7.
25 Smith, 291, 13 May 1682.
26 *Pepysiana*, 2612 ff 530–612.
27 *Naval Minutes*, 148.
28 A.Bryant, *Charles II*, 334.
29 Bryant, *Charles II*, 334.
30 Ogg, 602.
31 HMC Dartmouth II, 39–40. Rawl. A f 176. 'Journal of the Commission appointed to enquire into the true state of Tangier's property'.
32 E.M.G.Routh, *Tangier: England's Last Outpost*, 247.
33 *Tangier Papers*, 251–2.
34 *Tangier Papers*, 253.
35 Evelyn to Pepys, 10 Aug 1683, Howarth, 152–3.
36 Pepys's Journal 'Towards Tangier', Sunday 19 Aug.
37 'Towards Tangier'.
38 All Souls Ms 10, quoted Ollard.

39   'Towards Tangier', 7–8.
40   Ibid., 8.
41   Ibid., 9.
42   Ibid., 9.
43   Ibid., 17.
44   Ibid., 16.
45   Rawl. C 859 f 249, quoted Bryant.
46   *Tangier Papers*, 8, 109–11.
47   *Tangier Papers*, 12, 106, 109, 113.
48   Rawl. A 196 ff 1, 102, 105. Routh, *Tangier*, 259.
49   *Tangier Papers*, 23–4.
50   Ibid., 24.
51   Routh, *Tangier*, 251, 254–5.
52   Dartmouth Ms Report.
53   *Tangier Papers*, 164.
54   *Tangier Papers*, 119.
55   B. Meakin, *The Moorish Empire*, 154.
56   Pepys to Dartmouth, 22 Dec–1 Jan 1683–4, Howarth.
57   Pepys to Dartmouth, 5–15 Jan 1684, Howarth, 165.
58   Evelyn, 16 Sep 1685.
59   'Towards Tangier', 169.
60   Pepys to Dartmouth, 3–13 Feb 1684, Howarth, 166–7.
61   Bryant, 3–58.
62   *Tangier Papers*, 173.
63   Ibid., 205.
64   Ibid., 206.
65   Extracts from captain's log of HMS *Grafton*. PRO Adm. 51, 407.
66   Notes General, 175.
67   Log Book, 3 Mar 1684.
68   Ibid., 9 Mar 1684.
69   Ibid., 292.
70   *Tangier Papers*, 224.
71   Ibid., 225.
72   Ibid.
73   Ibid., 295.
74   *Tangier Papers*, 224.
75   Ibid., 245.
76   Ibid., 295–6.
77   Ibid., 241–2.
78   Ibid., 244.

*Chapter 19: James becomes King –
Monmouth invades England*

1   Pepys to Dartmouth, 6 Apr 1684, Howarth, 167.
2   Dartmouth to Pepys, 8 Apr 1684, Smith, 45.
3   Evelyn, 7 Jun 1684.
4   Evelyn to Pepys, 8 Jun 1684, *Further Correspondence* I, 23–4.
5   Memoirs, 7.
6   *Tangier Papers*.
7   Bryant III, 105.
8   Admiralty Letters XI, 209–10.
9   Bryant III, 124–5.
10   Ollard, 284.
11   Rawl. A 189 f 1.
12   Rawl. C 859 ff 191–4.
13   *Naval Minutes*, 223.
14   J. Ehrman, *The Navy in the War of William III*, 201.
15   *Tangier Papers*, 241.
16   Admiralty Letters X, 42, 57–8.
17   Ibid., 44.
18   Pepys Library, Magdalene College, Cambridge.
19   Memoirs, 819.
20   Rawl. A 190 f 25.
21   Evelyn, 1 Feb 1685.
22   Bryant, *Charles II*, 362.
23   Ailesbury, Memoirs I, 87–8.
24   Ibid., 89.
25   Ibid., 88–9.
26   Ibid., 90.
27   Burnett, *The Theory of the Earth*, 296.
28   Ogg.
29   Rawl. 537. 'A Description of the Ceremonial Proceedings of the Coronation of Their Most Illustrious, Serene and Sacred Majesties King James II and His Royal Consort'.
30   J. S. Clarke (ed.), *The Life of James II*, II, 404–6.
31   Burnet IV, 540.

32 C.J.Fox, *A History of the Early Part of the Reign of James II*, Appendix.
33 *Naval Minutes*, 272–3.
34 Ollard, 285.
35 Howarth, 127–8, 14 Mar 1682.
36 Ollard, 286.
37 Luttrell I, 343.
38 Evelyn, 16 May 1685.
39 Luttrell I, 344.
40 Evelyn, 22 May 1685.
41 *Journal of the House of Lords*, XIV, 30 Mar 1685.
42 Admiralty Letters XI, 137. See studies of Monmouth, P.Earle and R.Clifton.
43 N.Luttrell, *Brief Historical Relation of State Affairs* I, 346.
44 Ogg, 147.
45 Ibid., 148.
46 Admiralty Letters XI, 125–7, 7 Jul 1685.
47 Ogg, 154.
48 Rawl. A 193 f 136.
49 Tanner, *Samuel Pepys and Trinity House*.
50 Evelyn, 20 Jul 1685.
51 Evelyn, 17 Sep 1685.
52 Howarth, 169–70.
53 Evelyn, 2 Oct 1685.
54 Rawl. A 465 ff 112–13.
55 Grey VIII, 360–7.
56 CJ IX, 735–6.
57 Evelyn, 9 Nov 1685.
58 Evelyn, 12 Nov 1685.
59 Ogg, 168–9.
60 Pepys Ms 1490, 14–15.
61 Ibid., 142–53, quoted Ollard.

Chapter 20: The Special Commission – the trial of the bishops

1 Heath (ed.), *The Letters of Samuel Pepys and His Circle*, 206–7, 24 Jan 1687.
2 Mrs Evelyn to Pepys, 7 Sep 1687, Howarth, 183.
3 Pepys to Balty, 11 Dec 1686.

4 J.P.W. Ehrman, *The Navy in the War of William III*, 203.
5 Ibid., 205–6.
6 Ibid.
7 Ibid., 206.
8 Harleian Ms 7476, British Library.
9 Ehrman, *The Navy in the War of William III*, 206–7.
10 Rawl. A 179 f 40, quoted Bryant III, 168.
11 Admiralty Letters XI 531–2, 7 Jan 1687.
12 Evelyn, 5 May 1686.
13 Dr Peachell to Pepys, 23 Feb 1687.
14 F.P. and M.M.Verney, *Memoirs of the Verney Family* II, 457.
15 Ibid.
16 Verney, *Memoirs* II, 457, give a vivid account of these events.
17 Macaulay, *A History of England* II, 378.
18 Ibid., 381.
19 *State Trials* IV, 363, quoted Bryant.
20 Ibid.
21 Ibid., 395.
22 Ibid.
23 Admiralty Letters XIV, 222, 10 Jun 1688.
24 Verney, *Memoirs* II, 444.
25 Smith, 119.
26 Verney, *Memoirs* II, 400–401.
27 Ogg, 210. Recent work (W. Speck, *Reluctant Revolutionaries*) tends to focus on Anglican rather than Protestant opposition.
28 Rawl. A 186 ff 57–69.

Chapter 21 – Prince William invades England

1 Smith, 220.
2 Pepys to James Houblon, 10 Jul 1689.
3 Bryant III, 228.
4 Houblon to Pepys, 11 Jul 1689.
5 Lady Tuke to Pepys, 2 Mar 1687.
6 Evelyn, 19 Apr 1687.
7 Brayhooke IV, 238.

8   Admiralty Letters XIV, 407–9.
9   Bryant III, 267–9.
10   LBK, 121, Admiralty Letters.
11   Smith, 166–7.
12   Ibid.
13   Rawl. A 186 f 438.
14   Pepys to Dartmouth, 10 Nov 1688.
15   Rawl. A 186 f 353, quoted Bryant.
16   Ogg, 215.
17   Ehrman, *The Navy in the War of William III*, 206–7.
18   HMC Rep. XI App. pt. 5, 169.
19   Macaulay, *A History of England* II, 487.
20   Rawl. A 186 f 374. HMC Rep. XI App. pt. 5, 190, 198.
21   Ogg, 215.
22   Smith, 177.
23   Pepys to Dartmouth, 10 Nov 1688.
24   The King to Dartmouth, 12 Nov 1688, Smith II, 337–8.
25   Evelyn to Pepys, 23 Dec 1688, Howarth.
26   K. Felling, *A History of the Tory Party*, 232–4.
27   Macaulay, *A History of England* II, 150.
28   Bryant III, 313.
29   Macaulay, *A History of England* II, 532.
30   Ibid.
31   Ibid., 507.
32   Ogg, 217.
33   Barrillon, 1 Nov 1688, Dalrymple.
34   Admiralty Letters XV, 447.
35   Macaulay, *A History of England* II, 553.
36   Ibid.
37   Dartmouth to Pepys, 14 Dec 1688, Smith II, 191.
38   Hatton, *Correspondence*, 11, 124–5.
39   Steele, 1, 408b, 10 Apr 1692, quoted Ogg.
40   Evelyn, 13 Dec 1688.
41   Bryant III, 346.

42   Macaulay, *A History of England* II, 586.
43   Ibid.
44   17 Dec 1688.
45   Hewer to Pepys, 19 Dec 1688.
46   Dartmouth to Pepys, 28 Dec 1688.
47   Dartmouth to the Prince of Orange, 20 Dec 1688.
48   Pepys to Dartmouth, 2 Jan 1688.
49   Evelyn, 9 Jan 1689.
50   Hippolitus, De Luzancy to Pepys, 18 Jan 1688.
51   Admiralty Letters XV, 527.
52   Rawl. A 186, 125 6.
53   HMC Rep. XII, App. Pt 6.
54   Bodleian Ms, *English History C*, 299.
55   A. Browning, *Thomas Osborne* I, 420–1.
56   Rawl. A 186 f 112.
57   Admiralty Letters XV, 598.
58   Ms I, 38 Whitehall, 14 Jul 1690.
59   Ibid.
60   Pepys to John Jackson, 8 Apr 1700.
61   J. R. Tanner, *Mr Pepys*, 270.
62   Ehrman, *The Navy in the War of William III*, 283–5.
63   Ibid.
64   Burchett to Pepys, 21 Feb 1699.
65   Burchett to Pepys, 7 Jun 1700.
66   Ehrman, *The Navy in the War of William III*, 284.
67   Rawl. A 170 f 169, quoted Ollard.
68   Rawl. A 170 f 66.

Chapter 22 – Correspondence with Sir Isaac Newton

1   Tanner, *Mr Pepys*, 272.
2   Pepys to Evelyn, 7 Aug 1700.
3   Pepys to Sir Leoline Jenkins, 24 Jul 1676.
4   *Further Correspondence*, 301.
5   Rawl. A 178, 209.
6   Rawl. A 170 f 60.
7   *Review of English Studies*, Jul 1931, 267.

8   Pepys to John Jackson, 9 May
    1700, Howarth, 297.
9   Ibid.
10 D. 25 Jul 1663.
11 Evelyn, 26 May 1603.
12 Balty to Pepys, 28 May 1689.
13 Balty to Pepys, 1689, Heath, 223.
14 Pepys to Haddock, Sunday 21 Apr
    1689, Heath, 224–5.
15 Balty to Pepys, 20 Mar 1692.
16 Pepys to Hewer, 2 Nov 1680.
17 Pepys to Newton, 22 Nov 1693.
18 Ibid.
19 Newton to Pepys, 16 Dec 1693.
20 Pepys to Newton, 9 Dec 1693.
21 Pepys to Newton, 21 Dec 1693.
22 Pepys to George Tollett, 14 Feb
    1694.
23 D.Douglas, *English Scholars*.
24 Pepys to Reay, 21 Nov 1699,
    Further Correspondence I, 241.
25 *Further Correspondence* II, 305–6.
26 Pepys to Dr Gale, 15 Sep 1692,
    Further Correspondence I, 60
27 Pepys to Evelyn, 16 Sep 1692,
    Further Correspondence I, 63.
28 Wallis to Pepys, 24 Oct 1699,
    Further Correspondence II, 209–10.
29 Pepys to the Archbishop, 14 Nov
    1699, *Further Correspondence* II,
    239.
30 Ibid., 197–8.
31 Pepys to Jackson, 9 May 1700,
    Further Correspondence I, 333.
32 R.K.Merton, *Science in
    Seventeenth-Century England*, 443;
    R.E.W.Maddison, *Studies in
    Boyle*.
33 See also Shadwell's *The Virtuoso*.
34 *Certain Philosophical Questions*,
    1676. Eugene Klaaren gives a
    more balanced account.
35 Newton to Pepys, 13 Sep 1693.
36 Newton to Locke, 16 Sep 1693.
37 Rawl. A 171 f 217, 'Notes From

    the Discourses Touching
    Religion'.
38 Ibid.
39 D. 10: 350–4. Rawl. A 171 f 217.
40 Ibid.
41 Richard Popkin, *Isaac la Peyrère*, 1.
42 Rawl. A 171 f 217.
43 Ray Monk, *Ludwig Wittgenstein*,
    267. Information Dr Sophie
    Botros.

Chapter 23 – Retirement and death

1   Evelyn to Pepys, 9 Aug 1700,
    Further Correspondence II, 38.
2   Pepys to Evelyn, 19 Nov 1701,
    Howarth, 334.
3   Evelyn to Pepys, 10 Dec 1701.
4   Wanley to Pepys, 15 Apr 1701,
    Howarth 330–1.
5   Pepys to Evelyn, 7 Aug 1700,
    Further Correspondence II, 35–6.
6   Evelyn to Pepys, 9 Aug 1700,
    Further Correspondence II, 38–9.
7   Academy XXXVIII, 200.
8   *Further Correspondence* II, 35.
9   *Further Correspondence* I,
    Introduction, xxii.
10 Pepys to Sir George Rooke, Apr
    1703.
11 Jackson to Hewer, 20 Apr 1703.
12 Ibid.
13 Evelyn, 13 May 1703.
14 John Jackson's account of his
    uncle's death.
15 Ibid., 313.
16 Ibid.
17 Evelyn, 26 May 1703.
18 *Further Correspondence* I, xiii.
19 Wheatley, *Samuel Pepys and the
    World He Lived In* I, 111.

Appendix

1   Historical Mss Commission ninth
    report, pt 11, 406.
2   *Further Correspondence* II, 311–12.

Select Bibliography

Earl of Ailesbury, *Memoirs*, 1890

R.C.Anderson (ed.) *Journal of the First Earl of Sandwich*, 1928

J.Aubrey, *Brief Lives*, 2 vols, 1898

G.Barry, *Taverns*, 1914

W.G.Bell, *The Great Fire of London*, 1920

D.Brewster, *Isaac Newton*, 2 vols, 1855

Sir A.Bryant, *Pepys in the Making*, 1933

Sir A.Bryant, *The Years of Peril*, 1935

Sir A.Bryant, *Pepys: Saviour of the Navy*, 1938

Sir A.Bryant, *Charles II*, 1931

R.Chandler, *Parliamentary Proceedings*, 1674–5

R.Chandler, *Debates*, 1742

E.Chappell (ed.), *Shorthand Letters of Samuel Pepys*, 1933–5

E.Chappell (ed.), *Pepysiana*, 1937

E.Chappell (ed.), *The Tangier Papers of Samuel Pepys*, 1935

J.S.Gordon Clark, *A Sketch Pedigree in Tabular Form of the Descendants of John and Margaret Knight*, 1960

W.Cobbett, *State Trials*, 1909

J.S.Corbett, *England in the Meditarranean*, 2 vols, 1904

W.T.Costello, *Scholastic Curriculum*, 1958

Earl of Clarendon, *The State Letters of Henry, Earl of Clarendon*, 1609–1674

Sir D'Arcy Power, *Some Bygone Operations*, 1930

E.S. de Beer (ed.), *The Diary of John Evelyn*, 6 vols, 1955

D.Defoe, *Journal of the Plague Year*, 1895

P. de la Force, *Pepys in Love*, 1986

D.C.Douglas, *English Scholars*, 1939

J.P.W.Ehrman, *The Navy in the War of William III*, 1953

A.Grey, *Debates 1667–94*, 10 vols, 1769

F.Hargrave, *State Trials*, 1776

F.R.Harris, *Life of Edward Montagu, First Earl of Sandwich*, 2 vols, 1912

J.E.N.Hearsey, *The Tower*, 1960

H.T.Heath (ed.), *The Letters of Samuel Pepys and His Family Circle*, 2 vols, 1955

J.Holland, *Two Discourses of the Navy*, Vol. 7, 1894

R.G.Howarth, *Letters and Second Diary of Samuel Pepys*, 1932

J.J.Keevil and J.L.S.Coulter, *Medicine and the Navy*, 1957–63

J.Kenyon, *The Popish Plot*, 1984

E.Klaaren, *The Religious Origins of Modern Science*, 1975

R.Latham (ed.), *The Diary of Samuel Pepys*, 10 vols

M.Lewis, *A Short Model of a Bank*, 1678

C.C.Lloyd, *The British Seaman*, 1970

N.Luttrell, *Brief Historical Relation of State Affairs*, 6 vols, 1969

Lord Macaulay, *A History of England*, 1898

A.T.Mahan, *Sea Power*, 1957

H.M.McAfee, *Pepys on the Restoration Stage*, 1916

C.Marburg, *Mr Pepys and Mr Evelyn*, 1935

W.Matthews (ed.), *Charles II's Escape*, 1936

A.K.Merton, *Science and Technology in the Seventeenth Century*, 1936

M.H.Nicolson, *Pepys's Diary and the New Science*, 1965

R.North, *Examen*, 1740

D.Ogg, *England in the Reign of Charles II*, 2 vols, 1934, 1955

R.Ollard, *Man of War*, 1969

R.Ollard, *Pepys: A Biography*, 1974

M.Oppenheim, *The Royal Navy*, 1896

F.M.Page, *Estates of Crowland Abbey*, 1896

G.Penn, *Memorials of Sir William Penn*, 2 vols, 1833

J.R.Powell, *The Rupert and Monck Letter Book*, Vol. 112, 1666

W.C.Pepys, *Genealogy of the Pepys Family*, 1952

J.Pollock, *Popish Plot*, 1903

M. and C.H.B.Quennell, *Everyday Things*, 1918–31

E.M.G.Routh, *Tangier: England's Last Atlantic Outpost*, 1912

C.P.Rogers, *The Dutch in the Medway*, 1970

C.Russell, *The Reign of Charles I*, 1979

G.D.Scott, *Biographical Sketch*, 1885

Sir J.Sitwell, *The First Whig*, Vol. 1, 1900

G.D.Scull, *The Family of Scott*, 1882

J.D.Smith, *The Life, Journals and Correspondence of Pepys*, 2 vols, 1825

T.Sprat, *The Royal Society*, 1959

J.R.Tanner (ed.), *A Descriptive Catalogue of the Naval Manuscripts in the Pepysian Library at Magdalene College, Cambridge*, 1903–23

J.R.Tanner (ed.), *Samuel Pepys's Naval Minutes*, 1926

J.R.Tanner, *Mr Pepys*, 1925

J.R.Tanner (ed.), *Private Correspondence and Miscellaneous Papers of Samuel Pepys 1679–1703 in the possession of J. Pepys Cokerell*, 2 vols, 1926

J.R.Tanner (ed.), *Further Correspondence of Samuel Pepys 1662–1679*, 1929

A.W.Tedder, *The Navy of the Restoration*, 1889

H.W.Turnbull, *Newton's Letters*, 1959

Verney, *Memoirs of the Verney Family*, 1925

V.Wedgwood, *First Earl of Stafford*, 1961

H.B. Wheatley, *Samuel Pepys and the World He Lived in*, 1880
H.B. Wheatley, *Pepysiana*, Vol. 10 of H.B. Wheatley's edition of the Diary, 1899
W.H. Whitear (ed.), *More Pepysiana*, 1927
A. Williamson, *Diary*, Vol. 22

Index

A figure 2 in brackets after a page reference means that there are two separate references to the subject on that page. P. stands for Samuel Pepys.